THE ESSENTIAL GUIDE
to
Federal Labor Relations

What You Need to Know to be Successful

Third Edition

Joseph Swerdzewski

Copyright © 2014 Joseph Swerdzewski and Associates. Printed and bound in the United States of America. All rights reserved. No part of this book may be reproduced or transmitted in any form or by any means, electronic or mechanical, including photocopying, recording, or by an information storage and retrieval system – except by a reviewer who may quote brief passages in a review to be printed in a magazine, newspaper, or on the Web – without the written permission from the publisher. For information, please contact Joseph Swerdzewski and Associates, 6585 Highway 431 South, Suite E 457, Hampton Cove, AL 35763; (256) 503-2226.

Although the author and publisher have made every effort to ensure the accuracy and completeness of information contained in this book, we assume no responsibility for errors, inaccuracies, omissions, or any inconsistency herein.

First Edition © Copyright 2008
Second Edition © Copyright 2012
Third Edition © Copyright 2014

ISBN: 978-0-9910121-3-8

ATTENTION CORPORATIONS, UNIVERSITIES, COLLEGES, AND PROFESSIONAL ORGANIZATIONS: Quantity discounts are available on bulk purchases of this book for educational, or training purposes. Special books or book excerpts can also be created to fit specific needs.

Written by: Joseph Swerdzewski

Edited by: Joseph Swerdzewski & Nina Soden

Cover Design by: Nina Soden

Layout Design by: Julie Csizmadia

Published by: Joseph Swerdzewski

TABLE OF CONTENTS

Introduction
The Essential Guide to Federal Labor Relations
What You Need to Know to be Successful 1

Chapter One
A Status Check on Labor Relations
at your Facility 3
   1. Status of the Bargaining Unit 4
   2. Status of the Collective Bargaining Agreement 4
   3. Status of Knowledge of the Rights and Obligations of Unions, Employees and Management in Federal Sector Labor
      Relations 5
   4. The Status of the Relationship between Labor and Management 5
   Key Points in Chapter One 5

Chapter Two
Representation Issues 7
   What are Representation Issues? 8
   Agencies Whose Employees are Excluded by Law 8
   Status as a Labor Organization 8
   Organizing Employee - Basic Representation Petition 8
   Collection of Showing of Interest 9
   Appropriateness of Unit Questions 9
   Positions Excluded from Bargaining Units 10
   Employees Specifically Excluded from Bargaining Units by Statute: . 11
   Decision and Order by the Regional Director of the FLRA 13
   Election Agreement 13
   Secret Ballot Election 14
   Observers 14
   Voting Procedures 14
   Mail Ballots 14
   Challenged Ballots 14
   Objections and Challenges 15
   Certifications and Bars to Elections 15
   Post-Certification Events Calling for Petitions to the FLRA 15
   Amendment of a Certification 15
   Clarification of a Bargaining Unit 16
   Reorganizations or Other Unusual Circumstances Affecting the Continued Appropriateness of a Unit 16
   Other Types of Petitions 17
   Key Points in Chapter Two 18

Chapter Three
Rights Given to Management in the Statute 19
   Section 7106. Management Rights 20
   Why are Management Rights Important? 20
   The Right to Assign Work and Direct Employees 20
   The Right to Establish Internal Security Practices 21
   The Right to Discipline Employees 22
   The Right to Hire and Select Employees 23
   The Right to Determine the Budget of the Agency 23
   The Right to Layoff Employees 24
   The Right to Contract Out 25
   The Right to Determine the Agency's Organization 25
   The Right to Determine the Number of Employees and Personnel by Whom Agency Operations will be conducted. . . .25
   Why Are Management Reserved Rights Important? 26
   The Right to Take Actions during an Emergency 26

Other Management Rights 26
Management Rights Case Study. 28
Key Points in Chapter Three 29

Chapter Four
Union Rights 31
The Right to be the Exclusive Representative of Employees 32
The Right to Engage in Collective Bargaining 32
The Right to be Present at Meetings Management Has with Employees 33
The Right to Assist a Labor Organization 34
The Right to Negotiate Over Receiving Information 34
The Right to Request Information 34
Reasonably Available 34
Relevant and Necessary. 35
No Right to Information Prohibited from Release by Law. 35
Standards of Conduct 35
The Right to Binding Arbitration 36
The Right to File Exceptions to Arbitration Awards 36
The Right to File a Negotiability Appeal. 37
The Right to Seek Federal Services Impasses Panel (FSIP) Assistance 37
The Right to File Representation Petitions 37
The Right to File Unfair Labor Practice Charges. 38
The Right to Official Time 38
The Right to Collect Dues 39
Union Rights Case Study 40
What Union Rights Are Affected by the New Policy?. 40
Key Points in Chapter Four 40

Chapter Five
Employee Rights 43
The Right to Form a Labor Organization 44
The Right to Join or Not Join a Labor Organization 44
The Duty of Fair Representation 44
The Right to Assist a Labor Organization 45
The Right to Representation During A Weingarten Meeting 45
Right to File An Unfair Labor Practice Charge. 45
Right to File A Grievance 46
Right to Be Represented by a Representative of the Employee's Choice 46
Employee Rights Case Study. 46
What Employee Rights Are Affected by the Supervisor's Statements to John? 46
Key Points in Chapter Five. 46

Chapter Six
How Rights Are Enforced 49
The Federal Labor Relations Authority 50
How to Enforce Your Rights 50
Who Can File Unfair Labor Practice Charges?. 51
You Can't Take Two Bites from the Apple – the "d Bar" 51
Investigation, Prosecution, Settlement and Dismissal of Unfair Labor Practice Charges 51
Unfair Labor Practices Committed By Management 52
Why Do Unions File Unfair Labor Practices? 52
Common Unfair Labor Practices Charges Filed Against Management 53
Flagrant Misconduct. 54
To Sponsor, Control or Assist a Labor Organization 56
What Happens If Union or Management Commits an Unfair Labor Practice? 58
Common Remedies 58
Grievance Arbitration 59
Grievance Procedure 60
Problems in Processing Grievances. 60
Problems with Arbitrability 61

Arbitration	61
Arbitration Process	61
Arbitration Remedies	61
FLRA Administrative Appeals	61
Review of Regional Director Decision and Order on Representation Issue	61
Exceptions to Arbitration Awards	62
Negotiability Appeals	62
Unfair Labor Practice Case Study	62
Grievance Case Study	63
Key Points in Chapter Six	63

Chapter Seven
How to File a ULP and What Happens After That

When You can File a ULP:	66
What Must a Charge Contain	66
Must State Who is Charged	66
What the Charge Must Say	66
Investigation Statements and Evidence	67
Amended Charges	68
Resolution of Charge Before Decision	68
Dismissal of Charge	68
Final Investigative Report	68
Settlement Agreements	68
Unilateral Settlement Agreements	69
ULP Hearing	69
Key Points in this Chapter Seven	69

Chapter Eight
What Do You Need To Know About Your Collective Bargaining Agreement? 71

What Does This Contract Mean?	72
Custom and Usage	72
The Practice is Different from the language of the Collective Bargaining Agreement	72
Official Time	73
Scope of the Bargaining Unit	74
Overtime	74
Details and Reassignments	74
Grievance Procedure	74
Collective Bargaining	74
Disciplinary Actions	75
Hours of Work	75
Leave	75
Merit Promotion	75
Performance Management	75
Duration	75
Collective Bargaining Agreement Case Study	76
Key Points in Chapter Eight	76

Chapter Nine
What You Need to Know About Collective Bargaining 77

What is Collective Bargaining?	78
Performance of a Mutual Obligation	78
Duly Authorized Representatives	78
Meet At Reasonable Times	78
Bargain in a Good Faith Effort to Reach Agreement	78
Conditions of Employment	79
Who Can a Union Bargain For?	79
When Do You Have to Bargain?	80
The De Minimis Standard	80
Limitations on the Right to Bargain	81
Compelling Need for Agency Regulations	81

See §2424.11 of FLRA Rules and Regulations.. 81
What about Impact and Implementation Bargaining? 82
Bargaining over Procedures 82
Bargaining over Appropriate Arrangements 83
Five Part Appropriate Arrangements Test. 83
Conclusion: Provision is Negotiable 84
What are Permissive Subjects of Bargaining?. 85
What is a Past Practice? 85
Four Elements that Must Exist for There to be a Past Practice. 85
Illegal Past Practices 86
The Bargaining Process 86
Covered by Doctrine 87
Ground Rules 88
Collective Bargaining Case Study. 89
Key Points in Chapter Nine 90

Chapter Ten
What You Can and Cannot Say or Do to Union Representatives and Employees 91
Statements: Oral or Written 92
Robust Debate 92
Freedom of Expression 92
Discriminatory Actions 93
Flagrant Misconduct 93
What Managers Can and Cannot Say and Do Case Study 93
Key Points in Chapter Ten 94

Chapter Eleven
Meetings with Employees that Require
a Union Representative 95
Formal Discussions 96
Role of Union at a Formal discussion 97
Weingarten Meetings 97
Other Meetings 97
Case Study – Formal Discussions 98
Case Study – Weingarten Meeting 98
Key Points in Chapter Eleven 99

Chapter Twelve
An Effective Labor Management Relationship. 101
Common Barriers to an Effective Labor Management Relationship 102
Interest-Based Bargaining. 103

Chapter Thirteen
Pre-Decisional Involvement 105
The National Council on Federal Labor Management Relations Guidance on Pre-decisional Involvement 106
What is Pre-Decisional Involvement? 106
What is the Value of Pre-Decisional Involvement? 106
What are the Barriers to Pre-Decisional Involvement? 106
When Should Pre-Decisional Involvement Be Used? 107
Steps to Developing A Labor-Management Pre-Decisional Involvement Process 108
Develop A Formalized Process for Pre-Decisional Involvement 109
Train the Participants in Pre-Decisional Involvement on Problem Solving Skills 109
Select an Appropriate Issue for Pre-Decisional Involvement and Implement Process 109
Key Points in Chapter Thirteen 109

Chapter Fourteen
Title 38 and Employees of the U.S. Department of Veterans Affairs, Veterans Health Administration 111
Introduction. 112
A Brief Chronology of Positions at the Veterans Health Administration 112
Hybrid Employees and Collective Bargaining 113
Non-hybrid (Pure), Title 38 Employees and Collective Bargaining 114
What are the Section 7422 exemptions? 115

Current Procedures for Seeking a Determination on Section 7422 Issues 115
Alternative Approach to Resolving 38 U.S.C. Section 7422 Questions 116
Section 7422 Case Study 116
Key Points in Chapter Fourteen 117

Appendix A
Title 5 of the United States Code:
Government Organization & Employees 119
Subchapter I 120
Subchapter II 125
Subchapter III 135
Subchapter IV 138

Appendix B
10 Cases Recommended for Reading 141
Case #1 Flagrant Misconduct Standard 143
Case #2 Bad Faith Bargaining 152
Case #3 Definition of Working Conditions 159
Case #4 Discrimination Against Union Representatives 163
Case #5 Appropriate Arrangements 171
Case #6 Particularized Need Criteria for Information Requests by the Union 204
Case #7 Past Practice 212
Case #8 Appropriate Unit Criteria for Determining Whether a Petitioned for Bargaining Unit is Appropriate 218
Case #9 Right to Assign Work 223
Case #10 Limitation on Bargaining – Federal Statute 225

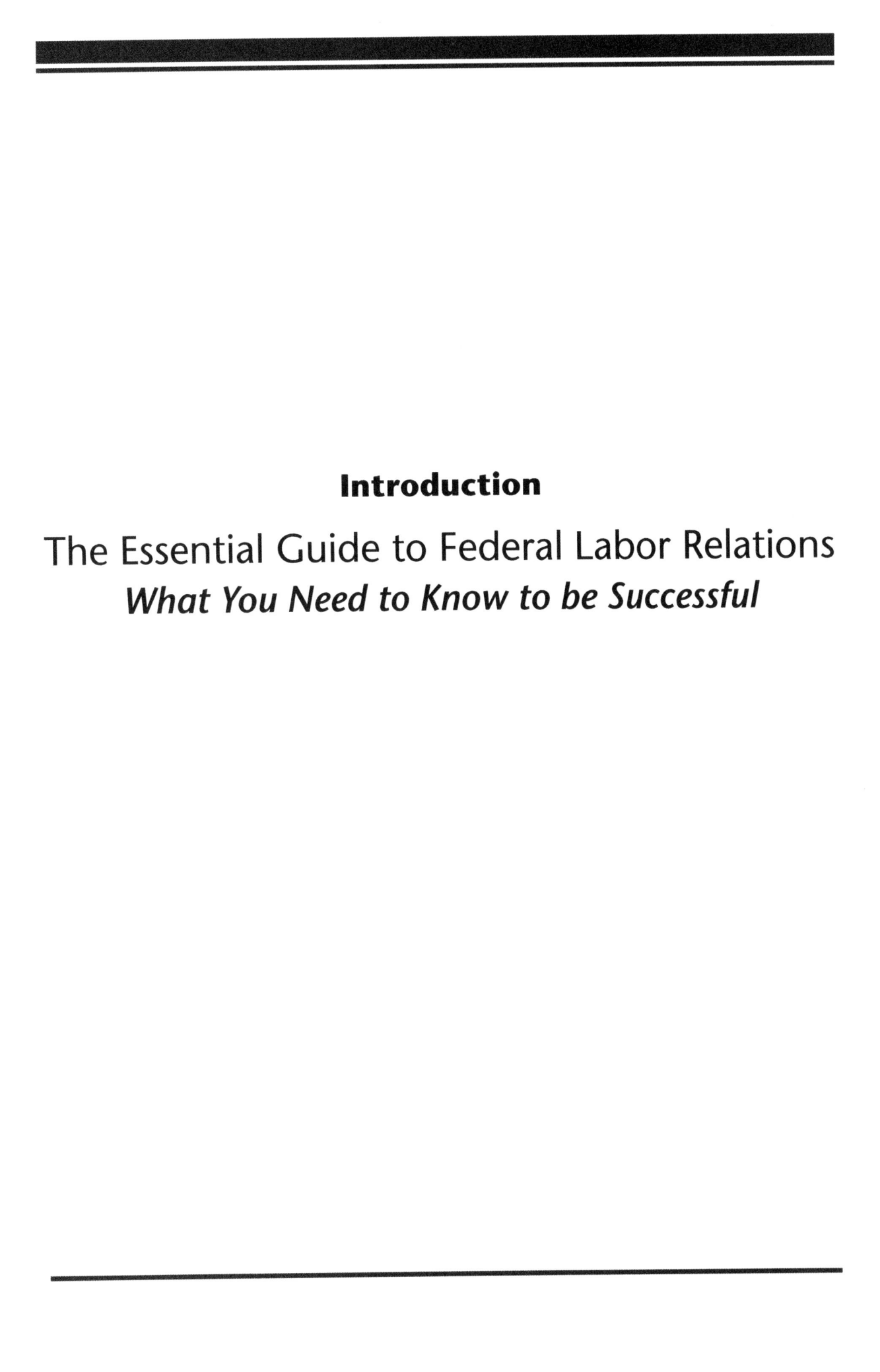

Introduction

The Essential Guide to Federal Labor Relations
What You Need to Know to be Successful

Introduction: The Essential Guide to Federal Labor Relations-What You Need to Know to be Successful

Some of you may have read Labor Law and Labor Relations – A Practical Guide to Federal Labor Relations. It is a good introduction to federal sector labor relations, intended for managers, supervisors and union stewards who need a working knowledge of labor relations in the federal government. This book goes beyond the level of understanding contained in Labor Law and Labor Relations. It is written for the person who needs more than a working knowledge and must deal in more depth with labor relations issues. It contains case citations, where appropriate, but does not rely heavily on an extensive recitation of cases. It is intended to be a resource you can pick up in order to get a quick answer to a problem, with the understanding that more in-depth research on esoteric issues may be necessary. The Third Edition has been updated to include recent case decisions of note and adds a chapter on Pre- Decisional Involvement.

Agency labor relations specialists are not the only practitioners of federal labor relations. This book is also aimed at union representatives at all levels, human resource specialists who need a more advanced understanding of labor relations, and, importantly, managers who must handle day to day labor relations responsibilities.

To be successful in labor relations, participants in labor relations must have a thorough understanding of some key concepts. As the federal government has taken a more rights-based enforcement approach to labor relations, both union and management must have a greater understanding of their rights under the Federal Service Labor Management Statute and of how to enforce them. In writing this book, I have tried to elucidate those critical issues which an individual with responsibility for labor relations needs to understand in order to make good decisions. I have attempted to provide quick, useful information in an understandable manner for people who need more than the basics of labor relations.

The Statute establishes boundaries to the relationship between union and management, which are in the form of rights given to the participants in each labor management relationship. Each party to this relationship must know these boundaries and how to effectively deal with each other in the federal sector labor relations environment. The enforcement of rights provided under the Statute is one important way in which both sides can achieve their goals in labor relations. However, the truly effective labor relationship achieves a necessary balance between enforcing rights and developing an effective relationship based on trust and communication.

Appendix A to this book contains the Federal Service Labor Management Relations Statute (Statute). While most people do not make a habit of sitting down and reading statutory language, having a copy of the Statute handy can frequently solve a dispute or, at least, provide a better understanding of what the Statute actually says as compared to what either side is guessing it says. Appendix B contains my top ten list of Federal Labor Relations Authority (FLRA) Cases, which I believe that anyone who wants to be truly knowledgeable in federal labor relations should read. Each of these cases was selected to give the reader an understanding of a key concept. There are well over 68 volumes of FLRA cases, which would take up a good sized book case. There are clearly many more cases which could be of help in better understanding the law. Providing these ten is not meant to deter you from further research.

Chapter One

A Status Check on Labor Relations at your Facility

Chapter One: A Status Check on Labor Relations at your Facility

The current status of labor relations at your facility has an impact on how successfully labor relations are conducted. The following are significant labor relations issues which affect the collective bargaining relationship of labor and management. I suggest that you look at each of these issues and decide if there are actions you should or could take, or questions which must be answered, to resolve outstanding labor relations concerns.

1. Status of the Bargaining Unit

One thing certain about the federal government is that it will continually change. As management changes, the new leadership frequently has different ideas about how the organization should be structured. Congress may also decide that certain departments or agencies should be consolidated or merged with another. The Base Realignment and Closure Commission (BRAC) results are an example of the impact of Congressional action on the scope of bargaining units, as is the creation of the Department of Homeland Security. All of these changes can have a significant impact on the scope of bargaining units.

If an agency is reorganized, one of the first questions which may arise is whether the existing bargaining units remain appropriate. This question is dealt with in more detail in Chapter Two – Representation Issues. The basic question is whether these employees still share a community of interest with the employees in the existing bargaining unit, or whether, as a result of the reorganization, they share a community of interest with employees in the new organization they are joining. The question of community of interest is decided based upon how the unit employees interact with other employees and those common or shared working conditions policies that apply to them. The next question often is whether the bargaining unit transferred to the new organization substantially intact, such that the new organization could be considered the successor to the previous organization that had a collective bargaining relationship with the employees' exclusive representative.

The scope of a bargaining unit determines whom the union represents and whether management has an obligation to bargain over changes in working conditions for certain employees. Bargaining units which are not properly aligned with the current structure of the organization can lead to difficulties for unions in representing the employees, as well as to problems for management in making changes in working conditions.

If there are outstanding issues or questions concerning the scope of the bargaining unit, either labor or management should file a representation petition with the FLRA.

2. Status of the Collective Bargaining Agreement

The current status of your collective bargaining agreement has a significant impact on how labor and management engage in labor relations. Collective bargaining agreements expire at the end of the term in the agreement, unless the parties agree to extend the agreement or the agreement "rolls over" (continues on for a term set forth in the agreement). The terms contained in expired agreements continue on as past practices. Once an agreement has expired, either party to the agreement can seek to make changes in working conditions by giving notice to the other party and engaging in collective bargaining. They are no longer bound by the terms of the agreement themselves but only to the extent the terms created past practices. For purposes of the "covered by doctrine" the terms of the agreement are treated as though they are still in effect until new terms are bargained. See Chapter 8 for an understanding of the "covered by" doctrine.

Any permissive subjects of bargaining contained in an expired agreement continue on until a party to the agreement notifies the other party that it no longer wishes to be bound by the contract clauses which concern permissive subjects. This must be a formal notification. The concept of permissive subjects of bargaining is covered in more detail in the Chapter on Collective Bargaining.

If a contract has expired, another union has the right to file a petition to seek to represent the employees currently in the bargaining unit unless precluded from doing so by the national constitution of the union. A collective bargaining agreement that is currently in effect prevents another union from filing such a petition.

If the contract is about to expire, it is important to read the duration article in the contract to determine when to notify the other party that you wish to renegotiate the contract. Missing the deadline in the contract will, in many cases, cause the contract automatically to roll over for another year. If the contract has expired, in most cases the party wishing to reopen the contract must simply notify the other party to the contract of their desire to negotiate a new contract.

An updated contract is important for both parties to the relationship. The contract represents an agreement between labor and management on the working conditions of employees in the bargaining unit. An outdated agreement may result in old practices remaining in effect, which could jeopardize the effectiveness and efficiency of the agency, as well as the union's ability to properly represent the employees in its bargaining unit.

3. Status of Knowledge of the Rights and Obligations of Unions, Employees and Management in Federal Sector Labor Relations

The Statute establishes the rights of labor, management and employees in a unionized environment in the federal sector. The Statute establishes the boundaries to the relationship between labor and management and sets forth both rights and obligations that union and management must observe in dealing with each other. It also establishes the rights employees have been given under the law which must be observed by both union and management. If managers and union representatives don't understand these boundaries, they may make mistakes which end in litigation or seriously damage the trust in their relationship. A working knowledge of the Statute and labor relations processes can greatly assist the parties in establishing a productive labor management relationship and avoiding time consuming, expensive litigation as well as protect the rights of employees.

4. The Status of the Relationship between Labor and Management

Labor relations is both understanding and obeying the Statute and maintaining an effective relationship between union and management. It cannot be overstated how important the relationship between the union and management is to the successful conduct of labor relations. The personalities of union leaders and management representatives have a major impact on how labor relations is conducted at a facility. Effective labor relations is not achieved solely by being knowledgeable about how to enforce your rights under the law, but also by knowing how to work effectively with the other side to the relationship. An effective working relationship can help the parties work through difficult and complex issues which otherwise could lead to acrimonious litigation and endless strife.

A relationship based on trust and open communication is invaluable. It allows the parties to engage in interest-based and win-win negotiations, which will almost invariably lead to better, more effective results for both parties to the negotiation.

Key Points in Chapter One

1. Determine whether the scope of the currently described bargaining units is appropriate. If there have been organizational changes do the bargaining units make sense as currently arranged.

2. Is your collective bargaining agreement out of date or has it expired. Does it provide the working conditions necessary to an effective and efficient conduct of the agencies mission and meet the needs of the employees.

3. Managers and union representatives must having a working knowledge of the Statute to avoid needless conflict based on misunderstanding the Statute.

4. Good labor relations are characterized by knowing the Statute and having an effective union management relationship.

Chapter Two

Representation Issues

Chapter Two: Representation Issues

The right of employees to be represented in a bargaining unit begins with the filing of a petition by a union to represent employees it believes share a community of interest. However, many other representation issues can arise after the initial granting of a certification to a union. It is vital to have an understanding of the representation process in order to know how to deal with the many issues which can arise concerning the status of bargaining unit employees.

What are Representation Issues?

Representation issues begin with the most fundamental of the rights given to eligible employees under the Statute: the right to be represented by a labor organization for purposes of collective bargaining. From this right spring many, if not most, of the other rights and responsibilities associated with representation by a union. Representation issues (in some cases also known as "questions concerning representation" or "questions relating to, or affecting, representation") arise from the exercise of this right by employees and unions, and from questions raised by agency management regarding how to honor these statutory rights while preserving the effective functioning of their agency. Representation issues essentially involve the question of who should be in the group of employees represented by the union; who should not be in that group because representation by a union might raise conflicts of interest with their jobs; and what the size and shape of the group should be when compared to the agency's organizational structure. Similar questions may crop up later if, for example, reorganizations substantially alter the mission, size or scope of an agency or its bargaining unit(s).

Agencies Whose Employees are Excluded by Law

One of the first questions to be answered is whether any employees of the agency are eligible to be represented by a union. Certain agencies are exempted from coverage by law because of the type of work they do – e.g., employees of the FBI, the CIA, the National Security Agency, the General Accountability Office, the Federal Labor Relations Authority, etc. See Section 7103(a)(3) of the Statute, as well as laws passed subsequently which exclude certain agencies from full or partial coverage of the Statute (e.g., the Dept. of Homeland Security).

Status as a Labor Organization

A second early question is whether the organization seeking to represent employees is a labor organization as defined by the Statute. Normally, whether or not a labor organization is authorized to represent a group of federal employees is not in doubt, because most of the unions representing federal employees have been in existence for decades and have clearly met all statutory requirements to constitute a labor organization. Occasionally, a group of employees may form a new association or organization to represent employees of an agency. If there is any doubt as to whether this association is legally entitled to represent employees, a challenge to its status may be filed with the FLRA.

Organizing Employee - Basic Representation Petition

When a labor organization initially seeks to represent a group of employees, it must present a petition to the FLRA on official FLRA forms accompanied by a "showing of interest" from at least 30% of the employees in the group (unit) it wishes to represent. This "showing of interest" may consist of signatures on a petition or authorization cards, evidence that the employees are already members of the union, or any other evidence that the FLRA feels sufficiently demonstrates that at least 30% of employees are interested in having an election on the question of union representation.

The showing of interest petitions or authorization cards must clearly state that the employee(s) signing are authorizing the union to represent them or wish to have an election to determine whether they should be represented by a union. All cards or petitions must also bear a date of signing in order to be counted, and the union should also include an alphabetized list of the employees comprising its showing of interest. It's normally wise for a union to collect more signatures than the required 30%, since some employees who sign may not be deemed eligible for representation, or may leave their jobs before the signatures are presented to the FLRA, so their names will be not be considered in the total of valid signatures. (Note: the adequacy – e.g., whether cards are properly signed and dated and total 30% – of the showing of interest is a matter to be determined by the FLRA alone and may not be challenged by any party, although if the petition is dismissed for insufficient signatures, the petitioner may file an appeal on limited grounds.)

If the agency or a competing labor organization contends that the showing of interest has been tainted in some way – for example, by supervisory involvement or coercion in the signing of cards or petitions, or by fraudulently obtained or forged signatures – they may file a challenge to the validity of the showing of interest with the FLRA, which will investigate the allegations.

Collection of Showing of Interest

There are some simple rules governing the collection of signatures for a showing of interest, although that simplicity can be deceiving, since a fair number of cases have resulted from alleged violations of the rules. As a general proposition, employees have the right to solicit signatures in work areas during non-work times (this includes paid breaks); they may distribute union or election-related materials in non-work areas during non-work times. Absent unusual circumstances, non-employee union organizers may visit the facility premises and non-work areas for the purpose of organizing employees to the same extent that other members of the public are allowed to be on the premises for other purposes. Once a petition is filed, unions with equivalent status (i.e., the petitioner and any other union which have qualified as an intervenor) should be furnished with equivalent access to employees.

After an official petition has been filed with the regional office of the FLRA, the FLRA office will begin processing the petition to determine if it warrants an election. Other labor organizations may become intervenors in the proceeding by submitting a showing of interest of 10% of the employees or other evidence, such as a current or expired contract, showing that it already represents the employees.

Appropriateness of Unit Questions

One of the first questions to be addressed in evaluating a petition for election is whether the unit of employees among whom the election is sought comprises an "appropriate unit." An appropriate unit is one which conforms to the agency's organizational lines in a logical way, so that the employees share common interests, personnel policies, working conditions, job functions and missions, and supervisory hierarchy. In other words, if a union were to represent certain employees, it would make sense to negotiate a contract or other issues relative to these employees, to the exclusion of other employees of the agency. The FLRA must be satisfied that the unit, or group of employees among whom an election will be held, is appropriate for purposes of collective bargaining. There may be more than one such "appropriate" unit – e.g., a district-wide, region-wide, or nationwide unit – and the unit which is the subject of the petition need only be an appropriate unit, not the most appropriate one.

If the agency and labor organization(s) who are parties to the case, and/or the FLRA, cannot agree about the appropriateness of the unit described in the petition, the FLRA will normally schedule an investigative hearing to explore the facts and the positions of all the parties. (In some cases it may be possible to submit stipulated evidence to the FLRA in order to avoid a hearing.) These hearings are non-adversarial, and strict rules of evidence don't apply. The FLRA has the regulatory authority to require the parties to meet to try to resolve the issues in dispute prior to any hearing. Some of the evidence the FLRA will wish to examine in order to make a decision on the appropriate unit issue may include:

1. Similarity of mission and functions (duties, work assignments and job titles) of the positions of employees in the desired unit as contrasted to employees in other units thought to be appropriate; the numbers and types of employees in these units;

2. Amount of contact between employees in the daily/weekly performance of their duties;

3. The amount of interchange of employees between various components of the unit, whether permanently (e.g., transfers between components for promotions or other reasons) or temporarily (for temporary details or short-term absences of employees);

4. The supervisory hierarchy and chain of command; at what level decisions affecting the employees' functions, working conditions or personnel policies are made;

5. The geographic proximity of employees in the unit(s) thought to be appropriate;

6. Whether there are local concerns or working conditions unique to the unit sought by the petition as compared to other possible units7. Where personnel policies and labor relations policies are made and/or administered for employees in the units in question; where personnel files are maintained; the scope of authority of the responsible personnel office in administering personnel and employee or labor relations policies;

8. Who, at what level, would negotiate for the agency if it were necessary to bargain changes in working conditions or a collective bargaining agreement;

9. The limitations, if any, on the ability of responsible agency officials to bargain over matters of concern to the employees in the proposed unit(s);

10. Whether the proposed unit would hinder effective administration of labor relations policies or collective bargaining agreements because it would result in the possible proliferation of many small units;

11. The history of collective bargaining, if any, within the agency;

12. Evidence concerning the efficient use of resources in administering labor relations in one unit as compared to another;

13. Evidence concerning the effect of the proposed unit on agency operations in terms of cost, productivity, and use of resources.

(**Note:** evidence will always be taken regarding/contrasting the various units the parties believe should be the unit found appropriate for election with respect to all of the items described above.)

The types of evidence or testimony explored at hearing as described above are not meant to be all-inclusive. The FLRA will take at hearing whatever evidence it believes is relevant to the particular issues of a case. The questions/evidence outlined above generally fall into three categories, referred to as "community of interest" of the employees, "efficiency of agency operations," and "effectiveness of dealings" between the agency and union. The FLRA should make a specific ruling on each of these areas in its written decision following hearing.

Other types of issues may also be raised at the hearing, or they may be the only issues requiring a hearing. For example, whether or not the agency and union(s) agree on the unit for election, they may disagree on who should be included in or excluded from the unit based on conflict of interest considerations. That is, they may not agree on who is a supervisor, management official, confidential employee, employee engaged in federal personnel work in other than a purely clerical capacity, or one engaged in internal audit or national security work as described by the Statute and clarified in FLRA case law.

If the number of positions/employees not agreed upon amounts to more than 15% of the total number of employees in the proposed unit, the FLRA will normally require that evidence be taken from representative employees at hearing in order to decide these issues before an election is held. If fewer than 15% of the positions in the proposed unit are in dispute, the employees in those positions will be provided the opportunity to cast a challenged ballot, and the parties may attempt to resolve these challenges before the ballots are counted. However, if the unresolved challenged ballots remaining are not determinative of the outcome of the election, that is, won't change the result of the election, the FLRA will not investigate or decide whether the disputed positions are included or excluded from the bargaining unit. If the employees vote to have the union represent them, the agency or union may later file a petition seeking clarification of the positions with respect to their inclusion in the unit.

Note: the parties to an election (agency and union(s)) should be wary of agreeing to the included/excluded status of positions prior to an election purely for the sake of expediency, in the interest of getting to a quick election. If they have agreed that certain positions are in or out of the unit, this agreement may be considered by the FLRA to be binding unless it can be shown that substantial changes in the duties and responsibilities of the position have subsequently taken place.

Positions Excluded from Bargaining Units

Whether preceding or following the election, any investigation or hearing conducted by the FLRA will explore certain evidence in order to determine the bargaining unit status of particular categories of employees. The FLRA decides employees' eligibility based on their actual duties at the time of a hearing, not on duties that may exist in the future. A sizeable body of FLRA case law exists concerning each of the categories of employees excluded from bargaining units by the Statute. It is important that unions and agencies examine these cases as they apply to the particular positions in dispute before proceeding to hearing. The FLRA regional offices may provide assistance regarding the case law which is applicable to a given situation, and the FLRA's website has a search facility as well.

In almost all cases, the FLRA will want evidence at a hearing to include such things as position descriptions; vacancy announcements; supervisory chain of command; geographic location; mission of the agency and its organizational hierarchy; length of time the employees have held the jobs in question; and the duties the employee is actually performing on a daily, weekly or other regular basis. If an employee has been in the position for only a short time, evidence should include what (s)he has been told regarding the duties (s)he is expected to perform; what training (s)he has been to or is scheduled to go to; what duties the predecessor employee performed; and if there are employees in similar positions, what their duties are. The FLRA will normally not decide the unit eligibility of positions which are vacant, unless it is necessary to decide whether an individual has access to the contractual grievance procedure or it is necessary in order to decide a grievance at arbitration.

Employees Specifically Excluded from Bargaining Units by Statute:

Internal Audit Functions

Employees who are engaged in internal audit or investigative functions are excluded per Section 7112(b)(7) of the Statute. These are employees whose duties require them to investigate or audit programs or contracts in order to verify the honesty and integrity of employees, or conversely, to uncover fraud, waste or abuse by employees. They need not be directly investigating employees, and they need not regularly find employees in violation of ethical or legal requirements in order to be excluded from a unit. See Small Business Administration 34 FLRA 392 (1990)

National Security

Section 7113(b)(6) of the Statute excludes from bargaining units employees who are engaged in intelligence, counterintelligence, investigative, or security work which directly affects national security. Since the events of September 11, 2001, this provision of the Statute has been invoked more frequently. The FLRA has held that security work means a duty or activity relating to securing, guarding, shielding, protecting or preserving something, and may include the "design, analysis or monitoring of security systems or procedures," as well as "the regular use of, or access to, classified information." (Dept of Justice, 52 FLRA 1093) "National security" was held by the FLRA to include "sensitive activities of the government that are directly related to the protection and preservation of the military, economic, and productive strength of the United States, including the security of the government in domestic and foreign affairs, against or from espionage, sabotage, subversion, foreign aggression and any other illegal acts which adversely affect the national defense." (Dept. of Energy, Oak Ridge, TN, 4 FLRA 644).

Confidential Employees

Confidential employees are defined in Section 7103 (a) (13) of the Statute as"... an employee who acts in a confidential capacity with respect to an individual who formulates or effectuates management policies in the field of labor-management relations." Not every employee who has private or confidential information concerning some aspect of an agency's function or mission is excluded from representation in a bargaining unit. Rather, there must be evidence of (1) a confidential working relationship between an employee and a supervisor or manager, and (2) significant involvement by the supervisor or manager in labor-management relations. See U.S. Dept of Labor, Office of the Solicitor 37 FLRA 1371 (1990)

For example, an administrative assistant to a manager who is on the agency negotiating team and helps decide negotiations strategies or proposals, and the secretary to a manager who regularly decides step 3 grievances or agency positions on unfair labor practices, might well be found to be confidential employees if they have regular access to confidential information concerning these matters. A person who actually formulates or carries out labor management relations or policies is also him- or herself a confidential employee. Advising management on negotiations, developing proposals for bargaining, preparing arbitration cases for hearing, or helping decide positions on grievances or unfair labor practice cases would be duties creating a conflict of interest such that an individual would be deemed to be a confidential employee and therefore excluded from a bargaining unit.

Personnelists

Employees whose duties require them to engage in federal personnel work "in other than a purely clerical capacity" are excluded from bargaining units by Section 7112(b)(3) of the Statute. Employees may be excluded if they use independent judgment to initiate personnel actions or make recommendations to management regarding personnel actions, organizational structure, or staffing levels, because their duties might conflict with bargaining unit interests. If, on the other hand, their duties involve only routine, clerical screening of personnel actions for technical sufficiency, or the recording of actions and maintenance of files, they may be included in a bargaining unit. See Dept of Treasury, IRS 36 FLRA 138, 144 (1990).

Management Officials

For purposes of exclusion from bargaining units and representation, "management officials" are defined somewhat narrowly by the Statute in Section 7103(a) (11). Not everyone normally considered to be a manager by the agency or by employees meets the statutory definition. To be excluded from a bargaining unit, an individual must create, establish, prescribe, decide upon or bring about "general principles, plans or courses of action for an agency." Employees in this category must use independent judgment in formulating policies or participating in this process. If an individual recommends policies or courses of action for an agency, the FLRA will look to see how often those recommendations are adopted. Merely carrying out or implementing policies is not sufficient to render someone a management official.

Supervisors

A common misconception is that the definition of a supervisor for purposes of bargaining unit representation is the same as that employed by the Office of Personnel Management for classification or pay purposes. It is not. Under the Statute, there is no certain number of employees an individual must supervise in order to be categorized as a supervisor. Therefore, if an individual meets the definition of supervisor with respect to only one employee, that individual may be excluded from a bargaining unit. Whether or not an agency has classified an employee as a supervisor, the FLRA will examine the duties and responsibilities of the employee under the lens established by the Statute and will make a determination which applies solely to the question of eligibility for representation in a bargaining unit and not to other matters.

To be a supervisor under Section 7103(a)(10) of the Statute, an individual must consistently use independent judgment in: hiring, directing, assigning, promoting, rewarding, transferring, furloughing, laying off, recalling, suspending, disciplining, or removing employees, adjusting grievances for employees, or effectively recommending any of these types of actions. The authority to take these actions must not be merely routine or clerical in nature. In any dispute between an agency and a union regarding an employee claimed to be a supervisor, the FLRA will require documentary evidence or testimony to show that one or more of these responsibilities is possessed by an employee. If a case goes to hearing, the FLRA will typically want to take evidence and testimony from the alleged supervisor, as well as that individual's supervisor and supervisee(s). In order for an individual to be deemed a supervisor, he/she need only be found to perform, or to effectively recommend, one of the responsibilities listed above.

The most difficult, or ambiguous, of the supervisory criteria are the authorities to assign and direct, in part because these call into play the requirement of "consistent use of independent judgment." Many agencies employ individuals in the capacity of "lead" employees, who may dole out work, give technical advice, or routinely sign off on completed work. If these tasks do not require independent judgments regarding the nature of the work contrasted with the abilities of the employees, or do not involve, for example, establishing work priorities, directing next steps for a project, or returning work for correction or additional work, the "team leader" might not be found to be a supervisor. See U.S. Dept of Treasury, Office of Chief Counsel 3 FLRA 1255 (1988), and U.S. Dept of Army, AVSCOM, St. Louis, MO 36 FLRA 587 (1990).

Although the preparation of performance appraisals is not, by itself, a specific statutory criterion in deciding supervisory status, if these appraisals are used by management in deciding rewards, promotions or discipline, they may be indicative of supervisory status. Other secondary evidence which may be pertinent to a decision of supervisory status are such things as whether the individual attends supervisory meetings, has attended supervisory training, or has the authority to grant time off, although the authority to grant or deny leave, standing alone, is not sufficient to confer supervisory status. See Dept. of the Interior, BIA, Navajo Area Office, 45 FLRA 646 (1992).

If an individual exercises supervisory authority only seasonally, or only on an intermittent basis when the regular supervisor is absent, that individual may be excluded from a bargaining unit (and representation by the union) only for the period during which they are actually performing supervisory duties.

Professional Employees

Because "professional employees" may have interests in common with one another which are not shared with other employees, they may be included in a bargaining unit with nonprofessional employees only if they are provided an opportunity to vote regarding whether they want to be in a separate unit consisting only of professional employees, or whether they prefer to be included with nonprofessional employees in one unit.

Professional employees as defined by Section 7103(a)(15) of the Statute are employees who work in fields requiring knowledge of an advanced, specialized type typically acquired through a college or university or hospital (e.g., a medical degree), as contrasted with on-the-job training, apprenticeship programs, or knowledge acquired from a general academic background (e.g., B.A. degree in liberal arts). The employees' work must also be intellectual and varied in nature, must require the consistent exercise of independent judgment, and must not be susceptible to being standardized in terms of productivity or output. For example, a doctor providing treatment to patients in a military or Veterans Administration hospital would clearly be a professional employee under the Statute. Someone who was educated as an attorney, but who is working in a job which doesn't require a law degree (e.g., in an employee relations specialist position), would probably not be considered to be a professional employee.

Temporary and Part-time Employees

The federal government employs a large number of employees in positions which are other than full-time, permanent positions. These may be called "temporary," "term," "intermittent," "seasonal," "on-call," "part-time," "permanent part-time," or some combination of these terms. Whether these employees can be included in a bargaining unit for purposes of union representation depends on the amount or length of time they are expected to work, as well on the commonality of interests they share with other employees in the unit. If the employees demonstrate a "substantial and continuing interest" in the working conditions shared with permanent employees, and if they have a "reasonable expectation of continued employment," rather than a brief, one-time appointment, they may be included in a bargaining unit. Probationary employees are not considered temporary employees and are normally included in bargaining units if they can reasonably expect to continue employment at the end of their probationary period. See U.S Army Engineer Activity, Capital Area, Ft. Myer, VA 34 FLRA 38 (1989)

Decision and Order by the Regional Director of the FLRA

After the close of a hearing, and after the parties have had an opportunity to submit briefs concerning their positions and applicable legal precedent, a Regional Director (RD) of the FLRA will issue a Decision and Order deciding the outcome of the dispute(s) and explaining his/her rationale for the decision and the evidence on which it is based. In a Decision and Order involving issues which must be decided before any election can be held, the RD will either dismiss the petition (if the petitioner does not wish to withdraw it) or direct an election; this decision and order may be appealed to the Authority in Washington, D.C. by any party adversely affected by the decision. The Authority's decision on appeal is final and cannot be appealed to Federal Court.

Election Agreement

If there are no disputes, or if any employee eligibility disputes or issues regarding the appropriateness of the unit have been resolved by the parties prior to the completion of a hearing, the agency and union may enter into an agreement for election, which must be approved by the Regional Director of the FLRA. If the parties cannot agree on such details as the date, time and place of an election, the Regional Director of the FLRA Region processing the petition will decide those details. In an agreement for election, the parties will also:

1. set a cutoff date for eligibility to vote in the election (normally the payroll period ending date preceding the agreement for election), and agree upon procedures for updating the list and checking its accuracy before the election, since employees must be employed on the cutoff date as well as on the date of election in order to be able to vote;

2. agree on the type of election – manual ballot, mail ballot, or some combination of the two; decide on procedures for absentee ballots for employees expected to be on temporary duty elsewhere on the date of the election;

3. decide whether multiple polling sites are necessary, or whether split voting shifts are necessary;

4. if more than one union is on the ballot, decide on the position and wording of their names on the ballot, as well as provisions for a run-off election, if necessary; and

5. agree on any procedures necessary for identification of voters.

All of these details will have to be approved by the Regional Director of the FLRA, so the FLRA agent assisting the parties in reaching the agreement will be a good resource for input and advice concerning what procedures might be best under the circumstances. Side agreements regarding campaigning by the union(s) before election may be entered into, but will not be approved or enforced by the FLRA.

Secret Ballot Election

Elections are conducted by secret ballot. Anything that breaches the secrecy of a ballot may be grounds for voiding the ballot cast; if enough ballots are affected, such a breach may be grounds for overturning an election. An agent of the FLRA is usually responsible for the conduct of the election, and the parties should seek the agent's advice if questions or problems arise before or during the election.

Observers

The parties to the agreement are entitled to have an equal number of observers at manual ballot election sites, during the count and tally of ballots in both mail and manual ballot elections, as well as during the mailing of ballots in mail or mixed mail/manual ballot elections. They are entitled to official time from the agency for this purpose. Observers for the agency should not be employees eligible to vote in the election, nor should they be supervisors, management officials, or anyone in a position which might be closely associated with management (e.g., confidential secretary to the head of the facility) such that employees could feel intimidated by their presence at the polls. Observers for the union must be federal employees (even if on leave without pay) and should not hold an elected office in the union.

No observers are allowed to keep lists of employees who vote, although they may have a list of employees whom they intend to challenge as ineligible to vote. Observers should not deposit ballots for voters or otherwise handle ballots. No union insignia or electioneering material should be worn by any observers. Any problems or potential problems noted by observers should be brought to the attention of the FLRA agent conducting the election. If, for example, an observer notices electioneering taking place in the voting line, or recognizes a voter who is blind or cannot read or write, he should point these matters out to the FLRA agent.

Voting Procedures

The polls must be opened and closed on time at the hours specified in the election agreement. No voting may take place before or after the hours specified, although those employees in line at the closing time should be allowed to vote. Even if all of the observers believe, and agree, that all eligible voters have voted before the closing time, the polls will remain open until the specified closing time. All voters must state their name to the observers in order to be allowed to vote, even if the observers know the individual. Voters are provided a ballot by the FLRA agent conducting the election and given an opportunity to vote in secret (in a voting booth or other area where the marking of the ballot cannot be seen) after they have been determined by the observers to be on the eligibility list. Voters must vote in secret; if a voter insists on marking his or her ballot publicly, the ballot may be confiscated by the FLRA agent. If a voter spoils a ballot, he/she must return it to the FLRA agent before receiving another.

Voters not found on the eligibility list, as well as all voters contended to be ineligible to vote by a party to the election, will be provided a ballot and a challenged ballot envelope by the FLRA agent. The challenged ballot envelope will note the voter's name and the reason for the challenge. The voter will mark his ballot in secret, place it in the challenged ballot envelope and then in the ballot box. All voters should deposit their own ballots in the ballot box, absent a handicapping condition or other unusual circumstance. No voter should leave the voting area with a ballot, marked or otherwise. After voting, no voters should be allowed to remain in the area.

Mail Ballots

In mail ballot elections, the FLRA mails a packet of materials to each eligible and challenged voter. These packets contain a ballot, explanatory election materials prepared by the FLRA, a secret ballot envelope, and an outer envelope bearing the return address of the FLRA (or in some cases, of a post office box rented by the FLRA) and a place for the signature of the voter certifying that he/she voted the ballot inside. Ballots will not be counted if the outer envelope does not contain the signature of the voter.

Challenged Ballots

In either type of election, before counting and tallying ballots, challenged ballots will first be separated from the remaining ballots. The parties, with the assistance of an FLRA agent, will attempt to resolve the challenges. Those that can be resolved by agreement of the parties will be opened and commingled with the rest of the ballots, and all ballots will then be counted. Any ballots with identifying markings will be declared void by the FLRA, and if a ballot is unclear (more than one choice apparently marked, for example), the FLRA will give the parties a chance to decide if they can agree on its meaning; if not, it won't be counted at that time. If: 1) a union receives a majority of the valid votes cast (note: not a majority of eligible voters); 2) unresolved challenged ballots are not sufficient to affect the outcome of the election; and 3) objections to the election are not filed by the agency or a competing union and/or are not found by the FLRA to have merit and to have affected the outcome of the election: the union will be deemed to have won the election. It will then be certified by the FLRA Regional Director as the exclusive representative of the employees in the appropriate unit.

Objections and Challenges

Ballots are usually challenged on the basis of eligibility issues, which were discussed previously. If these contested ballots are sufficient to change the outcome of the election, the FLRA may investigate or conduct a hearing, taking evidence from representative employees in the categories in question.

Objections may be filed to the election based upon the actual conduct of the election or to acts or communications which occurred before the election (generally between the filing of the petition and the date of the election and ballot count) which may have affected its outcome. Objections may be based upon, for example:

1. Errors made by the FLRA agent in conducting the election;
2. Procedural irregularities;
3. Electioneering in the polling site;
4. Conduct by employees, union adherents, or agents of management in or near the polling site which may have influenced the ability of voters to cast a ballot free from coercion;
5. Communications to employees by any party which might have significantly misled them regarding the consequences of voting;
6. Bribery, fraud or other serious misconduct which affected the free choice of voters.

Objections may be filed only by a "party" to the election – that is, one of the unions who is on the ballot (the petitioner, the incumbent union, or other intervener), an employee petitioner in a decertification election, or the agency. They must be filed with the FLRA within five working days of the service of the tally of ballots, and must clearly state the objections and the reasons for them. Within ten days following the service of the objections, the objecting party must submit evidence in writing supporting the objections. The FLRA will investigate and/or conduct a hearing as it deems necessary, and will issue a Decision and Order considering each objection and its merit. If it does not find merit in the objections, it will dismiss them. If it does find merit to any objection(s) sufficient to have affected the outcome of the election, it will order a re-run of the election. In either case, any party adversely affected by the RD's decision may file an appeal with the Authority before any certification is issued by the Region, and certification will be delayed until the Authority renders a decision on the appeal.

Certifications and Bars to Elections

When all objections and challenges, if filed, have been decided and the outcome of an election is clear, the RD will issue a certification; s/he will issue a "certification of results of election" if no union obtained a majority of the valid votes, and a "certification of representative" if a union did win the election. Both of these documents serve to bar the filing of any new petitions for election for one year.

If a union has been certified as the exclusive representative, it will normally seek to negotiate a collective bargaining agreement during the one year certification bar period. If it is successful in doing so, the contract will bar the filing of a petition for an election for up to three years. (So, for example, a five year agreement will bar a petition for election for only three years. A three year contract is a also a bar for only three years, and a rival union may file a petition during a window period of 105 to 60 days prior to the expiration of a three year contract; if no such petition is filed, the contract may be "rolled over" or renewed and will again serve as a bar for the duration of the renewal, up to another three years.)

Post-Certification Events Calling for Petitions to the FLRA

Sometimes after a union has been elected as the exclusive representative of a bargaining unit, events will occur which change the names or composition of parts of the unit. In these circumstances, it may be desirable or necessary to file a petition to make changes to the certification or to sort out what employees remain in the bargaining unit.

Amendment of a Certification

Petitions to amend a certification of representative often involve simple, uncontested changes to names of agency organizational components which do not affect or alter the size or scope of the unit. Even if the changes seem minor and obvious, it's a good idea to file these petitions, since over the years many such changes may take place and it may ultimately be difficult to trace the history of the unit and to identify its composition.

Another event calling for the filing of an amendment of certification is more complex, and involves changing the designation of the exclusive representative. There are specific procedures, referred to as "Montrose" procedures or criteria (after the VA, Montrose, NY case in which the criteria were first set forth), which must be followed in order for the FLRA to certify a change in a union designation resulting from a merger of unions or a requested change in affiliation. (For example, two national unions may merge; members of a local union may want to merge with another local of the same union; a local union of one national union may want to affiliate with a different national union; or it may wish to become a new, independent union.) The Montrose procedures require that:

1. The current exclusive representative must call a special meeting of all members of the incumbent union, for the express purpose of discussing the proposed change in affiliation/designation and its ramifications;

2. Adequate advance notice of the meeting must be given to all members;

3. The meeting must be held at a time and place convenient to all members (this may prove difficult, if not impossible, if there are widespread geographic areas or 24-hour shifts involved, but the union should do the best it can and should probably consult with the FLRA Regional Office on any current case law on these circumstances – it may be possible to use a mail ballot, for example);

4. All members should be given an adequate amount of time at the meeting to discuss the proposed change and the consequences of the change; and

5. All members should also be given an opportunity to vote by secret ballot, with the ballot clearly specifying the change and any inherent consequences of the change.

Note that bargaining unit employees who are not union members need not be given the foregoing options, nor are members of the receiving union given them.

Another important requirement is that any change in affiliation should not affect the continuity of the employees' representation. In this regard, the FLRA will look at such things as:

1. Whether the officers or representatives of the union will change;

2. Whether local control or autonomy will change;

3. Whether the gaining union will administer any existing contract;

4. Whether any organizational or administrative changes are so significant that they would effectively change the union's identity;

5. Whether existing union funds will be transferred intact; and

6. Whether the dues structures are similar.

Also note that a petition to amend a certification cannot in any way change the size or scope of the bargaining unit itself.

Clarification of a Bargaining Unit

Petitions are commonly filed to clarify the status of certain positions in the agency with respect to their inclusion in the bargaining unit, either because of changes in duties that have taken place since the date of the election or because the position is newly created. The FLRA will investigate or hold a hearing to take evidence on these positions, and will look at the same types of factors previously discussed in the election eligibility section re: supervisors, confidential employees, etc.

Reorganizations or Other Unusual Circumstances Affecting the Continued Appropriateness of a Unit

As we all know, upon being appointed, high level supervisors and managers in the federal government secretly pledge to reorganize something under their control in order to leave a new and improved legacy from the last person in the job. Sometimes the changes they make substantially alter the structure or organization of the agency, which then calls into question the continued viability of the bargaining unit. Congress occasionally passes laws which have a similar effect. Whatever the source of these reorganizations, either the agency or the union may believe that the organizational changes have taken employees out of the bargaining unit, added some in, or so muddied the waters that no one knows for sure what union, if any, represents the employees or what the composition of the unit is.

When these changes arise, it is a good idea to begin looking at the effects on the unit early on, and perhaps to involve the FLRA in discussions of what recourses and possible outcomes there may be, as well as how to narrow the areas of dispute. However, if possible, it is best to wait until most all changes, or changes affecting a substantial and representative number of the employees involved, have actually occurred before filing any petition. The FLRA normally prefers to decide the effects of reorganizations after they have taken place or when a phase-in plan is imminent and definite. The type of evidence described above in the section on appropriate unit questions will be examined with respect to the circumstances existing both before and after the changes affected by the reorganization.

Some of the outcomes of a petition asking the FLRA to decide the continued appropriateness of the unit are:

1. The Regional Director decides that the character and scope of the unit haven't changed significantly, and he/she dismisses the petition;

2. The FLRA decides that a gaining agency (or component of an agency) is the successor employer of a group of employees transferred to it, and that the union which formerly represented the employees continues to represent them because the transferees represent a majority of the employees in the new unit. The FLRA will also look to see if the mission, duties, functions, management structure, locations, and working conditions in the gaining entity have also remained substantially similar;

3. A bargaining unit, part of a bargaining unit, previously unrepresented employees, or a group of newly created positions not covered by the original unit description, may be "accreted to" (commingled with or functionally, physically, or operationally integrated into) another existing bargaining unit, which remains appropriate with the addition of the new employees. Providing that the transferred employees do not constitute a majority of employees in the combined unit, the exclusive representative in the gaining unit would then represent the transferred employees along with the rest of the employees in its unit;

4. Employees may be transferred to a component and integrally combined with a much larger group of unrepresented employees, and the FLRA may decide that the certified bargaining unit is no longer appropriate, or that the union can't be shown to represent a majority of the employees in the new unit, and therefore the union is not its exclusive representative;

5. One or more units of employees may be combined to form a new organization or unit, and the FLRA may decide that the new unit is appropriate and order an election to decide which of the unions formerly representing the employees should represent the new unit;

6. One or more units of employees are combined, but the FLRA finds that substantial portions of these units can't be identified within the new unit, which also includes formerly unrepresented employees, and the FLRA decides that no union exclusively represents the employees and that an election is not warranted.

Please be aware that since reorganizations are often quite complex and are rarely alike, the FLRA continues to develop case law to address the range of circumstances which they present. It is a good idea to consult with the FLRA and to do research into case law on these subjects before taking a final position on what effects a reorganization has had on your bargaining unit.

Other Types of Petitions

Petitions may also raise questions concerning whether a union is defunct or whether it continues to represent a majority of employees. These petitions are filed almost exclusively by agencies.

Defunctness

In order to establish defunctness, it must be shown that a union is either unable or unwilling to represent employees in the bargaining unit. In some instances, the national union of a "defunct" local agrees with an agency that the local can no longer represent employees and will submit a disclaimer of interest in the unit. Normally, if defunctness is shown, the FLRA will issue a document withdrawing the certification.

Petition Challenging Continued Majority Status of Union

Agencies may also file petitions questioning the continued majority status of the union. In such cases, the petitioner must submit to the FLRA a document outlining its "objective considerations" – in essence, the unbiased facts and reasons – supporting its claim that the union no longer represents a majority of the employees. These include such factors as: the absence of any collective bargaining agreement or requests to bargain over management-initiated changes over a substantial period of time; a lack of grievances or other representation on behalf of unit employees; few if any employees on dues withholding; few if any local officers or stewards; and other evidence that the union has gone dormant. This type of petition should be filed in accordance with the timeliness requirements of the FLRA regulations (i.e., after expiration of a contract, or in the open window period of a contract with an automatic renewal clause). If the FLRA agrees that a valid question concerning representation (or in this case, a good faith doubt of continued representation) exists, it may order an election among the employees to determine whether they wish to continue to be represented.

Decertification Petition

Petitions may also be filed by employees requesting that an election be held to determine the majority status of the union. These "decertification" petitions must be filed in accordance with the timeliness requirements of the FLRA's regulations and must be accompanied by a 30% showing of interest from the employees in the unit. If these requirements are met, absent other defects in the petition, the FLRA will require an election among the unit employees to determine if the union continues to represent them.

Severance Petition

Occasionally, a union will file a petition seeking to "sever" part of a unit, normally along craft or specialized occupational lines like police or firefighters, from a larger, facility-wide unit. This is largely hopeless, since the petitioner must show that the incumbent has essentially not fairly or effectively represented the group of employees in question either in its contract terms or in connection with daily working conditions, grievances, etc., or that other unusual circumstances exist (e.g., a substantial change in the scope or character of the unit has occurred due to a reorganization; or inequities in working conditions exist between the employees sought and employees in the same jobs in other units). Also, the severance should not result in the fragmentation of units.

Consolidation Petition

Agencies and labor organizations both sometimes find it desirable to consolidate smaller bargaining units into a larger unit, for ease of negotiations, to reduce costs of labor relations or representation, and for other reasons relating to a more streamlined operation or the ability to negotiate matters at a national level of their organizations. A petition to consolidate units may be filed jointly by an agency and a labor organization having exclusive recognition, or by either. The consolidated unit should itself constitute an appropriate unit, ensuring a community of interest among employees, effective dealings and efficiency of agency operations. Thus, consolidated units will not be considered to be appropriate if they promote fragmentation or otherwise are not formed along meaningful geographic and organizational lines. The parties may agree to consolidate units without an election, although employees must be given an opportunity to request an election if they collect a showing of interest of 30% in the proposed consolidated unit (this rarely happens); also, professional employees must ordinarily be allowed to vote on whether they wish to be in a consolidated unit with nonprofessional employees.

Dues Allotment Petition

Another type of petition, infrequently filed, permits a union to request certification for the limited purpose of negotiating a dues allotment agreement with an agency. The petitioning union must submit a showing of 10% union membership, and the unit involved must meet all criteria for an appropriate unit.

Key Points in Chapter Two

1. Representation issues involve the basic statutory right of employees to organize and be represented by a union in a group of employees that logically conforms to the agency's structure and facilitates bargaining.

2. Certain types of positions are excluded from any bargaining unit because the work they do might cause them to have a conflict of interest with representation by a union.

3. There are many different purposes for representation petitions – among others, there are some to determine if employees want to be represented by a union, some to determine who should be in the bargaining unit represented by the union, and some to sort out the lines and composition of the bargaining unit following changes in the agency.

4. There's a sizeable body of case law concerning representation issues, as well as relatively complex procedures governing them, and it may be helpful to explore that case law and/or to seek assistance from the FLRA if you are confronted with a situation which you think might require a petition.

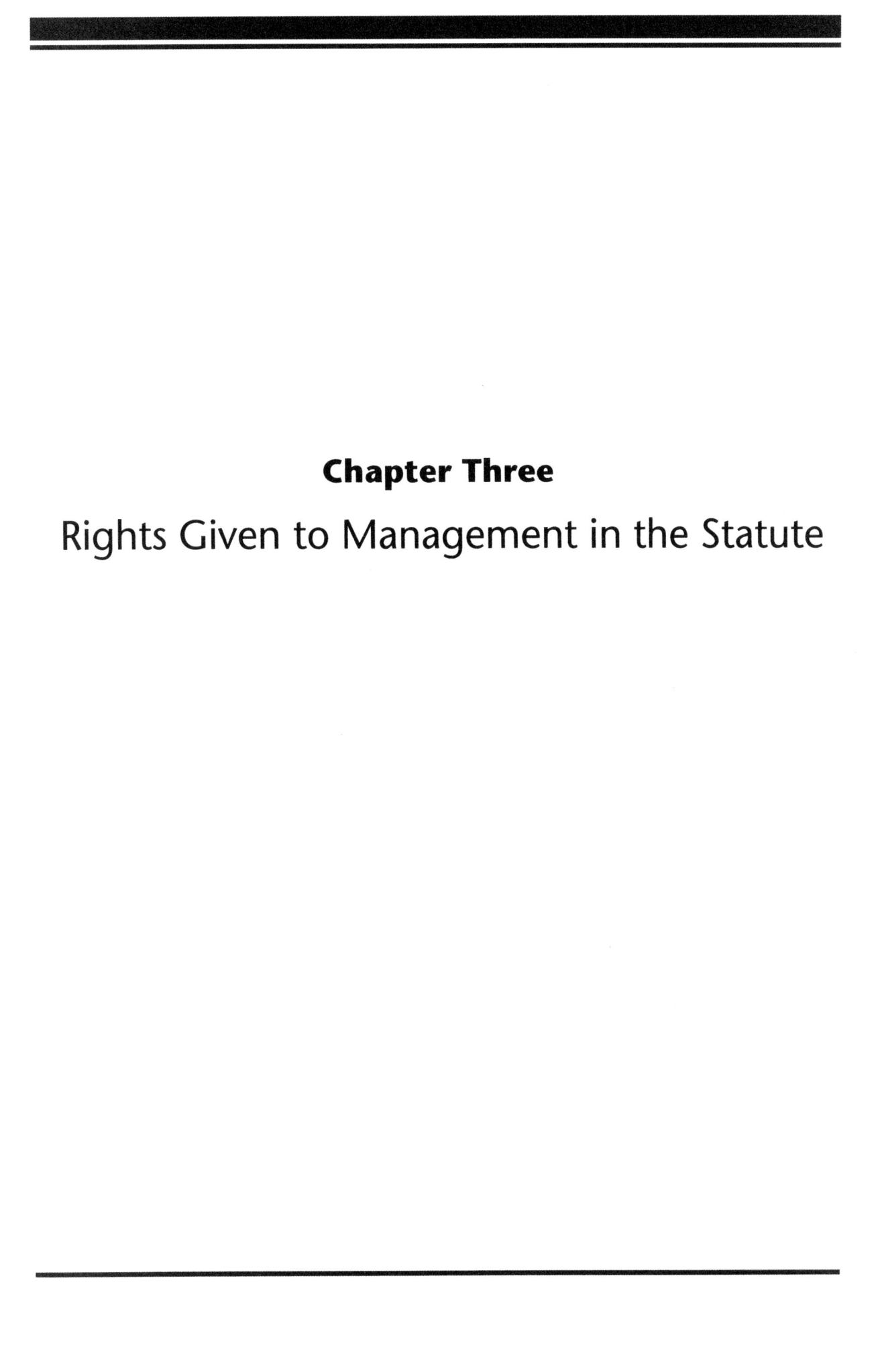

Chapter Three
Rights Given to Management in the Statute

Chapter Three: Rights Given to Management In the Statute

I often joke that if a private sector negotiator were able to negotiate into a private sector collective bargaining agreement the rights given to federal management by the Statute, he or she would be given an island in the Bahamas as a bonus. Management has significant rights given to it under the Statute. These consist of reserved management rights contained in Section 7106(a) of the Statute, which affect collective bargaining and rights given in other parts of the Statute. These management rights are called "reserved" rights because they are reserved to management and cannot be bargained away through negotiations with a union. Section 7106(a) removes from the duty to bargain management functions which Congress deemed essential to the effective conduct of agency business. This provision sets forth a list of management rights which allows management to manage the workforce and carry on the business of the government. These rights are very significant and cover most things a manager may want to do to manage his/her employees and accomplish the mission of the agency. Management receives these rights automatically by operation of the Statute. In the private sector, many of these rights are subjects over which management must bargain. It is important that both management and union understand these rights because they place significant restrictions on what can be bargained in the federal sector. The reserved rights that managers will most often exercise in their daily role of managing the workforce are discussed in this chapter. Because of the importance of management rights under the Statute, the management rights provision of the Statute is set forth in its entirety below.

In addition, management has a significant number of rights given to it by the Statute that are not specifically related to collective bargaining. This chapter will also explore these rights and explain how they function in the federal sector labor relations system.

Section 7106. Management Rights

(a) Subject to subsection (b) of this section, nothing in this chapter shall affect the authority of any management official of any agency –

(1) to determine the mission, budget, organization, number of employees, and internal security practices of the agency; and

(2) in accordance with applicable laws –

(A) to hire, assign, direct, layoff, and retain employees in the agency, or to suspend, remove, reduce in grade or pay, or take other disciplinary action against such employees;

(B) to assign work, to make determinations with respect to contracting out, and to determine the personnel by which agency operations shall be conducted;

(C) with respect to filling positions, to make selections for appointments from –

(i) among properly ranked and certified candidates for promotion; or

(ii) any other appropriate source; and

(D) to take whatever actions may be necessary to carry out the agency mission during emergencies.

Why are Management Rights Important?

Two aspects of management rights are important to understand. First, if an action of management is the exercise of a management right, a union cannot tell management through the collective bargaining process that it cannot exercise this right. The union cannot propose "Don't Do It", in other words. The union cannot, for example, bargain over management's decision to assign work to employees. It cannot tell management not to assign the work. However, it does have the right to bargain over mitigating the adverse effects on employees from the exercise of the rights. In the example just used, the union can propose to mitigate the effect of the new work assignment by proposing that employees be given adequate training for the new assignment. Training may reduce the adverse effect of not knowing how to do the new assignment, which could adversely affect an employee's appraisal.

The Right to Assign Work and Direct Employees

On a daily basis, managers assign work and direct employees. Assignment of work includes where and when employees work, what kind of work they do and to whom work is assigned. This is probably, for most managers or supervisors, the right they will most often exercise. In addition to assigning work, managers and supervisors usually "direct" employees on a daily basis, which under the Statute is defined as supervising or guiding employees in the performance of their duties. The right to direct employees is exercised through determining the quantity, quality and timeliness of their work production and establishing priorities for its accomplishment. The union cannot negotiate what duties employees perform, the location of those duties, or the tours of duty established for employees. However, if management makes significant changes in employees' duties, it may have to bargain over how these changes adversely affect the employees. In most cases, when changes in the assignment of duties have been found to be subject to negotiations, the changes involved new or different duties from those the employee normally is assigned.

Example 1: Management wishes to assign employees new tasks requiring the use of a computer and the employees have never used computers in their work. Management has the right to make this change. It is the exercise of management's right to assign work. The union cannot prevent management from making the change; however, management may have to notify the union before it makes the change, depending on how significant the change is. In this case, if the employees have never used computers in their work, introducing the use of computers could be considered a significant change in working conditions. An example of an adverse effect on employees from the requirement to use computers is the potential for the failure to effectively use the computers; inadequate performance could lead to a performance-based action against the employee for not meeting his/her productivity goals.

One key question when management introduces new technology into the work place is how significant the change is. If the change or its impact is significant, management may have an obligation to negotiate with the union. Determining the significance of a change and its impact on employees involves the concept of "de minimis," which will be discussed in the Chapter 7, What You Need to Know about Collective Bargaining.

The issues in negotiations may include such things as adequate training for the employees on how to use a computer, the effects on the employees' performance appraisals from this new requirement, and what happens to employees who are not capable of learning this new task.

Example 2: Management decides to change the location of its office. It is a management right to change the office location. Management has the right to assign the location where work will be performed. The union cannot tell management not to move or change its office location. However, as in the first example, if the change in location adversely affects bargaining unit employees, management may have an obligation to bargain before it makes the move. Management is not bargaining over the decision to move, but rather over the adverse effects on employees from the move. Bargaining over relocations is a common issue in the federal sector. There are many working condition issues involved in relocation of an office. Because of all the potential issues, the difficult part of bargaining over relocations is timing the bargaining so it is completed before the relocation is to take place. Implementing a relocation without notice to the union or prior to completing bargaining can be an unfair labor practice.

The issues in negotiations may include such things as where employees will park at the new location, the arrangement and size of the offices, and the safety and security of the new work site.

Example 3: Management decides to assign employees to a new shift that never existed before. The union cannot propose that management not establish the new shift. If management needs a new shift, it has the right to establish one. The issue to be negotiated will be the adverse effects on the employees from the exercise of the management right to assign work at a new time. Establishment of new shifts is another common issue in federal sector labor relations. If there are frequent changes in a certain type of working condition, such as shift changes, it may be better for union and management to mitigate the effects of such repetitive changes by including a provision covering prospective shift changes in their collective bargaining agreement. They can thereby avoid continuous bargaining over the subject.

Some potential negotiation issues include mitigation of the effects of the new shift on employees' child care arrangements, educational pursuits and public transportation availability, among others. For example, the negotiations may result in giving the employees affected by the shift change adequate time to rearrange their schedules to accommodate the new shift.

The Right to Establish Internal Security Practices

Management has the right to establish practices and policies and to take actions which are part of its plan to safeguard the persons and property of the government. This should not be confused with national security. The right to establish internal security practices involves those safeguards management puts in place to protect its employees and the property of the government, not how the government protects the American people. When management establishes an internal security practice, the union does not have the right to second guess whether the practice is the best way to protect employees or property. Management need only show that there is reasonable link between the practice it has put in effect and the protection of employees and property.

Example 1: The manager of a unit has decided to install a new lock on the front entrance to its offices. In the past, all employees had keys that provided free access to the office at all hours. Not all employees will be given a key to the new lock. Only managers will receive keys. The new lock has been installed because there has recently been a series of thefts of office equipment. Many employees who arrive early because of their bus or carpool schedules must now wait outside the building until a manager lets them in. In the past, employees had access to the building to perform work on weekends. Under the new system, the building will not be open on weekends.

The union cannot demand that the locks not be changed, nor can the union seek to negotiate whether limiting the availability of keys to the office door is the best approach to securing the building against theft of equipment. Under the circumstances, a connection can be shown between limiting the availability of keys to the door and safeguarding the property of the government. The restriction on who receives keys does have an adverse effect on employees, however. Being required to wait outside the building in inclement weather will be a significant change in working conditions of employees.

Proposals which may be made in negotiations over the change could include changing office hours or the hours of work of certain employees to coincide with the transportation schedule of employees or allowing exceptions for certain employees to have early key access to the building if management deems them trustworthy. The negotiability of these proposals will depend on the extent to which they interfere with management's rights. Do these proposals excessively interfere with the internal security practice management intended to implement? In determining whether the proposals are negotiable, the extent of the interference with management rights will be balanced against the benefit to employees from the union's proposal. This balance between interference with management rights and the benefit to employees is an integral part of the test applied to bargaining over

appropriate arrangements. The concept of appropriate arrangements bargaining will be discussed in detail in Chapter Eight.

Example 2: Management has established a new policy that all employees who drive a government vehicle may not talk on a cell phone while operating the vehicle. State law, in some of the states where the change will take place, does not prohibit speaking on a cell phone while driving. Management must show there is a connection between speaking on a cell phone while driving and protecting government vehicles and personnel from damage from accidents.

The union may argue that state law does not prohibit the use of cell phones while driving, so the federal government does not have authority to override state law. The FLRA has decided that individual state laws do not prohibit the federal government from implementing policies inconsistent with state law. In a case where a military base required employees to wear motorcycle helmets when driving their motorcycles on the military base even though state law did not require helmets, the FLRA found that state law did not control what happened on a military base. It also found a connection between wearing helmets and protecting the personnel of the government.

While the union in this example cannot stop the restriction on the use of cell phones, it may still make proposals to mitigate the adverse effects of the change. Issues which may be negotiated include warnings posted in all government vehicles advising employees not to use their cell phones and notices posted on agency bulletin boards announcing the new policy.

The Right to Discipline Employees

Management has the right to discipline employees and to take whatever actions are necessary to maintain discipline in the workplace. This right includes the right to suspend, remove, reduce in pay and grade or take any other disciplinary actions. The union does not have the right to negotiate over what or whether discipline will be given to employees.

Unions do have the right to negotiate over how management exercises the right to discipline employees. As an example, a union may negotiate that in disciplining employees, management must show "just cause" when taking a disciplinary action. "Just cause" means that management would have to be able to justify the reasons why it took a disciplinary action against an employee.

Unions also may negotiate the process used for disciplining employees. This may include such things as when responses will be made to disciplinary actions and information that will be provided to the union about the disciplinary action.

While unions cannot negotiate discipline, they may challenge disciplinary actions using a negotiated discipline article in the collective bargaining agreement, the negotiated grievance procedure, or if the action is considered an adverse action (such as a suspension for over 14 days or a removal action), they may appeal on behalf of the employee to the Merit Systems Protection Board.

Example: An employee is consistently tardy. The employee's manager issues a one day suspension to the employee for tardiness. The union representative contacts the manager for a meeting about the suspension. The manager agrees and meets with the representative. At the meeting, the union rep tells the manager that management had an obligation to issue a letter of reprimand to the employee first before issuing the suspension. The union rep further disputes the tardiness of the employee, indicating that everyone in the section was usually a little late and that this employee was singled out for discipline for improper reasons.

Management has no obligation to negotiate the discipline for the employee. In most contracts, the union has the right to grieve disciplinary actions. In the processing of the grievance, management and union may agree on reducing a disciplinary penalty in resolution of the grievance. However, if there is no resolution and the grievance goes to arbitration, the discipline may be reduced by the arbitrator if found inappropriate. The union might also grieve that the employee should have received counseling for a first offense because of a contract provision requiring progressive discipline. The normal approach to disciplining an employee is to use progressive discipline. Progressive discipline involves using progressively greater levels of discipline to try to change the behavior of an employee. It is management's choice whether it uses a progressive approach or not based on the nature of the offense. Management will have an obligation to support the use of a suspension for a first offense committed by the employee and to demonstrate that the penalty chosen was appropriate for the offense.

The Right to Hire and Select Employees

Hiring in the federal sector can be a complex process. It is subject to many rules and regulations and, importantly, merit principles. Assuming that management has followed these rules, regulations, and principles, it can hire or promote whomever it chooses. It has the right to make selections from among properly ranked and certified employees and from any appropriate source. In the private sector, hiring can be mandated in some cases by a union hiring hall and in others by union membership considerations. However, in the federal sector the union cannot mandate whom management hires.

Unions nevertheless have the right to negotiate over the procedures used to hire employees. These procedures are frequently contained in an agency or facility merit promotion plan or in a provision of a collective bargaining agreement. Negotiable merit promotion procedures may include such things as what vacancy announcements say and where they are posted, how interviews are conducted, and the employees' right to appeal if they believe they improperly were denied a promotion. Nonselection alone cannot be the basis for a grievance. However, such issues as improperly reviewing an employee's qualifications for a position may be the subject of a grievance. Along with the rules and regulations pertaining to selection, any collective bargaining agreement provisions concerning merit promotion must also be followed.

Example: Management has decided to reorganize a work unit. Among a number of other changes affecting employees, management is going to create a new position at the GS-13 level in the unit. There are currently no GS-13 positions in the unit. The new position will be a higher level version of an existing position which is currently in use. This new position will also include new duties not previously performed by employees.

The union has demanded to bargain over the reorganization. It proposes that the new GS-13 positions be filled on the basis of seniority by employees who currently work in the unit and are deemed qualified for the position by management. Management has no obligation to negotiate over this proposal. It has the right to select employees from any available source. Limiting the selection to existing employees interferes with this right.

The Right to Determine the Budget of the Agency

Management has the right to determine its budget. This right is sometimes confusing to managers. Things the union proposes in negotiations will often cost money. Money comes from an agency's budget. Therefore, it would seem logical that union proposals which cost money interfere with management's right to determine its budget. However, the right to determine a budget does not mean that the union cannot seek to negotiate over items which will cost the government money. For the most part, every time labor and management negotiate there are cost consequences. Negotiations themselves cost money. The time spent by the negotiators, the room where negotiators meet, and travel and per diem expenses for negotiators all cost money. These are costs necessary to fulfill a statutory mandate to engage in collective bargaining.

A union proposal runs afoul of management's right to determine its budget if it tries to include a specific cost item in the agency's budget or if the cost of the proposal is significant. The significance of the cost is in relation to the agency's budget as a whole, not just the dollar value of the individual item.

Example: Management has moved a number of offices to a new location which is served by public transportation. Employees were not able to use public transportation in the past to get to the office. Parking, which in the past was free, is now extremely expensive in the new location. The union has proposed that employees receive $50 a month in transit subsidy money for employees who use public transportation to get to work. This amount is consistent with existing requirements for money given to employees for transit subsidy purposes. Many employees at other agency locations have been receiving transit subsidy money for a number of years. Management calculates what it would cost for all employees to receive the transit subsidy and arrives at a figure of over $25,000 a year to subsidize their travel. It does not have money in its budget to pay this cost. It declares the union's proposal nonnegotiable because it does not have the money and therefore the proposal interferes with its right to determine its budget.

A union proposal violates management's right to determine its budget if it attempts to place a specific item in the agency's budget or if the cost is significant. The union's proposal in this example does not try to put an item in the budget. The significance of the cost is based on the agency's budget as a whole. If a work unit has a budget of $8 million and the whole organization has a budget of $100 million, the $25,000 cost would not be significant. While this may be negotiable as not interfering with management's right to determine its budget, this does not mean that management must agree to the proposal. While management cannot refuse to bargain over the proposal, it could counter-propose a lesser amount for the subsidy or, depending on the circumstances, no subsidy at all. There is a difference between a proposal being non-negotiable and being unreasonable. A union proposal may be negotiable and not violate the management rights provision of the Statute, but it may be unreasonable. If the agency proposes $10,000 in a transit subsidy while the union proposes $25,000, and they are unable to reach agreement, the dispute can be submitted to the Federal Service Impasses Panel (FSIP) for resolution. FSIP, which was created to resolve federal sector labor management bargaining impasses, would have authority to decide which proposal is more reasonable and should be adopted, or it can direct an entirely new resolution of its own.

The Right to Layoff Employees

Management has the right to layoff employees. In the federal sector this is done predominantly through reductions in force (RIF). The Office of Personnel Management (OPM) has issued a series of government wide regulations that govern RIFs. These regulations must be followed by all government agencies subject to them. While unions cannot propose that employees not be subject to a RIF, they can negotiate over the procedures for conducting a RIF. However, their proposals cannot run afoul of the OPM RIF regulations.

Example: Management has determined it must conduct a reduction in force because Congress has not provided adequate funding for the agency. Based on this budget shortfall, the agency must RIF 14 employees. It notifies the union representing these employees that it will be conducting a RIF.

The union proposes that instead of conducting the RIF of employees, management should delete all management bonuses for the current year and eliminate all travel and training. It also proposes that the employees subject to the RIF be provided training and outplacement assistance.

The union cannot negotiate over management's decision to conduct a RIF. Its proposal to delete all management bonuses is nonnegotiable because it deals with working conditions of employees who are not in the bargaining unit. It also cannot propose elimination of all travel and training, because this proposal interferes with management's right to assign work to employees. Sending someone to training and on travel is the assignment of work. However, its proposal to provide training and outplacement assistance may very well be a negotiable proposal, because it seeks to mitigate the adverse effects of the RIF on the employees.

The Right to Contract Out

Management has the right to contract out work performed by federal employees. The Office of Management and Budget (OMB) has issued a circular (OMB Circular A-76) which establishes the process an agency must follow in determining to contract out government work. Contracting out has been the subject of much litigation in the federal labor relations arena and much controversy. Recent studies show that the agencies keep work in-house and win contracting out competitions with the private sector approximately 90% of the time. That is the good news. The bad news is the drastic cuts agencies must sometimes make in staff and budgets to win the competition. The pros and cons of contracting out are not the subject of this book, however.

Unions have sought in a variety of ways to negotiate over contracting out. The answer has consistently been that they do not have the right. This is based on the statutory preclusion of bargaining over contracting out and OMB Circular A-76. Since the OMB Circular is considered a government-wide regulation, unions cannot negotiate provisions in their collective bargaining agreements which are inconsistent with it. Unions have also sought to grieve an agency's failure to follow A-76. The FLRA has found these proposals nonnegotiable also, because A-76 already contains an administrative appeal process.

However, unions can bargain over the adverse effects of contracting out on the employees whose jobs are lost, as well as on the employees who are left behind to do the agencies' work with fewer employees or with new processes. If employees are displaced through contracting out, in many cases there will ultimately be a RIF. The union can bargain over the RIF as discussed above. It can also bargain over the changes in working conditions for employees resulting from the retention of the work in-house.

The Right to Determine the Agency's Organization

The right of an agency to determine its organization refers to the administrative and functional structure of an agency, including the relationships of personnel through lines of authority and the distribution of responsibilities for delegated and assigned duties. It encompasses the determination of how an agency will structure itself to accomplish its mission and functions. This determination includes such matters as the geographic locations in which an agency will provide services or otherwise conduct its functions, how various responsibilities will be distributed among the organizational subdivisions, how an agency's organizational grade level structure will be designed, and how the agency will be divided into organizational entities such as sections, branches and divisions.

Example: An agency decides to consolidate 3 of its sections into one new large section and then add the section to a new division. As a result of this consolidation, among other changes, employees in this new section have different lines of supervision, new supervisors, new functional responsibilities and for some, a new location for their desks in generally the same work area.

The union proposes that the unit be consolidated into 2 new sections instead of 3. It bases its proposal on a recent study of the organization, done by an outside contractor, which recommends the two-section arrangement. The issue is not whether management has made the right decision, but whether there is an obligation to bargain over the union's proposal. A union argument that the reorganization is a bad decision and is contrary to the contractor's recommendation is of no value in determining the negotiability of a proposal. The determination of negotiability will be based on the Statute, regardless of whether management made a good or bad decision. By the same token, when management has clearly made a decision beneficial to employees, the correctness of the decision does not lessen the obligation to bargain over a proposal made by the union which is clearly negotiable. The question remains whether the proposal, as a matter of law, is negotiable under the Statute.

In this case, the union's proposal would be considered nonnegotiable because it interferes with management's right to determine its organization. Proposals made by the union concerning the changes in working conditions brought about by the new sectional arrangement, to the extent they are negotiable appropriate arrangements, must be bargained by the agency.

The Right to Determine the Number of Employees and Personnel by Whom Agency Operations will be conducted.

In interpreting these rights, the FLRA has often equated them with the permissive subjects of bargaining dealing with numbers, types and grades of employees assigned to an organization found in Section 7106 (b) (1). It is clear that a union cannot negotiate over how many employees management will employ to accomplish the mission of the agency. The permissive right further expands what it means to bargain over employees assigned to an organization. However, since the subject of numbers, types and grades is permissive, there is no obligation on the part of management to bargain over these issues however management may bargain over a permissive subject at its option.

Why Are Management Reserved Rights Important?

When management is exercising a management reserved right given to it under the Statute the union cannot propose that management not exercise the right. It cannot stop management from doing what management has decided to do. The union can only bargain over mitigating any adverse effects on employees from the exercise of that right. If an action does not entail the exercise of a management right, the union has the right to bargain over management's decision to take the action. A negotiable proposal in that case would include not taking the action at all. The fact that a proposal is negotiable does not require that it be agreed to. It simply means in most cases that it does not run afoul of management rights.

How negotiations work and what management must negotiate about will be more fully explained in Chapter Seven, What You Need to Know about Collective Bargaining.

The Right to Take Actions during an Emergency

Under Section 7106(a)(2)(D) of the Statute, an agency has the right to take whatever actions may be necessary to carry out the agency mission during emergencies. This provision, in essence, exempts management from its obligation to engage in bargaining before it makes a change in working conditions. The intention of this provision is to allow management to act quickly in times of emergency.

This is a very misunderstood provision of the Statute. The problem with the provision is that Statute does not define what type or degree of emergency triggers this exemption. As there is no definition of what an emergency is, it is left to case-by-case determinations, and agencies act at their peril in determining a particular event to be an emergency. When the union disagrees with the agency's determination of emergency in a particular event, it files an unfair labor practice charge with the FLRA, claiming that management unilaterally changed working conditions without bargaining. The agency is then subjected to a third party (the FLRA) second guessing its decision and actions. One alternative is for management and union to define in their collective bargaining agreement what they consider to be an emergency which would exempt bargaining. This approach can, however, make the application of this agreed-upon definition potentially subject to a grievance to be resolved by an arbitrator.

Example: A hurricane is quickly approaching a military base. In order to protect the base and its personnel, management cancels the third shift of maintenance operations to prevent maintenance employees from entering the base and being exposed to hurricane conditions. However, at the same time, it places second shift employees on mandatory overtime, which requires them not to leave the base. Once the hurricane has passed, it instructs the third shift employees to work the second shift for the next month to help clean up the mess left by the storm.

The union files an unfair labor practice claiming management unilaterally changed working conditions by cancelling the third shift and requiring second shift employees not to leave the base during the hurricane. These actions were taken without first bargaining with the union. Management claims its actions were exempt from the duty to bargain because there was an emergency. While management may be correct that its actions were exempt from pre-implementation bargaining, it still has an obligation to bargain with the union after the emergency is over. Any agreement would be applied retroactively.

Other Management Rights

Management also has rights given to it under the Statute which are not contained in the management rights provision of the Statute. As you will see, although management has the right to challenge the actions of a union, agencies frequently deem being proactive by filing unfair labor practices or grievances not to be a desirable approach.

The Right to File Unfair Labor Practices

Management has the right to file an unfair labor practice alleging that a union violated the Statute. Unfair labor practices are found in Section 7116. They are intended as a means of regulating the relationship between labor and management and insuring that they are complying with the Statute. Unfair labor practices filed by management may concern such issues as bad faith bargaining by the union or unlawful work stoppages or slow downs. Unfair labor practices will be more fully explained in Chapter Five, How to Enforce Your Rights.

Unfair labor practices over work stoppages can lead to decertification of a union. This occurred in 1982 when the air traffic controllers union went on strike. Strikes are illegal in the federal sector, and following the filing of an unfair labor practice by the FAA, the union representing the controllers was decertified. Unfair labor practices can only be filed against a union as an institution, not against individual union representatives.

Historically, management in the federal sector has not filed a large number of unfair labor practices against unions. In fact, unions file many times more unfair labor practices against management in any given year than management files against unions. This is because some agencies have strict prohibitions against the filing of unfair labor practice charges. Because of the management rights provision of the Statute, many agencies do not see the value of unfair labor practices since their rights are already very extensive. In their view, there is nothing that can be gained through an unfair labor practice that they do not already have under the Statute. Additionally, many agencies, rather than file an unfair labor practice when they believe the union is doing something wrong, will simply take the action they deem appropriate and wait for the union to file an unfair labor practice against them. They obviously take this approach at their peril. If they acted precipitously or improperly, they may have make-whole remedies and back-pay remedies to deal with later, not to mention almost certain damage to their labor-management relationship.

The Right to File Grievances

All collective bargaining agreements in the federal sector must include a grievance arbitration provision ending in binding arbitration. The right to file grievances extends to employees, unions and management. Management may file grievances concerning alleged union violations of the collective bargaining agreement. However, for the same reasons they do not file unfair labor practices, many agencies do not file grievances against unions.

The Right to File Petitions to Change the Scope of the Bargaining Unit or to Challenge the Representation Status of the Union

If management believes there have been changes in the employee composition of a bargaining unit, it may file a petition to challenge the current makeup of the unit. Reorganizations frequently change the scope of bargaining units. For example, management may petition to have the unit description changed to reflect which employees should be in the unit after the reorganization. They may also challenge whether the union maintains its majority status as the representative of the employees. This challenge may also come about as a result of reorganization. The types of petitions which may be filed in these circumstances are discussed in Chapter 2.

The Right to File Exceptions to the Decision of an Arbitrator

If management (or the union) does not agree with the decision of an arbitrator, it may file exceptions to the arbitrator's award with the FLRA. Section 7122 of the Statute provides as follows:

Section 7122. Exceptions to Arbitral Awards

(a) Either party to arbitration under this chapter may file with the Authority an exception to any arbitrator's award pursuant to the arbitration (other than an award relating to a matter described in section 7121(f) of this title). If upon review the Authority finds that the award is deficient–

(1) because it is contrary to any law, rule, or regulation; or

(2) on other grounds similar to those applied by Federal courts in private sector labor-management relations; the Authority may take such action and make such recommendations concerning the award as it considers necessary, consistent with applicable laws, rules, or regulations.

(b) If no exception to an arbitrator's award is filed under subsection (a) of this section during the 30-day period beginning on the date the award is served on the party, the award shall be final and binding. An agency shall take the actions required by an arbitrator's final award. The award may include the payment of back-pay (as provided in section 5596 of this title).

The grounds for exceptions discussed in the section include:

1. Bias on the part of the arbitrator

2. Arbitrator exceeded his authority

3. Arbitrator failed to provide a fair hearing

4. Award is deficient as contrary to law or regulation

5. Award fails to draw its essence from the parties' collective bargaining agreement

6. Award is based on a non-fact

An exception must be based on more than disagreement with the award. It must be supported by one or more of the grounds for exception. The FLRA, in reviewing an award, is reluctant to overturn the award unless it is clearly deficient on one of these grounds.

The Right to Seek Federal Services Impasses Panel Assistance

Management has the right to seek the assistance of FSIP to resolve impasses in negotiations. Section 7119 of the Statute provides for Impasses Panel assistance as follows:

Section 7119. Negotiation impasses; Federal Service Impasses Panel

(a) The Federal Mediation and Conciliation Service shall provide services and assistance to agencies and exclusive representatives in the resolution negotiation impasses. The Service shall determine under what circumstances and in what matter it shall provide services and assistance.

(b) If voluntary arrangements, including the services of the Federal Mediation and Conciliation Service or any other third-party mediation, fail to resolve a negotiation impasse –

(1) either party may request the Federal Service Impasses Panel to consider the matter, or

(2) the parties may agree to adopt a procedure for binding arbitration of the negotiation impasses, but only if the procedure is approved by the Panel.

(c)(1) The Federal Service Impasses Panel is an entity within the Authority, the function of which is to provide assistance in resolving negotiation impasses between agencies and exclusive.

The job of the FSIP is to resolve disputes when labor and management do not agree. It does not have the statutory authority to resolve questions concerning whether a proposal is negotiable as a matter of law.

Example. Labor and management are negotiating over the amount of official time a union representative should receive and they cannot agree. Management believes the representative should receive 10 hours a month and the union has proposed 20 hours. If this dispute is taken to the FSIP by either management or the union, the FSIP will decide the issue. It could agree with management or the union or it could fashion a different resolution from that proposed by either side. FSIP does not have authority to decide whether as a matter of law management has an obligation to negotiate over official time. That issue can normally only be resolved by the FLRA, unless the negotiability issues involved in the dispute concern subjects that have clearly been settled by the Authority.

Management Rights Case Study

Management has decided to move a work unit to new location as a result of a soon-to-be-announced reorganization. The new location is in a city 50 miles away from the current location. Management has chosen the new location because it is closer to a large segment of the public that uses the services of the unit. At the current location, employees enjoy free parking, but at the new location, they will have to pay for parking. At the new location, employees will also be in cubicles instead of private office space. As part of the reorganization, employees who were in the claims section will now be part of the customer response unit. In this new unit, employees will both process claims and answer phone inquiries. In the past, these responsibilities were done by separate units.

What management rights are being exercised by this management action?

1. Moving to a new location is the exercise of management's right to assign work. Management has the right to assign where work will be done.

2. Moving to a new city is the exercise of management's right to determine its organization. Management has the right to establish the geographic locations of its work units.

3. Assigning new duties for the unit is the exercise of management's right to assign work. Management has the right to assign any type of duties to employees that it wishes to assign.

4. Parking is not the exercise of a management right. Management may have to negotiate over whether the parking will be paid or will not be paid by the government. Unless the cost of parking is significant enough to meet the test discussed earlier in this chapter, management may not be able to assert that a proposal for paid parking violates management's right to determine its budget.

5. The union cannot propose that management not make the change. The relocation of the office will result in many working condition changes for the employees. The union may make proposals to

mitigate the various adverse effects on employees of the office relocation.

Key Points in Chapter Three

1. Management has significant reserved management rights given to it in the Statute. In determining its labor relations obligations, management should determine if it is exercising a management right.

2. When management exercises a management right, the union may not make proposals which prevent management from exercising the right. However, the union does have the right to bargain over proposals to mitigate the adverse effects on employees from the exercise of the right.

3. The management right to assign work includes where, when, and how employees do their job, what kind of work they do, and to whom work is assigned. The right to direct employees is exercised through supervising employees, determining the quantity, quality and timeliness of their work production, and establishing priorities for its accomplishment.

4. Management has the right to discipline employees and to take whatever actions are necessary to maintain discipline in the workplace. This right includes the right to suspend, remove, reduce in pay and grade, or take any other disciplinary actions. While unions cannot negotiate over discipline, they do have the right to grieve disciplinary actions.

5. Management has the right to determine its budget. A union may make proposals which cost the government money, as long as the proposals do not include a specific cost item in the agency's budget or the cost of the proposals is not significant when considered in comparison to the agency's budget as a whole. The cost of a union proposal may not make the proposal nonnegotiable, but it may affect how the FSIP looks at management's and the union's competing proposals in resolving a dispute.

6. Assuming management has followed the rules, regulations and merit principles applying to hiring in the federal government, it can hire or promote whomever it chooses. It also has the right to make selections from among properly ranked and certified employees and from any appropriate source. A union cannot negotiate whom management must hire or limit management's right to select from any appropriate sources. It may negotiate over the appropriate arrangements and procedures used in making selections and promoting employees.

7. Management has the right to layoff employees. In the federal sector this is done predominantly through reductions in force (RIF). The Office of Personnel Management (OPM) has issued a series of government-wide regulations that govern reductions in force. These regulations must be followed by all government agencies subject to them. While unions cannot propose that employees not be subject to a RIF, they can negotiate over the appropriate arrangements for employees adversely affected by a RIF.

8. Management has the right to contract out work performed by federal employees. The Office of Management and Budget (OMB) has issued a circular (OMB Circular A-76) which establishes the process an agency must follow in determining to contract out government work. Unions cannot bargain over contracting out, but they can bargain over the adverse effects of contracting out on the employees whose jobs are lost and on the employees who are left behind to do the agencies' work with fewer employees or with new processes.

9. The right of an agency to determine its organization refers to the administrative and functional structure of an agency, including the relationships of personnel through lines of authority and the distribution of responsibilities for delegated and assigned duties. This right encompasses the determination of how an agency will structure itself to accomplish its mission and functions. Unions cannot bargain over how an agency organizes itself, but they can bargain over the effects on employee working conditions of changes in the way an agency is organized.

10. Under Section 7106(a)(2)(D) of the Statute, an agency has the right to take whatever actions may be necessary to carry out the agency mission during emergencies. This provision, in essence, exempts management from its obligation to engage in bargaining before it makes a change in working conditions. The union may bargain post implementation over the adverse effects of the changes made during the emergency.

Chapter Four
Union Rights

Chapter Four: Union Rights

As is the case with management, unions have significant rights given to them by the Statute. These rights are sometimes called "institutional" rights because they are rights of the union, as an institution, rather than rights of the employees who are members of the union. We will discuss employee rights in the next chapter. This chapter will explore union rights and explain how they interface with management rights.

Unions exist in the federal sector because Congress, through the Statute, gives them the right to be a legal entity with rights and obligations. An organization in the federal sector can be called an exclusive representative (union) only if it meets certain criteria for labor organizations under the Statute and if employees in a secret ballot election have chosen to be represented by the union. This is unlike the private sector, where a union may be recognized by management as the exclusive representative without a vote. All unions in the federal sector, unless they were godfathered in by the Statute in 1978, can become an exclusive representative of federal employees only as result of an election. Section 7111 of the Statute establishes who can be an exclusive representative:

Section 7111. Exclusive recognition of labor organizations

(a) An agency shall accord exclusive recognition to a labor organization if the organization has been selected as the representative, in a secret ballot election, by a majority of the employees in an appropriate unit who cast valid ballots in the election.

To obtain this right, a union must file a petition with the FLRA seeking to be the exclusive representative of a group of employees in a proposed bargaining unit. The agency has the right to contest the scope of the proposed bargaining unit in what is called a representation proceeding. (See Chapter 2 – Representation Issues) Employees in a bargaining unit cannot be supervisors, management officials, confidential employees, or engaged in intelligence, counterintelligence, investigative or security work which directly affects national security. The employees must also share a community of interest and the proposed bargaining unit must lead to efficiency of agency operations and effectiveness of dealings.

The Right to be the Exclusive Representative of Employees

When employees vote for a union to represent them, the union becomes their exclusive representative and no other group can represent the interests of employees in the bargaining unit. In dealing with issues affecting employees' working conditions, management must deal only with the employees' exclusive representative and not directly with the employees.

Section 7114. Representation Rights and Duties

(a)(1) A labor organization which has been accorded exclusive recognition is the exclusive representative of the employees in the unit it represents and is entitled to act for, and negotiate collective bargaining agreements covering, all employees in the unit. An exclusive representative is responsible for representing the interests of all employees in the unit it represents without discrimination and without regard to labor organization membership.

Employees will sometimes go to management and complain about the union and seek to represent themselves over working conditions issues. Management has the right to deal with an individual employee over issues which pertain only to that employee. As an example, a manager can meet with an employee without a union representative being present over the employee's personal leave issue. However, a manager cannot meet with his/her staff and negotiate with them over a new approach to the granting of leave. When a manager meets with bargaining unit employees to negotiate with them over their working conditions without a union representative present, this is called a bypass of the union and can be an unfair labor practice.

The union is the exclusive representative of all employees in the bargaining unit whether they are members of the union or not. A bargaining unit is defined as the employees who were certified to be in the bargaining unit by the FLRA after an election. The Statute requires that the union must represent all employees in the bargaining unit whether they are members of union or not. Unions have a duty to fairly represent all employees in the bargaining unit regardless of union membership. Breaching this duty can be an unfair labor practice on the part of a union.

The Right to Engage in Collective Bargaining

The most important right unions have is to represent employees in collective bargaining over working conditions. Collective bargaining means one agent – the union – bargaining for the collective good of all the employees in the bargaining unit. Instead of having to bargain with each individual employee about the working conditions of that employee, management may – and must – bargain only with the union, which represents the interests of all employees and binds all employees to one agreement.

Unions generally engage in collective bargaining over a new contract or when management changes working conditions during the term of an existing contract. If management intends to make a change in working conditions, depending on the issue it may have to negotiate over the decision to make the change itself or over the adverse effects of the change on employees. During the term of an existing collective bargaining agreement, a union also has the right to initiate bargaining over new working conditions if those working conditions were not previously bargained over in contract bargaining. To be effective in federal sector collective bargaining, a union must know the Statute's approach to collective bargaining, the processes for challenging management's determinations on the negotiability of union proposals and how to be successful before FSIP.

The Right to be Present at Meetings Management Has with Employees

Unions have the right to be present at certain meetings that management conducts with bargaining unit employees. Management and union may include in a collective bargaining agreement the right of the union to be present at certain other types of meetings management holds with employees. These are contractually developed rights to be present at meetings. As an example, some collective bargaining agreements provide an employee the right to have a union representative present during an employee-manager meeting to discuss the employee's performance. This is not a right given by the Statute; it is a negotiated right found only in the parties' collective bargaining agreement. The enforcement of this right would be through the grievance procedure.

Management regularly has meetings with its employees. The Statute provides the right for the union to be present at various types of meetings management conducts with bargaining unit employees. These rights are provided to unions irrespective of whether they are placed in a collective bargaining agreement. In fact, many collective bargaining agreements mirror these statutory rights in various articles of the agreement. Placing them in the collective bargaining agreement gives the union the option of filing either a grievance or an unfair labor practice when management violates the right. However, to the extent the contractual provision changes the statutory right by either expanding or limiting the right, enforcement of this changed right must be done through the grievance procedure. As an example, some collective bargaining agreement provisions provide that when management conducts an investigatory examination with an employee in connection with potential disciplinary action, management must affirmatively tell the employee he/she is entitled to representation by the union. This is not required by the Statute. If management fails to tell an employee of the right to representation contained in the collective bargaining agreement a grievance must be filed to enforce this contractual right. The Statute provides explicitly for two types of meetings at which management must provide the union the right to be present.

Section 7114. Representation Rights and Duties

(2) An exclusive representative of an appropriate unit in an agency shall be given the opportunity to be represented at –

(A) any formal discussion between one or more representatives of the agency and one or more employees in the unit or their representatives concerning any grievance or any personnel policy or practices or other general condition of employment; or

(B) any examination of an employee in the unit by a representative of the agency in connection with an investigation if –

(i) the employee reasonably believes that the examination may result in disciplinary action against the employee; and

(ii) the employee requests representation.

(3) Each agency shall annually inform its employees of their rights under paragraph (2)(B) of this subsection.

These are formal discussions and investigative examinations (so-called "Weingarten" meetings). In numerous decisions, the FLRA has established the criteria for when a union must be given the opportunity to be present at formal discussions and Weingarten meetings. The requirements and respective roles and rights of management and union at meetings held with employees will be discussed in great detail in Chapter Nine. Meetings with Employees that Require a Union Representative.

The Right to Assist a Labor Organization

Employees have the right to be union representatives or seek the support of the union. An employee who becomes a union representative is protected against discrimination by management because of their status or actions as a union representative. Managers may not make statements that interfere with an employee's right to be a union representative, steward or official. Employees engaged in representational activities are regarded as being engaged in "protected activity." Management may not take action against an employee engaged in protected activity unless the actions of the employee are considered flagrant misconduct, which results in the loss of this protected status. Flagrant misconduct would include acts such as assaulting a manager during a representational activity.

The Right to Negotiate Over Receiving Information

Unions may negotiate in a collective bargaining agreement the right to receive information concerning a variety of subjects. The right to negotiate for information should not be confused with the right to request information under the Statute. In a collective bargaining agreement, both union and management can be required to provide information. Under Section 7114 of the Statute, only management may be required to provide information. For example, many collective bargaining agreements specify what information management must supply about disciplinary actions. Collective bargaining agreements may also dictate what data a union must provide to management about official time usage. If a duty to supply information is contained in a collective bargaining agreement, a failure to provide it in accordance with the contract may be subject to the grievance procedure.

The Right to Request Information

The information right is contained in Section 7114(b)(4):

Section 7114. Representation Rights and Duties

(b) The duty of an agency and an exclusive representative to negotiate in good faith under subsection (a) of this section shall include the obligation –

(4) in the case of an agency, to furnish to the exclusive representative involved, or its authorized representative, upon request and, to the extent not prohibited by law, data –

(A) which is normally maintained by the agency in the regular course of business;

(B) which is reasonably available and necessary for full and proper discussion, understanding, and negotiation of subjects within the scope of collective bargaining; and

(C) which does not constitute guidance, advice, counsel, or training provided for management officials or supervisors, relating to collective bargaining;...

Unions have a statutory right to request information which is normally maintained by management, is relevant and necessary to the unions' representational role, and does not constitute guidance, advice, counsel, or training provided for management officials or supervisors. Information requests under the Statute must be only for data which in existence. An agency does not have to create new data in order to comply with a request for information. However, an agency may be required to do a search of records contained in a computer data base.

Reasonably Available

The information requested must be reasonably available. The FLRA looks very closely at what could be considered burdensome requests for huge amounts of data. The FLRA will determine whether it takes "excessive or extreme means" to obtain the information. When there are questions raised about the burdensome nature of the requested information, the FLRA requires the parties to look at alternative ways the information can be provided.

No Right to have Questions Answered in Information Request

A request for information does not include the right to have questions answered. While asking a question does entail obtaining information, it is not the type of information which can be obtained under this section of the Statute. Requesting answers to questions is a legitimate function of the collective bargaining process and may be pursued as part of the good faith bargaining requirement of the Statute. Failure or refusal to answer questions necessary to fulfill the obligation to engage in good faith collective bargaining could be viewed as bargaining in bad faith.

Relevant and Necessary

To meet requirement that information requested under the Statute be relevant and necessary to the union's representational role, the union must explain the representational purpose for the information in its request. This explanation should describe the "particularized need" for the information. To support a particularized need for information, the union must articulate with specificity why it needs the information, including the uses to which the information will be put and the connection between those uses and the union's representational responsibility. It must also respond to requests to clarify what is being requested. A union's failure or refusal to respond to a request to clarify an information request may be deemed a valid reason not to provide the information. On the other hand, if management does not understand the request, it cannot simply refuse to respond to the union's request and then defend its failure on the basis that it did not understand the request. Under the Statute, it has an obligation to seek clarification.

No Right to Information Prohibited from Release by Law

The Statute prohibits requiring the release of information that would be prohibited from release by law. A union cannot request information which violates the privacy of employees as set forth in the Privacy Act and Freedom of Information Act. The restrictions on release of personal information found in the Freedom of Information Act and the Privacy Act must be followed in releasing information under the Statute. Information will not be required to be disclosed under the Statute if its disclosure would constitute a clearly unwarranted invasion of personal privacy. In many situations, requested information which contains personal identifiers, such as name or social security number, can be provided in a sanitized (personal identifier is redacted to protect the individual's privacy) format.

The union does not have to disclose confidential information about individual employees it is representing. Management, in seeking clarification of an information request, cannot condition its release of information on the union providing confidential details about individual grievants. The union also does not have to disclose its theory for the grievance. Information requests from the union usually concern collective bargaining subjects and grievances; however, they may be made for any information which is relevant to the full range of a union's representational responsibilities.

Example: The union is representing an employee in a grievance concerning overtime. The contract article on overtime provides that overtime will be fairly distributed to employees based on the work needs of the agency. The article further provides that employees can volunteer for overtime and that management will consider volunteers first when filling overtime needs.

An employee comes to the union complaining that she has not received any overtime in the past six months even though she is on the volunteer list. She contends that all the overtime has been given to the same employee. She does not consider this fair. The union decides to file a grievance. In preparing the grievance, the union representative decides she needs information about overtime in the work unit to verify the employee's story.

The union submits a request for information under the Statute. It requests all the overtime records for the section for the last year. This request includes the names of the employees receiving overtime, the dollar amount of overtime each employee received, and the overtime volunteer list for the section. Management refuses to give the information to the union on the basis of the Privacy Act. It asserts that disclosure of the names of employees would invade their privacy.

In order to support its position, management would have to show that the information requested is in a system of records protected by the Privacy Act. If it is not able to show that a system of records has been established to place the information under the protection of the Privacy Act, it will not be successful in this claim. For the most part, individual names of employees are not considered to be protected by the Privacy Act. However, if the release of information along with the employee's name could be embarrassing and stigmatizing to the employee involved, it may be withheld from release. Payroll data is not generally considered stigmatizing information, because the public is entitled to know how much money federal employees are paid.

Under the circumstances of this case, the agency would have to release the information to the union. Even though only one employee may be involved, the information concerning payment of overtime would not be embarrassing or stigmatizing to employees.

Standards of Conduct

All labor organizations representing employees in the federal sector must comply with the Standards of Conduct contained in the Statute. These standards are enforced by the Assistant Secretary of Labor for Labor Management Relations of the U.S. Department of Labor. Failure to comply with these requirements can lead to the union being placed in trusteeship with the management of the union being placed in the hands of a trustee other than the officers of the union.

Section 7120. Standards of Conduct for Labor Organizations

(a) An agency shall only accord recognition to a labor organization that is free from corrupt influences and influences opposed to basic democratic principles. Except as provided in subsection (b) of this section, an organization is not required to prove that it is free from such influences if it is subject to governing requirements adopted by the organization or by a national or international labor organization or federation of labor organizations with which it is affiliated, or in which it participates, containing explicit and detailed provisions to which it subscribes calling for –

(1) the maintenance of democratic procedures and practices including provisions for periodic elections to be conducted subject to recognized safeguards and provisions defining and securing the right of individual members to participate in the affairs of the organization, to receive fair and equal treatment under the governing rules of the organization, and to receive fair process in disciplinary proceedings;

(2) the exclusion from office in the organization of persons affiliated with communist or other totalitarian movements and persons identified with corrupt influences;

(3) the prohibition of business or financial interests on the part of organization officers and agents which conflict with their duty to the organization and its members; and

(4) the maintenance of fiscal integrity in the conduct of the affairs of the organization, including provisions for accounting and financial controls and regular financial reports or summaries to be made available to members.

The Right to Binding Arbitration

All collective bargaining agreements in the federal sector must have a grievance arbitration provision which ends in binding arbitration. Section 7121(b)(1) (C)(iii) provides:

Section 7121. Grievance Procedures

(b)(1) Any negotiated grievance procedure referred to in subsection (a) of this section shall –

(ii) provide that any grievance not satisfactorily settled under the negotiated grievance procedure shall be subject to binding arbitration which may be invoked by either the exclusive representative or the agency.

Next to collective bargaining, this is the most significant right unions have. Through the contractual grievance procedure, unions and employees have the right to grieve such issues as disciplinary actions and violations of law and regulation. As noted above, management also has the right to file grievances. Grievances are ultimately heard by an impartial arbitrator selected by the union and management. Both union and management have the right to appeal arbitrators' decisions to the FLRA. The decisions of an arbitrator can be enforced by the FLRA or a federal court, after noncompliance with the award has been pursued through the unfair labor practice procedure.

The Right to File Exceptions to Arbitration Awards

If the Union (or an agency) does not agree with the decision of an arbitrator, it may file exceptions to the arbitrator's award with the FLRA. Section 7122 of the Statute provides as follows:

Section 7122. Exceptions to arbitral awards

(a) Either party to arbitration under this chapter may file with the Authority an exception to any arbitrator's award pursuant to the arbitration (other than an award relating to a matter described in section 7121(f) of this title). If upon review the Authority finds that the award is deficient –

(1) because it is contrary to any law, rule, or regulation; or

(2) on other grounds similar to those applied by Federal courts in private sector labor-management relations; the Authority may take such action and make such recommendations concerning the award as it considers necessary, consistent with applicable laws, rules, or regulations

(b) If no exception to an arbitrator's award is filed under subsection (a) of this section during the 30-day period beginning on the date the award is served on the party, the award shall be final and binding. An agency shall take the actions required by an arbitrator's final award. The award may include the payment of back pay (as provided in section 5596 of this title).

The grounds for exceptions discussed in the section include:

1. Bias on the part of the arbitrator
2. Arbitrator exceeded his authority
3. Arbitrator failed to provide a fair hearing
4. Award is deficient as contrary to law or regulation
5. Award fails to draw its essence from the parties' collective bargaining agreement
6. Award is based on a non-fact

The Right to File a Negotiability Appeal

If management declares a union proposal nonnegotiable, the union has the right to file an appeal with the FLRA challenging the declaration of non-negotiability. Section 7117 of the Statute provides for such an appeal:

Section 7117. Duty to bargain in good faith; compelling need; duty to consult

(c)(1) Except in any case to which subsection (b) of this section applies, if an agency involved in collective bargaining with an exclusive representative alleges that the duty to bargain in good faith does not extend to any matter, the exclusive representative may appeal the allegation to the Authority in accordance with the provisions of this subsection.

(2) The exclusive representative may, on or before the 15th day after the date on which the agency first makes the allegation referred to in paragraph (1) of this subsection, institute an appeal under this subsection by –

(A) filing a petition with the Authority; and

(B) furnishing a copy of the petition to the head of the agency.

(3) On or before the 30th day after the date of the receipt by the head of the agency of the copy of the petition under paragraph (2)(B) of this subsection, the agency shall –

(A) file with the Authority a statement –

(i) withdrawing the allegation; or

(ii) setting forth in full its reasons supporting the allegation; and

(B) furnish a copy of such statement to the exclusive representative.

(4) On or before the 15th day after the date of the receipt by the exclusive representative of a copy of a statement under paragraph (3)(B) of this subsection, the exclusive representative shall file with the Authority its response to the statement.

(5) A hearing may be held, in the discretion of the Authority, before a determination is made under this subsection. If a hearing is held, it shall not include the General Counsel as a party.

(6) The Authority shall expedite proceedings under this subsection to the extent practicable and shall issue to the exclusive representative and to the agency a written decision on the allegation and specific reasons therefore at the earliest practicable date.

This right will be discussed in more detail in Chapter Six – How to Enforce Your Rights.

The Right to Seek Federal Services Impasses Panel (FSIP) Assistance

The Union has the right to seek FSIP assistance. FSIP resolves collective bargaining disputes where labor and management cannot agree. For example, if management proposes that the walls of all employee offices be blue and the union proposes white, and after extensive bargaining they are unable to agree on the question, the FSIP will resolve the dispute if requested by union or management. In most cases, the FSIP will require the parties to use the services of the Federal Mediation and Conciliation Service to assist in mediating the dispute before it will assert jurisdiction over the dispute. If management asserts that the union proposal over the color of the walls is nonnegotiable, the Union must file a negotiability appeal with the FLRA. However, if the issue concerning wall color has been clearly decided by the Authority, the FSIP may rely on that precedent and decide the matter.

The Right to File Representation Petitions

The union has the right to seek to be the representative of a new bargaining unit or to seek clarification or amendment to an existing bargaining unit through the filing of a petition with the FLRA. For example, such petitions are filed after reorganizations which affect the scope of the bargaining unit. Reorganizations can result in the expansion of the bargaining unit or in a reduction in the size of the unit. Representation petitions are dealt with in more detail in Chapter Two.

The Right to File Unfair Labor Practice Charges

Unfair labor practices are violations of the Statute. Unions, agencies and employees have the right to file unfair labor practice charges. Typical unfair labor practice charges concern an alleged failure to bargain, statements made to employees by union or agency representatives which may violate the Statute, and the failure to notify the union of meetings at which it may have the right to be present. Unfair labor practice charges are filed against an agency or a union, not against individual supervisors or union representatives. Unfair labor practices are covered in more detail in Chapter Six.

The Right to Official Time

Official time is the source of much controversy in the relationship between the union and management. Official time was provided for in the Statute as an alternative to a union shop. The union shop is an arrangement negotiated into some private sector contracts, which requires that all employees join the union or pay the equivalent of union dues to the union. Congress felt that if the unions were to be required to represent all employees regardless of union membership, this would place a financial burden on them. The alternative crafted by Congress to the union shop was official time. Under the Statute, union representatives are entitled to statutorily mandated official time and contractually negotiated official time. Section 7131 of the Statute establishes this right as follows;

Section 7131. Official Time

(a) Any employee representing an exclusive representative in the negotiation of a collective bargaining agreement under this chapter shall be authorized official time for such purposes, including attendance at impasse proceeding, during the time the employee otherwise would be in a duty status. The number of employees for whom official time is authorized under this subsection shall not exceed the number of individuals designated as representing the agency for such purposes.

(b) Any activities performed by any employee relating to the internal business of a labor organization (including the solicitation of membership, elections of labor organization officials, and collection of dues) shall be performed during the time the employee is in a non-duty status.

(c) Except as provided in subsection (a) of this section, the Authority shall determine whether any employee participating for, or on behalf of, a labor organization in any phase of proceedings before the Authority shall be authorized official time for such purpose during the time the employee otherwise would be in a duty status.

(d) Except as provided in the preceding subsections of this section –

(1) any employee representing an exclusive representative, or

(2) in connection with any other matter covered by this chapter, any employee in an appropriate unit represented by an exclusive representative, shall be granted official time in any amount the agency and the exclusive representative involved agree to be reasonable, necessary, and in the public interest.

Unions have the right under the Statute to be granted official time for participating in collective bargaining, including impasse proceedings. They do not have to negotiate this right; they are given it by the Statute (see Section 7131(a)). The statutory right to official time for collective bargaining does not include official time for preparation for bargaining. This is a subject for bargaining in the ground rules for negotiations. Under the Statute, the union and management may negotiate additional discretionary official time beyond what is mandated in Section 7131(a) for representational purposes in any amount they agree is reasonable and necessary and in the public interest (See Section 7131(d)). Official time negotiations over discretionary official time can be a very contentious issue between labor and management, and many collective bargaining agreement official time provisions end up before FSIP. To support their need before the FSIP for official time, unions must be able to support their contentions with evidence, not just argument or conjecture. Support for the need for official time can also be shown by describing the representational purposes the time will be used for and the relationship of the amount of time requested to the size of the bargaining unit. Management may provide evidence refuting these arguments in its response opposing a certain amount of official time.

Under no circumstances may official time be used for internal union business such as solicitation of membership, union elections and collection of dues.

Employees on official time are paid the normal wages for their position. While on official time, they are not performing their normally assigned duties. In some cases, this leaves managers shorthanded. The granting of official time and the potential for its abuse are the source of much consternation to many managers. How much official time union officials are to receive and the procedures for obtaining official time (other than official time prescribed by Section 7131(a) or (c)) are usually covered by negotiated provisions of collective bargaining agreements. In many cases, disputes over official time are not an issue of having inadequate provisions concerning official time; rather, they stem from the way these provisions are enforced. Unions complain that they are enforced too narrowly, and management complains that union representatives abuse their use of time. For the most part, disputes over official time are subjects for the grievance procedure. The denial of official time based on management's interpretation of the official time provisions of a contract is rarely an unfair labor practice.

It is the responsibility of managers to ensure that union representatives are following the correct procedures in their use of official time. It is the responsibility of union representatives not to abuse the use of official time. If an abuse of official time becomes apparent to employees in the bargaining unit, this can lead to diminished respect for the union by employees who feel that union representatives aren't pulling their weight in the work unit. On the other hand, improper denial of official time can result in the union being unable to properly represent the bargaining unit employees.

Example: The union contract provides that union stewards receive reasonable official time for their representational activities. The contract also requires that a union representative must request the use of official time before it is taken. A union steward requests 4 hours of official time from his manager to prepare a grievance for an employee. The manager denies the request on the grounds that 4 hours is not reasonable. The union steward has always received 4 hours of official time to prepare grievances and therefore believes that a past practice has developed of receiving 4 hours.

The issue for the union is what forum to choose to contest the denial of official time if it disagrees with the manager. Should the union file an unfair labor practice claiming management violated an existing past practice of granting 4 hours for preparing a grievance, or should it file a grievance because the manager did not act appropriately in denying the union steward's request for reasonable official time? In most cases, it is best to file a grievance to contest this type of denial of official time. The grievance would contest the manager's decision that the request was not reasonable under the circumstances (and it could also raise the issue of a change in practice, since nothing prevents unfair labor practice issues from being presented in the grievance/arbitration forum.)

To prove an unfair labor practice filed with the FLRA alleging a change in an established past practice of granting 4 hours for grievance preparation, the union would have to provide evidence that the practice was widespread and involved more managers and stewards than those involved in this incident. If it is able to prove this practice, the union can argue that the contract has been modified by the practice that has developed between management and the union. In most cases, this is a heavy burden.

The Right to Collect Dues

One of the rights unions have is to collect dues from bargaining unit employees. Unions have the right to have dues allotments made by employees be collected by management and remitted to the union. How dues deductions are handled is the subject of agreement between management and the union. Locals of a national union, in almost all cases, must submit a portion of the dues collected to the national union to defray the operational costs of the national union and its support to the local field structure. There are very strict U.S. Department of Labor requirements for union accountability of union dues collected.

Section 7115. Allotments to Representatives

(a) If an agency has received from an employee in an appropriate unit a written assignment which authorizes the agency to deduct from the pay of the employee amounts for the payment of regular and periodic dues of the exclusive representative of the unit, the agency shall honor the assignment and make an appropriate allotment pursuant to the assignment. Any such allotment shall be made at no cost to the exclusive representative or the employee. Except as provided under subsection (b) of this section, any such assignment may not be revoked for a period of 1 year.

(b) An allotment under subsection (a) of this section for the deduction of dues with respect to any employee shall terminate when –

(1) the agreement between the agency and the exclusive representative involved ceases to be applicable to the employee; or

(2) the employee is suspended or expelled from membership in the exclusive representative.

If management fails to properly collect or remit dues to the union, it may have liability for the moneys not collected or remitted. Only bargaining unit employees may have dues deducted from their pay checks. For periods when an employee is not in the bargaining unit, such as on temporary detail to a supervisory position, dues should no longer be collected. Also, when employees receive promotions to positions outside the bargaining unit, dues deductions should cease.

Union Rights Case Study

A manager has decided to make a change in how leave is approved. There is no provision in the collective bargaining agreement that covers employees requesting leave. The manager calls all six of his employees together to discuss the change. He asks for their input on how best to handle requests for leave, particularly holiday leave. A number of employees suggest a holiday leave rotational system based on seniority. He suggests a variation of this which allows for employees with hardships to obtain an opportunity for leave not based on their seniority. The employees seem to like this approach. Based on this discussion, he implements a new overtime policy. The union calls to complain about the new policy.

What Union Rights Are Affected by the New Policy?

The union has the right to act as the exclusive representative of employees in the bargaining unit. Management may not negotiate directly with employees over working conditions. This is called bypassing the exclusive representative. If management holds a meeting where it deals directly with employees rather than the union, it violates the union's right to act as the exclusive representative of employees.

The union has the right to be offered the opportunity to be present at meetings with bargaining unit employees in which personnel policies, practices or working condition are discussed. This type meeting is called a formal discussion. However, if no union representative chooses to attend, the meeting can proceed as scheduled. A meeting with employees to discuss leave, which is a working condition, would be considered a formal discussion if the meeting also meets the indicia of formality discussed in Chapter Ten – Meetings with Employees that Require Union Representation. In the circumstances of this case study where the manager did not just discuss leave policy but also negotiated directly with the employees, the absence of the union if notified does not amount to a waiver of the union's right to represent the employees. Conducting the meeting in the union's absence could be an unfair labor practice even though the union had been notified.

Implementing a new leave policy would be a change in working conditions. The union has the right to engage in collective bargaining over changes in working conditions before management implements the change. Even though all the employees seem to agree and be in favor of the change, this does not relieve a manager of his/her responsibility to notify the union and engage in collective bargaining. The fact that the employees may like the new policy does not in any way mitigate the failure to meet with the union over the policy.

Key Points in Chapter Four

1. Congress has given unions the legal right in the Statute to represent employees if they petition the FLRA to be the exclusive representative of the employees and a majority of votes cast by employees are in favor of union representation.

2. When employees are represented by a union, management may not bypass the union and deal directly with them concerning working conditions. A bypass is an unfair labor practice.

3. Unions have the right to engage in collective bargaining with management by negotiating over new collective bargaining agreements, initiating bargaining over new working conditions issues, and bargaining over changes in working conditions. This is by far the most important right given to unions in the Statute.

4. Unions are entitled to be present at certain types of meetings management holds with bargaining unit employees. The requirement for the union to be present at these meetings may derive from the provisions of the parties' collective bargaining agreement or be required by the Statute. Meetings, or rights with respect to meetings, which come about through the contract can only be enforced by the grievance procedure. Violations of the Statute can

be enforced by the unfair labor practice procedure or the grievance procedure.

5. All collective bargaining agreements in the federal sector must have grievance – arbitration provisions which end in binding arbitration.

6. Unions have the right to negotiate provisions in their collective bargaining agreements which require management to provide certain types of information. Unions also have the right to request information under the Statute. In submitting a request for information, unions must show a particularized need for the information requested. They also have a responsibility to respond to requests from management for clarification of their requests for information.

7. Unions have the right to receive official time for performing representational activities. Official time for collective bargaining is provided as a specific right under the Statute. Other types of official time are subject to negotiation between union and management.

Chapter Five

Employee Rights

Chapter Five: Employee Rights

The Statute gives individual employees, regardless of union membership, important rights. The Statute also gives employees processes to enforce these statutory rights. In addition to rights given directly to employees, the Statute gives employees protection against actions taken by management or the union, since employees may often find themselves caught in the middle of the combat between them. Employees, in a bargaining unit, also enjoy the rights given to the union as an institution by being members of the bargaining unit. This chapter will explore the rights employees have been given under the Statute.

The Right to Form a Labor Organization

Employees have the right to form labor organizations. A union only becomes an exclusive representative if the employees in the proposed bargaining unit vote for it following the filing of a petition with the FLRA for an election among all employees in the proposed bargaining unit. Employees have the right to form a union without fear of penalty or reprisal for engaging in that activity. Even before a union comes into existence, employees are protected by the Statute for engaging in activities to form the union. If an employee who is seeking to form a union is threatened, coerced, or discriminated against by management, the employee may file an unfair labor practice against management claiming a violation of the Statute. An unfair labor practice may be filed even though the union is not yet in existence.

Example: An employee, on non-work time, in non-work areas, gathers signatures for a petition seeking an election for a union. Management tells the employee to stop gathering signatures in the facility. Management also tells the employee that it will remember who the union supporters were if the union is voted in by the employees.

The employee files an unfair labor practice charge alleging that management interfered with the employee's right to form a labor organization. Management cannot restrict an employee from gathering signatures in a non-work area during non-work time. However, management can restrict employees from interfering with the work of the agency by gathering signatures or campaigning for the union in work areas during work time.

Telling the employee it will remember who the supporters of the union were would be considered an unlawful threat and an unfair labor practice.

The Right to Join or Not Join a Labor Organization

Employees have the right to join or not join the union. Employees in the federal sector cannot be required to join a union as a condition of their employment. They are still represented by the union whether they join or not. Management may not take action against an employee or restrain or coerce an employee because the employee joined or did not join the union. By the same token, the Union cannot discriminate against employees who do not join the union and deny them representation concerning issues over which the union has exclusive control.

Example: A union has the right to provide representation to only union members in EEO cases before the Equal Employment Opportunity Commission (EEOC). They do not have to provide representation to nonmembers, because the EEOC complaint process is not under the union's exclusive control. However, if there is an EEO dispute resolution process in the collective bargaining agreement the union cannot deny nonmembers access to the process and will have to represent the nonmembers to the same extent that it represents members in the contractual process. A union cannot make joining the union a condition for providing representation to an employee with respect to an issue or process contained in the collective bargaining agreement.

The Duty of Fair Representation

The union also cannot engage in arbitrary, bad faith, or discriminatory conduct towards any bargaining unit member in a matter within the union's exclusive control. Assuming that union membership is not a factor, negligence or miscommunication resulting in the failure to provide adequate representation does not breach the duty of fair representation, as long as it is not demonstrated that the employee was deliberately and unjustifiably treated differently from other bargaining unit employees.

Example: A bargaining unit employee seeks the assistance of the union in filing a grievance against management concerning the denial of holiday leave. Management denied the leave request on the day the employee spoke to the union representative. The collective bargaining agreement provides that a first step grievance must be filed within 15 calendar days of the occurrence. The union representative, who spoke to the employee, tells the employee he will file the grievance as soon as he gets back to the union office. The union representative met the employee for the first time when the employee requested assistance and had never spoken to the employee before. The representative goes back to the office and immediately is involved in a number of crises. He forgets to file the grievance within the 15 day time frame.

The employee files an unfair labor practice alleging the union violated the duty of fair representation. It is clear the union representative was negligent in failing to file the grievance after telling the employee he would. The union representative led the employee to believe he would file the grievance, and the employee relied on this assurance. The FLRA has found such a failure on the part of a union to be deliberate and unjustifiable and a violation of the duty of fair representation.

The Right to Assist a Labor Organization

Employees have the right to be union representatives. Employees who become union representatives are protected against interference with their right to represent the union and from discrimination by management because of their status or actions as a union representative. Managers cannot make statements which interfere with an employee's right to be a union representative, steward or official. Employees engaged in representational activities are considered to be engaged in protected activity. Management may not take action against an employee engaged in protected activity as long as the actions of the employee are not considered to be flagrant misconduct, which results in the loss of this protected status. Flagrant misconduct consists of acts such as assaulting a manager, without provocation and not in self-defense, during a representational activity.

Example: An employee became a union steward 3 years ago. She has handled a number of contentious grievances challenging management actions. She has applied for a number of promotions but has not been promoted, even though she is near the top of the best qualified list each time. She is known as a very competent employee. She asked her supervisor why she had not been promoted. The supervisor has worked with the employee for a number of years and has established a friendship outside the office. In order to help the employee get ahead, she tells her: "There is nothing wrong with your work. If you would just get out of the union, I'm sure the next time a promotion comes up you'd be selected."

The employee files an unfair labor practice alleging that she has been discriminated against because of the denial of promotions. The statement made by the supervisor can be seen as an interference with the employee's right to be a union representative. To prove that she was discriminated against with respect to the promotions she didn't receive, the employee must prove that but for her union activity, she would have been promoted.

The right to assist a labor organization also protects the right of employees to seek the assistance of the union. An employee has the right to file a grievance and seek assistance from the union regarding complaints against management. Interference, restraint, or coercion of an employee in exercising this right is an unfair labor practice.

The Right to Representation During A Weingarten Meeting

An employee who reasonably believes that an examination by management (questioning) in connection with an investigation will lead to discipline has the right to request that a union representative be present to represent him/her in the meeting. The union does not have the right to be present unless the employee requests its presence. Management has no obligation under the Statute to inform the employee that he or she is entitled to a union representative.

This is the "Weingarten" right. It gets its name from a 1975 U.S. Supreme Court case in the private sector, NLRB v. Weingarten. The Weingarten case involved an employee who worked at a lunch counter in a retail store called Weingarten. She was questioned by a store loss prevention specialist about a report that she had not paid enough for chicken she had purchased at the lunch counter. She was suspected of not paying the correct amount for the number of pieces of chicken she had purchased. She repeatedly asked for a union representative to represent her in this interrogation. She was denied the representative. The Supreme Court found that she was entitled to a representative and that management should have provided one. In enacting the Statute, Congress had the Weingarten decision in mind and made the right found by the Supreme Court a statutory right for federal employees. The Weingarten right will be discussed in greater detail in Chapter Ten – Meetings with Employees That Require A Union Representative.

Right to File An Unfair Labor Practice Charge

Individual employees have the right to file unfair labor practice charges against both management and the union. They do not have to go through the union to file a charge; they can file it on their own. Common unfair labor practice charges filed by employees against management concern statements by supervisors which interfere with the employee's right to seek the assistance of the union or to be a union member, and allegations of discrimination because of their union activities. Common charges against the union deal with the failure to fairly represent employees. Many of these deal with union negligence in the handling of the representation of an employee in a grievance.

Right to File A Grievance

An unfair labor practice and a grievance cannot be filed over the same issue. This is called trying to get "two bites at the apple." If both are filed over the same issue, then the party being filed against has the right to request the arbitrator or Office of General Counsel of the FLRA to dismiss the grievance or unfair labor practice, whichever was filed second. However, if for example, an employee files a grievance over not receiving overtime, this does not preclude the union from filing an unfair labor practice claiming that the change in the overtime policy was implemented without bargaining. These would be considered two different issues by two different parties.

Right to Be Represented by a Representative of the Employee's Choice

An employee may be represented by a representative of his/her choice, including an attorney, in a matter concerning his/her employment. However, if the representative is to represent the employee under the negotiated grievance procedure, the employee must receive the permission of the union to be represented by a representative other than the union.

Section 7114. Representation Rights and Duties

(a)(5) The rights of an exclusive representative under the provisions of this subsection shall not be construed to preclude an employee from –

(A) being represented by an attorney or other representative, other than the exclusive representative, of the employee's own choosing in any grievance or appeal action; or

(B) exercising grievance or appellate rights established by law, rule, or regulation; except in the case of grievance or appeal procedures negotiated under this chapter.

Employee Rights Case Study

Eugene Debs works as a computer analyst. He is also the union steward for the section he works in. He has been friends with his supervisor for a number of years going back to before he was a union representative and before the supervisor became a supervisor. He recently complained to his supervisor that he had not been promoted when a promotion action was taken, even though he was on the best qualified list. As a friend, the supervisor told him he should "think about getting out of the union if he wanted to get promoted." The supervisor also told him he "spends so much time on union business, supervisors are not going to want to promote someone who is never there to do the job." She further added that "being a union representative has gotten John a reputation as a troublemaker." This was intended to be friendly advice.

What Employee Rights Are Affected by the Supervisor's Statements to John?

John has the right to join a labor organization. Telling him he should get out of the union in order to be promoted interferes with his right to be a member of the union. Even though the statements were meant to be friendly advice, they can be understood to be coercive.

John also has the right to act as a union representative. Statements cannot be made which interfere with John's right to assist the union. The advice was intended to be from one friend to another. However, the issue is whether a reasonable employee would feel coerced by the statements. If a reasonable employee would feel coerced or threatened by the statements, they are an unfair labor practice.

Key Points in Chapter Five

1. The Statute gives employees important rights and also protects them from improper actions by either union or management.

2. Employees have the right to form a labor organization. They are protected from unlawful actions by management even before the union is certified as the exclusive representative.

3. Employees have the right to assist the union without fear of penalty or reprisal. This right applies both to union representatives and employees seeking the assistance of the union.

4. Employees have the right to request union representation if they are being examined in connection with an investigation and they reasonably believe disciplinary action will be taken.

5. Employees have the right to join or not to join the union but must still be represented by the union regardless of union membership. The union has the duty of fair representation towards all bargaining unit employees.

6. Employees have the right to file grievances on their own behalf without union representation. However, the union has the right to be present during the steps of the grievance procedure and any settlement discussions.

7. Employees have the right to be represented by a representative of their own choice, except for processes governed by the negotiated agreement such as the negotiated grievance procedure.

Chapter Six
How Rights Are Enforced

Chapter Six: How Rights Are Enforced

This chapter will explain how to enforce the statutory rights explained in the preceding chapters through the use of the unfair labor practice process. It will also explain how to enforce contractual rights contained in a collective bargaining agreement by use of the grievance process. It will explain negotiability appeals, exceptions to arbitration awards and appeals of Regional Director decisions on representation case issues which may be filed with the FLRA. In understanding how to enforce your statutory rights, it is helpful to understand the agency that is responsible for the enforcement of the Statute.

The Federal Labor Relations Authority

The enforcement of the provisions of the Statute is the responsibility of the FLRA. The FLRA was established by Congress to regulate labor relations between labor and management in the federal sector. It is very similar in structure and function to the National Labor Relations Board, which governs labor relations in the private sector. The three member panel of the FLRA is appointed by the President and confirmed by the Senate. One of the three members must be from a different political party from that of the President. The General Counsel is also appointed by the President after confirmation by the Senate. The Federal Service Impasses Panel has seven members appointed by the President. They do not go through the Senate confirmation process. The FLRA and the FLRA General Counsel also act as the Foreign Service Labor Relations Board for disputes concerning foreign service officers, who are predominantly employed by the Department of State.

The three members of the FLRA hear negotiability appeals, exceptions to arbitration awards, appeals of Regional Director decisions on representation cases and appeals from decisions of administrative law judges on unfair labor practice charges. Within the FLRA is the Office of Administrative Law Judges who preside over unfair labor practice hearings. The General Counsel of the FLRA investigates and prosecutes unfair labor practice charges and also processes representation petitions, which includes investigating petitions, holding hearings, issuing decisions on petitions and conducting elections. The work of the General Counsel is done by Regional office staff located in seven regional offices. The Federal Service Impasses Panel resolves negotiations disputes. These are normally disputes in which the parties cannot agree on terms, rather than disputes regarding whether proposals are negotiable.

How to Enforce Your Rights

There are a number of avenues for employees, unions and management to enforce their rights in federal sector labor relations. The two predominant ways are through the filing of unfair labor practice charges and grievances. Decisions of the FLRA on unfair labor practice cases may be appealed to the federal circuit courts and therefore receive federal court enforcement. For our purposes, we will deal with the administrative processes short of court action. Unions and management may also enforce their rights through the FLRA by filing negotiability appeals (union only), exceptions to arbitration awards and appeals of representation decisions of the FLRA Regional Directors.

The filing of unfair labor practice charges is a process established under the Statute to seek redress for violations of the unfair labor practice provisions of the Statute. Grievance/arbitration procedures mandated by the Statute are established in the collective bargaining agreement to resolve disputes over rights and obligations contained in the agreement. The two processes have many things in common and at the same time, many differences. The most important common feature is that they both provide for a neutral third party with jurisdiction to make binding decisions over disputes in the workplace. Someone other than the union or management will make the ultimate decision on a dispute.

They are quite different in that unfair labor practices deal with violations of the Statute, while grievances deal with violations of the parties' contract. In the unfair labor practice process, violations of law are prosecuted by the General Counsel of the FLRA before administrative law judges of the FLRA. In the grievance process, unions and management represent themselves before impartial arbitrators whom they have selected. Unfair labor practices must be filed within 6 months of the occurrence which is the basis for the charge. Grievances must be filed within the contractual time frames contained in the contract. The unfair labor practice process costs nothing to the filer of the charge. The costs of grievance arbitration are normally shared by the parties. The cost of a one-day arbitration can amount to well over four thousand dollars.

Who Can File Unfair Labor Practice Charges?

The easy answer is that anyone can file a charge, just as anyone can file a lawsuit over just about anything. The real question is whether the allegations fall within the jurisdiction of the FLRA, and therefore, whether the FLRA will process the charge. Unfair labor practice charges may be filed both by employees and by unions against management, and by employees and agencies against unions.

5 CPR Section 2423.3. Who May File Charges

(a) Filing charges. Any person may charge an activity, agency or labor organization with having engaged in, or engaging in, any unfair labor practice prohibited under 5 U.S.C. 7116.

(b) Charging Party. Charging Party means the individual, labor organization, activity or agency filing an unfair labor practice charge with a Regional Director.

(c) Charged Party. Charged Party means the activity, agency or labor organization charged with allegedly having engaged in, or engaging in, an unfair labor practice.

You Can't Take Two Bites from the Apple – the "d Bar"

Under the Statute you may not file both an unfair labor practice and a grievance over the same matter. This is commonly called a "d" bar, referring to the fact that Section 7116(d) bars the later-filed action.

Section 7116. Unfair Labor Practices

(d) Issues which can properly be raised under an appeals procedure may not be raised as unfair labor practices prohibited under this section. Except for matters wherein, under section 7121(e) and (f) of this title, an employee has an option of using the negotiated grievance procedure or an appeals procedure, issues which can be raised under a grievance procedure may, in the discretion of the aggrieved party, be raised under the grievance procedure or as an unfair labor practice under this section, but not under both procedures. If you do file both, the later-filed charge or grievance may be dismissed either by the FLRA or an arbitrator. However, if an employee files a grievance over a right given to the employee in a collective bargaining agreement, the union may file an unfair labor practice over the same subject if it seeks to protect union institutional rights affected by the action of management.

Example. An employee believes he has not fairly been given overtime under the contract and files a grievance under the negotiated grievance procedure. The union believes management's action in changing how overtime is distributed is a change in working conditions for which management has a duty to bargain. Under these circumstances, the union's unfair labor practice would not be "d" barred.

Investigation, Prosecution, Settlement and Dismissal of Unfair Labor Practice Charges

The General Counsel of the FLRA has the statutory responsibility to investigate, prosecute, settle, or dismiss unfair labor practice charges. Processing of unfair labor practice charges is done by the Regional Offices of the FLRA. The Regional Office which has jurisdiction over where the parties to a case are located will handle the charge and assign a field agent to investigate. The investigation of charges can be done on site or by telephone. If the Regional Director of the FLRA believes that the evidence shows that a violation of the Statute occurred, (s)he will issue a complaint. The complaint will be prosecuted by attorneys from the Regional Office. Prior to prosecution, the Regional Office will send the parties a proposed settlement agreement, which contains terms acceptable to Regional Director for resolution of the charge. The Regional Director has the authority to accept a settlement even if the party filing the charge does not agree with the settlement's terms. If a settlement agreement is approved by the Regional Director, no hearing is necessary.

If there is no settlement of the complaint, a hearing on the charge will be held by a FLRA administrative law judge. The judge may either dismiss the complaint or find a violation (or, if there is more than one allegation, decide to do some of each). If there is no disagreement with the finding of a violation, the remedy ordered by the judge must be complied with by the party found to have violated the Statute. If a party does not agree with the decision of the judge either to dismiss or find a violation, it may appeal the decision to the three members of the FLRA. The decision of the FLRA may be appealed to a Federal Circuit Court of Appeals and eventually even up to the U.S. Supreme Court.

If the Regional Director decides there is no merit to the unfair labor practice charge, it will be dismissed. If the party who filed the charge disagrees with the decision to dismiss the charge, it may file an appeal with the Office of General Counsel. The Office of General Counsel will issue a decision on the appeal. The grounds for granting an appeal are contained in the Regulations of the FLRA:

5 CPR Section 2423.11. Determination not to issue complaint; review of action by the Regional Director

(e) Grounds for granting an appeal. The General Counsel may grant an appeal when the appeal establishes at least one of the following grounds:

(1) The Regional Director's decision did not consider material facts that would have resulted in issuance of complaint;

(2) The Regional Director's decision is based on a finding of a material fact that is clearly erroneous;

(3) The Regional Director's decision is based on an incorrect statement of the applicable rule of law;

(4) There is no Authority precedent on the legal issue in the case; or

(5) The manner in which the Region conducted the investigation has resulted in prejudicial error.

Unfair Labor Practices Committed By Management

The Statute sets forth what are unfair labor practices committed by management. On its face, the language of the Statute is often difficult to understand. However, the language has been given meaning by over 68 Volumes of decisions by the FLRA and by federal court decisions. While many work place actions may be unfair, they are not an unfair labor practices unless they fit within one of the categories described in the law.

Section 7116. Unfair Labor Practices

(a) For the purpose of this chapter, it shall be an unfair labor practice for an agency –

(1) to interfere with, restrain, or coerce any employee in the exercise by the employee of any right under this chapter;

(2) to encourage or discourage membership in any labor organization by discrimination in connection with hiring, tenure, promotion, or other conditions of employment;

(3) to sponsor, control, or otherwise assist any labor organization, other than to furnish, upon request, customary and routine services and facilities if the services and facilities are also furnished on an impartial basis to other labor organizations having equivalent status;

(4) to discipline or otherwise discriminate against an employee because the employee has filed a complaint, affidavit, or petition, or has given any information or testimony under this chapter;

(5) to refuse to consult or negotiate in good faith with a labor organization as required by this chapter;

(6) to fail or refuse to cooperate in impasse procedures and impasse decisions as required by this chapter;

(7) to enforce any rule or regulation (other than a rule or regulation implementing section 2302 of this title) which is in conflict with any applicable collective bargaining agreement if the agreement was in effect before the date the rule or regulation was prescribed; or

(8) to otherwise fail or refuse to comply with any provision of this chapter.

Individual managers are not personally liable for damages in unfair labor practice cases. They also cannot be disciplined by the FLRA or arbitrators for violating the Statute. This does not mean that an agency could not take a personnel action against a supervisor for violating the law; it means that the FLRA cannot impose disciplinary action. These rules also apply to union representatives. Unfair labor practices can often cost an agency a significant amount of time and expense to deal with them. They also may result in significant awards of back pay.

Why Do Unions File Unfair Labor Practices?

Unions file unfair labor practice charges for a variety of reasons. Charges are usually filed because there is a legitimate dispute between labor and management which requires the services of an objective third party to resolve it. Unfair labor practices are also often filed by unions to get management's attention to a problem in the workplace. Importantly, they can lead to the deterioration of the relationship between labor and management. A large number of unfair labor practice filings are usually indicative of problems in the relationship. Often the allegation in an unfair labor practice charge is not the basis of the problem, but is a symptom of a much bigger problem. Solving the problems between labor and management often takes more than just resolving individual unfair labor practice charges. It requires trying to resolve the underlying issues in the relationship.

Common Unfair Labor Practices Charges Filed Against Management

The following is a presentation of common unfair labor practice charges filed against management. This is not an exhaustive listing of all the potential unfair labor practices that may be filed, but it is representative of those a manager and union representative may deal with most often.

Statements That Interfere with Employee Rights – Section 7116 (a) (1)

It is an unfair labor practice to interfere with, restrain or coerce an employee in the exercise of any right given to the employee in the Statute. From our discussion in Chapter Four, we have a basic understanding of employee rights. However, there are no definitions in the Statute of what it means to interfere with, restrain or coerce an employee in the exercise of these rights. These definitions are developed based on the facts of individual cases presented to the FLRA. One type of violation for interference, restraint and coercion is based on statements made to employees. Statements made by managers that a reasonable employee would understand to be threats or intimidation because the employee engaged in activity protected under the Statute can be unfair labor practices. Statements that can be violations usually concern an employee's membership in a union, use of the grievance procedure or actions as a union steward.

Not all statements by managers concerning labor relations are prohibited. Managers have the right under the Statute to express opinions about labor relations as long as they are not coercive. The freedom of speech given to managers in Section 7116(e) of the Statute must be used judiciously. If a manager's opinion has an undercurrent of a threat, it will not receive the protection of the Statute.

Section 7116 (e)

(e) The expression of any personal view, argument, opinion or the making of any statement which–

(1) publicizes the fact of a representational election and encourages employees to exercise their right to vote in such election,

(2) corrects the record with respect to any false or misleading statement made by any person, or

(3) informs employees of the Government's policy relating to labor-management relations and representation

Example. A manager tells an employee he/she should not join the union because the union is made up of a bunch of troublemakers. This statement can result in an unfair labor practice charge alleging that the statement interferes with the employee's right to join the union. Based on this statement, a reasonable employee would conclude that management thinks it is bad thing to be in the union and will hurt the employee's career. While management has the right to express an opinion about unions, it does not have the right to coerce employees into not joining the union. Unfair labor practice charges over statements made to employees are a common type of charge. Chapter Ten – What You Can and Cannot Say and Do to Employees and Union Representatives covers this issue in more detail.

Discrimination against Union Representatives or Employees – Section 7116 (a) (2)

It is an unfair labor practice to encourage or discourage membership in a union by discrimination in connection with hiring, tenure, promotion, or other conditions of employment. This is discrimination based on engaging in or refraining from union activity, not for EEO reasons. Common issues asserted as discrimination are disciplinary actions and denial of promotions. To prove discrimination, a charging party must show that the employee engaged in protected activity. This proof is called the prima facie case. Absent a showing that the employee engaged in such activity, there cannot be a finding of discrimination. Assuming there is a prima facie case of discrimination, the charging party must then prove that but for discrimination, the action taken by management would not have occurred. Management also has the opportunity to prove that it would have taken the same action irrespective of the employee's union or other protected activity.

Example. John Jones is a steward. He represents employees in disciplinary actions taken by management. He just received a letter of reprimand for being tardy 3 times last week. He does admit that he was late for work, however he believes he is being singled out for discipline because he is a union steward. He files an unfair labor practice charge.

John must first show that he was involved in protected activity. His representation of employees would meet the test. He has proven a prima facie case of discrimination. It must next be proven that but for the union activity, management would not have taken the action against John. If management can prove that all employees who are tardy three times in one week receive a letter of reprimand John's case will be dismissed. However, if John can show that other employees are similarly tardy and no one has received discipline, he will have proven discrimination based on his union activities.

Flagrant Misconduct

Union representatives and employees who engage in flagrant misconduct lose the protection of the Statute. In determining whether an employee has engaged in flagrant misconduct, the FLRA balances the employee's right to engage in protected activity, which "permits leeway for impulsive behavior," against the employer's right to maintain order and respect for its supervisory staff on the jobsite. Relevant factors to be considered in striking this balance include: (1) the place and subject matter of the discussion; (2) whether the employee's outburst was impulsive or designed; (3) whether the outburst was in any way provoked by the employer's conduct; and (4) the nature of the intemperate language and conduct.

Example. Jane Smith is a union steward. She filed a grievance for an employee who was grieving a failure to receive overtime. The grievant believed the responsible manager was giving the overtime to a distant cousin of the manager. A meeting on the grievance was scheduled in a conference room close to the work site. In the meeting with the manager concerning the employee's grievance, the manager denied the claim that he gave the overtime to another employee because the employee was a distant relative of his. The manager also denied that he gave any preference to the employee who was alleged to be his distant relative. He further denied that he had any relatives working for him. The discussion became very heated, and the manager yelled at Jane that he was not going to put up with any one challenging what he did. Jane called him a liar for denying that he had any relatives working on his staff. He ended the meeting and stormed out.

The next day, Jane received a proposed suspension of 5 days for insubordination for making the statement to the manager. Jane filed an unfair labor practice charge alleging that the suspension was in retaliation for engaging in protected union activity. Management asserted, as a defense to the charge, that Jane engaged in flagrant misconduct by calling the manager a liar and therefore lost the protection of the Statute.

The meeting to discuss the grievance was conducted in a conference room at a pre-arranged time. The outburst appeared to be impulsive, in response to the manager yelling at the union representative. The meeting appeared to be heated, with both sides engaging in robust debate. The language used was not intemperate under the circumstances. These factors could lead to a finding that Jane did not engage in flagrant misconduct by calling the manager a liar.

Failure to Provide Information – Section 7116 (a) (8)

Unions have the right to request information under Section 7114 (b) (4) of the Statute. This right was discussed in the Chapter Four, Union Rights. The failure to provide information can be an unfair labor practice. Section 7116(a) (8) of the Statute provides that to fail or refuse to comply with any provision of the Statute is an unfair labor practice. This is how information requests, Weingarten meetings and formal discussions become unfair labor practices, even though they are not specifically named in the list of unfair labor practices found in Section 7116.

Example. The union requests the investigative file relied on by management for a disciplinary action taken against a bargaining unit employee it is representing. This file contains statements given by employees during the investigation, copies of a description of the work site where the incident which is the basis of the action took place, and notes made by the investigator of the incident. Management refuses to provide the file, claiming that to do so would interfere with the privacy of employees who gave statements.

Any information which is relied upon by management to support a disciplinary action of an employee must be provided by management. Statements of employees relied on by management must be provided to the union. There is no privacy right of an employee if the statements were taken as part of an official investigation of conduct and used by management as the basis of its decision to take disciplinary action. The description of the work site would also have to be disclosed to the union. However, the notes of the investigator would not have to be provided. They are used as part of management's deliberative process in taking the action and need not be disclosed unless specifically cited as a basis for taking the action.

Failure to Bargain in Good Faith with the Union – Section 7116 (a) (5)

It is an unfair labor practice to fail or refuse to engage in collective bargaining over a new collective bargaining agreement. If management refuses to begin negotiations over a new collective bargaining agreement, such refusal is an unfair labor practice. However, if there is a dispute as to the meaning of the duration clause of a collective bargaining agreement, that issue should be resolved through the grievance process.

Example. The collective bargaining agreement provides that either party to the agreement that wishes to reopen the agreement must provide written notice in writing to the other party 30 days before the agreement's expiration. The agreement has no definition of whether a day is a calendar day or a work day. The union provides management 30 calendar days' notice of its desire to reopen. Management asserts that the notice is untimely and refuses to engage in bargaining. The union files an unfair labor practice charge. The dispute is a question of contract interpretation, which is better handled by a grievance than an unfair labor practice charge. The unfair labor practice process cannot ordinarily be used to interpret contracts. That is the role of an arbitrator. The unfair labor practice charge would be dismissed.

It is also an unfair practice to implement a change in working conditions without providing the union adequate notice and an opportunity to bargain. Change bargaining is the predominant form of collective bargaining in the federal sector which managers and union representatives become involved with. Very few managers and union representatives are involved in negotiating a term collective bargaining agreement.

As part of accomplishing the mission of the agency, managers make changes in the way employees do their job and how they are managed. The Statute requires that the union be notified of changes which have an adverse effect on bargaining unit employees. Not only must management notify the union of the change, but in most circumstances, it cannot implement the change until completion of bargaining. It is important to understand that employees and managers may look at changes in working conditions very differently. To a manager, if the change is good for employees, (s)he may not understand why there would be an obligation to bargain. However, what a manager thinks is good and what an employee thinks is good may be two very different things.

Implementing a change such as requiring employees to work rotating shifts is a change in their working conditions. Management has the right to make the change, but must notify the union before it makes the change so that union and management can bargain over mitigating the adverse effects on employees. Chapter Eight – What You Need to Know about Collective Bargaining covers this subject in more detail.

Example. Management implemented a change in the way leave is requested. This affects all the employees in the section. Management failed to notify the union or give it an opportunity to request bargaining. Leave is a working condition. Changes to how or when leave is requested would be a change subject to bargaining. However, the change must be significant enough for bargaining to be required. In determining whether a change is significant enough to warrant bargaining the FLRA employs what is called the de minimis test. This test determines the significance of the change. The union could file an unfair labor practice charge claiming that management violated the law by implementing the change. Management may be ordered to put the leave system back to the way it was before the change. While it may have the right to make the change, management must bargain over proposals from the union that attempt to mitigate the adverse effects of the change on the employees before its implementation.

Engaging in Bad Faith Bargaining – Section 7116 (a) (5)

It is frequently alleged by unions that management engaged in bad faith bargaining. Bad faith bargaining is an unfair labor practice. To prove bad faith bargaining, the union must provide evidence to answer the following questions:

1. Did the parties approach negotiations with a sincere resolve to reach agreement?

2. Were the parties represented by duty authorized representatives prepared to discuss and negotiate any condition of employment?

3. Did the parties meet as frequently as necessary?

4. Did the parties avoid unnecessary delays?

5. Did the parties explore and discuss each other's position?

Failure to Provide the Union The Opportunity to be to Be Present at a Formal Discussion – Section 7116 (a) (8)

It is an unfair labor practice for management to hold a meeting with bargaining unit employees to discuss personnel policies, practices, or general working conditions of employees without providing the union the opportunity to be present. A formal discussion is not an individual discussion with an employee about an issue related to just that employee, but rather is a discussion of general working conditions that have an effect on a number of employees.

Example. A manager is conducting a regularly scheduled staff meeting with her section. At this meeting, she discusses the policy on how employees are assigned to offices, holiday leave requests and new work schedules. The meeting is held in the staff conference room. All employees are required to attend. The staff has been unhappy with how offices are assigned at the facility. She discusses possible options to correct the employees' complaints.

She has not invited the union to be present because she considers the meeting to be a regularly scheduled event with no changes in working conditions discussed. She has held numerous staff meetings over the years and never provided the union the opportunity to be present.

Even though this was a regular staff meeting, she discussed general working conditions of employees. The meeting also was formal in nature, meeting the indicia of formality required by the Statute for formal discussions. For a meeting to be a formal discussion there need not be a discussion of changes in working conditions. Assignment to offices, holiday leave requests, and work schedules are all working conditions.

Failure to Provide a Representative in a Weingarten Meeting – Section 7116 (a) (8)

The failure to provide a representative requested by an employee when management is conducting an examination in connection with an investigation is an unfair labor practice. An employee has the right to representation when he/she reasonably fears that discipline will result from the questioning. The employee must make the request. Management does not have an obligation to tell the employee that the employee has a right to a representative.

Example. Tom Jones is a fellow employee of Roy Rogers. His cubicle is next to the cubicle of Rogers. Under the arrangement of the office, it is common to be able to overhear what goes on in the next cubicle and also to see what your next door neighbor is working on. Rogers has been called in by management for questioning about his alleged review of personal taxpayer information which he did not have access to in the normal course of his job. The agency that both Tom and Roy work for has strict standards of conduct regarding accessing this information. It also has a requirement that if an employee has knowledge of wrongdoing on the part of a fellow employee, the employee must report any suspected wrongdoing to management. Tom has just been informed that he is being asked to meet with his supervisor to discuss whether he knew what Roy was doing. He is told that he is not the subject of the inquiry, but that management would like to ask him a few questions. He requests a union representative.

Is Tom entitled to a rep? The issue will be whether he had a reasonable fear of discipline. It is not necessary to be the subject of an investigation to have a reasonable fear of discipline. Tom can reasonably fear discipline because he did not disclose to management what he knew about what Roy was doing. He could reasonably fear that he might be disciplined for his failure to disclose what he knew.

To Sponsor, Control or Assist a Labor Organization
Section 7116 (a) (3)

Management cannot put into place what in the past have been called company unions, which are unions under the control of management. Managers cannot denigrate the union, but by the same token, managers cannot illegally provide support to the union. Managers may however, join the union that represents their employees. In some agencies, managers join the union to obtain union-sponsored insurance benefits. While there is no prohibition on managers being members of the union representing their employees, the managers cannot participate in the management of the union, hold office in the union, or act as advisors to the union.

To Discriminate Against an Employee for Participating in the Processes under the Statute – Section 7116 (a) (4)

The Statute protects employees who supply evidence to the FLRA in an unfair labor practice investigation or representation proceeding. It also protects employees who testify in a FLRA hearing. The unfair labor practice process may be used by employees to protect their rights to access to the FLRA.

To Fail or Refuse to Cooperate in Impasse Panel Procedures – Section 7116 (a) (6)

The Statute mandates that both labor and management engage in impasse panel procedures. Another area of unfair labor practice activity is when agencies refuse to comply with an order of the FSIP. It is an unfair labor practice to fail or refuse to comply with an impasses panel decision. However, in some circumstances, it may first be necessary to show that the agency implemented a change contrary to the order of FSIP before a violation may be found. The violation would then be a bargaining violation, as opposed to a violation for failure to comply with an impasse panel order.

Unfair Labor Practices Committed by Unions

Unfair labor practices can be committed by unions as well as management. Unfair labor practices committed by unions are violations of Section 7116 (b) and (c) of the Statute. Management unfair labor practices are filed predominantly by unions against management. However, unfair labor practices filed against unions are filed predominantly by employees against the union. Management in the federal sector historically has filed a small percentage of the unfair labor practice charges filed with the FLRA. The following are the types of unfair labor practices that may be filed against unions:

Section 7116 (b)

(b) For the purpose of this chapter, it shall be an unfair labor practice for a labor organization –

(1) to interfere with, restrain, or coerce any employee in the exercise by the employee of any right under this chapter;

(2) to cause or attempt to cause an agency to discriminate against any employee in the exercise by the employee of any right under this chapter; or

(3) to coerce, discipline, fine, or attempt to coerce a member of the labor organization as punishment, reprisal, or for the purpose of hindering or impeding the member's work performance or productivity as an employee or the discharge of the member's duties as an employee;

(4) to discriminate against an employee with regard to the terms or conditions of membership in the labor organization on the basis of race, color, creed, national origin, sex, age, preferential or nonpreferential civil service status, political affiliation, marital status, or handicapping condition;

(5) to refuse to consult or negotiate in good faith with an agency as required by this chapter;

(6) to fail or refuse to cooperate in impasse procedures and impasse decisions as required by this chapter;

(7) (A) to call, or participate in, a strike, work stoppage, or slowdown, or picketing of an agency in a labor-management dispute if such picketing interferes with an agency's operations, or

  (B) to condone any activity described in subparagraph (A) of this paragraph by failing to take action to prevent or stop such activity; or

(8) to otherwise fail or refuse to comply with any provision of this chapter. Nothing in paragraph (7) of this subsection shall result in any informational picketing which does not interfere with an agency's operations being considered as an unfair labor practice.

(c) For the purpose of this chapter it shall be an unfair labor practice for an exclusive representative to deny membership to any employee in the appropriate unit represented by such exclusive representative except for failure –

(1) to meet reasonable occupational standards uniformly required for admission, or

(2) to tender dues uniformly required as a condition of acquiring and retaining membership.

Failure of the Duty of Fair Representation – Section 7116 (b) (1)

A union has the obligation to fairly represent all employees regardless of whether or not the employee is a member of the union. Employees file unfair labor practice charges against unions when they believe the union treated them differently because they were not a member of the union or when they believe the union was negligent in the representation it provided. These are the most common unfair labor practice charges filed against unions.

Bargain in Bad Faith – Section 7116 (b) (5)

It is an unfair labor practice for a union to bargain in bad faith. Both union and management have a statutory obligation to bargain in good faith. Bargaining in good faith means that you bargain with a sincere desire to reach agreement. Management may file a bad faith bargaining unfair labor practice charge when it believes the union is unnecessarily stalling or delaying negotiations. Often, unions feel that their best strategy is to delay negotiations as long as possible, because that will delay management's implementation of a change. Since in many cases there may be little that the union can bargain about, delay is the best way to wear down management and hopefully prevent the inevitable. These dilatory tactics become an unfair labor practice when the union's conduct evidences that its actions are intended solely to delay negotiations and not reach an agreement.

What Happens If Union or Management Commits an Unfair Labor Practice?

An important question is what happens if union or management is found to have committed an unfair labor practice. As stated previously, individual managers and union representatives who violate the Statute are not personally liable for the violations and therefore are not personally prosecuted. The agency or the union which they represent is prosecuted.

In theory, the remedy for a violation of the Statute should be the same whether it comes through a settlement at the unfair practice charge stage or is ordered by the FLRA after a hearing. The reality is that if labor, management, and the FLRA can come to a settlement prior to litigation, quite often the remedy is different than one which is obtained after a hearing. Additionally, if the remedy being offered by the party charged with the unfair labor practice is reasonable, but the party filing the charge does not agree to the settlement, the FLRA has authority to accept the settlement unilaterally without the agreement of the charging party. The charging party may, however, file an appeal of the unilateral settlement to the General Counsel.

When dealing with unfair labor practice charges. The Office of General Counsel is acting much like a District Attorney. It does not represent the party who filed the charge; it represents the Statute, just as a District Attorney does not represent the victim but the state. In the same way that a District Attorney can accept a plea bargain without the consent of the victim, the General Counsel can accept a settlement opposed by the party filing the charge.

Common Remedies

The FLRA is vested with wide discretion to fashion appropriate remedies for violations of any provisions of the Statute. When it has decided to prosecute an unfair labor practice charge, the FLRA Office of General Counsel will determine the appropriate remedy for the violation. It will in all cases send the parties A Notice to All Employees or, in the case of a union, A Notice to All Employees and Members. This Notice will describe the remedy which the FLRA Office of General Counsel is seeking in the case. The parties may decide to settle the case without a hearing, and in many cases, the Notice will be the basis of the settlement. However, if the case goes to hearing and the Administrative Law Judge hearing the case finds a violation of the Statute, the judge in his/her decision and order will determine the remedy for the violation. In all cases heard by a judge the remedy will include a Notice.

A posted notice, in most cases, is an acknowledgement that a violation occurred, what the violation was and that the party signing the notice agrees that no further violations will occur in the future. Who signs the Notice often is a point of contention between the parties to the settlement. In the case of unfair labor practices charges against management, notices are usually signed by the highest ranking manager where the violation took place. They may also be signed by the Secretary of the Department or a military commander. Who signs the notice is based on where the violation took place, the nature of the violation and who would be an appropriate official to indicate to the readers the importance of the Notice. In the case of a union, they are signed by the union president or other high ranking union official.

In cases involving bargaining violations, a status quo ante remedy may be pursued. Status quo ante means putting things back to the way they were before the violation. Such a remedy may entail significant costs to an agency which is required to return conditions in the workplace to the way they were before the violation took place. In some cases, it is impossible to put Humpty Dumpty back together again. In those cases, all that can be done is to put things back as closely as possible to the way they were.

In deciding the appropriateness of a status quo ante remedy, the FLRA makes a determination on a case by case basis, by balancing the nature and circumstances of the particular violation against the degree of disruption in government operations that would be caused by such a remedy. In making this determination, the FLRA considers, among other things, (1) whether, and when, notice was given to the union by the agency concerning the change decided upon; (2) whether, and when, the union requested bargaining on the procedures to be observed by the agency in implementing such action and/or concerning appropriate arrangements for employees adversely affected by such action or change; (3) the willfulness of the agency's conduct in failing to discharge its bargaining obligations under the Statute;(4) the nature and extent of the impact experienced by adversely affected employees; and (5) whether, and to what degree, a *status quo ante* remedy would disrupt or impair the efficiency and effectiveness of the agency's operations.

If a status quo remedy is not ordered, the parties may be ordered to bargain over the change and apply the result either prospectively or retroactively to when the violation first occurred. Retroactive bargaining orders are often used when a status quo ante remedy would not be practical. They are of particular use in cases involving monetary benefits for employees. A retroactive bargaining order affords the parties the ability to negotiate and implement the results of their agreement retroactively, thereby approximating the situation that would have existed had the agency fulfilled its statutory obligations.

Back pay is also a possible remedy. If management commits an unjustifiable or unwarranted personnel action, employees affected by it may receive back pay to make them whole for the act. In appropriate circumstances, committing an unfair labor practice can be found to be an unwarranted personnel action. Back pay can be awarded in an unfair labor practice case where an employee was not promoted solely because he was a union representative. Back pay also has been awarded in cases where management changes an overtime policy which results in employees who should have received overtime being denied overtime. Employees are entitled to back pay even in situations where they did not actually work the overtime, but would have worked it if wrongful changes in working conditions had not been made.

5 USC Section 5596. Back Pay Due to Unjustified Personnel Action

(b) (1) An employee of an agency who, on the basis of a timely appeal or an administrative determination (including a decision relating to an unfair labor practice or a grievance) is found by appropriate authority under applicable law, rule, regulation, or collective bargaining agreement, to have been affected by an unjustified or unwarranted personnel action which has resulted in the withdrawal or reduction of all or part of the pay, allowances, or differentials of the employee –

(A) is entitled, on correction of the personnel action, to receive for the period for which the personnel action was in effect-

(i) an amount equal to all or any part of the pay, allowances, or an amount equal to all or any part of the pay, allowances, or differentials, as applicable which the employee normally would have earned or received during the period if the personnel action had not occurred, less any amounts earned by the employee through other employment during that period; and

(ii) reasonable attorney fees related to the personnel action which, with respect to any decision relating to an unfair labor practice or a grievance processed under a procedure negoti a t e d in accordance with chapter 71 of this title, or under chapter 11 of title I of the Foreign Ser v i c e Act of 1980, shall be awarded in accordance with standards established under section 7701 (g) of this title; and...

(2) (A) An amount payable under paragraph (1)(A) (i) of this subsection shall be payable with interest.

(B) Such interest –

(i) shall be computed for the period beginning on the effective date of the withdrawal or reduction involved and ending on a date not more than 30 days before the date on which payment is made;

(ii) shall be computed at the rate or rates in effect under section 6621(a)(1) of the Internal Revenue Code of 1986 during the period described in clause (i); and

(iii) shall be compounded daily.

Grievance Arbitration

Next to collective bargaining, grievance arbitration is the most important right unions and employees have under the Statute. The Statute requires all collective bargaining agreements to have a grievance procedure ending in binding arbitration. Binding arbitration gives a neutral third party authority to make decisions which can be enforced against either the union or management. Some managers may look at this as the arbitrator having the authority to second guess the manager's decision. While, in a sense, this may seem to be the outcome, the purpose behind having a neutral third party decide disputes is to give credibility to decisions in the workplace and also to give employees belief in the fairness of the decisions. Grievance arbitration is intended to be an inexpensive and quick process for resolving disputes.

Grievance Procedure

The grievance procedure is found in the collective bargaining agreement. Unlike the unfair labor practice procedure which is set out in Statute and regulations, the grievance procedure is a product of negotiations between management and the union. It describes a series of steps (in most cases three or four) which must be followed to attempt to resolve the grievance before it is submitted to arbitration. The reason for having various steps is to elevate the grievance to successively higher levels of management in an attempt to have unbiased managers look at what is being grieved. The intention of the grievance procedure is to resolve the grievance at the lowest level possible. In most cases, grievances by employees are handled by union representatives.

Problems in Processing Grievances

A common problem in processing grievances is timeliness. The timeliness of actions taken under the grievance procedure is determined by the provisions of the agreement. It is important that both the grievant and the party responding to the grievance follow the time deadlines found in the grievance procedure. If the grievance procedure indicates that a grievance is to be filed within 15 calendar days of the occurrence on which the grievance is based, a grievance filed 20 calendar days after the occurrence will be considered untimely and likely be denied. However, most agreements also provide that a grievance must be filed within a certain number of days from when the employee became aware, or should have become aware, of the act or occurrence on which the grievance is based. If an employee just found out today about an act which violated the employee's right under the contract, the time period for filing a grievance would start from today.

If management is late in responding to a grievance at a step of the grievance procedure, this would not be an unfair labor practice, nor would the union, in most cases, automatically win the grievance. Some contracts provide that if management is untimely in processing a grievance, the grievant automatically wins the remedy requested. Only a small minority of contracts contain this provision. If management is untimely in responding or fails to respond to a grievance at any step of the grievance procedure, the union has the right to move the grievance to the next step of the grievance procedure. On the other hand, if the grievant is late in taking an action required under the grievance procedure, the grievance can be declared untimely and be denied. However, the union can challenge the determination of untimeliness before an arbitrator. The issue of the timeliness of the processing of the grievance becomes a threshold issue for the arbitrator to resolve.

Example. An employee just discovered that he has been repeatedly denied overtime over the course of the last 3 months. He found this out by obtaining a copy of the overtime roster which was just issued for the last quarter. He files a grievance alleging that he was denied overtime for the last 3 months. The grievance procedure provides that a grievance must be filed within 15 calendar days of the action being grieved. Management denies the grievance for all overtime not given to the employee for periods more than 15 calendar days before the grievance was filed. The arbitrator will determine if the employee could reasonably have known of the denial of overtime more than 15 calendar days before the grievance was filed. If management can prove that the employee knew of the denial of overtime, it can limit the scope of the grievance to only the alleged denials that occurred within 15 calendar days of the filing of the grievance.

Scope of the Grievance Procedure. What employees, the union, or even management may file grievances over is found in the collective bargaining agreement. The agreement will describe what issues are subject to the grievance procedure. Most contracts have what is called a full scope grievance procedure, which allows grievances on any issue under the contract and any violation of law, rule or regulation. However, the scope of the grievance procedure may be limited through negotiations. For example, some grievance procedures limit employees' rights to bring certain kinds of issues under the grievance procedure, because they are already provided for by a statutory appeal procedure under the Merit System Protection Board or the Equal Employment Opportunity Commission. Grievances are commonly filed over such subjects as proposed disciplinary actions, promotions, overtime and employees' appraisals.

Problems with Arbitrability

When a grievance is filed, an agency or union may declare the grievance non-arbitratable because it is outside the scope of the grievance procedure. As with timeliness, this is a threshold issue for the arbitrator to decide if the grievance is taken to arbitration. An agency or union may not refuse to go to arbitration because they have declared a grievance non-arbitrable. Refusing or failing to participate in the grievance arbitration process can be an unfair labor practice. Refusing to go to arbitration denies a hearing on whether the party claiming it was non arbitrable was correct.

Arbitration

If the grievance cannot be resolved, the grievant may request arbitration. An individual employee can file a grievance on his/her own behalf. However, the employee can only take the grievance to arbitration with the permission of the union. The arbitrator is usually selected by labor and management by using a process of "striking for arbitrators." A list (in most cases, containing five names) of arbitrators is requested and then the union and management alternately strike names off the list of arbitrators whom they find objectionable, ending up with the least objectionable person. Arbitrators are private citizens who make their livelihood hearing and deciding different types of cases.

Arbitration Process

The rules for how the arbitration will be conducted are established by the individual arbitrator. There are no set rules which must be followed. However, the arbitrator must conduct a fair hearing and be unbiased in his/her decision-making. After the arbitration hearing, the arbitrator will issue a decision, which is also called an award. If either union or management disagrees with the decision, they can file an exception to the award to the three members of the FLRA. This is discussed below in the Exceptions to Arbitration Awards section.

Arbitration Remedies

Remedies for violations of the contract in disciplinary actions include rescission of the action and back pay. In most cases, before awarding a remedy ordering the promotion of an employee, an arbitrator must be able to show that absent the violation of the contract, the employee would have received the promotion. Quite often the remedy an arbitrator awards is the subject of an appeal claiming that the award violates the law. As with unfair labor practices, supervisors and union officials are not personally liable for the contract violation or personally responsible for complying with the award.

FLRA Administrative Appeals

Beyond grievances and unfair labor practices, unions and management may enforce their rights through use of administrative appeal procedures established under the Statute. These administrative appeal processes govern representation case issues, negotiability appeals and exceptions to arbitration awards. Each of these processes has different administrative rules and regulations that govern their use. It is advisable to have a basic understanding of them, since they are frequently used in the federal sector. To use these processes, the filing party must understand and follow the FLRA Regulations that deal with each process. They can be found on the FLRA website at www.FLRA.gov. Excerpts of the regulations have been cited below. To be effective in pursuing appeals, you must read all parts of the regulations that apply to the appeal you wish to file.

Review of Regional Director Decision and Order on Representation Issue

If union or management disagrees with a Decision and Order of a Regional Director on a representation issue, it may file an appeal to the FLRA. If the FLRA does not accept the appeal within 60 days of receipt from the appellant, the decision of the Regional Director becomes final. The FLRA Regulations establish the rules for filing appeals of a Regional Director Decision and Order:

Section 2422.31 Application for Review of a Regional Director Decision and Order

(a) Filing an application for review. A party must file an application for review with the Authority within sixty (60) days of the Regional Director's Decision and Order. The sixty (60) day time limit provided for in 5 U.S.C. 7105(f) may not be extended or waived.

(b) Contents. An application for review must be sufficient to enable the Authority to rule on the application without recourse to the record; however, the Authority may, in its discretion, examine the record in evaluating the application. An application must specify the matters and rulings to which exception(s) is taken, include a summary of evidence relating to any issue raised in the application, and make specific reference to page citations in the transcript if a hearing was held. An application may not raise any issue or rely on any facts not timely presented to the Hearing Officer or Regional Director.

(c) Review. The Authority may grant an application for review only when the application demonstrates that review is warranted on one or more of the following grounds:

(1) The decision raises an issue for which there is an absence of precedent;

(2) Established law or policy warrants reconsideration; or,

(3) There is a genuine issue over whether the Regional Director has:

(i) Failed to apply established law;

(ii) Committed a prejudicial procedural error;

(iii) Committed a clear and prejudicial error concerning a substantial factual matter

Exceptions to Arbitration Awards

If either union or management disagrees with the award of an arbitrator, it may take exceptions to the award by filing an appeal with the three member panel of the FLRA. Two of the bases for appeal are that the arbitrator did not conduct a fairing hearing or that the arbitrator was biased. Arbitrators' awards are not frequently overturned by the FLRA on these bases. The most common basis on which an arbitrator's decision is overturned is that the award violates a law or regulation.

An exception cannot be based solely on disagreement with the arbitrator, but must set forth arguments recognized by the FLRA as legitimate grounds for appeal. The FLRA Regulations establish the rules for filing exceptions to arbitration awards:

Section 2425.1 Who May File an Exception; Time Limits for Filing; Opposition; Service

(a) Either party to arbitration under the provisions of chapter 71 of title 5 of the United States Code may file an exception to an arbitrator's award rendered pursuant to the arbitration.

(b) The time limit for filing an exception to an arbitration award is thirty (30) days beginning on the date the award is served on the filing party.

(c) An opposition to the exception may be filed by a party within thirty (30) days after the date of service of the exception.

(d) A copy of the exception and any opposition shall be served on the other party.

Negotiability Appeals

A union has the right to file a negotiability appeal when management declares during negotiations that a union proposal is nonnegotiable because it violates management rights. This appeal is filed with the three member panel of the FLRA. The FLRA will decide whether the union's proposal violates management rights or whether management will be ordered to bargain over the proposal. Negotiability appeals are most often filed during negotiations for a new collective bargaining agreement. The negotiability appeals process must be used by the union to enforce its right to bargain when management has not made a change in working conditions, but has declared a proposal nonnegotiable. If the FLRA finds the proposal negotiable, it will issue an order to management to bargain over the proposal. This bargaining order does not require management to return to the status quo in existence before the negotiability appeal was filed, nor will it require the payment of back pay, because there have been no changes to working conditions. The FLRA regulations establish the procedures for filing a negotiability appeal:

Section 2424.22 Exclusive Representative's Petition for Review; Purpose; Content; Severance; Service

(a) Purpose. The purpose of a petition for review is to initiate a negotiability proceeding and provide the agency with notice that the exclusive representative requests a decision from the Authority that a proposal or provision is within the duty to bargain or not contrary to law, respectively. As more fully explained in paragraph (b) of this section, the exclusive representative is required in the petition for review to, among other things, inform the Authority of the exact wording and meaning of the proposal or provision as well as how it is intended to operate, explain technical or unusual terms, and provide copies of materials that support the exclusive representative's position.

Unfair Labor Practice Case Study

A manager has decided to change how his unit is organized to better accomplish the mission. The change will entail new job duties for some employees, relocating some employees to different buildings and new work hours for all his staff. He calls a staff meeting to explain all the changes to the employees. At this meeting, he agrees with the suggestion of one staff member to limit the change in hours to only two out of three of the sections in the unit. When asked whether the union has been informed, he states that union representatives are only interested in themselves and won't help any of the employees. Besides, he adds, he needs to make these changes fast, and the union only will slow him down. After the meeting, he implements new work hours and changes in the employees' office locations and job duties.

What are the potential unfair labor practices which may have been committed by the manager's actions?

Conducting a staff meeting to explain the changes could be a formal discussion. A meeting with employees in which personnel practices, policies or general working conditions are discussed is a formal discussion, if the criteria for formality are also met. Management is obligated to provide the union an opportunity to be present at such a meeting.

Negotiating or dealing directly with employees over working condition changes such as the hours of the work units is considered a bypass of the union and is an unfair labor practice.

Unilaterally implementing changes to employees' work hours, office locations and job duties without providing notice and an opportunity to bargain to the union would constitute a failure to bargain in violation of the Statute.

The manager's comments concerning the union might be considered to interfere with or coerce employees in their rights to seek assistance from their union representatives, although it could also be argued to be merely personal opinion on the part of the manager.

Grievance Case Study

The collective bargaining agreement has a provision which provides that employees can request one day of leave by submitting a leave request slip two days before the requested date, and if it is not denied that day, then normally it should be considered by the employee as granted. Sally Smith followed the agreement and submitted a leave slip for leave two days in advance of her requested leave day. Her supervisor did not act on her request that day. The next day a new work assignment came in requiring all employees to complete the task. The supervisor called Sally in to her office and cancelled her leave. She told the supervisor she could not do that because it violated the contract.

She filed a grievance. You are responsible for deciding the grievance at the second level. What should you do?

The issue is what the contract means and whether the employee or management interpreted it correctly. Many employees believe that leave is a right and they can take it whenever they want to. In this case, the employee believed that the contract granted an absolute right to her day of leave. The contract in fact said that "normally" when leave is requested and not denied that day, it is considered approved. The new work assignment could be argued by management not to be a "normal" situation, giving the supervisor to the right to cancel the leave. The employee could argue that the situation that came up that day happens all the time and therefore is a normal occurrence.

This is classic example of differing interpretations of the contract. To be better able to defend or pursue an action subject to a grievance, it is often helpful to know what was said at the bargaining table about the provision of the contract in dispute. This is called bargaining history. Bargaining history can be persuasive proof of what the contract means on certain issues.

Key Points in Chapter Six

1. An unfair labor practice is a violation of the Statute.

2. A grievance is filed over a violation of the collective bargaining agreement.

3. The filer of an unfair labor practice and a grievance may not get two bites of the apple by filing both over the same issue.

4. Unfair labor practices are prosecuted by the Office of General Counsel of the FLRA.

5. Unions and management represent themselves in cases before an arbitrator.

6. A manager or union official cannot be held personally liable for damages or have disciplinary action taken against them by the FLRA for an unfair labor practice or a grievance.

7. If management declares a union proposal nonnegotiable, the union has the right to file a negotiability appeal with the FLRA. Management cannot file negotiability appeals.

8. If either the union or management disagrees with an award of an arbitrator, it may file an exception to the award with the FLRA.

9. If either union or management wishes to file an appeal of an unfair labor practice decision of an

administrative law judge, a representation decision of a Regional Director, exceptions to an arbitration award, or a negotiability appeal, it must follow the regulations of the FLRA in filing the appeal.

Chapter Seven

How to File a ULP and What Happens After That

When You can File a ULP:

If, after an event occurs that you - union official, management, or employee or their representative - believe constitutes an unfair labor practice (see, pretty much all the rest of this book) you may file an unfair labor practice charge with the Regional Office of the FLRA where the unfair labor practice allegedly took place, or if it occurred in more than one regional office jurisdiction, with any of the Regional offices in which it is occurring. The charge must be filed within six months of the date on which the unfair labor practice occurred, or within six months of the date on which the unfair labor practice was discovered by the charging party, if the charging party was prevented from discovering the unfair labor practice because of concealment or failure of the Charged Party to perform a duty owed to the Charging Party – for example, a failure by an agency to notify the union of a change in working conditions, which the union does not discover until months after its implementation. (However, if the unfair labor practice is discovered within 6 months of its occurrence, the charging party still has only 6 months from the date of occurrence within which to file a charge. Thus, if a charging party finds out about a ULP 3 months after its occurrence, it has another 3 months to file a charge; on the other hand, if the charging party discovers the UP 7 months after its occurrence, it would have 6 months from the date of the discovery – 13 months from the occurrence – to file the charge, absent other actions or inaction which might affect its rights. See, Dept. of Labor, 20 FLRA 296 and Department of Homeland Security, U.S. Customs and Border Protection, 65 FLRA 422.)

What Must a Charge Contain

The FLRA's regulations, which may be found on its website (at www.flra.gov), spell out specifically what a charge must contain when filed with the General Counsel's Regional Office. Briefly, however, the charge must be filed on forms prescribed by the General Counsel (hereafter, GC) or on substantially similar forms which contain the same information. The forms may be downloaded from the FLRA's website. A charge must be signed by the filing party, and may be mailed, faxed or hand-carried into a Regional Office. A copy must also be served on the Charged Party (agency or union against which the charge is filed). Any evidence which supports the charge should be provided to the Regional Office either with the charge or as soon as possible thereafter. This information would include names and telephone numbers of witnesses, and any documentary evidence, notes, contractual provisions, or correspondence relevant to the allegations in the charge. If the evidence is voluminous, it would be advisable to contact the agent assigned to investigate the charge to determine how and when the Region wants the evidence provided.

Must State Who is Charged

At a minimum, the charge must contain the name and address of the Charged Party and the name and telephone number of its representative; the same information should be provided for the Charging Party. The charge must include information concerning whether the allegations forming the basis of the charge have also been raised in other forums, such as the negotiated grievance procedure, in a negotiability appeal, FSIP proceeding, or with the EEOC, MSPB, FMCS, etc. As discussed in Chapter 6 of this book, Section 7116(d) of the Statute prevents a charging party from filing both a grievance and an unfair labor practice over the same issue where the aggrieved party is also the same in both matters. In addition, if an issue "can properly be raised under an appeals procedure," it may not be raised as an unfair labor practice. Thus, if an employee alleges that he/she received a 30-day suspension or was terminated because of activities on behalf of a union, since those matters can be raised with the Merit Systems Protection Board (unless the employee is in a probationary status or does not have MSPB appeal rights for some other reason), the issue cannot be filed in an unfair labor practice charge.

What the Charge Must Say

The charge must contain "a clear and concise statement of the facts alleged to constitute an unfair labor practice...," and the date and place where it allegedly occurred. That is, the basis of the charge needs to be specific enough to allow the Charged Party to determine what it is being charged with and when and where the alleged violation of the Statute took place. Although the names of specific managers and employees involved need not be identified on the face of the charge, this information will need to be provided to the FLRA and revealed to the Charged Party so that it has an adequate opportunity to defend itself. The following are examples of what might constitute an adequate statement of the basis of the charge:

"On or about September 5, 2011, the supervisor of the Accounting Division of the WHO's facility in Oklahoma City, OK violated Section 7116 (a)(1) of the Statute by telling an employee that he should not join the union because he would be considered a troublemaker, like the other union members, and would never get anywhere in WHO."

"On or about March 7, 2011, Wrigley Spearmint AFB violated Section 7116(a)(2) of the Statute when it passed over the union vice-president for a promotion because he was active in the union. Although the union vice-president was among the best qualified candidates for the position, he was denied the promotion because he had filed grievances against the selecting official and upper management officials."

"Since on or about June 23, 2010, the XYZ agency, at its St. Louis, MO location, has failed or refused to bargain concerning the proposed relocation of its offices from Kirkwood, MO to East St. Louis, IL, in violation of Section 7116(a)(1) and (5) of the Statute. The agency has begun to implement the relocation by building out the new space and by moving some of the employees to the new location on August 1, 2010, without bargaining with the union."

"On April 18, 2011, the head of the facilities management section of the Rah Rah Agency's Regional Office in Sacramento, CA held a formal discussion with employees of that section without notifying the union or providing it an opportunity to be present. In addition, on the following day, the supervisor of the machinery shop called employee Roy Rogers into his office and examined him in connection with an investigation into missing tools. Although Mr. Rogers requested a representative, the supervisor refused to allow him to have one. These actions violated Section 7116(a)(1) and (8) of the Statute."

"On or about August 17, 2011, the United Workers of the World, Local 2323, requested information concerning a proposed RIF in the Honolulu Area facility of the Maui Waui agency. To date the agency has not responded to the union's request, even though the union reiterated its request on September 7, 2011. The RIF is scheduled to take place in November 2011, and the union needs the requested information in order to be able to represent employees at the facility. The agency's failure to respond or to provide the requested necessary information violates Section 7116(a)(1), (5) and (8) of the Statute. Copies of the union's information requests are attached."

"Since on or about May 14, 2011, the UWWW, Local 17, has bargained in bad faith by refusing to meet or to schedule bargaining sessions and by engaging in dilatory tactics in an effort to delay implementation of the agency's proposed staff realignments. The union's actions constitute a violation of Section 7116(b)(1) and (5) of the Statute."

Investigation of Unfair Labor Practice charge and Rights of the Parties in the Investigation

Once a charge has been filed, a Regional Office agent or attorney will be assigned to investigate the case. He or she will attempt to clarify the charge if it is not clear on its face and may also assist the parties in identifying and resolving the issues underlying the charge. The Regional Office has discretion regarding when and how to investigate the charge – for example, by phone or on-site – although it will normally consider any requests to expedite the investigation or to perform an on-site or telephone investigation if there are compelling reasons given for doing so. In addition, it will conduct an expedited preliminary investigation if there appears to be a basis for seeking a temporary restraining order.

Investigation Statements and Evidence

Investigation of a charge normally entails the taking of sworn statements from the Charging Party's witnesses and of seeking any and all documentary evidence bearing on the allegations raised in the charge. If the Charged Party is willing to permit sworn statements to be taken from its witnesses, these will be taken as well, unless the evidence obtained from the Charged Party witnesses indicates that further proceedings aren't warranted and the charge will likely be dismissed, absent withdrawal. The Charging Party must make its witnesses and evidence available to the investigating agent; failure to do so may result in dismissal of the charge for lack of cooperation. The Charged Party is not required to provide witnesses and evidence, although it may often be to its benefit to do so in order that the Regional Director may make an informed decision based on all available facts and versions of events. It is in the Charged Party's best interest, at the very least, to provide a statement of its position regarding the allegations. All witness statements and evidence obtained during the investigation remain confidential until and unless a decision is made to proceed to a hearing, a complaint has been issued, and trial preparations are underway.

Both the Charging Party and the Charged Party have the right to submit evidence to the Regional Office which they feel is relevant to the case even if the investigating agent does not agree as to its relevance, in order that it can be considered by the Regional Director in making a decision.

Amended Charges

If the investigation uncovers evidence of additional violations (usually related to the charge or to the same affected individual, union or agency charging party), the charge may be amended to include the new allegations, providing they are still timely, and the Charged Party will be provided an opportunity to respond to those allegations. The Charging Party (or affected individual) may also opt to file a separate charge raising the allegations. The Regional Office has an obligation to notify affected parties of evidence indicating possible violations of the Statute, although it will also advise the potential charging party that any new allegations or charges will need to be fully investigated and that no determination on the merits has been or will be made until the investigation is complete.

Resolution of Charge Before Decision

The Regional Director or the agent assigned to the case may, during the investigation and before a determination on the merits of the charge, assist the parties in resolving the underlying issues, which would result in an informal agreement and withdrawal of the charge. These informal agreements are not precedent-setting, are not admissions of wrong-doing, and are not enforced by the Regional Office. However, they can be very valuable instruments in getting the parties to resolve their differences quickly and to move forward without further involvement by third parties.

Dismissal of Charge

The agent assigned to the investigation may conclude during the investigation that the charge was not timely filed or that the evidence doesn't support the allegations. In that event, the agent may (often, but not necessarily, with the approval of the Regional Director) suggest that the Charging Party withdraw the charge. If the charge is withdrawn, no explanation of the reasons for withdrawal will be given to the Charged Party by the agent or the Regional Director. If the Charging Party does not opt to withdraw the charge at this point, it is entitled to have a determination made by the Regional Director based upon the evidence taken/submitted at that point. It should be noted that, if the agent investigating the case (or the RD) determines that the Charging Party's evidence does not support the allegations, the Region will normally not seek evidence from the Charged Party, but will base its decision solely on the Charging Party's evidence. The reason for this is so that the investigation does not expend the Region's and the Charged Party's time and resources unnecessarily. Of course, if the Regional Director does not agree with the agent's assessment of the case, more evidence may be requested from either or both parties.

Final Investigative Report

Following completion of the investigation, the FLRA agent will provide a report to the Regional Director outlining the facts of the case, the evidence, and relevant case law bearing on the allegations. If the Regional Director believes that no additional information is necessary in order for him or her to render a decision, (s)he may decide to dismiss the case, absent its withdrawal, or to issue a complaint, absent settlement. Again, if the Charging Party decides to withdraw the charge, no explanation for the withdrawal will be provided by the Region to the Charged Party. If the charge is not withdrawn, the Regional Director will dismiss the case in a letter describing the reasons for the decision to dismiss; this determination/dismissal may be appealed to the General Counsel. Any appeal of the dismissal must be filed within time frames set out in the FLRA's regulations, and must contain the grounds on which the Charging Party bases its appeal. The regulations set forth potential grounds for appeal at Section 2423.11, which may be accessed through the FLRA website. The General Counsel will review the appeal and the Regional Director's decision and will either deny the appeal or remand the case to the RD for further investigation or issuance of a complaint.

Settlement Agreements

If the Regional Director determines that the evidence shows probable cause to believe that one or more violations of the Statute has occurred, the Region will ordinarily attempt to settle the violations found before any complaint is issued. Frequently, if the parties do not agree quickly concerning how to settle the matter, the Region will prepare and send to the parties a settlement agreement containing the terms it believes will equitably resolve the violations found. As discussed in Chapter 6, the settlement agreement will contain a Notice to All Employees or Notice to All Employees and Members which should be posted in all places where notices to employees are customarily posted. Traditionally, this has meant official bulletin boards or other boards or places where notices concerning employee rights or benefits may be posted. Recently, the General Counsel of the FLRA has announced that the OGC through its Regional Offices will seek to have notices posted electronically in cases where agency or union respondents customarily communicate with their employees or members electronically. As also discussed in Chapter 6, the settlement agreement may provide for status quo ante remedies, bargaining with retroactive application, or back pay when appropriate, and never include punitive damages. A settlement agreement entered into by the parties and approved by the Regional Director at this stage of the proceedings will be tailored to the specific violations found and will be enforced by the Region (through issuance or re-issuance of the complaint) if the Charged Party fails or refuses to implement its provisions. Like other settlement agreements entered into at prior steps of a case investigation, this settlement agreement does not establish precedent. Each case is looked at individually and on its own merits. However, if repeated violations of the same type are committed by a particular Charged Party, the Region may up the ante in later cases by seeking stronger remedies or a formal settlement agreement which would be approved by the Authority and be enforceable in federal court.

Unilateral Settlement Agreements

If the Charged Party declines to enter into a bilateral settlement agreement with the Charging Party, the Region will issue a complaint and the case will proceed to a hearing before an Administrative Law Judge of the FLRA. If the Charged Party is agreeable to entering into the settlement agreement, but the Charging Party will not agree to it, the Regional Director may choose to approve a unilateral settlement agreement between the Region and the Charged Party. If the RD approves a unilateral settlement agreement, a letter explaining the grounds for its approval will be issued to the Charging Party, which may appeal this decision to the General Counsel, who can overturn the Regional Director's decision.

ULP Hearing

If a complaint is issued and no settlement agreement is reached by the parties and approved by the Regional Director, the case will be set for hearing through issuance of a complaint, which will specifically set forth the facts comprising the alleged violations of the Statute. The Charged Party/Respondent must respond to each allegation of the complaint. At this point, if not before, the legal departments of agencies or unions and the legal staff of the Office of the General Counsel's Regional Offices take over handling the case, and the usual arguments and filings- motions, amendments, subpoenas, pre-hearing disclosures and conferences, including conferences with the Administrative Law Judge or a settlement judge - are filed or take place. The parties may stipulate facts directly to the Administrative Law Judge or to the Authority, in appropriate cases, and any party may file a motion for Summary Judgment with the Administrative Law Judge. However the case proceeds, if it goes to an Administrative Law Judge for a decision after hearing or after a Motion for Summary Judgment, the Judge will render a decision based on the facts before him, as well as based on his credibility determinations regarding any disputed witness testimony. His or her decision may be appealed to the FLRA. The Authority will, after a review of the parties' briefs, the Judge's decision and review of the trial transcript, as appropriate, render a decision, which may be appealed to the Circuit Court of Appeal which has jurisdiction over the location where the alleged violation(s) took place. Although very few federal sector cases have been appealed as far as the Supreme Court, this is possible.

Key Points in this Chapter Seven

1. An unfair labor practice charge must be filed on forms provided by the FLRA (or forms containing substantially similar information), normally within 6 months of the date of occurrence of the alleged unfair labor practice, unless the Charging Party was prevented from discovering it within 6 months of its occurrence.

2. If a matter can be filed under a statutory appeals procedure – e.g. MSPB procedures, it may not be filed as an unfair labor practice charge. If a matter has been raised by or on behalf of an affected party under a negotiated grievance procedure, it may not subsequently be filed as an unfair labor practice.

3. The Charging Party must cooperate in the investigation by the FLRA Regional Office by providing all witness testimony, documentation and other relevant evidence in its possession. Failure to do so may result in dismissal of the charge for lack of cooperation.

4. The Charged Party is not required to cooperate in the FLRA's investigation to the same degree as the Charging Party, but it is often in its best interest to do so. If the evidence provided by the Charging Party during the investigation does not indicate that an unfair labor practice occurred, the Region normally will not seek to gather information from the Charged Party.

5. If a charge is withdrawn by the Charging Party at any time during the investigation, the FLRA Regional Office will not provide any explanation for the withdrawal to the Charged Party.

6. If a charge is not withdrawn by the Charging Party, the Regional Director of the FLRA will render a decision on the merits of the case, either deciding to dismiss it in whole or in part, or to issue a complaint.

7. The Regional Office will assist the parties in resolving the issues under- lying the charge at all stages of the investigation. After the Regional Director has determined that a complaint should issue in a case, the Region will fashion a settlement agreement tailored to the specific violations of law found, which will normally include a Notice to Employees and/or Members, which will be posted in locations where notices to employees/members are customarily posted.

8. Depending on the decision made by the Regional Director, Administrative Law Judge, and Authority, there are various rights to appeal their decisions to the federal circuit courts of appeal..

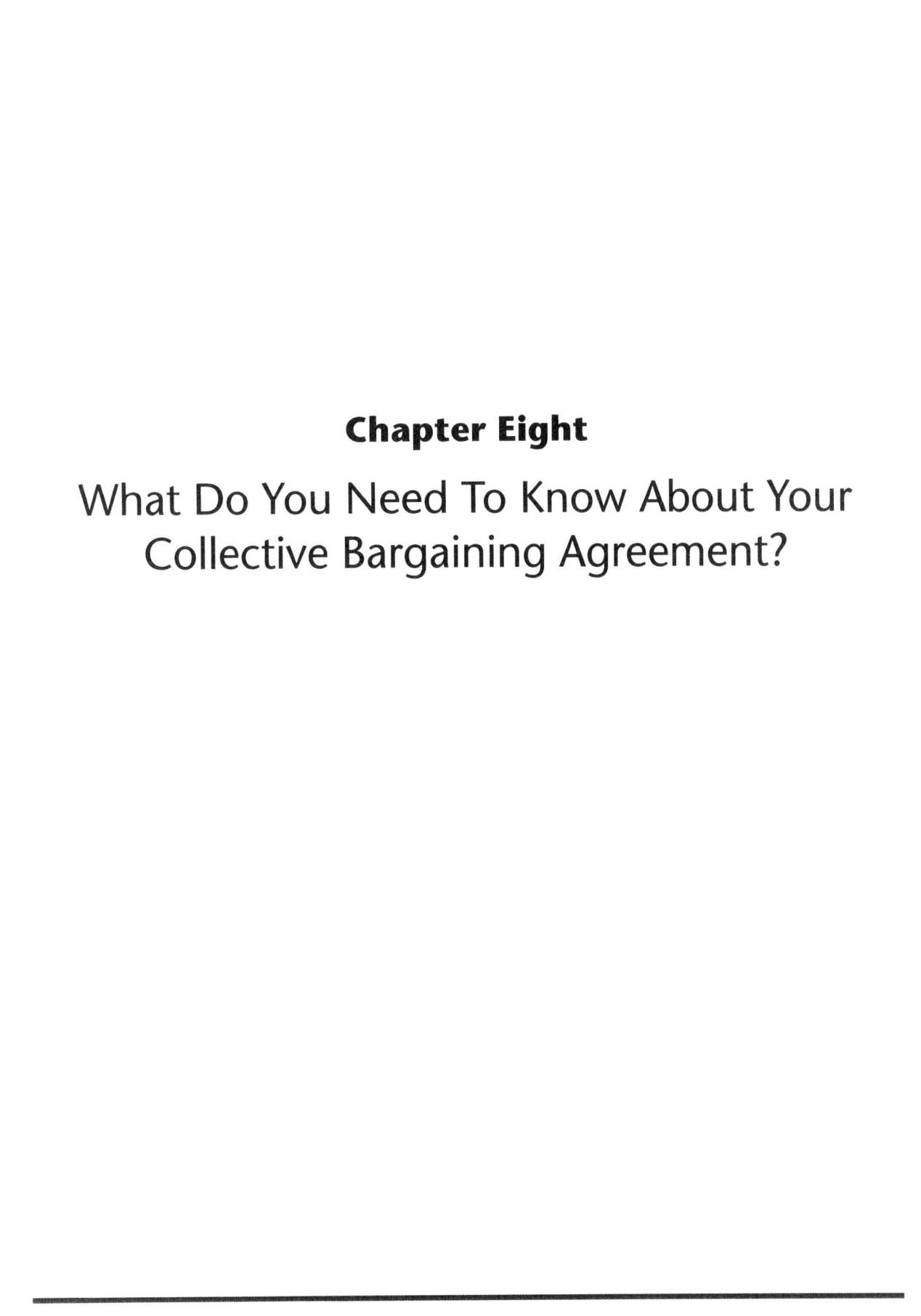

Chapter Eight
What Do You Need To Know About Your Collective Bargaining Agreement?

Chapter Eight: What Do You Need To Know About Your Collective Bargaining Agreement?

To be effective as a manager, supervisor, or union representative, you must know both what the Statute requires of you and what your collective bargaining agreement provides. A collective bargaining agreement is one of the most important documents created in a mutual endeavor by union and management. It establishes working conditions for employees, processes for how labor and management will work together and how disputes will be resolved. It takes a tremendous effort on the part of both labor and management to negotiate and come to agreement on its terms.

All contracts are the product of the environment in which they were negotiated and a function of the type of work and the mission of the government entity entering into it. It is impossible in this chapter to set forth all the variations of the provisions which labor and management may have negotiated into the contract. However, there are common provisions which will be found in most all collective bargaining agreements. In this chapter, we will discuss some of the most significant issues that apply to contracts and the common provisions which are found in them.

What Does This Contract Mean?

This is a common question. It is amazing how two sides to an agreement can have significantly differing interpretations of what they both agreed to. The first rule of interpretation is that what it says is what it means. If, in order to justify your interpretation of the agreement, you have to come up with an argument which is clearly at odds with the plain language of the agreement, you probably are not going to be successful.

Example 1. The agreement says employees must request leave 7 days in advance. If a manager were to take the position that he/she could require leave requests to be submitted ten days in advance, that directive would be inconsistent with the plain language of the agreement.

When a contract article contains language which is based on a standard such as fairness or reasonableness, this provides an arbitrator the opportunity to decide whether management's action was fair or reasonable based on what the arbitrator concludes that a fair or reasonable manager would or would not have done. The arbitrator will be substituting his/her judgment for that of the manager.

Example 2. You have a contract which states that an employee will be treated fairly in promotion actions. The arbitrator will determine in his/her own judgment whether the employee was treated fairly. Both the union and management will be able to argue whether the action was fair, but it will be the arbitrator's judgment as to the final decision. Standards such as fairness and reasonableness give an arbitrator wide latitude in making decisions.

The best supporting evidence for what a contract means is what was said at the time it was being negotiated. This "bargaining history" gives life to the words. In situations where it is difficult to understand a provision of the contract, it is always wise to review the bargaining history to seek an understanding of what it means. This history can be very persuasive when presented to an arbitrator. Bargaining history consists of the notes and recollections of the bargainers as to what took place at negotiations on a particular topic. The best practice for both management and the union is to have as accurate a record as possible of what took place at the bargaining table. Individually or jointly, the parties should have someone at the bargaining table taking notes of what is said during negotiations.

Custom and Usage

Practices you have adopted to carry out the provisions of the contract often come to define the contract over time. This custom and usage gives meaning to a contract by the actions of the parties as they use the contract over time. How management and employees have come to apply a provision of a contract becomes its meaning.

Example. The contract has a provision for assignment of overtime that says it will be rotated among the employees. A practice has developed that volunteers are requested first before it is assigned on a rotating basis. This practice can become an interpretation of the contract provision on overtime. Seeking volunteers first is not inconsistent with the wording of the agreement, but gives meaning to how the union and management operated under it

The Practice is Different from the language of the Collective Bargaining Agreement

Many agencies and unions have master agreements which cover many thousands of employees, with thousands of managers spread throughout the country. It is not uncommon that different approaches to applying contract terms develop. Different practices may come to exist in different parts of the bargaining unit. This can also happen when the bargaining unit only covers a few hundred employees. It can become a problem when a new supervisor tries to change the practice that has developed in his or her work unit to be consistent with the contract.

Example. The contract provides that employees must submit leave requests 7 days in advance. The previous supervisor of the unit did not enforce this requirement, but allowed employees to request leave at any time. A new supervisor has just been named. She wishes to change the practice to be consistent with the contract. She notifies the employees that she will be requiring a request for leave to be made 7 days in advance, consistent with the requirements of the contract. Such a change may result in complaints that the new supervisor is changing an existing past practice. The supervisor's answer is that she is bringing the unit back into compliance with the contract.

Unless the union and management agreed to a change in the contract provision, the supervisor has the right to bring the unit back into conformance with the contract. A practice altering the contract can only change the contract if the parties to the collective bargaining agreement agree to such a change. However, a practice which merely clarifies the contract may be considered a past practice which cannot be changed without bargaining. Such a clarification becomes a part of the contract, which both parties may rely upon.

Official Time

Every contract has an official time provision which describes the amount of official time union representatives will receive and the process to be used in granting it. Official time is time granted to union representatives to perform the representational activities described in the provision. A union representative who receives official time is paid at the same rate of pay for official time hours as he/she is paid for their job for the agency.

Official time provisions usually provide for official time in one of three ways: 1) Union representatives may receive a certain portion of their duty time as official time. For example, a union president may receive 50% of their time as official time. This means they are guaranteed up to 20 hours a week on union representational activity. However, they cannot be granted any more than 20 hours a week of official time. 2) Union representatives may have what is called bank time. Under bank time, union officials have a certain number of hours of official time to use throughout the leave year. This time – for example, 1000 hours – is put into a "bank." The time can be used at any time during the year, but once it used up there is no more official time. The union representative must then take leave of some kind to perform union representational activities. 3) The last kind of official time is "reasonable" official time. Under this type of official time provision, the union representative can receive a reasonable amount of official time to perform representational duties. What is reasonable is requested on a case by case basis by the union representative and either agreed to or not by the supervisor. Reasonable official time is the most common approach to the use of official time in the federal sector.

Managers run into problems with reasonable official time when they are too lenient or too stringent in the granting of the time. What is reasonable can frequently become the basis for disputes, because the reasonableness of a request may be subject to interpretation. Reasonable official time is usually a question of what the reasonable union representative would need to use to perform the representational activity for which the time is requested. If, however, a manager freely grants all requests for official time, no matter how lengthy, then in the union representative's mind this may create a practice of unlimited official time.

Example. A union representative requests 4 hours of official time to meet with an employee to discuss a grievance. The union contract provides that union representatives will receive reasonable official time for representational purposes. The supervisor believes 4 hours is excessive for the meeting. The supervisor has the right to tell the representative that he believes 4 hours is excessive and that unless the representative can justify more than 2 hours, the supervisor is only going to grant 2 hours of time. To justify this position, the supervisor tells the representative that he believes an initial interview should only take 2 hours and if the representative needs more than that, he will consider an additional request.

The union representative may grieve the denial of 4 hours as an unreasonable action by the supervisor; however, if the supervisor is able to show that 4 hours is unreasonable under the circumstances, he will be found to have acted reasonably

Failure to enforce the processes put in place in the contract for the granting of official time can result in abuse of the use of official time. Abuse of official time can be a serious problem at an agency or activity. It is the job of managers to ensure that abuse does not occur. An important role for managers who supervise union representatives is to ensure that union representatives are following the rules with respect to official time. It is not always the easiest task, but is necessary to ensure the contract is being complied with by the union. By the same token, union officers and stewards have an obligation to use official time conscientiously, both to avoid disputes with management to the extent possible and to demonstrate to employees that they are taking both their representational responsibilities and their duties for the agency seriously.

Scope of the Bargaining Unit

All contracts have an article which describes who is in the bargaining unit covered by the agreement. This is usually one of the first provisions in the agreement. It is important for each supervisor and union representative to know who is in the bargaining unit, because the union can only represent employees who are in the unit. With the constant state of reorganization of many federal agencies, it is sometimes difficult to know the bargaining unit status of employees. However, in drafting this article it is important to make certain that the description of the employees in the bargaining unit is consistent with the unit description in the certification of unit issued by the FLRA Regional Director. A contract cannot expand or contract the membership of a bargaining unit. The FLRA is the only entity which can decide whether there has been a change in the status of employees in or out of the bargaining unit. This cannot be done by agreement of the parties. It takes the filing of a representation petition to make these changes.

Overtime

Many contracts have a provision on how overtime will be assigned. If your unit has overtime potential, you will need to know the procedures for assigning employees to overtime. A union cannot negotiate over whether management can require employees to work overtime. Assignment of overtime is an assignment of work, which is a management right. However, a union can negotiate over procedures and appropriate arrangements when management exercises its right to assign overtime.

A common overtime provision establishes that overtime will be distributed fairly among the employees. This provision does not interfere with management's right to assign overtime to employees; it merely ensures that employees will be treated fairly when it is distributed.

Another common overtime provision provides that management will distribute overtime for similarly situated employees on the basis of seniority. This does not interfere with management's right to assign employees to overtime, because it distributes the overtime to employees who do exactly the same job at the same level. In essence the workers are fungible.

Details and Reassignments

These provisions, found in most agreements, explain the process for detailing and reassigning employees. If management is going to detail or reassign employees, it must follow the procedures set forth in this article of the contract. Once again, the union cannot interfere with management's right to reassign or detail employees. The union can make proposals which provide for procedures for selecting employees for details or reassignments, however it cannot interfere with management's right to determine the qualifications for who it selects for reassignment.

Grievance Procedure

A grievance process is required to be included in all contracts. It sets time periods for filing grievances, as well as for management responses and who is to respond at various levels. Failure to follow the procedure gives the union the right to elevate the grievance to the next level. The grievance procedure must end in binding arbitration. The grievance procedure should set forth the scope of what is covered by the grievance procedure and the steps of the grievance process. In the federal sector, most grievance procedures have a broad scope which is consistent with the language of the Statute. Grievance procedures normally have 3 to 5 steps, ending in arbitration. At each step, the deciding official for that step must make a decision on the grievance unless the parties are able to settle the grievance as a result of the grievance meeting.

Collective Bargaining

Most contracts have a provision which establishes how bargaining over changes in working conditions will be done. Quite often it establishes when the union will be notified of a change and the period of time it has to respond with proposals. This provision may establish the amount of notice of the change that must be given to the union and provide for how much time the union has to request bargaining. Failure to give notice and implementation of a change without bargaining can be an unfair labor practice. If management gives the union the contractually required notice of the change and the union fails to request bargaining, management has the right to implement the change without fear of being found to have committed an unfair labor practice.

Collective bargaining provisions also often establish what bargaining can take place at the local level in large consolidated bargaining units consisting of many locations. The basic rule is that all bargaining must take place at the level where the contract is signed. However, bargaining can take place at lower levels of the organization if the contract delegates authority to those levels to bargain. If an agency has a large bargaining unit, it is important to know where bargaining takes place, so management understands to whom notice of changes must be given.

Disciplinary Actions

Contract provisions on disciplinary actions often explain the various types of actions and how or when the actions should be taken by managers. They also will, in many cases, explain the role of the union and time periods for responses to the actions. In taking a disciplinary action, a manager must also know what appeal rights employees have. Appeal rights are often found in the disciplinary action article. Frequently, this article will describe the difference between a disciplinary action and an adverse action. An adverse action, which includes, among other things, a suspension of more than 14 days, is able to be appealed to the Merit Systems Protection Board, while other "disciplinary" actions can only be appealed as grievances under the grievance procedure.

Hours of Work

Hours of work articles are in almost all contracts. They explain what is considered the normal administrative work week, as well as employee tours of duty. Tours of duty are a permissive subject of bargaining, which management must bargain over only if it elects to do so.

Although alternative work schedules are frequently a standalone article in a contract, they are just as often included in an hours of work article. Alternative work schedules (AWS) bargaining has been established by the Federal Employees Flexible and Compressed Work Schedules Act of 1982. The courts have also ruled that flexible and compressed work schedules are fully negotiable. In Bureau of Land Management v. Federal Labor Relations Authority, 864 F.2d 89 (9th Cir. 1988), (Bureau of Land Management), the court held that "[i]n order for employees to have the flexibility and choice envisioned by the [Flexible and Compressed Work Schedules] statute, both the overall contours of the employees' available choices and the manner in which an individual's choice is exercised within those contours, must be subjects included within the terms of the collective bargaining agreement and hence negotiable."

Such negotiations include such things as flextime, credit hours, compressed work hours and core work time. The contract provision will also often explain how to remove employees from an AWS schedule or how to change AWS schedules.

Leave

Granting of leave is an exercise of management's right to assign work. A union cannot propose that employees will be granted leave. They can negotiate over procedures management will use for granting leave. These procedures outline how or when employees will request annual leave and how it will be granted. However, many also contain information about other types of leave, such as military leave, sick leave and administrative leave.

Merit Promotion

Most contracts have a merit promotion article. Merit promotion is the process used by management in the federal government to promote internal employees to new positions. Selection of employees for a promotion is the exercise of management's right to select from all appropriate sources. Merit promotion is covered extensively by Office of Personnel Management Regulations. These government-wide regulations on merit promotion further restrict what can be bargained over by the union. However, unions may bargain over the procedures used by management to select employees for promotion. They cannot bargain over who will be selected, only the selection procedures that will be used.

Performance Management

Performance management articles are in most contracts in various forms. Performance management is the exercise of management's right to assign work and to evaluate employees who are assigned the work. Many aspects of performance management, such as performance standards and critical elements, are nonnegotiable. However, unions may negotiate over how employees participate in the performance management process and how they can appeal management's appraisal of their work.

Duration

The duration article establishes how long the agreement will be in effect. Most federal sector agreements use a 3 year term. The duration article also determines how a contract can be reopened at the end of the term or midterm. In most cases, it will also provide for the way in which the contract may be rolled over for an additional term if neither party opens the contract. The duration clause can be very important, because it establishes how to end the contract and what happens during negotiations for a successor agreement.

This list is not an exclusive or exhaustive list of important contract articles which you need to know about. They are some of the important articles you should look at in your own contract. It is essential that all managers, supervisors and union representatives are familiar with all provisions of their collective bargaining agreement.

Collective Bargaining Agreement Case Study

Your collective bargaining agreement has a provision which provides as follows:

Participation in the Flexiplace program will be voluntary for both the employee and supervisor, and both parties must be comfortable with and agree to the Flexiplace schedule. Participation in the program requires advanced supervisory approval. An employee must receive reasonable notice of any termination of an employee's participation in the Flexiplace program and be provided an adequate amount of time to make transportation arrangements.

Mary Smith has been on Flexiplace for over two years. Her prior supervisor was very happy with the arrangement. The current supervisor is not a believer in Flexiplace. She sends Mary a letter on Friday telling her that effective Monday she will begin reporting to work at the office.

The union, on her behalf, responds that Mary has a past practice of working from home and that the supervisor cannot unilaterally change the practice without bargaining. The union further asserts that she did not receive adequate advance notice of the termination of her flexiplace schedule or adequate time to find transportation to the office. The transportation she did find was an expensive taxi that she had to take each day the first week until she could arrange a van pool. The union is asking she be reimbursed for her expenses beyond what a van pool would have cost.

The collective bargaining agreement clearly provides management with the right to terminate Mary's Flexiplace schedule. The agreement also provides that both the employee and supervisor must be comfortable with the arrangement. If the supervisor is not comfortable, he or she may terminate Flexiplace. However, it also requires adequate advance notice and adequate time to find transportation to the office.

It could be difficult for management to prove that a weekend is adequate advance notice of the termination or an adequate amount of time to find alternate transportation. The question will be how reasonable two days notice given over a weekend is and why additional notice could not have been given.

Key Points in Chapter Eight

1. The collective bargaining agreement establishes working conditions for employees and processes for how labor and management will work together and how disputes will be resolved.

2. The plain language of the contract is the first place to look to interpret the contract.

3. An important source of information to support the interpretation of the contract is the bargaining history, which is what was said at the bargaining table.

4. How employees, management and the union operate under the contract may be used to define what the contract means.

5. Words such as "usually," "normally," and "reasonable" can lead to many interpretations. "Usually" and "normally" can be defined by evidence of what has happened in the past. "Reasonable" is usually defined by what a reasonable person would have done under the circumstances. What is reasonable may be left to the experience of the arbitrator brought in to resolve a dispute over whether management acted reasonably.

Chapter Nine
What You Need to Know About Collective Bargaining

Chapter Nine: What You Need to Know About Collective Bargaining

Collective bargaining is the all-important labor relations process by which unions and management negotiate over working conditions affecting employees. In the private sector, the key issues are wages, hours, and benefits. Those issues in the federal sector are almost always nonnegotiable because they are covered by statutes. All issues covered by federal law or government-wide rules or regulations cannot be negotiated. For the most part, negotiations in the federal sector are over how management exercises its management rights. We have learned in an earlier chapter what management rights are. This chapter will deal with what collective bargaining is and how it works in the federal sector.

What is Collective Bargaining?

The definition of collective bargaining in the Section 7103 (a) (12) provides:

"collective bargaining, means the performance of the mutual obligation of the representative of an agency and the exclusive representative of employees in an appropriate unit in the agency to meet at reasonable times and to consult and bargain in good faith effort to reach agreement with respect to the conditions of employment affecting such employees and to execute, if requested by either party, a written document incorporating any collective bargaining agreement reached, but the obligation referred to in this paragraph does not compel either party to agree to a proposal or to make a concession."

To understand this definition we will look at each part of it:

Performance of a Mutual Obligation

Both labor and management have the obligation to engage in collective bargaining. This is not just a union right but also a management right and obligation. Bargaining must be carried out by both parties to the collective bargaining relationship.

Duly Authorized Representatives

This obligation must be carried out by a representative of the agency and of the exclusive representative. Both sides must be represented by duly authorized representatives. Quite often unions complain that they have the right to deal directly with the head of an agency when engaged in collective bargaining. The person who represents management in negotiations need not be the head of an agency or a facility, but must have authority to bind the agency to an agreement. It is an unfair labor practice to send someone to the negotiating table who does not have authority to bind their principal. However, this does not mean the designated representative cannot seek assistance from their legal advisors or seek guidance from their boss. It means that when they sign an agreement, the agreement must be enforceable. If they have no authority to sign an enforceable agreement, they cannot act as a representative.

Example. Mary Smith has been designated to represent management in collective bargaining negotiations over the relocation of an office. The union has proposed that offices be assigned based on seniority. Mary does not know if the proposal is negotiable or if it is agreeable to the rest of the managers. She tells the union she wants to contact her legal office to seek an opinion as to the negotiability of its proposal. She further states that she wants to talk to the director about how seniority will work.

The union tells her that she is committing an unfair labor practice because she does not have the authority to agree to its proposal. The fact that she is asking for legal advice is not an unfair labor practice. She has the right to seek advice from whomever she chooses. Asking her boss what he/she thinks of the proposal is also not a violation of law. If she tells the union she has no authority to enter into an agreement, the union has the right to request negotiations with the person in management who has the authority to negotiate.

Meet At Reasonable Times

Both sides have an obligation to meet at reasonable times and convenient places, to meet as frequently as necessary, and to avoid unreasonable delays. Neither side can dictate when bargaining will take place or where it will be held. Often these issues will be decided in a negotiated ground rules agreement which sets forth how, where, and when negotiations will be conducted. If there is no ground rules agreement, both sides still have an obligation to be reasonable in establishing the process for bargaining.

Bargain in a Good Faith Effort to Reach Agreement

Both union and management have an obligation to negotiate in good faith. Good faith bargaining requires both union and management to approach negotiations with a sincere resolve to reach an agreement. A common allegation is that one side or the other is engaging in bad faith bargaining. This can result when one side takes a hard and seemingly intractable position on an issue.

There is no requirement that you agree to the other side's proposals. There is only a requirement that you try to resolve your differences. You are entitled to disagree. In the federal sector, because management has the right to declare a union proposal nonnegotiable, management is not often found to have engaged in bad faith bargaining. The situations in which management has been found to have bargained in bad faith have generally occurred when management has made statements that it never intended to reach agreement regardless of the union proposals. These types of statements do not evidence a sincere effort to reach agreement.

Unions are sometimes charged with bad faith bargaining for unduly delaying negotiations. Many times, federal sector unions feel that their best recourse is to prolong negotiations, because they are not able to negotiate what they want because of management rights. The strategy is to delay so that management doesn't implement the change or makes a mistake, such as early implementation, resulting in an unfair labor practice. In some of these circumstances, management has been found not to be prepared for negotiations. If management alleges bad faith by the union, it must be able to show that it is ready, willing and able to negotiate. One way to expedite negotiations is to negotiate a set of standard ground rules for all negotiations, so that new ground rules need not be developed for each set of negotiations.

Conditions of Employment

The only issues unions and management are required to bargain over are conditions of employment. Conditions of employment are defined as personnel policies, practices and matters affecting working conditions of employees. Section 7103 (a) (14) provides:

(14) "conditions of employment" means personnel policies, practices, and matters, whether established by rule, regulation, or otherwise, affecting working conditions, except that such term does not include policies, practices, and matters –

(A) relating to political activities prohibited under subchapter III of chapter 73 of this title;

(B) relating to the classification of any position; or

(C) to the extent such matters are specifically provided for by Federal statute;

When a union seeks to bargain over a change in working conditions it must first show that the matter being changed is a working condition. Working conditions must pertain to bargaining unit employees and to the work situation or employment relationship of those employees. Federal laws and government-wide regulations are not considered working conditions. Classification of positions is also excluded from the definition of what is a working condition, along with political activities prohibited by law.

Example. Management has decided to make a change. For many years there had been a holiday party held during work time in the work area. It was purely a social event. Many former employees would come back to participate in the party. The party had grown into a major event taking up a significant part of the time of a number of employees the week before the party. Management has decided to restrict the party to lunch time and no former employees will be invited.

The union has threatened an unfair labor practice charge over the change unless the party is restored to its previous way of being conducted and retirees are allowed to attend.

It is not a change in working conditions to eliminate attendance at the party by retirees. They are not members of the bargaining unit and therefore, any change with respect to them would not be a change in working conditions. This also applies to any changes that affect supervisors. The party itself was not a working condition. The party was held as a morale activity. The FLRA has found that there is no duty to negotiate over issues related to morale because morale is not a working condition. The changes can be made without bargaining. However, if the party had a work related aspect, such as being used to give out awards, or was an award itself, it would be a working condition.

Who Can a Union Bargain For?

A union can only submit proposals with respect to changes which affect bargaining unit employees. A union can also only bargain to establish working conditions of employees in the bargaining unit. Proposals may not establish working conditions for non-employees or employees who are not in the bargaining unit. Bargaining over working conditions for employees not in the bargaining unit – such as non-employees, employees in other bargaining units, and supervisors – would be a permissive subject of bargaining. If a union proposal has a direct effect on non-bargaining unit employees, it is nonnegotiable.

Example: Management has just awarded a contract to have contract employees do help desk work side-by-side with bargaining unit employees. The contract states that the contract employees will receive preference for assignment to shifts to cover the desk. The union contract establishes a seniority system for bidding on shifts for bargaining unit employees. The first day of work for the contract employees, management gives preference to the contract employees for assignment to the help desk. The union files a grievance on behalf of an employee, as well as an unfair labor practice charge.

The union cannot bargain on behalf of non-bargaining unit employees. However, management cannot unilaterally change the working conditions of bargaining unit employees because it has entered into a contract with a contractor. While the union cannot make proposals which directly affect contract employees, it can propose to mitigate the adverse effects of a management action. Management cannot repudiate the contract provision on assignment to the help desk because it has hired contractors.

When Do You Have to Bargain?

Management and union must bargain over a collective bargaining agreement. This is called a term agreement, because it has a specific time period (term) that it is in existence. This agreement sets forth provisions covering many of the working conditions for employees, including a grievance procedure. Management must also bargain over changes in working conditions that occur during the term of the agreement, if they concern issues not already negotiated in the agreement and if the union requests to bargain. Lastly, management must bargain when the union initiates bargaining over working condition issues which were not covered in the collective bargaining agreement. Most managers are only involved in bargaining over issues related to changes in working conditions. This section will only deal with change bargaining, because very few managers and union representatives will be involved in negotiating collective bargaining agreements or with union-initiated bargaining proposals.

The De Minimis Standard

There is no labor relations definition of what constitutes a change. It is clearly doing something different than was done in the past. The quantum of the change is important. You must only bargain over changes which are more than de minimis. The de minimis standard looks to the nature and extent of the effect or reasonably foreseeable effect of the change on conditions of employment. This is a legal definition adopted by the FLRA to set a standard for when a change is significant enough to require bargaining. However, there are very loose criteria for what is de minimis which makes it difficult to understand when or how to apply the standard.

Example 1. Management decides to change the requirement for employees to use a pencil to fill out forms while they are in the field. Employees were permitted to use a pencil first in the field, then to use a pen in the office when submitting the final corrected version of the form. Under the new policy, they may only use a pen and not change the form once it has been completed.

Is the change de minimis? The requirement of mandating a pen versus a pencil in and of itself is not a significant change and would not require bargaining. The question, though, is whether not allowing correction of the form once it is completed is a significant change. If not being able to change the form would have an adverse effect on the employees' appraisals, for example, that change would require bargaining.

Example 2. Management decides to change the way employees request leave. In the past, leave was requested by using a standard agency form and leaving it on the supervisor's desk at least two days before the requested day of leave. Now the form, which contains exactly the same information as before, is printed on blue paper and is half the size of the standard form. It must now be submitted three days ahead of time.

Is the change de minimis? The change in the size of the form is not significant. The issue is how significant is the change requiring an additional day of notice of the request. The union would have to show the adverse effect on employees of being required to request leave an additional day in advance. This is a situation where it is difficult to determine what the significance of the change might be. Notifying the union of the change will give management an opportunity to understand what employees may be concerned about with respect to the change. If the union cannot show that there are reasonably foreseeable adverse effects from the change, there is no obligation to bargain.

It is sometimes very difficult to tell when a change is de minimis. When in doubt as to whether a change is significant enough to require bargaining, the best approach is to notify the union of the change. If the union cannot show that there are reasonably foreseeable adverse effects from the change, there is no duty to bargain and management can implement. Management has an obligation to notify the union if a change is more than de minimis, but it only has to bargain if the union can identify adverse effects from the change and make proposals which mitigate these effects (assuming that the substance of the change itself is not bargainable).

Limitations on the Right to Bargain

Federal Law and Government-Wide Rules and Regulations

One of the key issues in collective bargaining is what can be negotiated. The Statute places a number of limitations on a union's right to bargain in the federal sector. Unions cannot bargain over federal laws and government-wide rules and regulations. Government-wide rules and regulations are official declarations of policy which apply to the federal civilian workforce as a whole and are binding on federal agencies and officials. A government-wide regulation is generally applicable throughout the federal government Examples of government wide regulations are: EEOC Regulations; Office of Government Ethics Regulations – 5 CFR 2600; Office of Personnel Management Regulations; Office of Management and Budget Circulars; and Federal Travel Regulations.

Where law specifically provides for a matter, it is not a condition of employment subject to bargaining. However, mere reference to a matter in a law is not sufficient to preclude bargaining. A statute may be specific as to some matters, but not as to others. If an issue is specifically provided for in a statute or government-wide regulation, it means the agency has no discretion to bargain over the content of the statute or government-wide regulation. Where an agency has discretion in a law or regulation, it is obligated to exercise that discretion through bargaining.

Compelling Need for Agency Regulations

Unions may bargain over agency as opposed to government wide regulations. The duty to bargain extends to agency regulations unless there is a compelling need for the regulation. To prove compelling need an agency must:

1. Identify a specific agency-wide regulation,

2. Show that there's a conflict between its regulation and the union's proposal, and

3. Demonstrate that its regulation meets the compelling need criteria of §2424.11 of the FLRA regulations.

To avoid the duty to bargain over an agency regulation, the agency regulation must meet one or more of the following compelling need criteria:

1. Rule or regulation is essential as distinguished from helpful or desirable to accomplishment of mission, or

2. Rule or regulation is necessary to insure maintenance of merit principles, or

3. Rule or regulation implements mandate to Agency or Primary National Subdivision, which implementation is non-discretionary in nature.

See §2424.11 of FLRA Rules and Regulations.

Management Rights

By far the greatest majority of bargaining in the federal sector concerns the exercise of management rights. Management rights were discussed earlier in Chapter 3, however we will look more closely at them now. Management's reserved right are found in Section 7106 of the Statute:

§ 7106. Management Rights

(a) Subject to subsection (b) of this section, nothing in this chapter shall affect the authority of any management official of any agency –

(1) to determine the mission, budget, organization, number of employees, and internal security practices of the agency; and

(2) in accordance with applicable laws –

(A) to hire, assign, direct, layoff, and retain employees in the agency, or to suspend, remove, reduce in grade or pay, or take other disciplinary action against such employees;

(B) to assign work, to make determinations with respect to contracting out, and to determine the personnel by which agency operations shall be conducted;

(C) with respect to filling positions, to make selections for appointments from –

(i) among properly ranked and certified candidates for promotion; or

(ii) any other appropriate source; and

(D) to take whatever actions may be necessary to carry out the agency mission during emergencies.

(b) Nothing in this section shall preclude any agency and any labor organization from negotiating –

(1) at the election of the agency, on the numbers, types, and grades of employees or positions assigned to any organizational subdivision, work project, or tour of duty, or on the technology, methods, and means of performing work;

(2) procedures which management officials of the agency will observe in exercising any authority under this section; or

(3) appropriate arrangements for employees adversely affected by the exercise of any authority under this section by such management officials.

When management does anything in the workplace, it is more than likely exercising its management rights. While unions cannot bargain over management's decision to exercise a right, they can bargain over appropriate arrangements for employees adversely affected by the exercise of those rights. They can also bargain over procedures to be used to exercise the rights.

What about Impact and Implementation Bargaining?

Many readers have heard of bargaining over "impact and implementation." This is still referred to as the legal requirement for bargaining when management exercises a management right. For purposes of this book, we will refer to the obligation to bargain over the exercise of management rights as bargaining over "procedures and appropriate arrangements." "Impact and implementation" is, in my opinion, an outmoded way of describing the approach to bargaining over management rights. When determining whether a proposal is negotiable, you must determine whether it is a negotiable procedure or a negotiable appropriate arrangement. Using the proper identification of the bargaining obligation will help direct you to an understanding of the correct test to be used to determine the negotiability of a proposal.

Bargaining over Procedures

The Statute gives unions the right to bargain over the procedures to be used when management exercises its rights. Section 7106 (b) (2) provides:

(b) Nothing in this section shall preclude any agency and any labor organization from negotiating–

(2) procedures which management officials of the agency will observe in exercising any authority under this section;

The Statute does not contain a definition for procedure(s), nor have any FLRA decisions defined what a procedure is. The difficulty in defining what a procedure is stems from the fact that many proposals which could be considered procedural in nature also could be considered substantive, because the procedure is itself the substance of what is being negotiated. It is easy to see the confusion between whether a proposal is a procedure or is substantive. When it receives a negotiability appeal from a union, the FLRA has resolved this dilemma of whether a proposal is a procedure by relying on its test for procedures only for those proposals which the union called procedures. If the union called the proposal an appropriate arrangement, then the FLRA uses the test for appropriate arrangements.

The basic test for whether a proposal is a negotiable procedure is whether the proposal directly interferes with the exercise of a management right. This is a fact-based test dependent on the nature of the particular proposal. The FLRA, after considering the arguments of both the union and management, will determine whether the proposed procedure directly interferes with the exercise of a management right, or whether it only "indirectly" interferes and is thus negotiable. Management attempts to convince the FLRA how the proposed procedure directly interferes with management's ability to exercise its reserved right, and the union tries to convince the FLRA to the contrary. It is obvious how important the viewpoints of the political appointees of the FLRA are to the eventual outcomes of cases decided by the FLRA. There is potential for different outcomes for the same fact pattern, based on the different composition of the FLRA as different Presidential Administrations come into office and change the members of the FLRA.

The following are an example of proposals the FLRA has found not to be procedures:

1. Proposals that condition the exercise of a management right on agreement of employees or their union;

2. Proposals that require management to assign particular individuals the task of evaluating employee performance;

3. Proposals that restrict use of competitive procedures;

4. Proposals that prevent management from holding employees accountable for performance of assigned work; and

5. Proposals that require agency to adjust performance expectations.

See AFGE, Local 3529, 57 FLRA No. 43

Example. Union and management are negotiating over a new procedure for the assignment of offices as a result of a prospective office move. The union proposed that offices be assigned based on seniority. Management declared the proposal nonnegotiable on the basis that it directly interferes with management's right to assign work and direct employees.

Management will have to show how the use of seniority to select offices would interfere with the assignment of work. For example, management could submit evidence on how the organization of the office space is necessary to the way work is performed in order to support its arguments regarding interference with the assignment of work. The union would have to prove that management can accomplish its tasks without interference if seniority is used for office assignment. The ultimate issue would be whether using seniority for office assignments directly interferes with management's right to assign work.

Bargaining over Appropriate Arrangements

Management has an obligation to negotiate over appropriate arrangements for employees adversely affected by the exercise of management rights. Section 7106 (b) (3) provides:

(b) Nothing in this section shall preclude any agency and any labor organization from negotiating –

(3) appropriate arrangements for employees adversely affected by the exercise of any authority under this section by such management officials.

The union has the right to make appropriate arrangements proposals which mitigate the adverse effects on employees of management's exercise of its rights. The FLRA has developed a five-part test for determining the negotiability of these proposals. This test provides a common sense approach to how to determine whether a proposal is negotiable as an appropriate arrangement.

Five Part Appropriate Arrangements Test

Part 1. Exercise of a Management Right

It must first be determined what management right is being exercised. A union can only bargain over appropriate arrangements when management is exercising a management right. If management makes a change which is not the exercise of a management right, the union may bargain over the decision itself and not just appropriate arrangements. This is called substantive bargaining.

Part 2. Adverse Effects

For there to be a duty to bargain there must be adverse effects from the exercise of the management right. In determining what proposals to make, the union should be looking at proposals which will mitigate the adverse effects on employees from management's exercise of its rights. These adverse effects need not only occur as soon as the change takes place, but can also be foreseeable. Foreseeable adverse effects are effects which may take place in the future as a result of the change. However, they cannot be hypothetical or speculative effects. They must have a basis in what realistically could happen.

Part 3. Tailored to Employees

A proposal must be tailored to the employees who will be adversely affected by the change. It cannot provide a benefit to employees who hypothetically may be affected in the future.

Part 4. Must Not Excessively Interfere with Management Rights

To be negotiable, a proposal may not excessively interfere with the exercise of management rights. Excessive interference is a fact-based test. In determining whether something excessively interferes, you must look at the extent to which the proposal interferes with management's ability to exercise its rights. If the proposal does not excessively interfere with the exercise of managements rights, it is negotiable. Excessive interference acknowledges that there may be interference with the exercise of the right; it just doesn't allow the interference to be excessive. Management must show the extent to which the proposal interferes with the exercise of its management right, and the union must show how the proposal does not excessively interfere with this right.

Part 5. Balance Intrusion on Management Right Against Benefit to Employees

In determining whether the proposal is appropriate, you must balance the intrusion on management rights against the benefit to employees. In mitigating the adverse effects of the exercise of management rights on employees, the proposal must provide a benefit to the employees. This benefit must be balanced against the proposal's intrusion on management rights. If the intrusion is greater than the benefit, the proposal will be found nonnegotiable. If the benefit is greater than the intrusion, the proposal will be negotiable.

*Example: *Article 16 Section 13 – Duty free lunch*

Once children are seated in the cafeteria, teacher partners may alternate lunchroom supervision duties to allow each partner a duty free time at lunch.

What is the management right?

Assignment of work under §7106(a)(2)(B)

What is the adverse effect on employees?

Teachers assigned lunchroom duties cannot do other things.

Employees have expectations that they will be allowed to eat lunch while not performing duties.

Were effects speculative or hypothetical?

No, employees were not able to eat their lunch with this additional duty.

Was proposal tailored to those affected?

Yes, it affected only employees who were working at lunchtime.

Did the proposal excessively interfere with a management right?

It did not excessively interfere because the children were being supervised at the time necessary during lunch.

How did benefits to employee compare with the intrusion on management rights?

Benefits afforded teachers are significant – ability to use duty-free time for personal reasons, preparation for class, etc. Management's ability to ensure supervision necessary to preserve lunchroom discipline would not be severely restricted – management could determine when it was not feasible to allow duty free time because of other requirements.

Conclusion: Provision is Negotiable

*Overseas Education Association, Fort Rucker Education Association and Department of Defense Dependent Elementary and Secondary Schools, Fort Rucker Department Schools, Fort Rucker, Alabama, 53 FLRA No. 76, 53 FLRA 941 (1997)

Example. Management has decided to require electricians to also do plumbing and plumbers to do electrical work. The new duties will start within a week. The new employees will be called plumtricians. The union is notified of the change.

The union submits an appropriate arrangements proposal which requires employees who must become plumtricians to be trained and receive certification in the new craft, before they are required to act as a plumtrician. As an example, plumbers will have to be certified as electricians before they can be given electrical work. Is this proposal negotiable?

The first question to be answered in applying the appropriate arrangements test is what management right is being exercised by management. Assigning the new duties to plumbers and electricians would be the exercise of the right to assign work.

Next, you must determine if there are adverse effects from the exercise of the right. Management is requiring electricians to do plumbing and plumbers to do electrical work. Employees who do not know how to do electrical work could be injured owing to their lack of knowledge. The same applies to electricians required to do plumbing. Potential injury would be an adverse effect of the change. Additionally, employees who do not know how to do their assigned duties may be demoted, fired or receive poor performance ratings. All of these possibilities are also foreseeable adverse effects of the change. The adverse effects do not appear to be hypothetical or speculative.

The proposal applies only to the employees who will be required to do these new duties. This is sufficiently tailored to meet the third part of the test.

Does the proposal, which requires employees to be certified and trained before being assigned these new duties, excessively interfere with management rights? The proposal would not allow management to assign the new duties until after the period of time it takes for the employees to be trained and certified. This is a clear interference with management rights. Is the interference excessive? The union argues that while it does interfere with management rights, it is not excessive, because management will be able to assign the duties upon employees' successful completion of the training and certification. The union also asserts that the delay is not an excessive interference because of the significant safety concerns for the employees. Management argues that the delay excessively interferes with its right to assign these new duties, because it unreasonably delays management's ability to have these employees start working as plumtricians.

The intrusion on management rights by mandating a delay in its ability to immediately assign the new duties must be balanced against the benefits to employees from being trained before they are asked to do the new work.

Each person reading this example may come up with a different answer to the question based on their background. There are arguments on both sides to support both the union and management position. If union and management cannot resolve the issue at the bargaining table and management declares the union's proposal nonnegotiable, it will be up to the FLRA to provide its judgment on whether this excessively interferes with management rights.

What are Permissive Subjects of Bargaining?

There are certain subjects over which management must bargain. These are called mandatory subjects of bargaining. When management exercises management rights, it must bargain over procedures and appropriate arrangements. There are also a number of subjects which are not mandatory, but which are instead "permissive" subjects of bargaining. A permissive subject is something management does not have an obligation to bargain about, but may engage in bargaining over if it chooses. The Statute establishes a number of issues in Section 7106(b)(1) which are permissive subjects of bargaining. Section 7106(b) provides:

(b) Nothing in this section shall preclude any agency and any labor organization from negotiating –

(1) at the election of the agency, on the numbers, types, and grades of employees or positions assigned to any organizational subdivision, work project, or tour of duty, or on the technology, methods, and means of performing work;

For example, if management wants to bargain over numbers, types and grades of employees, it may bargain over these issues, but it does not have to. Management may bargain over working conditions of non-bargaining unit employees, such as supervisors, but is not required to.

Management may begin bargaining over a permissive subject and change its mind and stop bargaining over that subject. However, if management enters into an agreement on a permissive subject, it cannot terminate the agreement until the agreement – or the collective bargaining agreement – expires, and management declares that it no longer wishes to be bound by it.

Unions also bargain over permissive subjects. An example is negotiating that bargaining can take place at levels in the organization below the level of certification and/or at which the collective bargaining agreement is signed. As an example, if the certification of unit is at the national level and the collective bargaining agreement is signed at the headquarters level of an agency, the union and management can agree that bargaining over local changes will take place at the regional level of the agency. The normal rule is that all bargaining must take place at the level of certification or at which the collective bargaining agreement is signed. By agreeing to bargain at a lower level, both management and the union have bargained over a permissive subject. The same rule as discussed in the previous paragraph – that once you bargain to agreement on a permissive subject, you are bound by it until it expires by its terms and is declared no longer to be effective, or is renegotiated – applies to unions as well as to management.

What is a Past Practice?

One of the most common issues raised between labor and management is the status of past practices. Unions frequently tell management that it may not make a change, because the change would be a change in a past practice. For the most part, past practices may be changed, but management must first bargain with the union over the change in practice. Some practices cannot be changed if they have become terms of the collective bargaining agreement. A practice which has become the custom for how an agreement is interpreted becomes a provision of the collective bargaining agreement and may not be changed until the agreement is renegotiated.

Four Elements that Must Exist for There to be a Past Practice.

Element 1. The practice must concern a working condition. Only something which is a working condition can become a past practice. To be a working condition, it must pertain to employees in the bargaining unit and it must directly affect the employment relationship of bargaining unit employees.

Example. If a practice develops of allowing retired employees to visit the work place, stopping their access is not a change in a past practice, because practices concerning non-bargaining unit employees are not working conditions. In other words, a practice concerning retired employees is not a working condition, because it does not pertain to bargaining unit employees and therefore cannot become the basis for a past practice.

Element 2. The practice must be exercised consistently. The consistent exercise of a practice is dependent on the nature of the practice. The more often a particular practice occurs over a given period of time, the more often it must be shown to have occurred. If something takes place once a year, then it must have occurred each year for a number of years. If something happens every day, it must have occurred every day for a period of months or for some other substantial period of time.

Example. If a practice develops of employees drinking beverages at their desks, there must be a showing that this practice was exercised consistently. It would not be sufficient to show that employees occasionally drank beverages. There must be evidence that employees regularly drank beverages at their desks, because drinking beverages is the type of practice which occurs on a regular basis. If the practice in question only occurs once a year, then there would need to be evidence that showed it occurred for a number of years in row.

Element 3. The practice must be in existence for a sufficient period of time, depending on the nature of the practice. The length of time a practice must be in existence depends on what the practice is. If a practice occurs frequently, the period required would be shorter. If the practice occurs infrequently, the period would have to be longer.

Example. Employees have been permitted two hours of administrative leave for donating blood each of the five times blood donations have been requested over the past year. This might be considered a sufficiently long period of time, since each time blood donations were requested, administrative leave was granted. However, if blood donations occurred only once a year, a one year practice would not be sufficient.

Element 4. The practice must be known by management and agreed to or acquiesced in by it. The actions – or inaction – of management can amount to an agreement to a past practice. If responsible management knows of the practice and either agrees to the practice or allows the practice to continue, this meets the requirement of this element.

Who constitutes responsible management can become a key question, depending on the nature of the practice. A practice which only affects an individual supervisor's unit and is not derived in any way from the collective bargaining agreement can be agreed to or acquiesced in by the supervisor of that unit. A practice which changes the meaning of a collective bargaining agreement can only be agreed to by management at the level at which the collective bargaining agreement was signed.

Example. A practice developed in Region 6 of the agency of allowing the Union President 100% official time for union activities. The agency collective bargaining agreement, which covers all the regions of the agency, provides that union officials will receive reasonable official time for union activities. The new Regional Director terminated the 100% official time for the Union President because he felt it was inconsistent with the contract. The union filed an unfair labor practice claiming that management terminated a past practice without bargaining.

A past practice cannot develop at the local level which is inconsistent with the collective bargaining agreement. The prior Regional Director could not agree to or acquiesce in a past practice that was inconsistent with the agency level collective bargaining agreement. He would not be considered a responsible management official with authority to change a provision of the collective bargaining agreement by practice, when that provision was agreed to at a higher level of the agency. The union would have to show that someone at the agency level knew of the practice in Region 6 and either agreed to the practice or acquiesced in it.

Illegal Past Practices

If a practice is found to be illegal because it violates law, management may immediately terminate the practice without first bargaining. It may, however, have an obligation to bargain post-implementation over the adverse effects on employees from the termination of the practice.

Example. Management just discovered that employees have been paid standby time in violation of law. It immediately terminated the practice. The union claims this was a past practice which can only be terminated after bargaining. If there is a dispute over the legality of the practice, the union can file an unfair labor practice or a grievance. If management is correct, then the only bargaining obligation management might have is to bargain after the change takes place over the adverse effects on employees.

The Bargaining Process

The collective bargaining process with respect to changes in working conditions is very much like a ping pong game. When the ball is hit over the net to you, you must then hit it back to the other side and vice versa. The following are the steps of the back and forth nature of collective bargaining over changes.

Step 1. The first thing management should do when deciding to make a change in working conditions is to review its collective bargaining agreement. If the collective bargaining agreement already covers the matter which is going to be changed, then management must follow the agreement and has no obligation to bargain. However, if the agreement does not cover the issue or matter which is the subject of the change, notice and an opportunity to bargain must be given to the union.

Example. Management needs a number of employees to work mandatory overtime each weekend for the next two months. Employees have not been required to work overtime for a long period of time. The collective bargaining agreement provides a process for selecting employees for overtime; however, this provision has never been used before because of a lack of overtime. The union requests to bargain over this "new" requirement.

Covered by Doctrine

If a provision of the collective bargaining agreement covers the matter which is the subject of the change, there is no obligation to bargain over the change. Agencies have the right to assert as a defense to a union demand to bargain the fact that the subject matter of the bargaining is covered by the existing collective bargaining agreement. This is called the "covered by doctrine". If the union and management negotiated over an issue during negotiations for a term agreement and agreed to a collective bargaining provision covering the issue, there is no requirement to bargain again over that issue during the term of the agreement. If the subject matter of the change is expressly contained in (specifically written in the agreement), there is no obligation by management to negotiate over the change. The parties must follow the contract. If the subject matter of the change is so "inseparably bound up with" a subject covered by the collective bargaining agreement to the extent that it is an aspect of matters already negotiated, there is no obligation to bargain.

Step 2. Management must provide the union notice of changes in working conditions which are more than de minimis. The notice must be adequate to give the union an understanding of the nature of the change, and it must provide an adequate opportunity for the union to respond to the change before the change is implemented.

The adequacy of the notice is dependent on the nature of the change. The more significant the change, the more notice required. Also, the more significant the change, the more time should be allowed the union to respond. The Statute does not have specific time periods for notice to the union or by when a union must respond. The FLRA uses a reasonableness standard to determine if, under the circumstances, the notice was adequate. It is important to look at your collective bargaining agreement to determine if it has requirements establishing how much notice is to be given. The notice periods in the contract are the ones management and union should follow in dealing with changes in working conditions. If management fails to follow the notice periods set forth in the contract, the union can file a grievance over late notice or no notice being given. If management, in the absence of a contractual notice period, fails to give reasonable notice of a change, it may be found to have committed an unfair labor practice.

Example 1. Management decides to implement a reduction in force (RIF). The collective bargaining agreement is silent on the amount of notice to be given when implementing changes. Management gives the union five work days' notice prior to implementation to request bargaining. The RIF involves 300 employees in three different work units in two locations.

Five days notice would not be sufficient notice of something as complicated as a RIF covering 300 employees. Considering the number of employees affected, the complexity of a RIF, and the multiple locations, more notice would be appropriate.

Example 2. Management decides to change the assignments to the night shift for one day because of conflicts for employees on the night shift. The supervisor of the night shift employees just found out the employees must go to a training class during the day one day that week. The supervisor immediately notified the union of the need to fill in the night shift with employees from other shifts to provide coverage for that one night. This notice was given on Monday, with Thursday being the day that employees would have to cover the night shift.

Absent a provision in the collective bargaining agreement covering such changes, under the circumstances, the notice was sufficient. The supervisor gave as much notice of the change as he himself had received.

Step 3. Upon receiving notice, the union must request bargaining. If there is a time frame for requesting bargaining specified in the collective bargaining agreement, the union's request for bargaining must comply with that requirement. If there is no specified contractual time period, the union has a reasonable period of time to request bargaining after receiving notice. As discussed in Step 2, the period of time to respond is dependent on the significance of the change. It must be clear in the union's request that the union is requesting bargaining. A request to have a meeting about the change may not be a sufficient request to bargain.

Example. Management decides to change the configuration of the parking lot and gives the union notice of the change. The notice indicates that there will be a temporary building project which will require the use of 25 spaces in the lot. Twenty-five employees will have to park one quarter mile away during the construction. The construction is to start in 30 days. Management requests that the union respond within 10 days. The union requests bargaining the day before the construction is to start.

Is this a timely request to bargain? Under these circumstances, the union's request would not be considered timely. Management gave the union adequate time to request bargaining, but the union waited until the last minute. This was not a complicated issue requiring more time to determine whether to request bargaining or to gather information. A bargaining request simply must request bargaining. Unless the collective bargaining agreement requires that proposals be submitted along with the request, a simple statement requesting bargaining is sufficient.

Step 4. Once the union requests bargaining, management must respond acknowledging the request. At that time, both union and management must establish ground rules, either in writing or informally, which establish how bargaining will be conducted. If management fails to acknowledge a timely request to bargain and implements the change, it may be subject to an unfair labor practice charge.

Ground Rules

Bargaining over ground rules can in some cases take as long as the negotiations over the subject matter of the change. Ground rules are not necessary for all negotiations. However, for more complex subjects, it is helpful to clearly set forth the agreed-upon process which negotiations will follow. A typical ground rules agreement will have some or all of the following issues covered:

1. Location where negotiations will be conducted
2. Time, date and duration of negotiations
3. Membership of the negotiation teams
4. Role of chief negotiators
4. How proposals will be exchanged
5. How a record of negotiations will be kept
6. Effect of signing off on individual articles of an agreement
7. Official time and travel and per diem
8. Impasse resolution

Step 5. Before bargaining takes place, often the union and management will meet to discuss the nature of the change and the adverse effects on employees from the change, and to provide or exchange information about the change. While such a meeting is not mandatory, it can be helpful in providing both sides with a better understanding of potential issues in dispute. Unions frequently request information from management about changes in working conditions. As has been previously discussed, unions have the right under Section 7114 (c)(4) to request information for representational purposes. Sharing information is often a useful process allowing the parties to the negotiations to understand the nature of the change, management's reasoning in deciding on the change, and the employees' concerns about it.

Step 6. The union must submit proposals to respond to the management change. A failure to timely submit proposals can be considered bad faith bargaining if it unduly prolongs the bargaining process. If the union does not timely submit proposals in accordance with formal or informal ground rules, management is free to implement. The failure to submit proposals may be considered a waiver of the right to bargain. However, unless the parties' ground rules specify that proposals must be submitted in advance of a meeting to negotiate, there is no Statutory requirement that the union provide its proposals in advance of bargaining – only that a timely request to bargain be made.

Step 7. Management has an obligation to respond to the union's proposals. Failing to respond to the union's proposals along with implementation of the change would be an unfair labor practice for implementing prior to completion of bargaining. If all the union proposals are nonnegotiable as violations of management rights or federal law, management must notify the union of its determination of non-negotiability. If the union fails to change the proposals or to acknowledge management's position on negotiability, management may implement the change. It implements at its peril, because if it is wrong about the negotiability of any proposal, it has committed an unfair labor practice for implementing in the face of negotiable proposals.

Step 8. If management declares some or all of the union's proposals nonnegotiable, the union must change its proposals, file a negotiability appeal with the FLRA or refute the management's allegation of non-negotiability. Management must give the union enough time to modify and resubmit its proposal after a declaration of non-negotiability, before it implements the change. The filing of a negotiability appeal by the union does not require management to stop implementing the change. If the union's appeal is successful, the FLRA will order prospective bargaining without *status quo* relief for the union. If the union chooses to file an unfair labor practice and the FLRA finds that management committed an unfair labor practice, the FLRA may order a *status quo ante* remedy. A *status quo ante* remedy would require management to put things back to the way they were before the violation of law and then commence bargaining.

Step 9. If there are no declarations of non-negotiability by management but the negotiators cannot come to agreement, either union or management has the right to request the services of the Federal Mediation and Conciliation Service (FMCS). It is the job of FMCS to assist the negotiators in reaching an agreement through mediation of the dispute. If FMCS is not able to resolve the dispute, it certifies that the parties have reached an impasse in the dispute to the Federal Service Impasses Panel.

Step 10. Either the union or management or both can request the services of the Federal Services Impasses Panel (FSIP). FSIP is a part of the FLRA. Its job is to resolve impasses. An impasse occurs when labor and management cannot agree on an issue or issues, and there are no issues of negotiability. FSIP cannot decide whether a proposal is negotiable, unless it is a matter of clearly settled law. It has authority to issue a decision establishing the actual terms of the agreement between labor and management. Both sides have the opportunity to present their positions on what FSIP should find. FSIP has independent authority to fashion whatever result it thinks is appropriate, even if it is different from what either side proposed. There is no appeal from a decision of FSIP. It is an unfair labor practice to fail to comply with an order of FSIP.

These 10 Steps are a digested version of the rules and processes concerning collective bargaining in the federal sector. As may be obvious at this point, it can be a very complex system for resolving workplace disputes.

Collective Bargaining Case Study

Mary Jones is a new supervisor. She has found a number of problems in her work unit and has decided to make a series of changes to better accomplish her unit's mission. Her first change entails requiring employees to come in to work 30 minutes earlier on Tuesdays and Thursdays. This is 30 minutes earlier than is required in the core hours' provision of the collective bargaining agreement. The collective bargaining agreement sets 8:00 AM to 5:00 PM to be the established core hours. However, she wants employees in earlier to be ready when the public arrives on these days at 8:00 AM. She will shorten the work day by 30 minutes each day so employees still only work 8 hour days.

Employees have been putting up pictures of family members, their favorite movie stars and their pets on the walls of their cubicles. She believes this is very unprofessional, and she wants them to be removed.

A practice has developed over a number of years of having a luncheon for the employees of the unit at a restaurant near the office on the third Friday of each month. These luncheons have generally lasted about 45 minutes past the normal end of the lunch hour. She wants to stop what she considers to be an illegal practice.

Her next change involves the use of the back door of the facility for entry to the workspace. She believes this is a security problem and will have an emergency door installed in place of the door now in use. Employees will not have entry through this door in the future. Not having the door available will require employees to enter the work space from the other side of the building, which will take employees an additional 10 minutes to walk from where they park their cars.

She called in her union steward and told him the changes she was going to make. He requested bargaining. What are the rights and obligations of the union and management?

The first change involves a change in the contract which establishes the core hours for employees. A collective bargaining agreement cannot be changed unless both union and management agree on amending the contract. Mary can seek to change the core hours when the contract comes open for renegotiation or if there is a mid-term reopener provision in the contract.

The next change involves pictures in employee cubicles. The first question is whether the pictures are a working condition. Is there a relationship between employees having pictures in their cubicles and their jobs? Mary can argue that there is no relationship between the pictures and performance of the employees' duties. Morale is not considered a working condition. The union can argue that having the pictures in the cubicles makes the employees more productive. This is an argument which unions have used successfully in persuading the FLRA that issues pertaining to radios and beverages such as coffee are considered working conditions and should be allowed in the work area. This is an argument Mary may win, but she will have to deal with the morale issues the change will cause.

The third change involves stopping the use of a back door for entering the facility. Mary is exercising her right to establish internal security practices when she makes this change. The union cannot propose that the door not be closed to entry by employees. However, the union may propose appropriate arrangements for employees who must now walk around the building to gain entry.

Key Points in Chapter Nine

1. The only issues unions and management have an obligation to negotiate over are conditions of employment.

2. Bad faith bargaining occurs when either union or management does not show a sincere resolve to reach agreement.

3. There is no obligation to bargain over changes which are de minimis. The de minimis standard deals with the significance of the change.

4. The terms "procedures and appropriate arrangements" bargaining have replaced "impact and implementation" bargaining when management exercises a management right.

5. For a procedure to be negotiable it must not directly interfere with Management's rights.

6. Appropriate arrangements proposals may not excessively interfere with the exercise of a management right.

7. The final determination as to whether a proposal is an appropriate arrangement requires balancing the proposal's intrusion on management rights against the benefit to employees.

8. Management and unions have no obligation to bargain over permissive subjects; however, once they reach an agreement on a permissive subject, the agreement is binding.

9. If something is not a working condition, it cannot be the basis or a past practice.

10. The FLRA resolves whether a union proposal is negotiable, while the FSIP resolves disputes when labor and management agree on the negotiability of proposals but cannot reach an agreement.

Chapter Ten
What You Can and Cannot Say or Do to Union Representatives and Employees

Chapter Ten: What You Can and Cannot Say or Do to Union Representatives and Employees

Union representatives and employees are protected by the Statute from statements or actions taken against them by management because they are assisting the union or seeking the assistance of the union. If they are engaged in protected activity, they have greater rights with respect to their activities than a regular employee. This is especially true for union representatives who are representing individual employees or are engaged in collective bargaining.

Statements: Oral or Written

A statement which interferes, restrains or coerces an employee in the exercise of rights given to the employee under the Statute is an unfair labor practice. Employee rights include the right to form, join or assist a union or to seek the assistance of a union. Statements may be made orally or in writing. Statements to union representatives which interfere, restrain or coerce them in the exercise of their right to assist the union are also unfair labor practices.

These types of disputes are difficult to resolve because they involve the credibility of the supervisor and the employee. They are often the only people involved in the conversation. It is the word of the employee against the word of the supervisor. If the statement is the basis of an unfair labor practice charge, the Office of General Counsel does not decide who is telling the truth. Its investigation will determine whether, under the circumstances, the evidence indicates that a statement was made and whether the statement, if made, would be an unfair labor practice. It will be up to the Administrative Law judge in an unfair labor practice hearing to decide who is telling the truth.

Robust Debate

Union representatives are entitled to greater latitude in speech and action than are other employees. They may vigorously defend the union and employees. Robust debate often equates to the use of language which, absent the protected activity of the union representative, would not be considered appropriate in the work place. In situations where a Union steward uses vulgarity or rough language, the question may become whether managers themselves use such language or whether such language is a regular occurrence in the workplace. Frequently, the heated nature of the conversation and the circumstances surrounding the discussion are the basis for determining whether the language or discussion was inappropriate.

The language will lose its protection if it amounts to flagrant misconduct. Flagrant misconduct is more fully discussed later in this chapter.

Freedom of Expression

Section 7116(e) of the Statute provides protection to supervisors and managers who make statements which are expressions of any personal view, argument, or opinion which informs employees of the government's policy relating to labor relations and representation if the expression contains no threat or reprisal or force or promise of benefit or was not made under coercive conditions. They also have the right to make statements which correct the record with respect to any false or misleading statement. This section of the Statute gives managers and supervisors the right to express their opinion concerning labor relations matters as long as it is not threatening or coercive to employees.

Example 1. John Pitts works as claims examiner in the District Office of his agency. He has been unhappy about how leave is granted around the holidays. He does not believe his supervisor is following the provisions of the collective bargaining agreement but instead is granting leave to her favorites first. John talked to his supervisor, Sally Burgh. He told her he was going to file a grievance over her practice. Sally did not want to get in trouble with higher level management. She had recently had another allegation that she played favorites in a promotion action. She decided to solve this one the way she solved the other. She told John that if he filed a grievance, higher level management would back her, he would get a reputation as a trouble maker, and she would see to it that he never got his leave request granted for holiday time off. She also told him she would deny having had this conversation with him.

Management, in its response to an unfair labor practice charge filed by the union, denies that the statements were made by Sally.

The first statement – that if John filed a grievance, higher level management would back her – was intended to restrain him from filing a grievance. A reasonable employee would understand that remark as an effort to stop him from grieving her holiday leave policy.

The second statement – that he would get a reputation as a troublemaker – was also intended to interfere with his right to file a grievance. While, on its face, it might be a true statement, unlike libel and slander where truth is a defense, the fact that this might be true is no defense to its coercive effect on John.

The last statement was clearly a threat that he would never obtain holiday leave if he filed a grievance.

These statements, if made, would be violations of the law. If the union and management are not able to resolve this dispute, the Office of General Counsel issues an unfair labor practice complaint. An administrative law judge will decide who is telling the truth. One of the things the judge will look at is the demeanor of the witnesses, which includes, among other things, who sounds more trustworthy. The judge will also look at whose story makes the most sense and whose facts are clearly presented. Two different judges could potentially make different decisions on the credibility of the same witnesses. This is always the chance you take when you are in litigation.

Example 2. At the end of the work day, Tom Hunts stopped by his supervisor's office to report on his last assignment. His supervisor, Sam Ville, had just completed reviewing a grievance that was filed over the movement of a desk two feet farther from the break room area. The union complained that this change was made without using the collective bargaining agreement procedures for office relocations. Sam was frustrated by the grievance. When Tom came in, Sam asked him if he was a member of the union. He then went on to say he had a silly grievance he was spending time on and he wished the union had better things to do with their time.

Management does not deny that Sam made the statements. It claims the statements were expressions of personal opinion and therefore did not violate the Statute.

It is not threatening or coercive for Sam to ask Tom whether he was a member of the union. Such a question does not contain a threat. Calling the grievance a silly grievance was also not threatening, nor did it denigrate the union for having filed it. Saying he wished the union had better things to do also could be seen as not coercive. Sam made these statements to one employee in a non-threatening or coercive atmosphere. They were expressions of his opinion and not intended to threaten the employee.

Discriminatory Actions

Actions by management which encourage or discourage employee membership in a union by discrimination in connection with hiring, tenure, promotion or other conditions of employment are unfair labor practices. When actions are taken against employees or union representatives that would not otherwise have been taken had they not engaged in union activity, the actions are considered discriminatory. The types of actions which have been found to be violations of the law include disciplinary actions, denials of promotions, removals during an employee's probationary term, denials of awards and denials of other benefits.

In a situation where the union claims that an employee or union representative was discriminated against by management, it must make a prima facie showing that the action taken against the employee was based on his/or her union activities. If management can show that it would have taken the action it took regardless of the union activities, it will not have violated the Statute. An employee may be engaged in union activities, but if management can show it would have taken the same action against any employee or treated any other employee the same way, discrimination will not be found.

Flagrant Misconduct

Union representatives and employees who engage in flagrant misconduct lose the protection of the Statute. Flagrant misconduct is conduct on the part of an employee which goes beyond the boundaries of what would be considered appropriate conduct under the circumstances. In determining whether an action or statement by a union representative is flagrant misconduct the following factors should be considered: (1) the place and subject matter of the discussion; (2) whether the employee's outburst or action was impulsive or designed; (3) whether the outburst or action was in any way provoked by the employer's conduct; and (4) the nature of the intemperate language and conduct. A union representative who, in a heated grievance discussion, pushes a manager and causes injury would clearly have engaged in flagrant misconduct. However, if the union representative was acting in self-defense, the conduct might not be considered flagrant misconduct. What is or is not flagrant misconduct is determined by the individual circumstances of each incident.

What Managers Can and Cannot Say and Do Case Study

Gayle Mayfield is the union steward for the Operations Branch of the District where she is a level one operations controller. She had filed over 20 unfair labor practices and 10 grievances in the past year. She is also active on the union negotiating team for the agency collective bargaining agreement. She spends approximately 50% of her time on union business. She had recently applied for a promotion to a level two operations controller position. The position requires being available full time to assist in operational issues. She has always received the highest performance ratings for her job and also was deemed best qualified for the promotion. She asked the supervisor who interviewed her for the promotion what her chances were of getting promoted. He told her the job required someone who could work full time at the job and she would have to consider the impact of the job on her union activities. She did not receive the promotion. An employee who was also rated best qualified but did not perform union activities was selected. Gayle filed an unfair labor practice charge against management.

To prove an employee was discriminated against based on performing union activities, the person filing the unfair labor practice charge must first show that the employee was engaged in union or other protected activities. If the employee was not engaged in protected activities, there can be no discrimination. In this example, Gayle Mayfield was an active union representative who clearly was heavily engaged in assisting the union. Additionally, the selecting supervisor told Gayle that she should consider the impact of the job on her union activities. Gayle has met her prima facie burden of showing protected activity.

Management now has the opportunity to show that it could justify the selection it made and would have made the same promotion decision regardless of Gayle's union activities. The employee who received the position was rated the same as Gayle. Gayle was told to consider the impact on her union activities of having to work full time in the new position. Management can argue that the statement was not coercive. The manager was seeking an accommodation with the employee over how she would handle her union duties in the new position. Management has the right to inquire as to the effect of Gayle's union duties on her ability to do the job, as long as the inquiry is not coercive or threatening in nature.

Key Points in Chapter Ten

1. Employees who are engaged in protected activity are protected from management actions taken against them because they are engaged in protected union activities.

2. Managers have freedom to express their opinions about unions as long as they are not threatening or coercive.

3. Union representatives who are performing in their union role may engage in robust debate with management.

4. Union representatives who engage in flagrant misconduct in their words or actions lose the protection of the Statute.

5. When an agency is charged with discrimination based on union activity, the agency can rebut the charge by showing it was justified in the action it took and it would have taken the same action regardless of whether the employee was engaged in union activity.

Chapter Eleven
Meetings with Employees that Require a Union Representative

Chapter Eleven: Meetings with Employees that Require a Union Representative

All managers and supervisors conduct various types of meetings with their employees. The Statute requires management to notify the union and provide it the opportunity to be present at some of these meetings. When a union is recognized as the exclusive representative of employees in a bargaining unit, it is obligated to represent the interests of the employees. Its rights and role as a representative are different depending on the type of meeting which is being conducted.

Formal Discussions

These are the most common meetings which are conducted by managers. A formal discussion is defined as a meeting between one or more representatives of the agency and one or more employees in the unit or their representatives concerning any grievance or any personnel policy or practices or other general conditions of employment. If such a meeting takes place, there is an obligation on the part of management to provide the union an opportunity to be present at the meeting. The basic elements of a formal discussion are:

Element 1. There must be a meeting. A meeting must be face to face, or perhaps by telephone or video conference with an employee or with employees. A letter announcing changes in practices or policies is not a meeting for purposes of a formal discussion.

Element 2. The meeting must be formal in nature. In determining formality the following questions should be answered:

a. How high in the management hierarchy was the caller of the meeting? The more senior the representatives, the more likely the meeting would be considered formal.

b. Did other management representatives attend? If a number of management representatives attend, that adds to the formality.

c. What was the site of the discussion? A meeting held away from the workplace is more formal than a meeting held at an employee's desk.

d. How was the meeting called? An impromptu meeting is less formal than a scheduled meeting.

e. How long was the discussion? The greater the length of the discussion the more likely it would be considered formal.

f. Was there a formal agenda? A written agenda is more formal than a verbal statement of what is to be discussed.

g. Was the meeting mandatory? A meeting which employees are required to attend is more formal than a voluntary meeting.

h. What was the manner in which the meeting was conducted? The more casual the meeting, the less formal it would be considered.

For a meeting to be considered formal, not all the above indicia of formality must be present. The significance of the issue being discussed will determine how formal the meeting must be. The more significant the subject of the meeting, the less formality will be required for the meeting to be a formal discussion.

Element 3. There must be a meeting between a representative of the agency and one or more employees. Supervisors are commonly the representatives of an agency for formal discussion purposes. Other levels of management also qualify as representatives of the agency. Staff of the human resources office and the agency legal office may also be considered representatives of management.

Element 4. The meeting must concern any grievance, personnel policy or practice or general condition of employment. Grievance has been broadly construed to include any complaint an employee may have. This includes complaints outside the contractual grievance procedure. The subject matter of a formal discussion must be general conditions of employment and not issues related to a specific employee. As an example, a meeting to discuss an individual employee's performance would not be a general working condition because it applies to only one employee. However, a discussion of performance management policy would be an appropriate subject for a formal discussion.

Element 5. The union must be provided adequate notice and the opportunity to attend the formal discussion. The amount of notice required to be given to the union for a formal discussion is based on the subject matter of the discussion. At a minimum, the union should receive as much notice as employees who will be attending the meeting. Unless the union otherwise specifies, the union representative who serves the employees who will be attending the meeting should be provided notice. However, the union has the right to specify who will represent it at a formal discussion and to whom notice should be provided. A formal discussion may proceed without a union representative if, after adequate notice, no representative attends the meeting. The union need only be given the opportunity. There is no requirement that the union attend.

Role of Union at a Formal discussion

The role of the union representative is to represent the interests of the bargaining unit at a formal discussion. The representative has the right to ask questions and seek clarification of what is being said. A formal discussion is not a negotiation session, nor is it an opportunity to cross-examine the management representatives at the meeting. A union representative must be allowed to speak and represent the bargaining unit; however, the representative is not entitled to take over the meeting.

Weingarten Meetings

The Statute provides an employee the right to request representation when the employee is being examined by management in connection with an investigation where the employee reasonably fears discipline. This is the so-called Weingarten right which is derived from a U.S. Supreme Court decision in the private sector (NLRB v. Weingarten) which established an employee's right to representation when being questioned by management. Congress placed this right in the Statute as a protection for employees who may not be able to properly respond when questioned by management.

Unlike the formal discussion right, where the union must be provided notice of formal meetings by management, the right of the union to represent an employee in a Weingarten investigation only occurs if the employee requests representation. Management has no affirmative duty to notify the union unless the employee makes a request for representation. However, some collective bargaining agreements provide an affirmative obligation on management to tell the employee they have the right to a representative. The basic elements of a Weingarten meeting are:

Element 1. There must be a meeting between an employee and a representative of the agency. A Weingarten meeting is characterized by a face to face encounter between an employee and a representative of management. The representative of management may be someone other than the employee's supervisor. Anyone who works for the agency who is acting on behalf of management may be considered a representative of management. This includes agency investigators and members of staff agencies such as the legal office. Investigators working for outside entities such as the FBI or local police departments would not be considered representatives of management.

Element 2. The purpose of the meeting must be to conduct an examination in connection with an investigation. Normally, an examination involves questions asked of the employee. The questions asked could range from why an employee was late to work to questions involving possible criminal activity. An investigation could be as simple as a supervisor wanting to know the whereabouts of an employee or as complex as a full blown criminal file being established.

Element 3. To be entitled to a representative, an employee must reasonably fear discipline. The nature of the types of questions being asked the employee must lead a reasonable employee to fear discipline. The fact that an individual employee may fear his or her supervisor does not give the employee the right to representation every time the supervisor wishes to talk to the employee.

Element 4. The employee must request representation. Management has no obligation to provide a representative unless one is requested. However, some collective bargaining agreements require notification of the union when a Weingarten meeting is to take place. A request for a representative does not have to specifically say a "union" representative. It must only make clear that a representative is wanted.

Element 5. A requested representative must be reasonably available. There is no requirement that an employee be provided a specific representative or that the investigation be held up until a specific representative is available. An investigation should not be scheduled during a time when management knows a representative will not be available. The union representative may play an active role in the investigation; however the representative may not take over the investigation. The investigator has the right to control the investigation and conduct it in any manner he or she chooses. The representative may ask questions and seek clarification of questions. The representative does not have the right to cross examine witnesses or the investigator.

Other Meetings

Management and the union often agree to other types of meetings at which a union representative is entitled to be present. These are contractually agreed upon meetings.

These types of meetings may include such issues as performance counseling where, under the Statute, the union would otherwise not be entitled to be represented. It is important to know the contractual provisions which may provide for greater rights of representation than are found in the Statute.

Case Study – Formal Discussions

Sally Manger is a new supervisor. She decides to hold a meeting with her employees to discuss her approach to managing the workplace and to get to know the employees. She specifically wants to talk about how leave is to be requested, how work assignments will be given out and generally her philosophy of managing. She set the meeting for 2:00 to 2:30PM in the 6th floor conference room. She sent each employee an invitation to the meeting which included the statement "If you have time, I would like you to attend the meeting. If you are too busy, you need not attend." At the meeting, Sally made notes of each employee's comments and specifically asked each employee to write down one question they would like answered.

The union has filed an unfair labor practice alleging that this was a formal discussion and that the union was not provided the opportunity to attend. Is this meeting a formal discussion, and if it is, why would it be a formal discussion?

The meeting is conducted by a manager with one or more employees participating. Leave as applied to all employees in the work unit would be a personnel policy, practice and general working condition of employees. It met the following indicia of formality: it was held away from the employee's work area. It was set for a prescribed time. It was of sufficient length. There was a prescribed agenda. It was held in formal manner with questions being asked of each employee. The issue of whether it was voluntary or mandatory would be most likely decided in favor of finding that it was mandatory. This would be the case even though the supervisor said to come if you can, since most employees would have considered it mandatory.

Case Study – Weingarten Meeting

Supervisor Pete Small has received an allegation that Clark Kant has engaged in sexual harassment of a female employee. He sets a meeting with Kant to investigate the allegation. Kant requests a union representative. His request is granted. Kant arrives at the meeting with Perry Meeson as his representative. Before Small asks one question, Meeson asks for a postponement of the investigation because Meeson just learned about it. Small denies the postponement. Meeson asks that Kant be given Miranda warnings. This request is also denied. Small asks one question. Before Kant can answer, Meeson answers for him. Small directs the question again to Kant. Meeson answers again. Small tells Kant he must answer the questions himself. Kant agrees to do so. Small asks three more questions before Meeson again answers for Kant. Finally Small tells Kant he must control his representative or the investigation will be concluded. Kant agrees. Twenty minutes later, Meeson asks for a recess to talk to "his client." Small denies the request. After 5 more questions, Small concludes the interview.

Review each of the decisions made by Small. Where they correct or did they act to deny Kant representation?

The issue with respect to all of the decisions of Small is whether they interfered with Kant's right to be adequately represented. Not granting a postponement did not interfere with representation. Management has the right to establish the time frame for its investigation and the methods it uses. As long as the timeframes and methods are reasonable, management has wide latitude in how it conducts an investigation

Small is not required to give Kant Miranda warnings. Miranda warnings are only given if criminal activity is being investigated. Investigation of potential administrative disciplinary action does not entitle a witness to Miranda warnings. If the Miranda warnings were given to Kant, he would have the right to not answer any questions. Small has the right to tell Kant to control his representative. He also has the right to conclude the investigation if the representative is abusive or disrupts the investigation. Small has the right to tell Kant that if he does not control his representative a decision will be made on disciplinary action without hearing Kant's side of the story. The investigator does not have to grant a request for a recess. It is a management right to determine how an investigation is conducted. However an investigation which does not allow the interviewee reasonable breaks may be challenged as being abusive.

Key Points in Chapter Eleven

1. Certain types of meetings conducted by management with employees require that the union be given an opportunity to be present.

2. A meeting must meet the requirements of formality to be considered a formal discussion.

3. A formal discussion must concern general working conditions and not just issues related to an individual employee.

4. The role of a union representative at a formal discussion is to clarify statements made and to ask questions. The union representative's role is not to take over the meeting.

5. A union representative is only entitled to represent an employee in a Weingarten meeting if the employee requests representation.

6. Any questioning by a manager which would lead a reasonable employee to fear discipline entitles an employee to request representation.

7. A union representative may not interfere with the conduct of the investigation. The representative may ask questions and assist the employee, but may not answer questions on behalf of the employee.

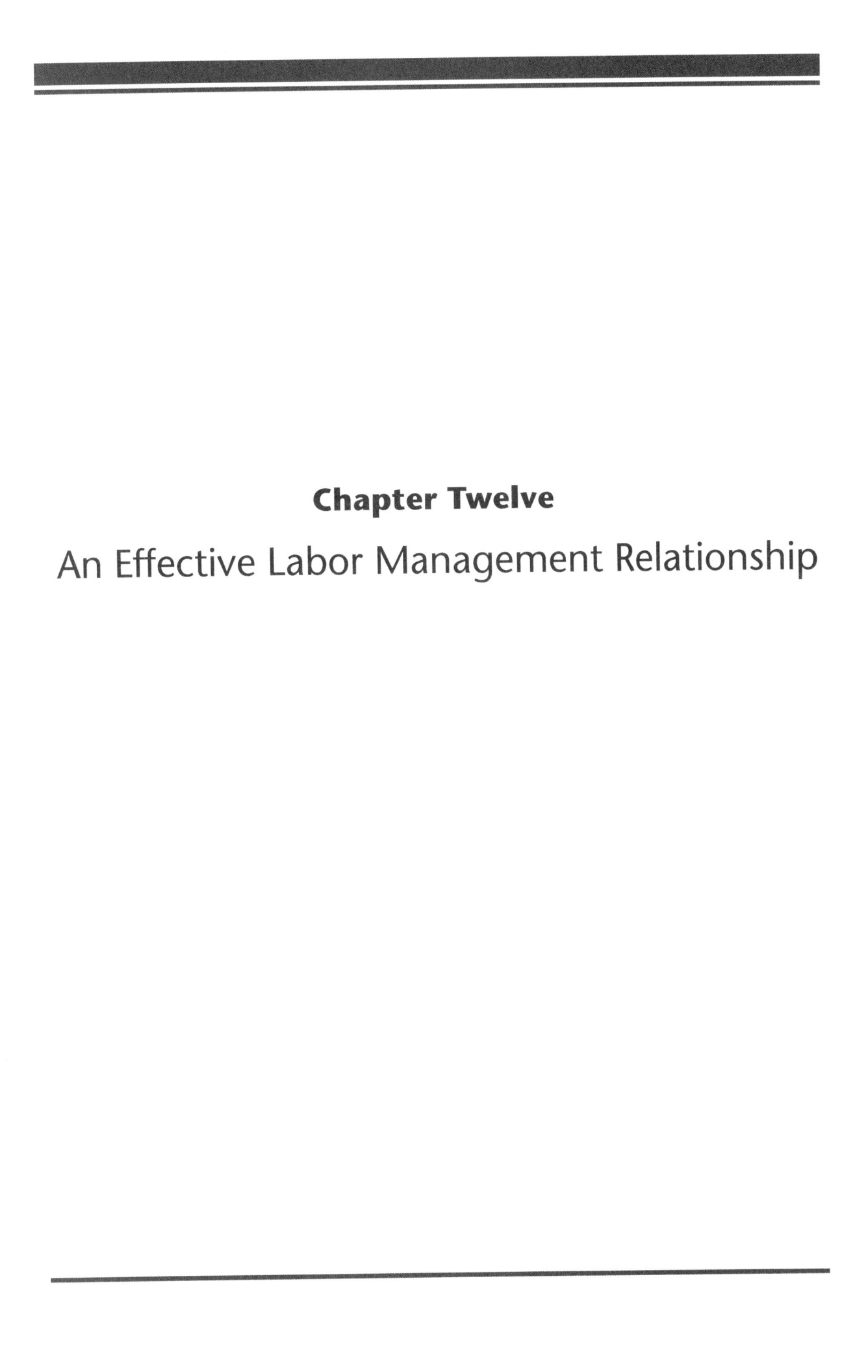

Chapter Twelve
An Effective Labor Management Relationship

Chapter Twelve: An Effective Labor Management Relationship

To be successful in labor relations, you must be able to combine knowing what your rights and obligations are with being able to maintain an effective labor management relationship. Labor relations is a relationship between people much like many other relationships. All effective relationships need boundaries which each party to the relationship knows and understands to regulate and maintain the success of the relationship. The rights and obligations which have been discussed in the previous chapters are the boundaries of the labor management relationship.

Beyond knowing the boundaries, both labor and management must know how to effectively deal with each other. Much of labor relations is based on people-to-people relationships – or how people deal with people. As with all relationships, there are often barriers to having an effective relationship. To establish or effectively maintain a successful relationship, the barriers to the relationship must be recognized and approaches to these barriers must be put in place. The most common barriers to an effective labor management relationship will be discussed in the next section.

Common Barriers to an Effective Labor Management Relationship

Lack of Trust

One of the most serious barriers to an effective relationship between labor and management is lack of trust. Most relationships are based on trust. The absence of trust creates serious problems in how labor and management deal with each other. Building trust in the relationship is a step by step process, with each party to the relationship taking small steps to show that they are worthy of trust. Sometimes, outside assistance is necessary to facilitate discussion which can lead to improvement in the level of trust. Change in leadership can be effective in giving new life to a mistrusting relationship. Whatever approach is taken, if trust is lacking in the labor management relationship, it is the most essential thing for both sides of the relationship to work on improving.

Past History

The failure to trust each other is quite often based on the past history of the relationship. The baggage of the past frequently shapes current actions and attitudes. People act based on their previous experience. Sometimes it is possible to repair the inaccurate perceptions of past dealings by opening a dialogue to air the circumstances that have lead to what may be misconceptions. It is not always possible to fix the problems of the past to engender a new relationship. One party or the other may have to risk taking the first step to change the current climate of distrust. Dumping the baggage of the past is not always possible, but often attempts at first steps can be valuable to developing a new relationship.

Communication

Communication is vital to all relationships. The more communication between labor and management, the more often trust will be developed. The less the communication, the more often distrust develops. Communication is often inextricably bound together with trust, so they both must be worked on together to achieve results with each.

There are two aspects of communicating on which both labor and management must work. The first aspect is the environment in which communication is not taking place. There must be the opportunity to communicate and there must be the desire to provide the information. Each party must ask themselves why they are not sharing information which is necessary for the relationship to work effectively. Overcoming the desire not to communicate is the first step to improving the communication between labor and management.

The second aspect is the systems in place which are available for communication to take place. If systems do not exist for the regular and orderly transfer of information, all too often information is not communicated. Approaches as simple as regularly scheduled meetings with union representatives and managers to discuss what is happening in the workplace can be the start of effective communications. Effective communication needs a pattern of communicating which can be relied upon by both parties.

Personalities

The people conducting the relationship can by themselves create barriers to the success of the relationship. Labor-management relations are dominated by people issues and by the people who conduct the relationship. An unreasonable participant in the relationship can by himself or herself lead to a counter-productive relationship between labor and management.

This is one of the most difficult problems to deal with in labor relations. In most cases, union officials are elected to represent employees. They can be removed only by being voted out of office by the bargaining unit or, in some cases, by executive action of the union leadership. It is rather infrequent that such processes remove a union official from office. By the same token, an ineffective or unreasonable management official or management labor relations representative can only be removed by action of management. As with union officials, such removals do not often take place.

The assertion that individuals on either side are being unreasonable often is seen merely as disagreement with positions taken by them and not as a valid assessment of the worth of an individual representative. If management does not like the union representative, the bargaining unit may consider that proof of the effectiveness of the representative. If the union does not like a particular manager or management representative, that is similarly seen as proof that they are doing their job well.

One solution to the problems created by individual personalities is to expand the scope of people involved in decision making. This can act to a certain extent to neutralize the offending manager or union representative. A broader number and variety of people who are involved in the relationship can lead to an opportunity to provide more information to more people and achieve more favorable results.

Interest-Based Bargaining

One approach to building a successful labor management relationship is to use interest-based bargaining, as opposed to traditional positional bargaining. In positional bargaining, each side to the bargaining puts forth one simple answer or solution to a problem. Each negotiating team's minds are already made up as to what the final outcome should be. The bargaining becomes a question of which side retreats the most from its stated position or which side is able to force or cajole the other side to its point of view. Positional bargaining is sometimes characterized by bullying and threats and is usually an exercise of power by the successful party.

Bargaining in the federal sector has historically been a combination of positional bargaining and rights-based bargaining. Rights-based bargaining relies on the assertion of statutory rights. In the federal sector, bargainers use the negotiability process to resolve questions concerning the assertion of management rights. The FLRA takes on the job of resolving contradictory positions of the parties on what their respective rights are. It decides issues parties cannot reach agreement on because of real or imagined infringements on management rights

under the Statute. The use of this system delays the completion of bargaining. The assertion of rights takes the form of strongly held positions. This combination of positional and rights-based bargaining can lead to protracted negotiations.

Interest-based bargaining is based on the concept of labor and management acting together as joint problem solvers. The outcome of interest-based bargaining is an agreement which addresses the interests of both sides. The interests are the needs, fears, worries and concerns of the participants in the bargaining. Interest-based bargaining is also known as "Win-Win" bargaining, where both sides are seen to be winners in the final outcome.

There are five principles of interest-based bargaining which are valuable to understand. Each standing alone has merit; however, it is the merging of these principles into a successful process which not only leads the parties to an agreement, but also yields the dividend of an improved relationship. The following is a general overview of the principles underlying interest-based bargaining:

Separate the People from the Problem

The resolution of problems can become entangled in the perceptions, emotions and assumptions of the people whose job it is to be the problem solvers. Often, an approach to bargaining is to attack the individual bargainers in an attempt to wear them down. By personally attacking a bargainer, the hope is that the bargainer will capitulate on what you want to avoid further attacks. This can become a test of wills and can be counterproductive to solving the real issue. By concentrating on the problem which is the objective of the negotiations, interest-based bargaining avoids the personal attacks.

Focus on Interests and not Positions

Positions are predetermined outcomes, while interests are needs to be satisfied. Interests are needs, wants and concerns the parties to the negotiation have. By focusing on interests, you are forced to look at the reasons underlying your positions. In looking at interests, you are asking why something is needed. Looking at interests is a way to start a discussion of what is really needed, as opposed to positions, which presuppose that one side already has all the answers.

Create Options for Mutual Gain

To create options for mutual gain, each side must recognize that there is more than one option to solve a problem. A necessary process for creating these new options is to use brainstorming. Brainstorming provides the opportunity to come up with the greatest possible number of options. Brainstorming opens new approaches to thinking about how to resolve a problem and creates new possibilities for solutions to provide joint benefit for both sides at the bargaining table.

Develop Your BATNA

Your BATNA is your Best Alternative To a Negotiated Agreement. Looking at your BATNA forces you to think through what you will do if an agreement is not reached. It provides a dose of reality as to what happens if you cannot come to agreement. Developing your BATNA is creating alternatives before you negotiate.

Define Objective Criteria

Objective criteria are used by the parties to the negotiation to determine which options meet the needs of the participants and which fail because they do not meet the mutually agreed upon criteria. Examples of objective criteria include fairness, acceptability to constituents, legality, cost effectiveness and tradition. Objective criteria provide a process for sorting out the options to determine which ones are most likely to solve the problem and meet the needs of the parties to the negotiation.

Understanding and being effective at interest based bargaining takes both experience with the process and a belief in its goals. A process which has as its foundation trust and communication may be a whole new world for some labor-management relationships. It provides a process for improving communication and making the first down payment on developing trust.

Developing a good labor management relationship requires both skill at dealing effectively with the other side and an understanding of what the limits to the relationship are and of how to ensure that those limits are observed and appreciated.

Chapter Thirteen

Pre-Decisional Involvement

Pre-decisional involvement is a voluntary process agreed upon by union and management which provides the union an opportunity to provide input to management on issues which may or may not be subject to collective bargaining. It is an essential aspect of collaborative labor relations in the federal sector because it engenders discussion about a variety of issues without regard to the statutory rules related to management rights. It is a required by Executive Order 13522 that management in the Executive Branch engage in pre-decisional involvement on all work place matters to the extent feasible. It can also be found in collective bargaining agreements as a contractual requirement.

The National Council on Federal Labor Management Relations Guidance on Pre-decisional Involvement

The National Council on Federal Labor Management Relations (National Council), established under Executive Order 13522, issued guidance on pre- decisional involvement on January 19, 2011. This guidance provides that the Executive Order requires that agencies should allow pre-decisional involvement (PDI) with unions in all workplace matters to the fullest extent practicable, without regard to whether those matters are negotiable subjects of bargaining under 5 U.S.C. 7106. The Guidance provides in relevant part the following:

1. Agencies should develop a shared understanding with employee representatives on how the pre-decisional involvement process can best be utilized for their workplace.

2. Generally agencies should begin the pre-decisional process as soon as possible after they determine that some decision or action is needed to address a particular issue or problem.

3. Pre-decisional discussions should be conducted confidentially among the parties to the discussion.

4. The goal of PDI is to allow employees, through their elected labor representatives, to have meaningful input which results in better quality decision-making, more support for decisions and timelier implementation.

5. Pre-decisional input does not bind or obligate an agency to reach a specific decision or take a specific action. Opportunities for pre-decisional involvement are valuable sources of input from employees through their representatives.

This guidance did not address the essential question of what issues are subject to pre-decisional involvement but rather left to the respective labor management parties to "a shared understanding of the process".

What is Pre-Decisional Involvement?

The concept of pre-decisional involvement developed during Clinton Administration as a concept for union involvement under the Clinton Partnership Executive Order. It is the voluntary involvement of unions by management prior to decisions being made. There is no defined legal status or legally enforceable right of unions to pre-decisional involvement. It evolves out of a collaborative relationship between labor and management. Involvement before final decision making is not a requirement of the Federal Service Labor Management Relations Statute (Statute) that governs labor relations in the federal sector. The Statute only requires that management give the union notice and complete collective bargaining prior to implementation of a change in working conditions. Pre-decisional involvement is an extralegal approach to improving management decision making with the assistance of the union.

While pre-decisional involvement is not legally enforceable it is a requirement placed on the Executive Branch by Executive Order 13522. It is a mutually agreed upon approach to improve the union's involvement and participation in changes in the work place. The degree of the union's involvement and the processes used for PDI should be agreed upon by the parties as recommended by the National Council.

What is the Value of Pre-Decisional Involvement?

The value proposition for pre-decisional involvement is based on improved decision making by management. With union involvement decisions made by management will have direct input from employees and their representatives which will greatly improve the quality of the decision making. It should also speed the implementation of new management initiatives by reducing the amount of time taken by traditional collective bargaining and also increase the quality of the implementation by having the support of the union and employees for the new changes about to take place.

What are the Barriers to Pre-Decisional Involvement?

The Statute is a major barrier to pre-decisional involvement. The rights based barriers the Statute establishes between the parties in traditional federal sector labor relations can easily be carried over to the pre-decisional process and lead to disputes over the law and not over the best solution. When both parties are concerned with giving up statutory rights, it leads to pre-decisional involvement being an adjunct to the traditional collective bargaining process rather than a new problem solving approach. The statutory rights of both labor and management need not be waived in the process but should be understood not as barriers to solutions but as guideposts for structuring durable answers to questions posed.

Lack of trust is the most frequently cited reason for not either engaging in pre-decisional involvement or for it not being successful. Communication of information necessary for union involvement requires trusting the party who is receiving the information to handle it appropriately. This lack of trust leads to less information being provided and with less information it is more difficult to be successful at problem solving which is the foundation on which of pre- decisional involvement is built. Since information of a confidential nature is often provided to the union in a PDI process how this information will be kept confidential must be discussed and agreed upon by the parties as noted by the guidance from the National Council.

Lack of problem solving skills is also a root cause of unsuccessful pre-decisional involvement. Both parties must understand how to engage in problem solving and be willing to use such skills to resolve disputes and develop new approaches to work place issues. The essence of pre-decisional involvement is labor and management learning to work together effectively to solve work place problems. To do this effectively they must learn new skills to aid them in looking at problems differently.

Lack of substantive knowledge of the subject matter by the unions is a significant barrier to pre-decisional involvement. Union representatives must represent all employees in the bargaining unit. Such representation covers a wide variety of jobs and agency functions. It is difficult for the union to have expertise in all functional areas of an agency. It is important that union representatives be given the opportunity to learn the substantive areas they will be in involved in to gain a greater understanding of the issues involved. If the union does not understand the substance of what is being done it is more likely to resist changes because of a lack of understanding of how the change will work and its effects on employees.

The example for use of PDI contained in guidance from the National Council dealt with the Agency budget process. For a union to be successful in providing input as envisioned in the guidance it must understand the budget process. This will often require an agency to provide substantive training on the agency budget process so the union can be effective in providing input on behalf of employees.

Unrealistic expectations are a major barrier to successful pre-decisional involvement. Both parties must have a mutual understanding of what each expects the result to be from pre-decisional involvement. If management expects it to be a substitute for collective bargaining that expectation must be understood and agreed to by the union. If the union expects it to be simply an opportunity to receive information while retaining its collective bargaining right, that expectation must be shared and understood by management. The failure to have mutually understood expectations damages the relationship between the parties and can lead to further mistrust.

When Should Pre-Decisional Involvement Be Used?

Involving the union pre-decisionally in the management decision making process should only occur when the parties to the labor management relationship have a level of trust justifying open and frequent communication. Traditional labor management relationships are not marked by a high level of trust and communication. In a traditional relationship both parties look upon the other with a mixture of wariness and often open distrust. However to be involved pre-decisionally management must provide a greater range and amount of information than it might otherwise provide in a traditional collective bargaining situation and the union must divulge to management its true concerns and issues. The union and management must both operate on a level of trust which will safeguard information and use it for the purposes of solving the immediate problem facing the parties rather than to buttress the union's or management's positions in traditional collective bargaining.

Involving the union pre-decisionally should be employed when the parties have agreed that they will use a problem solving approach for the issue presented. It is suited to an interest based or quasi interest based approach to problem solving. While the parties may not use a systematic interest based approach they must agree that they will use a problem solving approach which relies on interest based principles of full communication and attacking the problem and not the people.

Executive Order 13522 provides that "all workplace issues to the extent feasible "will be subject to pre-decisional involvement. However not all issues should be submitted to the pre-decisional involvement process. There are many issues which are more appropriately resolved using traditional collective bargaining approaches. However the parties should agree on criteria to use in assessing which problems are best served by pre-decisional involvement and which by more traditional labor relations dispute systems such as grievance arbitration or collective bargaining.

Steps to Developing A Labor-Management Pre-Decisional Involvement Process

A formalized pre-decisional involvement process will reduce misunderstanding about the process and increase over time the trust the parties have in the relationship and the process itself. The National Council guidance provides that the parties should develop a shared understanding on how pre-decisional involvement can best be utilized in the workplace. To be successful in engaging in pre-decisional involved the following steps should be considered:

Step 1. What issues are appropriate for pre-decisional involvement?

The parties need to develop criteria for what issues are subject to pre-decisional involvement. Different issues may be subject to pre-decisional involvement in a labor management forum. Other issues should be handled between supervisors and union representatives. The parties should work to determine what issues are handled at each level within an organization.

Step 2. When should the union be involved in pre-decisional involvement?

The union should be provided the opportunity to participate pre-decisionally at a point when a final decision had not yet been made on a matter. When the agency has determined to study or review a matter in order to make a decision is a point at which a union most often is interested in being involved. The National Council in its guidance provides agencies should begin the pre-decisional process as soon as possible after they determine that some decision or action is needed to address a particular issue or problem.

Step 3. Who should be involved?

In the case of pre-decisional involvement at the forum level the union should designate either forum members or other representatives on groups working pre-decisionally. At the supervisory level individual stewards and representatives may act on behalf of the union. The agency has the right to designate bargaining unit members to act as subject matter experts as an assignment of work in studying a problem. This does not diminish or replace the role of the union in the pre-decisional process.

Step 4. What are the expectations of the Union and Management?

A key step in the process is the development of a clear understanding of the expectations of both union and management with respect to collective bargaining after the pre-decisional process. Expectations are based on what the authority is of the group working pre-decisionally. Do they have decision making authority, recommending authority or advisory authority? The authority of the group will quite often determine whether the union waives its right to bargain. Many managers believe that union membership on study groups should result in no collective bargaining over the issues because the union had the opportunity to discuss the issue before a decision is made. Unions rarely waive their right to bargain pre-decisionally unless decisions that will be implemented are reached through consensus. If a final decision is made by a higher level than that which was represented on the pre-decisional group then the union will in most cases not be interested in giving up the right to bargain simply because they were on the committee. It must be clear to both management and the union whether the union has an expectation of bargaining after the pre-decisional process is completed.

Step 5. Develop the process for providing information to the union and for union input.

A major requirement of Executive Order 13522 is providing information to the union pre-decisionally. An agreed upon process for providing the information must be arrived at by union and management. An approach for union input to be provided also must be determined.

Step 6. Develop a problem solving approach

It is the expectation of the Executive Order that the participants in pre-decisional involvement will engage in problem solving. Each participant in the pre-decisional process must understand and be skilled in problem solving. The intent of the Executive Order is to solve workplace problems. Pre-decisional involvement will not be successful if the parties resort to traditional negotiating practices.

Develop A Formalized Process for Pre-Decisional Involvement

As with labor management dispute resolution systems such as the grievance procedure and ground rules for collective bargaining, pre-decisional involvement works best with an established formalized process. These procedures need not be extensive but should at a minimum contain an understanding of how pre- decisional involvement will work; the criteria for determining which issues will be submitted to pre-decisional involvement; and the potential expectations that each party will have in agreeing to engage in pre-decisional involvement.

Some of the issues that must be more fully developed in the process include the union's role at meetings, its access to and confidentiality of information and the process for resolving disputes. Developing an understanding of criteria that will be used in determining when pre-decisional involvement will be invoked is an important process which will reduce misunderstandings about its future use. Importantly expectations of the parties engaged in the process must be clearly understood before engaging in pre-decisional involvement. A group involved in pre-decisional involvement, as an example, may be granted authority to make decisions and therefore there may be an expectation by management that the union will waive its right to bargain over the issue. The group may have authority to make recommendations and therefore the union may want to retain its right to bargain. The involvement of the union may only be informational and therefore once again it may retain its right to bargain. The above are examples of expectations of the parties which must be clearly explained and understood before the process has begun to avoid any future disagreements or injury to the parties' relationship by misunderstandings of the outcomes of working cooperatively.

Train the Participants in Pre-Decisional Involvement on Problem Solving Skills

It is important that the parties who will be working together pre-decisionally be trained on problem solving skills using approaches such as interest based problem solving. While it is not necessary to use a strict interest based approach to how union and management work together interest based principals help the parties to understand how to work together more effectively in trying to solve work place issues. It is the principles of interest based problem solving which must be learned rather that a strict adherence to the interest based problem solving process.

Select an Appropriate Issue for Pre-Decisional Involvement and Implement Process

Once the process is understood and developed the parties should select an appropriate issue for this new process. At the beginning of any such engagement all the participants in the process should have an orientation into how pre-decisional involvement works and how it will work for them. When using a new approach to how labor and management will work together it is necessary to regularly monitor how the approach is working. There are great opportunities for misunderstandings and a need for necessary tweaks to the process developed. Constant vigilance of the process when first used provides each side with ways to adjust to each other before a crisis of confidence in the process develops.

Key Points in Chapter Thirteen

1. Pre-decisional involvement is a process not required by law but is a requirement placed on managers and supervisors under Executive Order 13522 and certain union collective bargaining agreements.

2. I t provides a union the right to provide input to management before management makes decisions.

3. Engaging in pre-decisional involvement does not result in a waiver of union bargaining rights or of management's ability to assert an issue is non-negotiable.

4. Pre-decisional involvement required by Executive Order 13522 is not enforceable through the unfair labor practice process. If pre-decisional involvement is made a provision in a collective bargaining agreement it may be enforceable through the grievance process contained in the collective bargaining agreement.

5. Determining how pre-decisional involvement works is subject to mutual agreement by union and management.

Chapter Fourteen

Title 38 and Employees of the U.S. Department of Veterans Affairs, Veterans Health Administration

Introduction

As you have read in the other chapters of this book, most employees of the Federal government who are eligible to be represented by a union are covered under the procedures of Title 5 of the Unites States Code, Chapter 71 (5 U.S.C.71). This chapter, chapter 71 of Title 5, is entitled the "Federal Service Labor- Management Relations Statute" (FSLMRS), and was enacted in 1978. Employees of the Department of Veterans Affairs, the Veterans Health Administration (VHA) some of whom are hired under the authorities of Title 38 of the United States Code, and not Title 5, present unique issues related to Federal sector labor-management relations.

The conglomeration of laws and regulations concerning these employees makes labor management relations at VA and VHA very complex. The interplay of Title 38 and Title 5 has been the topic of discussion and differing interpretations for over thirty years. Congress, the Federal Courts, the FLRA, the VA and labor unions all have weighed in on how the statutes should be interpreted and applied to these various VHA employees. Often one adjudicating party will overrule the other, which shifts the course of interpretations and consequently complicates labor management relations. Add to this the various administrations' philosophical approaches to labor management relations over the past thirty or so years, and the result is a somewhat confusing state of affairs. These issues are discussed in more detail below.

A Brief Chronology of Positions at the Veterans Health Administration

Congress established the Department of Medicine and Surgery, now the Veterans Health Administration (VHA), in 1946. For fear that the then current civil service regulations were not flexible enough to allow the hiring of sufficient numbers of medical personnel to treat the returning World War II veterans, a second, independent, personnel system was established for the VA. This new system was encoded under Title 38 and covered specified medical professions (e.g., physicians, dentist, podiatrists, registered nurses, psychologists, chemists, pharmacists, social workers, licensed physical therapists, etc.). At that time, Congress declared that the Secretary (then Administrator) of Veterans Affairs was authorized to "prescribe by regulation the hours and conditions of employment" of these employees "(n) notwithstanding any law, Executive order, or regulation" Pub.L. No. 79-293, Sec.7(b), 59Stat.at 677 (codified as amended at 38 U.S.C. Sec. 7421(a)). Congress reaffirmed in 1980 that VA medical personnel were governed exclusively by chapter 74 of Title 38 whenever Title 5 is inconsistent with Title 38. These original positions under Title 38 are often called "non-hybrid" positions.

In 1983 Congress established a new category of VA medical personnel. These are employees of VHA hired under Title 38 U.S.C. sections 7401(2), 7401(3) and 7405, who are covered under Title 38 for appointment, advancement and some pay purposes; but for all other purposes they are afforded the rights under Title 5. Although not found in law, the term "Hybrid" is used to refer to these occupations and employees because they are covered by provisions of both the Title 5 and Title 38 personnel systems. "Hybrid Title 38" employees include clinical staff positions, such as clinical and counseling psychologists, respiratory and physical therapists, and a host of other medical related occupations. Congress has adjusted the list of which positions may be hybrid positions many times throughout the ensuing years. Qualification standards for all Title 38 and hybrid Title 38 appointments in the VHA are determined by the Secretary of Veterans Affairs in accordance with 38 U.S.C. 7402.

In 1988 Congress established that "hybrid" employees are subject to Title 38 for appointment, promotion and advancement except that "all matters relating to adverse actions, disciplinary actions,... and grievance procedures..." are governed by chapter 71 of Title 5. See 38 U.S.C. 7403(f)(3).

In 1991, largely in response to the DC Circuit Court of Appeals' 1988 decision in Colorado Nurses Association v. FLRA, 851 F.2d 1486, Congress granted Title 38 "non-hybrid" (also often called "pure" or "full" title 38 employees) VHA employees (those appointed under 38 U.S.C. 7401(1) the right "to engage in collective bargaining" in accordance with chapter 71 of Title 5, with three significant exceptions. These exemptions are found in Title 38 Section 7422. These are often called "Section 7422 exemptions." Section 7422 (b) states:

Such collective bargaining (and any grievance procedures provided under a collective bargaining agreement) in the case of employees described in section 7421(b) of this title may not cover, or have any applicability to, any matter or question concerning or arising out of

(1) professional conduct or competence,

(2) peer review, or

(3) the establishment, determination, or adjustment of employee compensation under this title.

In May 2010, the Caregivers and Veterans Omnibus Health Services Act of 2010 (Pub.L 111-163) added Nursing Assistants as a new "Hybrid" Title 38 occupation under 38 U.S.C. 7401(3). In addition, this law gives the Secretary of Veterans Affairs authority to extend Title 38 status to "…such other classes of health care occupations as the Secretary considers necessary for the recruitment and retention needs of the Department", and the Department plans to convert numerous other health care occupations from Title 5 to Title 38 in the coming years.

So to summarize, under current law, VHA employs its hospital and clinical staff under three separate legal authorities. The authority under which a particular staff member is employed is a function of the duties the particular employee performs. The first category, Title 38 employees, or "non-hybrid" employees, are the critical, hands-on medical staff - physicians, dentists, registered nurses, physician assistants, etc. The second category, Title 38 "hybrid" employees, are clinical staff – clinical and counseling psychologists, respiratory and physical therapists, dental hygienists, licensed practical nurses, medical technologists, etc. Congress has added to the positions in this group several times since 1983. The final categories, Title 5 employees, are the traditional civil service employees – accountants, administrative clerks, human resource specialists, management analysts, computer assistants, etc. These Title 5 employees are included in either the General Schedule (GS) or the Federal Wage Schedule (FWS), (also called WG) pay systems. In 2010, approximately 40 percent of all VHA employees were Title 38, hybrid and non-hybrid, employees, and 60 percent were Title 5 employees.

The Title 5 system is a "rank in position" system. That is, each position is assigned a grade based upon classification standards, and a person/employee holds the grade of the position occupied. Under the Title 38 system, which is a modified "rank in person" system, standards boards assign a grade to each employee rather than to the position held. The Title 38 system has greater flexibilities, and this had allowed VA to pay higher salaries than would be possible under Title 5, and thereby compete more effectively for shortage occupations. Appointments under Title 38 are accepted from the competitive Title 5 appointment process. The Title 38 personnel system also allows VHA to develop and utilize VA-specific qualification standards which identify the education, license/certification/ registration and experience required for each occupation and position in order to ensure the optimum care for the veteran patients. In the VHA employees under both Title 38 and Title 5 often work side by side, and sometimes with one supervisor supervising employees under both systems.

Given the complexity of even the relatively brief background above, it can be seen that personnel matters, especially those related to labor management relations at the VHA, are unique and could obviously lead to differing interpretations of the myriad laws, regulations and collective bargaining agreements. Managers, supervisors, union officials and Labor Relations Specialists should tread carefully when confronted with the unique and specialized issues present at the VHA. As always, as discussed in Chapter Eight, in addition to knowing the applicable laws and VA regulations, when an issue arises you should always check the collective bargaining agreement(s) to ascertain if there are contract provisions that may also be applicable to your situation.

Hybrid Employees and Collective Bargaining

As indicated above, in 1983 Congress first established a class of positions which had a combination of benefits from both Title 5 and Title 38, primarily Title 5. These positions are listed in Title 38 section 7401(3). Congress has added to the members of this class over the years, but the current list of hybrid positions, as of 2011, is:

Scientific and professional personnel, such as microbiologists, chemists, and biostatisticians *(Note: Although codified in the law, 38 U.S.C. 7401(2), the VHA does not employ individuals in these occupations under the provisions of Title 38).

Audiologists, speech pathologists, and audiologist-speech pathologists

Biomedical engineers

Certified or registered respiratory therapists

Dietitians

Licensed physical therapists, physical therapy assistants, or prosthetic representatives

Licensed practical or vocational nurses

Medical instrument technicians, medical records administrators or specialists, medical records technicians, or medical technologists

Dental hygienists or dental assistants

Nuclear medicine technologists

Occupational therapists or occupational therapy assistants

Kinesiotherapists

Orthotist-prosthetists

Pharmacists or pharmacy technicians

Psychologists

Diagnostic radiologic technologists or therapeutic radiologic technologists

Social workers

Marriage and family therapists

Licensed professional mental health counselors

Blind rehabilitation specialists or blind rehabilitation outpatient specialists

Nursing Assistants

In 1988 Congress amended the VHA personnel provisions expressly to provide greater collective bargaining rights for these hybrid employees. (see 38 U.S.C. Sec. 7403(f)(3)). Section 7403 establishes the Secretary's exclusive power to prescribe regulations for the appointment, promotion and advancement of hybrid employees generally and also explicitly limits from this power certain negotiable matters. Specifically, Section 7403(f)(3) limits the Secretary's power by providing that… "all matters relating to adverse actions, reductions- in-force, the applicability of the principles of preference…, rights of part-time employees, disciplinary actions, and grievance procedures involving individuals appointed to [hybrid]… positions… shall be resolved under the provisions of Title 5 as though such individuals had been appointed under that title", notwithstanding any other provisions of Title 38 or other laws.

In one leading case on negotiability, U.S. Department of Veterans Affairs v. FLRA, 9 F3d 123 (D.C. Cir. 1993) the United States Court of Appeals for the District of Columbia Circuit held that while regulations for the promotion and advancement of hybrid employees are generally nonnegotiable; matters relating to the grievance procedures are negotiable in accordance with Title 5. In overturning the underlying FLRA decision, the Court clarified that the obligation to negotiate over "grievance procedures" did not include the broad obligation to negotiate over any topic that could conceivably be the subject of a grievance, but rather, it included the more limited obligation to negotiate (a) the procedures for filing of a grievance, (b) the scope of the grievance procedure and (c) questions concerning binding arbitration of grievances not satisfactorily resolved through grievance procedures.

In most matters concerning negotiations over conditions of employment of hybrid employees, you should generally follow the Title 5 guidance on negotiability found in Chapter Nine, and case law on negotiability. However, if the issue involves substantive criteria concerning the appointment, promotion or advancement of hybrid employees it is likely to be nonnegotiable. Some examples of such topics are time-in-grade requirements or qualifications, peer review requirements, and procedures to be followed by Professional Standards Boards in determining promotion actions of hybrid employees.

Non-hybrid (Pure), Title 38 Employees and Collective Bargaining

As interesting as the technical negotiability and grievability aspects of labor relations with respect to hybrid employees may be, the matters only become more interesting with respect to the pure Title 38, or non-hybrid, employees. These employees occupy the following positions:

- Physician
- Dentist
- Podiatrist
- Chiropractor
- Optometrist
- Registered Nurse
- Physician Assistant
- Expanded-function Dental Auxiliary

You will recall that in 1991 Congress amended Title 38 to provide non-hybrid employees collective bargaining rights in accordance with Title 5 Chapter 71, but with significant restrictions. Title 38 Section 7422 reads:

§ 7422. Collective bargaining

(a) Except as otherwise specifically provided in this title, the authority of the Secretary to prescribe regulations under section 7421 of this title is subject to the right of Federal employees to engage in collective bargaining with respect to conditions of employment through representatives chosen by them in accordance with chapter 71 of title 5 (relating to labor-management relations).

(b) Such collective bargaining (and any grievance procedures provided under a collective bargaining agreement) in the case of employees described in section 7421 (b) of this title may not cover, or have any applicability to, any matter or question concerning or arising out of (1) professional conduct or competence, (2) peer review, or (3) the establishment, determination, or adjustment of employee compensation under this title.

(c) For purposes of this section, the term "professional conduct or competence" means any of the following: (1) Direct patient care. (2) Clinical competence.

(d) An issue of whether a matter or question concerns or arises out of (1) professional conduct or competence, (2) peer review, or (3) the establishment, determination, or adjustment of employee compensation under this title shall be decided by the Secretary and is not itself subject to collective bargaining and may not be reviewed by any other agency.

(e) A petition for judicial review or petition for enforcement under section 7123 of title 5 in any case involving employees described in section 7421 (b) of this title or arising out of the applicability of chapter 71 of title 5 to employees in those positions, shall be taken only in the United States Court of Appeals for the District of Columbia Circuit.

The exact definition of what is meant by the language in Section 7422, (b), (c), and (d), and how it is to be interpreted, has been the source of continued discussion and disagreement between the VA and the unions that represent VA employees for decades.

First, and significantly, it must be recognized that in accordance with 7422 (d) (3) the Secretary has sole, full and final authority to determine what constitutes a matter of professional conduct or competence, peer review, or the establishment, determination or adjustment of non-hybrid employee compensation. Case law has clearly held that this authority is absolute, and is not subject to challenge with the FLRA, any other agency, arbitrators, or any court other than the United States court of Appeals for the District of Columbia. If the Secretary determines that a matter is covered by one of the provisions of Section 7422, then the issue is nonnegotiable, and is completely outside the scope of collective bargaining as discussed in Chapter Nine. This means that the substance of the matter, as well as the procedures for implementing the matter, or appropriate arrangements for employees adversely affected by the matter, are not subject to bargaining. And it bears repeating, the FLRA and arbitrators have no jurisdiction to review the Secretary's/USH's finding.

What are the Section 7422 exemptions?

The question of whether a topic involves one of the 7422 exemptions frequently arises in VA labor-management relations. The issue may pop up in grievances, disciplinary actions (other than major adverse actions), negotiations, unfair labor practices and litigation before the FLRA, arbitrators, courts or the FSIP. This is because, until the USH has made a finding, it is often not clear whether a particular issue or proposal falls under the 7422 exemptions or whether it is a peripheral matter. Peripheral matters may be subject to collective bargaining or review by appropriate forums.

Section 7422 states that collective bargaining may not apply to any matter or question concerning or arising out of professional conduct or competence (which is defined as relating to direct patient care or clinical competence), peer review, or the establishment, determination, or adjustment of employee compensation. Most Section 7422 disagreements between the unions and VA management are centered on issues of what, exactly, is a matter concerning or arising out of professional conduct or competence?

It is not possible in this book to give definitive answers as to whether topics that will arise in the workplace in negotiations or disciplinary actions will fall under the Section 7422 exemptions. Practitioners should review the prior findings of the Secretary, as well as FLRA and court decisions for similar subject matter. In addition, practitioners should make their best efforts to reason through the conflagration of laws and regulations and then explain to the opposing party the factors supporting their logic. In that way, even if agreement cannot be reached, at a minimum all participants will have a clearer understanding of the issues and principles involved.

Current Procedures for Seeking a Determination on Section 7422 Issues

The VA has established specific procedures for seeking a determination when there is a question as to whether a particular matter, issue, or proposal falls under the 7422 exemptions. Since these issues are often very complex, it is imperative that the parties at the level at which the issue arises, both union and management, are very clear in presenting their meaning and intent. On the management side, the decision of whether to request a determination requires coordination by managers, labor relations specialists, and VA Regional and General Counsel Attorneys. It is current VA policy that management should not assert a 7422 exemption prior to the USH having actually issued such a determination in writing. Rather, the VA policy is to ask the other parties to suspend proceedings pending the decision.

If the issue arises at the local or facility level with the union, it is generally advisable to explain management's concern as to why the issue may fall under the 7422 exemptions, and then attempt to resolve the matter without needing to obtain a determination. However, if such informal attempts fail, a request for a decision must be signed by the facility director and submitted through the VA Labor Management Relations Office. There are specific requirements as to format and information that must be included in the request (see the VA LMR website).

The VA LMR office maintains a list of previously issued findings on 7422 exemptions. This listing is available on line, http://www.va.gov/lmr/Title38- 7422.asp, along with a copy of the findings which explain the rationale for the decision. A few examples of matters that the USH has found to be nonnegotiable or non-grievable because they involved a matter or question that concerned or arose out of an exemption under Section 7422 are, specifically:

Professional conduct or competence:

- Compressed work schedules
- RN reassignment
- Policy on mandatory tuberculosis testing for all employees
- Proficiency rating and step increase
- VA Handbook 5011/9 Hours of Duty and Leave
- Requirement to complete continuing education during privileging period

Peer review:

- Professional Standards Board

- Union observers on Nurse Professional Standards Boards

Employee compensation:

- Specialized skills pay
- Physician specialty pay
- Nurse locality pay
- Scarce Medical Specialty pay
- Night differential/Weekend premium pay
- Overtime pay

Alternative Approach to Resolving 38 U.S.C. Section 7422 Questions

As Section 7422 (b) states, the VA may not bargain, or include in grievance procedures of a collective bargaining agreement, any matter concerning or arising out of professional conduct or competence, peer-review, or employee compensation for non-hybrid Title 38 employees. That is the current law, and it must be followed in good faith until or unless it is changed. However, exactly what this means has led to much litigation and exasperation between the labor unions and management. Management has the option to simply state that the matter is "not negotiable" or a "Section 7422 exemption" and end any discussion.

There is another way for all the parties to approach the situation, however. Consider for a moment that the legal restriction on management to not negotiate a topic, does not necessarily preclude management from discussing that topic with the union(s). After such discussions, especially if they are open, creative and substantive, management may be able to "unilaterally" reach a decision or course of action that all parties can live with. Such a decision or course of action would then not have been negotiated, but, rather, it would be a management decision reached after giving full consideration to all aspects of the matter. The management decision obviously could not be put into a negotiated agreement, but there is nothing precluding it from being adhered to as a management policy. If the union(s) then accepted the management policy, understanding that it could not be "negotiated", the matter could be resolved without having to request a USH determination or resorting to litigation.

Section 7422 Case Study

Registered Nurse Morrison received a proficiency rating from Supervisor Nathan, with which she was not pleased. AFGE Local 1756 filed a grievance on Nurse Morrison's behalf, alleging that Supervisor Nathan had not been Morrison's supervisor for the required minimum 90 days. The 90 day requirement is published VAMC policy. Nathan had supervised Morrison for 75 days. The union requested as a remedy that the rating be rescinded and Morrison be given a fair and accurate proficiency rating.

The parties met for the first step grievance, but it was not resolved. At step two, the management Deciding Official took the position that proficiency reports are not grievable, and did not issue a grievance decision. The union invoked arbitration, but before an arbitrator could be assigned management informed the union that the Agency was seeking a 7422 exemption determination from the USH. Management requested a determination on both the issue grieved and the remedy. Management alleged that proficiency ratings involved issues of professional conduct or competence within the meaning of 38 U.S.C. Section 7422.

The union argued that it was grieving the procedural error allegedly committed by Supervisor Nathan who acted inappropriately as the rating official.

There was, in fact, a VA Handbook requiring rating officials to have been in their supervisory role for a minimum of 90 days.

Previous USH decisions on proficiency reports held that proficiency reports are non-grievable when they involve the substantive rating of an employee or clearly constitute an assessment of a provider's patient care duties.

Is the grievance grievable and arbitrable? And are the requested remedies allowable under Section 7422?

The grievance was determined to be grievable because it involves a procedural requirement of proficiency reports and does not affect the substance of the decision underlying the employee's proficiency. The grievance deals with the timing of the issuance of the proficiency report, not the substance of the report, itself. Thus, it is not a matter concerning or arising out of professional conduct or competence or peer review within the meaning of Section 7422.

However, the requested remedies, that the rating be rescinded and Morrison be given a fair and accurate proficiency rating, do involve the substance of the rating itself. Thus, the remedies are matters or questions concerning or arising out of professional conduct or competence and peer review within the meaning of Section 7422.

Key Points in Chapter Fourteen

1. Employees of the VA and VHA may be appointed under Title 38 or Title 5 of the United States code, depending on what duties they perform.

2. Pure Title 38 employees are often referred to as "non-hybrid" and include nine professions of critical, medical staff such as physicians and registered nurses.

3. Employees appointed under Title 38, but given most of the rights of employees appointed under Title 5 are referred to as "hybrid." These include numerous professions of clinical staff, such as licensed practical nurses, clinical psychologists, etc.

4. Other, support professions such as HR Specialists, accountants, attorneys, computer clerks, etc. are appointed under Title 5 and are under the GS or the WG pay systems.

5. In 1991 "non-hybrid" employees were given the right to collective bargaining, subject to three significant exceptions under Section 7422. These exceptions are any matter or question concerning or arising out of (1) professional conduct or competence, (2) peer review, or ((3) the establishment, determination, or adjustment of employee compensation under Title 38.

6. What falls under the Section 7422 exceptions has been a matter of disagreement and litigation between management and the unions for decades.

7. The VA has established procedures for requesting a Section 7422 determination from the Secretary. Determinations are published on a VA website.

8. The current Executive Order 13522 by President Obama, which encourages collaborative approaches to collective bargaining, has reinvigorated VA and the unions representing VA employees to expand collaborative approaches that were begun under the Clinton E.O. 12871.

Appendix A

Title 5 of the United States Code: Government Organization & Employees

Appendix A: Title 5 of the United States Code Government Organization & Employees

Title 5 of the United States Code
Government Organization & Employees
Part III – Employees
Subpart F – Labor Management & Employee Relations
Chapter 71
Labor-Management Relations
Subchapter I

Subchapter I
General Provisions

Subchapter II
Rights & Duties of Agencies & Labor Organizations

Subchapter III
Grievances, Appeals, and Review

Subchapter IV
Administrative and Other Provisions

Subchapter I
General Provisions

7101 Findings and Purpose

(a) The Congress finds that –

(1) experience in both private and public employment indicates that the statutory protection of the right of employees to organize, bargain collectively, and participate through labor organizations of their own choosing in decisions which affect them –

(A) safeguards the public interest,

(B) contributes to the effective conduct of public business, and

(C) facilitates and encourages the amicable settlements of disputes between employees and their employers involving conditions of employment; and

(2) the public interest demands the highest standards of employee performance and the continued development and implementation of modern and progressive work practices to facilitate and improve employee performance and the efficient accomplishment of the operations of the Government. Therefore, labor organizations and collective bargaining in the civil services are in the public interest.

(b) It is the purpose of this chapter to prescribe certain rights and obligations of the employees of the Federal Government and to establish procedures which are designed to meet the special requirements and needs of the Government. The provisions of this chapter should be interpreted in a manner consistent with the requirement of an effective and efficient Government.

7102 Employees' Rights

Each employee shall have the right to form, join, or assist any labor organization, or to refrain from any such activity, freely and without fear of penalty or reprisal, and each employee shall be protected in the exercise of such right. Except as otherwise provided under this chapter, such right includes the right –

(1) to act for a labor organization in the capacity of a representative and the right, in that capacity, to present the views of the labor organization to heads of agencies and other officials of the executive branch of the Government, the Congress, or other appropriate authorities, and

(2) to engage in collective bargaining with respect to conditions of employment through representatives chosen by employees under this chapter.

7103 Definitions; Application

(a) For the purpose of this chapter

(1) "person" means an individual, labor organization, or agency;

(2) "employee" means an individual –

(A) employed in an agency; or

(B) whose employment in an agency has ceased because of any unfair labor practice under section 7116 of this title and who has not obtained any other regular and substantially equivalent employment, as determined under regulations prescribed by the Federal Labor Relations Authority; but does not include –

(i) an alien or non-citizen of the United States who occupies a position outside the United States;

(ii) a member of the uniformed services;

(iii) a supervisor or a management official;

(iv) an officer or employee in the Foreign Service of the United States employed in the Department of State, the International Communication Agency, the Agency for International Development, the Department of Agriculture, or the Department of Commerce; or (v) any person who participates in a strike in violation of section 7311 of this title;

(3) "agency" means an Executive agency (including a non-appropriated fund instrumentality described in section 2105(c) of this title and the Veterans' Canteen Service, Department of Veterans Affairs), the Library of Congress, the Government Printing Office, and the Smithsonian Institution, but does not include –

(A) the General Accounting Office;

(B) the Federal Bureau of Investigation;

(C) the Central Intelligence Agency;

(D) the National Security Agency;

(E) the Tennessee Valley Authority;

(F) the Federal Labor Relations Authority;

(G) the Federal Service Impasses Panel; or

(H) the United States Secret Service and the United States Secret Service Uniformed Division.

(4) "labor organization" means an organization composed in whole or in part of employees, in which employees participate and pay dues, and which has as a purpose the dealing with an agency concerning grievances and conditions of employment, but does not include –

(A) an organization which, by its constitution, bylaws, tacit agreement among its members, or otherwise, denies membership because of race, color, creed, national origin, sex, age, preferential or nonpreferential civil service status, political affiliation, marital status, or handicapping condition;

(B) an organization which advocated the overthrow of the constitutional form of government of the United States;

(C) an organization sponsored by an agency; or

(D) an organization which participates in the conduct of a strike against the Government or any agency thereof or imposes a duty or obligation to conduct, assist, or participate in such a strike;

(5) "dues" means dues, fees, and assessments;

(6) "Authority" means the Federal Labor Relations Authority described in section 7104(a) of this title;

(7) "Panel" means the Federal Service Impasses Panel described in section 7119(c) of this title;

(8) "collective bargaining agreement" means an agreement entered into as a result of collective bargaining pursuant to the provisions of this chapter;

(9) "grievance" means any complaint –

(A) by any employee concerning any matter relating to the employment of the employee;

(B) by any labor organization concerning any matter relating to the employment of any employee; or

(C) by any employee, labor organization, or agency concerning –

(i) the effect or interpretation, or a claim of breach, of a collective bargaining agreement; or

(ii) any claimed violation, misinterpretation, or misapplication of any law, rule, or regulation affecting conditions of employment;

(10) "supervisor" means an individual employed by an agency having authority in the interest of the agency to hire, direct, assign, promote, and reward, transfer, furlough, layoff, recall, suspend, discipline, or remove employees, to adjust their grievances, or to effectively recommend such action, if the exercise of the authority is not merely routine or clerical in nature but requires the consistent exercise of independent judgment, except that, with respect to any unit which includes firefighters or nurses, the term "supervisor" includes only those individuals who devote a preponderance of their employment time to exercising such authority;

(11) "management official" means an individual employed by an agency in a position the duties and responsibilities of which require or authorize the individual to formulate, determine, or influence the policies of the agency;

(12) "collective bargaining" means the performance of the mutual obligation of the representative of an agency and the exclusive representative of employees in an appropriate unit in the agency to meet at reasonable times and to consult and bargain in a good-faith effort to reach agreement with respect to the conditions of employment affecting such employees and to execute, if requested by either party, a written document incorporating any collective bargaining agreement reached, but the obligation referred to in this paragraph does not compel either party to agree to a proposal or to make a concession;

(13) "confidential employee" means an employee who acts in a confidential capacity with respect to an individual who formulates or effectuates management policies in the field of labor management relations;

(14) "conditions of employment" means personnel policies, practices, and matters, whether established by rule, regulations, or otherwise, affecting working conditions, except that such term does not include policies, practices, and matters–

(A) relating to political activities prohibited under subchapter III or chapter 73 of this title;

(B) relating to the classification of any position; or

(C) to the extent such matters are specifically provided for by Federal statute;

(15) "professional employee" means –

(A) an employee engaged in the performance of work

(i) requiring knowledge of an advanced type in a field of science or learning customarily acquired by a prolonged course of specialized intellectual instruction and study in an institution of higher learning or a hospital (as distinguished from knowledge acquired by a general academic education, or from an apprenticeship, or from training in the performance of routine mental, manual, mechanical, or physical activities);

(ii) requiring the consistent exercise of discretion and judgment in its performance;

(iii) which is predominantly intellectual and varied in character (as distinguished from routine mental, manual, mechanical, or physical work); and

(iv) which is of such character that the output produced or the result accomplished by such work cannot be standardized in relation to a given period of time; or

(B) an employee who has completed the courses of specialized intellectual instruction and study described in subparagraph (A)(i) of this paragraph and is performing related work under appropriate direction or guidance to qualify the employee as a professional employee described in subparagraph (A) of this paragraph;

(16) "exclusive representative" means any labor organization which –

(A) is certified as the exclusive representative of employees in an appropriate unit pursuant to section 7111 of this title; or

(B) was recognized by an agency immediately before the effective date of this chapter as the exclusive representative of employees in an appropriate unit –

(i) on the basis of an election; or

(ii) on any basis other than an election, and continues to be so recognized in accordance with the provisions of this chapter;

(17) "firefighter" means any employee engaged in the performance of work directly connected with the control and extinguishment of fires or the maintenance and use firefighting apparatus and equipment; and

(18) "United States" means the 50 States, the District of Columbia, the Commonwealth of Puerto Rico, Guam, the Virgin Islands, the Trust Territory of the Pacific Islands, and any territory or possession of the United States.

(b)(1) The President may issue an order excluding any agency or subdivision thereof from coverage under this chapter if the President determines that

(A) the agency or subdivision has as a primary function intelligence, counterintelligence, investigative, or national security work, and

(B) the provisions of this chapter cannot be applied to that agency or subdivision in a manner consistent with national security requirements and considerations.

(2) The President may issue an order suspending any provision of this chapter with respect to any agency, installation, or activity located outside the 50 States and the District of Columbia, if the President determines that the suspension is necessary in the interest of national security.

7104 Federal Labor Relations Authority

(a) The Federal Labor Relations Authority is composed of three members, not more than 2 of whom may be adherents of the same political party. No member shall engage in any other business or employment or hold another office or position in the Government of the United States except as otherwise provided by law.

(b) Members of the Authority shall be appointed by the President by and with the advice and consent of the Senate, and may be removed by the President only upon notice and hearing and only for inefficiency, neglect of duty, or malfeasance in office. The President shall designate one member to serve as Chairman of the Authority. The Chairman is the chief executive and administrative officer of the Authority.

(c) A member of the Authority shall be appointed for a term of 5 years. An individual chosen to fill a vacancy shall be appointed for the unexpired term of the member replaced. The term of any member shall not expire before the earlier of –

(1) the date on which the member's successor takes office, or

(2) the last day of the Congress beginning after the date on which the member's term of office would (but for this paragraph) expire.

(d) A vacancy in the Authority shall not impair the right of the remaining members to exercise all of the powers of the Authority.

(e) The Authority shall make an annual report to the President for transmittal to the Congress which shall include information as to the cases it has heard and decisions it has rendered.

(f)(1) The general Counsel of the Authority shall be appointed by the President, by and with the advice and consent of the Senate, for a term of 5 years. The General Counsel may be removed at any time by the President. The General Counsel shall hold no other office or position in the Government of the United States except as provided by law.

(2) The General Counsel may –

(A) investigate alleged unfair labor practices under this chapter,

(B) file and prosecute complaints under this chapter, and

(C) exercise such other powers of the Authority as the Authority may prescribe.

(3) The General Counsel shall have direct authority over, and responsibility for, all employees in the office of General Counsel, including employees of the General Counsel in the regional offices of the Authority.

7105 Powers and Duties of the Authority

(a)(1) The Authority shall provide leadership in establishing policies and guidance relating to matters under this chapter, and, except as otherwise provided, shall be responsible for carrying out the purpose of this chapter.

(2) The Authority shall, to the extent provided in this chapter and in accordance with regulations prescribed by the Authority

(A) determine the appropriateness of units for section 7112 of this title; (B) supervise or conduct elections to determine whether a labor organization has been selected as an exclusive representative by a majority of the employees in an appropriate unit and otherwise administer the provisions of section 7111 of this title relating to the according of exclusive recognition to labor organizations;

(C) prescribe criteria and resolve issues relating to the granting of national consultation rights under section 7113 of this title;

(D) prescribe criteria and resolve issues relating to determining compelling need for agency rules or regulations under section 7117(b) of this title;

(E) resolve issues relating to the duty to bargain in good faith under section 7117(c) of this title;

(F) prescribe criteria relating to the granting of consultation rights with respect to conditions of employment under section 7117(d) of this title;

(G) conduct hearings and resolve complaints of unfair labor practices under section 7118 of this title;

(H) resolve exceptions to arbitrator's awards under section 7122 of this title; and

(I) take such other actions as are necessary and appropriate to effectively administer the provisions of this chapter.

(b) The Authority shall adopt an official seal which shall be judicially noticed.

(c) The principal office of the Authority shall be in or about the District of Columbia, but the Authority may meet and exercise any or all of its powers at any time or place. Except as otherwise expressly provided by law, the Authority may, by one or more of its members or by such agents as it may designate, make an appropriate inquiry necessary to carry out its duties wherever persons subject to this chapter are located. Any member who participates in the inquiry shall not be disqualified from later participating in a decision of the Authority in any case relating to the inquiry.

(d) The Authority shall appoint an Executive Director and such regional directors, administrative law judges under section 3105 of this title, and other individuals as it may from time to time find necessary for the proper performance of its functions. The Authority may delegate to officers and employees appointed under this subsection authority to perform such duties and make such expenditures as may be necessary.

(e)(1) The Authority may delegate to any regional director its authority under this chapter--

(A) to determine whether a group of employees is an appropriate unit;

(B) to conduct investigations and to provide for hearings;

(C) to determine whether a question of representation exists and to direct an election; and

(D) to supervise or conduct secret ballot elections and certify the results thereof.

(2) The Authority may delegate to any administrative law judge appointed under subsection (d) of this section its authority under section 7118 of this title to determine whether any person has engaged in or is engaging in an unfair labor practice.

(f) If the Authority delegates any authority to any regional director or administrative law judge to take any action pursuant to subsection (e) of this section, the Authority may, upon application by any interested person filed within 60 days after the date of the action, review such action, but the review shall not, unless specifically ordered by the Authority, operate as a stay of action. The Authority may affirm, modify, or reverse any action reviewed under this subsection. If the Authority does not undertake to grant review of the action under this subsection within 60 days after the later of –

(1) the date of the action; or

(2) the date of the filing of any application under this subsection for review of the action; the action shall become the action of the Authority at the end of such 60-day period.

(g) In order to carry out its functions under this chapter, the Authority may –

(1) hold hearings;

(2) administer oaths, take the testimony or deposition of any person under oath, and issue subpenas as provided in section 7132 of this title; and

(3) may require an agency or a labor organization to cease and desist from violations of this chapter and require it to take any remedial action it considers appropriate to carry out the policies of this chapter.

(h) Except as provided in section 518 of title 28, relating to litigation before the Supreme Court, attorneys designated by the Authority may appear for the Authority and represent the Authority in any civil action brought in connection with any function carried out by the Authority pursuant to this title or as otherwise authorized by law.

(i) In the exercise of the functions of the Authority under this title, the Authority may request from the Director of the Office of Personnel Management an advisory opinion concerning the proper interpretation of rules, regulations, or policy directives issued by the Office of Personnel Management in connection with any matter before the Authority.

7106 Management Rights

(a) Subject to subsection (b) of this section, nothing in this chapter shall affect the authority of any management official of any agency–

(1) to determine the mission, budget, organization, number or employees, and internal security practices of the agency; and

(2) in accordance with applicable laws--

(A) to hire, assign, direct, layoff, and retain employees in the agency, or to suspend, remove, reduce in grade or pay, or take other disciplinary action against such employees;

(B) to assign work, to make determinations with respect to contracting out, and to determine the personnel by which agency operation shall be conducted;

(C) with respect to filling positions, to make selections for appointments from –

(i.) among properly ranked and certified candidates for promotion; or

(ii.) any other appropriate source; and

(D) to take whatever actions may be necessary to carry out the agency mission during emergencies.

(b) Nothing in this section shall preclude any agency and any labor organization from negotiating--

(1) at the election of the agency, on the numbers, types, and grades of employees or positions assigned to any organizational subdivision, work project, or tour of duty, or on the technology, methods, and means of performing work;

(2) procedures which management officials of the agency will observe in exercising any authority under this section; or

(3) appropriate arrangements for employees adversely affected by the exercise of any authority under this section by such management officials.

Subchapter II

Rights and Duties of Agencies and Labor Organizations

7111 Exclusive Recognition of Labor Organizations

(a) An agency shall accord exclusive recognition to a labor organization if the organization has been selected as the representative, in a secret ballot election, by a majority of the employees in an appropriate unit who cast valid ballots in the election.

(b) If a petition is filed with the Authority –

(1) by any person alleging--

(A) in the case of an appropriate unit for which there is no exclusive representative, that 30 percent of the employees in the appropriate unit wish to be represented for the purpose of collective bargaining by an exclusive representative, or

(B) in the case of an appropriate unit for which there is an exclusive representative, that 30 percent of the employees in the unit allege that the exclusive representative is no longer the representative of the majority of the employees in the unit; or

(2) by any person seeking clarification of, or an amendment to, a certification then in effect or a matter relating to representation; the Authority shall investigate the petition, and if it has reasonable cause to believe that a question of representation exists, it shall provide an opportunity for a hearing (for which a transcript shall be kept) after a reasonable notice. If the Authority finds on the record of the hearing that a question of representation exists, the Authority shall supervise or conduct an election on the question by secret ballot and shall certify the results thereof. An election under this subsection shall not be conducted in any appropriate unit or in any subdivision thereof within which, in the preceding 12 calendar months, a valid election under this subsection has been held.

(c) A labor organization which –

(1) has been designated by at least 10 percent of the employees in the unit specified in any petition filed pursuant to subsection (b) of this section;

(2) has submitted a valid copy of a current or recently expired collective bargaining agreement for the unit; or

(3) has submitted other evidence that it is the exclusive representative of the employees involved; may intervene with respect to a petition filed pursuant to subsection (b) of this section and shall be placed on the ballot of any election under such subsection (b) with respect to the petition.

(d) The Authority shall determine who is eligible to vote in any election under this section and shall establish rules governing any such election, which shall include rules allowing employees eligible to vote the opportunity to choose –

(1) from labor organizations on the ballot, that labor organizations which the employees wish to have represent them; or

(2) not to be represented by a labor organization. In any election in which no choice on the ballot receives a majority of the votes cast, a runoff election shall be conducted between the two choices receiving the highest number of votes. A labor organization which receives the majority of the votes cast in an election shall be certified by the Authority as the exclusive representative.

(e) A labor organization seeking exclusive recognition shall submit to the Authority and the agency involved a roster of its officers and representatives, a copy of its constitution and bylaws, and a statement of its objectives.

(f) Exclusive recognition shall not be accorded to a labor organization--

(1) if the Authority determines that the labor organization is subject to corrupt influences or influences opposed to democratic principles;

(2) in the case of a petition filed pursuant to subsection (b)(1)(A) of this section, if there is not credible evidence that at least 30 percent of the employees in the unit specified in the petition wish to be represented for the purpose of collective bargaining by the labor organization seeking exclusive recognition;

(3) if there is then in effect a lawful written collective bargaining agreement between the agency involved and an exclusive representative (other than the labor organization seeking exclusive recognition) covering any employees included in the unit specified in the petition, unless--

(A) the collective bargaining agreement has been in effect for more than 3 years, or

(B) the petition for exclusive recognition is filed not more than 105 days and not less than 60 days before the expiration date of the collective bargaining agreement; or

(4) if the Authority has, within the previous 12 calendar months, conducted a secret ballot election for the unit described in any petition under this section and in such election a majority of the employees voting chose a labor organization for certification as the unit's exclusive representative.

(g) Nothing in this section shall be construed to prohibit the waiving of hearings by stipulation for the purpose of a consent election in conformity with regulations and rules or decisions of the Authority.

7112 Determination of Appropriate Units for Labor Organization Representation

(a) The Authority shall determine the appropriateness of any unit. The Authority shall determine in each case whether, in order to ensure employees the fullest freedom in exercising the rights guaranteed under this chapter, the appropriate unit should be established on an agency, plant, installation, functional, or other basis and shall determine any unit to be an appropriate unit only if the determination will ensure a clear and identifiable community of interest among the employees in the unit and will promote effective dealings with, and efficiency of the operations of the agency involved.

(b) A unit shall not be determined to be appropriate under this section solely on the basis of the extent to which employees in the proposed unit have organized, nor shall a unit be determined to appropriate if it includes –

(1) except as provided under section 7135(a)(2) of this title, any management official or supervisor;

(2) a confidential employee;

(3) an employee engaged in personnel work in other than a purely clerical capacity;

(4) an employee engaged in administering the provisions of this chapter;

(5) both professional employees and other employees, unless a majority of the professional employees vote for inclusion in the unit;

(6) any employee engaged in intelligence, counter-intelligence, investigative, or security work which directly affects national security; or

(7) any employee primarily engaged in investigation or audit functions relating to the work of individuals employed by an agency whose duties directly affect the internal security of the agency, but only if the functions are undertaken to ensure that the duties are discharged honestly and with integrity.

(c) Any employee who is engaged in administering any provision of law relating to labor-management relations may not be represented by a labor organization –

(1) which represents other individuals to whom such provisions applies; or

(2) which is affiliated directly or indirectly with an organization which represents other individuals to whom such provision applies.

(d) Two or more units which are in an agency and for which a labor organization is the exclusive representative may, upon petition by the agency or labor organization, be consolidated with or without an election into a single larger unit if the Authority considers the larger unit to be appropriate. The Authority shall certify the labor organization as the exclusive representative of the new larger unit.

7113 National Consultation Rights

(a) If, in connection with any agency, no labor organization has been accorded exclusive recognition on any agency basis, a labor organization which is the exclusive representative of a substantial number of the employees of the agency, as determined in accordance with criteria prescribed by the Authority, shall be granted national consultation rights by the agency. National consultation rights shall terminate when the labor organization no longer meets the criteria prescribed by the Authority. Any issue relating to any labor organization's eligibility for, or continuation of, national consultation rights shall be subject to determination by the Authority.

(b)(1) Any labor organization having national consultation rights in connection with any agency under subsection (a) of this section shall –

(A) be informed of any substantive change in conditions of employment proposed by the agency, and

(B) be permitted reasonable time to present its views and recommendations regarding the changes.

(2) If any views or recommendations are presented under paragraph (1) of this subsection to an agency by any labor organization –

(A) the agency shall consider the views or recommendations before taking final action on any matter with respect to which the views or recommendations are presented; and

(B) the agency shall provide the labor organization a written statement of the reasons for taking the final action.

(c) Nothing in this section shall be construed to limit the right of any agency or exclusive representative to engage in collective bargaining.

7114 Representation Rights and Duties

(a)(1) A labor organization which has been accorded exclusive recognition is the exclusive representative of the employees in the unit it represents and is entitled to act for, and negotiate collective bargaining agreements covering, all employees in the unit. An exclusive representative is responsible for representing the interests of all employees in the unit it represents without discrimination and without regard to labor organization membership.

(2) An exclusive representative of an appropriate unit in an agency shall be given the opportunity to be represented at

(A) any formal discussion between one or more representatives of the agency and one or more employees in the unit or their representatives concerning any grievance or any personnel policy or practices or other general condition of employment; or

(B) any examination of an employee in the unit by a representative of the agency in connection with an investigation if –

(i) the employee reasonably believes that the examination may result in disciplinary action against the employee; and

(ii) the employee requests representation.

(3) Each agency shall annually inform its employees of their rights under paragraph (2)(B) of this subsection.

(4) Any agency and any exclusive representative in any appropriate unit in the agency, through appropriate representatives, shall meet and negotiate in good faith for the purposes of arriving at a collective bargaining agreement. In addition, the agency and the exclusive representative may determine appropriate techniques, consistent with the provisions of section 7119 of this title, to assist in any negotiation.

(5) The rights of an exclusive representative under the provisions of this subsection shall not be construed to preclude an employee from –

(A) being represented by an attorney or other representative, other than the exclusive representative, of the employee's own choosing in any grievance or appeal action; or

(B) exercising grievance or appellate rights established by law, rule, or regulation; except in the case of grievance or appeal procedures negotiated under this chapter.

(b) The duty of an agency and an exclusive representative to negotiate in good faith under subsection (a) of this section shall include the obligation

(1) to approach the negotiations with a sincere resolve to reach a collective bargaining agreement;

(2) to be represented at the negotiations by duly authorized representatives prepared to discuss and negotiate on any condition of employment;

(3) to meet at reasonable times and convenient places as frequently as may be necessary, and to avoid unnecessary delays;

(4) in the case of an agency, to furnish to the exclusive representative involved, or its authorized representative, upon request and, to the extent not prohibited by law, data--

(A) which is normally maintained by the agency in the regular course of business;

(B) which is reasonably available and necessary for full and proper discussion, understanding, and negotiation of subjects within the scope of collective bargaining; and

(C) which does not constitute guidance, advise, counsel, or training provided for management officials or supervisors, relating to collective bargaining; and

(5) if agreement is reached, to execute on the request of any party to the negotiation a written document embodying the agreed terms, and to take such steps as are necessary to implement such agreement.

(c)(1) An agreement between any agency and an exclusive representative shall be subject to approval by the head of the agency.

(2) The head of the agency shall approve the agreement within 30 days from the date the agreement is executed if the agreement is in accordance with the provisions of this chapter and any other applicable law, rule, or regulation (unless the agency has granted an exception to the provision).

(3) If the head of the agency does not approve or disapprove the agreement within the 30-day period, the agreement shall take effect and shall be binding on the agency and the exclusive representative subject to the provisions of this chapter and any other applicable law, rule, or regulation.

(4) A local agreement subject to a national or other controlling agreement at a higher level shall be approved under the procedures of the controlling agreement or, if none, under regulations prescribed by the agency.

7115 Allotments to Representatives

(a) If an agency has received from an employee in an appropriate unit a written assignment which authorizes the agency to deduct from the pay of the employee amounts for the payment of regular and periodic dues of the exclusive representative of the unit, the agency shall honor the assignment and make an appropriate allotment pursuant to the assignment. Any such allotment shall be made at no cost to the exclusive representative or the employee. Except as provided under subsection (b) of this section, any such assignment may not be revoked for a period of 1 year.

(b) An allotment under subsection (a) of this section for the deduction of dues with respect to any employee shall terminate when –

(1) the agreement between the agency and the exclusive representative involved ceases to be applicable to the employee; or

(2) the employee is suspended or expelled from membership in the exclusive representative.

(c)(1) Subject to paragraph (2) of this subsection, if a petition has been filed with the Authority by a labor organization alleging that 10 percent of the employees in an appropriate unit in an agency have membership in the labor organization, the Authority shall investigate the petition to determine its validity. Upon certification by the Authority of the validity of the petition, the agency shall have a duty to negotiate with the labor organization solely concerning the deduction of dues of the labor organization from the pay of the members of the labor organization who are employees in the unit and who make a voluntary allotment for such purpose.

(2)(A) The provisions of paragraph (1) of this subsection shall not apply in the case of any appropriate unit for which there is an exclusive representative.

(B) Any agreement under paragraph (1) of this subsection between a labor organization and an agency with respect to an appropriate unit shall be null and void upon the certification of an exclusive representative of the unit.

7116 Unfair Labor Practices

(a) For the purpose of this chapter, it shall be an unfair labor practice for an agency –

(1) to interfere with, restrain, or coerce any employee in the exercise by the employee of any right under this chapter;

(2) to encourage or discourage membership in any labor organization by discrimination in connection with hiring, tenure, promotion, or other conditions of employment;

(3) to sponsor, control, or otherwise assist any labor organization, other than to furnish, upon request, customary and routine services and facilities if the services and facilities are also furnished on an impartial basis to other labor organizations having equivalent status;

(4) to discipline or otherwise discriminate against an employee because the employee has filed a complaint, affidavit, or petition, or has given any information or testimony under this chapter;

(5) to refuse to consult or negotiate in good faith with a labor organization as required by this chapter;

(6) to fail or refuse to cooperate in impasse procedures and impasse decisions as required by this chapter;

(7) to enforce any rule or regulation (other than a rule or regulation implementing section 2302 of this title) which is in conflict with any applicable collective bargaining agreement if the agreement was in effect before the date the rule or regulation was prescribed; or

(8) to otherwise fail or refuse to comply with any provision of this chapter.

(b) For the purpose of this chapter, it shall be an unfair labor practice for a labor organization--

(1) to interfere with, restrain, or coerce any employee in the exercise by the employee of any right under this chapter;

(2) to cause or attempt to cause an agency to discriminate against any employee in the exercise by the employee of any right under this chapter;

(3) to coerce, discipline, fine, or attempt to coerce a member of the labor organization as punishment, reprisal, or for the purpose of hindering or impeding the member's work performance or productivity as an employee or the discharge of the member's duties as an employee;

(4) to discriminate against an employee with regard to the terms or conditions of membership in the labor organization on the basis of race, color, creed, national origin, sex, age, preferential or nonpreferential civil service status, political affiliation, marital status, or handicapping condition;

(1) to interfere with, restrain, or coerce any employee in the exercise by the employee of any right under this chapter;

(2) to encourage or discourage membership in any labor organization by discrimination in connection with hiring, tenure, promotion, or other conditions of employment;

(3) to sponsor, control, or otherwise assist any labor organization, other than to furnish, upon request, customary and routine services and facilities if the services and facilities are also furnished on an impartial basis to other labor organizations having equivalent status;

(4) to discipline or otherwise discriminate against an employee because the employee has filed a complaint, affidavit, or petition, or has given any information or testimony under this chapter;

(5) to refuse to consult or negotiate in good faith with a labor organization as required by this chapter;

(6) to fail or refuse to cooperate in impasse procedures and impasse decisions as required by this chapter;

(7) to enforce any rule or regulation (other than a rule or regulation implementing section 2302 of this title) which is in conflict with any applicable collective bargaining agreement if the agreement was in effect before the date the rule or regulation was prescribed; or

(8) to otherwise fail or refuse to comply with any provision of this chapter.

(b) For the purpose of this chapter, it shall be an unfair labor practice for a labor organization--

(1) to interfere with, restrain, or coerce any employee in the exercise by the employee of any right under this chapter;

(2) to cause or attempt to cause an agency to discriminate against any employee in the exercise by the employee of any right under this chapter;

(3) to coerce, discipline, fine, or attempt to coerce a member of the labor organization as punishment, reprisal, or for the purpose of hindering or impeding the member's work performance or productivity as an employee or the discharge of the member's duties as an employee;

(4) to discriminate against an employee with regard to the terms or conditions of membership in the labor organization on the basis of race, color, creed, national origin, sex, age, preferential or nonpreferential civil service status, political affiliation, marital status, or handicapping condition;

(5) to refuse to consult or negotiate in good faith with an agency as required by this chapter;

(6) to fail or refuse to cooperate in impasse procedures and impasse decisions as required by this chapter;

(7)(A) to call, or participate in, a strike, work stoppage, or slowdown, or picketing of an agency in a labor-management dispute if such picketing interferes with an agency's operations, or

(B) to condone any activity described in subparagraph (A) of this paragraph by failing to take action to prevent or stop such activity; or

(8) to otherwise fail or refuse to comply with any provision of this chapter. Nothing in paragraph (7) of this subsection shall result in any informational picketing which does not interfere with an agency's operations being considered as an unfair labor practice.

(c) For the purpose of this chapter, it shall be an unfair labor practice for an exclusive representative to deny membership to any employee in the appropriate unit represented by such exclusive representative except for failure

(1) to meet reasonable occupational standards uniformly required for admission, or

(2) to tender dues uniformly required as a condition of acquiring and retaining membership. This subsection does not preclude any labor organization from enforcing discipline in accordance with procedures under its constitution or bylaws to the extent consistent with the provisions of this chapter.

(d) Issues which can properly be raised under an appeals procedure may not be raised as unfair labor practices prohibited under this section. Except for matters wherein, under section 7121(e) and (f) of this title, an employee has an option of using the negotiated grievance procedure or an appeals procedure, issues which can be raised under a grievance procedure may, in the discretion of the aggrieved party, be raised under the grievance procedure or as an unfair labor practice under this section, but not under both procedures.

(e) The expression of any personal view, argument, opinion or the making of any statement which –

(1) publicized the fact of a representational election and encourages employees to exercise their right to vote in such election,

(2) corrects the record with respect to any false or misleading statement made by any person, or

(3) informs employees of the Government's policy relating to labor-management relations and representation, shall not, if the expression contains no threat or reprisal or force or promise of benefit or was not make under coercive conditions,

(A) constitute an unfair labor practice under any provision of this chapter, or

(B) constitute grounds for the setting aside of any election conducted under any provisions of this chapter.

7117 Duty to Bargain in Good Faith; Compelling Need; Duty to Consult

(a)(1) Subject to paragraph (2) of this subsection, the duty to bargain in good faith shall, to the extent not inconsistent with any Federal law or any Government-wide rule or regulation, extend to matters which are the subject of any rule or regulation only if the rule or regulation is not a Government-wide rule or regulation.

(2) The duty to bargain in good faith shall, to the extent not inconsistent with Federal law or any Government-wide rule or regulation, extend to matters which are the subject of any agency rule or regulation referred to in paragraph (3) of this subsection only if the Authority has determined under subsection (b) of this section that no compelling need (as determined under regulations prescribed by the Authority) exists for the rule or regulation.

(3) Paragraph (2) of the subsection applies to any rule or regulation issued by any agency or issued by any primary national subdivision of such agency, unless an exclusive representative represents an appropriate unit including not less than a majority of the employees in the issuing agency or primary national subdivision, as the case may be, to whom the rule or regulation is applicable.

(b)(1) In any case of collective bargaining in which an exclusive representative alleges that no compelling need exists for any rule or regulation referred to in subsection (a)(3) of this section which is then in effect and which governs any matter at issue in such collective bargaining, the Authority shall determine under paragraph (2) of this subsection, in accordance with regulations prescribed by the Authority, whether such a compelling need exists.

(2) For the purpose of this section, a compelling need shall be determined not to exist for any rule or regulation only if –

(A) the agency, or primary national subdivision, as the case may be, which issued the rule or regulation informs the Authority in writing that a compelling need for the rule or regulation does not exist; or

(B) the Authority determines that a compelling need for a rule or regulation does not exist.

(3) A hearing may be held, in the discretion of the Authority, before a determination is made under this subsection. If a hearing is held, it shall be expedited to the extent practicable and shall not include the General Counsel as a party.

(4) The agency, or primary national subdivision, as the case may be, which issued the rule or regulation shall be a necessary party at any hearing under this subsection.

(c)(1) Except in any case to which subsection (b) of this section applies, if an agency involved in collective bargaining with an exclusive representative alleges that the duty to bargain in good faith does not extend to any matter, the exclusive representative may appeal the allegation to the Authority in accordance with the provisions of this subsection.

(2) The exclusive representative may, on or before the 15th day after the date on which the agency first makes the allegation referred to in paragraph (1) of this subsection, institute an appeal under this subsection by –

(A) filing a petition with the Authority; and

(B) furnishing a copy of the petition to the head of the agency.

(3) On or before the 30th day after the date of the receipt by the head of the agency of the copy of the petition under paragraph (2)(B) of this subsection, the agency shall –

(A) file with the Authority a statement

(i) withdrawing the allegation; or

(ii) setting forth in full its reasons supporting the allegation; and

(B) furnish a copy of such statement to the exclusive representative.

(4) On or before the 15th day after the date of the receipt by the exclusive representative of a copy of a statement under paragraph (3)(B) of this subsection, the exclusive representative shall file with the Authority its response to the statement.

(5) A hearing may be held, in the discretion of the Authority, before a determination is made under this subsection. If a hearing is held, it shall not include the General Counsel as a party.

(6) The Authority shall expedite proceedings under this subsection to the extent practicable and shall issue to the exclusive representative and to the agency a written decision on the allegation and specific reasons therefore at the earliest practicable date.

(d)(1) A labor organization which is the exclusive representative of a substantial number of employees, determined in accordance with criteria prescribed by the Authority, shall be granted consultation rights by any agency with respect to any Government-wide rule or regulation issued by the agency effecting any substantive change in any condition of employment. Such consultation rights shall terminate when the labor organization no longer meets the criteria prescribed by the Authority. Any issue relating to a labor organization's eligibility for, or continuation of, such consultation rights shall be subject to determination by the Authority.

(2) A labor organization having consultation rights under paragraph (1) of this subsection shall--

(A) be informed of any substantive change in conditions of employment proposed by the agency, and

(B) shall be permitted reasonable time to present its views and recommendations regarding the changes.

(3) If any views or recommendations are presented under paragraph (2) of this subsection to an agency by any labor organization –

(A) the agency shall consider the views or recommendations before taking final action on any matter with respect to which the views or recommendations are presented; and

(B) the agency shall provide the labor organization a written statement of the reasons for taking the final action.

7118 Prevention of Unfair Labor Practices

(a)(1) If any agency or labor organization is charged by any person with having engaged in or engaging in an unfair labor practice, the General Counsel shall investigate the charge and may issue and cause to be served upon the agency or labor organization a complaint. In any case in which the General Counsel does not issue a complaint because the charge fails to state an unfair labor practice, the General Counsel shall provide the person making the charge a written statement of the reasons for not issuing a complaint.

(2) Any complaint under paragraph (1) of this subsection shall contain a notice –

(A) of the charge;

(B) that a hearing will be held before the Authority (or any member thereof or before an individual employed by the authority and designated for such purpose); and

(C) of the time and place fixed for the hearing.

(3) The labor organization or agency involved shall have the right to file an answer to the original and any amended complaint and to appear in person or otherwise and give testimony at the time and place fixed in the complaint for the hearing.

(4)(A) Except as provided in subparagraph (B) of this paragraph, no complaint shall be issued on any alleged unfair labor practice which occurred more than 6 months before the filing of the charge with the Authority (B) If the General Counsel determines that the person filing any charge was prevented from filing the charge during the 6-month period referred to in subparagraph (A) of this paragraph by reason of

(i) any failure of the agency or labor organization against which the charge is made to perform a duty owed to the person, or

(ii) any concealment which presented discovery of the alleged unfair labor practice during the 6-month period, the General Counsel may issue a complaint based on the charge if the charge was filed during the 6-month period beginning on the day of the discovery by the person of the alleged unfair labor practice.

(5) The General Counsel may prescribe regulations providing for informal methods by which the alleged unfair labor practice may be resolved prior to the issuance of a complaint.

(6) The Authority (or any member thereof or any individual employed by the Authority and designated for such purpose) shall conduct a hearing on the complaint not earlier than 5 days after the date on which the complaint is served. In the discretion of the individual or individuals conducting the hearing, any person involved may be allowed to intervene in the hearing and to present testimony. Any such hearing shall, to the extent practicable, be conducted in accordance with the provisions of subchapter II of chapter 5 of this title, except that the parties shall not be bound by rules of evidence, whether statutory, common law, or adopted by a court. A transcript shall be kept of the hearing. After such a hearing the Authority, in its discretion, may upon notice receive further evidence or hear argument.

(7) If the Authority (or any member thereof or any individual employed by the Authority and designated for such purpose) determines after any hearing on a complaint under paragraph (5) of this subsection that the preponderance of the evidence received demonstrates that the agency or labor organization named in the complaint has engaged in or is engaging in an unfair labor practice, then the individual or individuals conducting the hearing shall state in writing their findings of fact and shall issue and cause to be served on the agency or labor organization an order

(A) to cease and desist from any such unfair labor practice in which the agency or labor organization is engaged;

(B) requiring the parties to renegotiate a collective bargaining agreement in accordance with the order of the Authority and requiring that the agreement, as amended, be given retroactive effect;

(C) requiring reinstatement of an employee with back-pay in accordance with section 5596 of this title; or

(D) including any combination of the actions described in subparagraphs (A) through (C) of this paragraph or such other actions as will carry out the purpose of this chapter.

If any such order required reinstatement of any employee with back-pay, back-pay may be required of the agency (as provided in section 5596 of this title) or of the labor organization, as the case may be, which is found to have engaged in the unfair labor practice involved.

(8) If the individual or individuals conducting the hearing determine that the preponderance of the evidence received fails to demonstrate that the agency or labor organization named in the complaint has engaged in or is engaging in an unfair labor practice, the individual or individuals shall state in writing their findings of fact and shall issue an order dismissing the complaint.

(b) In connection with any matter before the Authority in any proceeding under this section, the Authority may request, in accordance with the provisions of section 7105(i) of this title, from the Director of the Office of Personnel Management an advisory opinion concerning the proper interpretation of rules, regulations, or other policy directives issued by the Office of Personnel Management.

7119 Negotiation Impasses; Federal Service Impasses Panel

(a) The Federal Mediation and Conciliation Service shall provide services and assistance to agencies and exclusive representatives in the resolution of negotiation impasses. The Service shall determine under what circumstances and in what matter it shall provide services and assistance.

(b) If voluntary arrangements, including the services of the Federal Mediation and Conciliation Service or any other third-party mediation, fail to resolve a negotiation impasse –

(1) either party may request the Federal Service Impasses Panel to consider the matter, or

(2) the parties may agree to adopt a procedure for binding arbitration of the negotiation impasses, but only if the procedure is approved by the Panel.

(c)(1) The Federal Service Impasses Panel is an entity within the Authority, the function of which is to provide assistance in resolving negotiation impasses between agencies and exclusive representatives.

(2) The panel shall be composed of a Chairman and at least six other members, who shall be appointed by the President, solely on the basis of fitness to perform duties and functions involved, from among individuals who are familiar with Government operations and knowledgeable in labor-management relations.

(3) Of the original members of the Panel, 2 members shall be appointed for a term of 1 year, 2 members shall be appointed for a term of 3 years, and the Chairman and the remaining members shall be appointed for a term of 5 years. Thereafter each member shall be appointed for a term of 5 years, except that an individual chosen to fill a vacancy shall be appointed for the unexpired term of the member replaced. Any member of the Panel may be removed by the President.

(4) The Panel may appoint an Executive Director and any other individuals it may from time to time find necessary for the proper performance of its duties. Each member of the Panel who is not an employee (as defined in section 2105 of this title) is entitled to pay at a rate equal to the daily equivalent of the maximum annual rate of basic pay then currently paid under the General Schedule for each day he is engaged in the performance of official business of the Panel, including travel time, and is entitled to travel expenses as provided under section 5703 of this title.

(5)(A) The Panel or its designee shall promptly investigate any impasse presented to it under subsection (b) of this section. The Panel shall consider the impasse and shall either –

   (i) recommend to the parties procedures for the resolution of the impasse; or

   (ii) assist the parties in resolving the impasse through whatever methods and procedures, including factfinding and recommendations, it may consider appropriate to accomplish the purpose of this section.

(B) If the parties do not arrive at a settlement after assistance by the Panel under subparagraph (A) of this paragraph, the Panel may --

   (i) hold hearings;

   (ii) administer oaths, take the testimony or deposition of any person under oath, and issue subpenas as provided in section 7132 of this title; and

   (iii) take whatever action is necessary and not inconsistent with this chapter to resolve the impasse.

(C) Notice of any final action of the Panel under this section shall be promptly served upon the parties, and the action shall be binding on such parties during the term of the agreement, unless the parties agree otherwise.

7120 Standards of Conduct for Labor Organizations

(a) An agency shall only accord recognition to a labor organization that is free from corrupt influences and influences opposed to basic democratic principles. Except as provided in subsection (b) of this section, an organization is not required to prove that it is free from such influences if it is subject to governing requirements adopted by the organization or by a national or international labor organization or federation of labor organizations with which it is affiliated, or in which it participates, containing explicit and detailed provisions to which it subscribes calling for –

(1) the maintenance of democratic procedures and practices including provisions for periodic elections to be conducted subject to recognized safeguards and provisions defining and securing the right of individual members to participate in the affairs of the organization, to receive fair and equal treatment under the governing rules of the organization, and to receive fair process in disciplinary proceedings;

(2) the exclusion from office in the organization of persons affiliated with communist or other totalitarian movements and persons identified with corrupt influences;

(3) the prohibition of business or financial interests on the part of organization officers and agents which conflict with their duty to the organization and its members; and

(4) the maintenance of fiscal integrity in the conduct of the affairs of the organization, including provisions for accounting and financial controls and regular financial reports or summaries to be made available to members.

(b) Notwithstanding the fact that a labor organization has adopted or subscribed to standards of conduct as provided in subsection (a) of this section, the organization is required to furnish evidence of its freedom from corrupt influences or influences opposed to basic democratic principles if there is reasonable cause to believe that --

(1) the organization has been suspended or expelled from, or is subject to other sanction, by a parent labor organization, or federation of organizations with which it had been affiliated, because it has demonstrated an unwillingness or inability to comply with governing requirements comparable in purpose to those required by subsection (a) of this section; or

(2) the organization is in fact subject to influences that would preclude recognition under this chapter.

(c) A labor organization which has or seeks recognition as a representative of employees under this chapter shall file financial and other reports with the Assistant Secretary of Labor for Labor Management Relations, provide for bonding of officials and employees of the organization, and comply with trusteeship and election standards.

(d) The Assistant Secretary shall prescribe such regulations as are necessary to carry out the purposes of this section. Such regulations shall conform generally to the principles applied to labor organizations in the private sector. Complaints of violations of this section shall be filed with the Assistant Secretary. In any matter arising under this section, the Assistant Secretary may require a labor organization to cease and desist from violations of this section and require it to take such actions as he considers appropriate to carry out the policies of this section.

(e) This chapter does not authorize participation in the management of a labor organization or acting as a representative of a labor organization by a management official, a supervisor, or a confidential employee, except as specifically provided in this chapter, or by an employee if the participation or activity would result in a conflict or apparent conflict of interest or would otherwise be incompatible with law or with the official duties of the employee.

(f) In the case of any labor organization which by omission or commission has willfully and intentionally, with regard to any strike, work stoppage, or slowdown, violated section 7116(b)(7) of this title, the Authority shall, upon an appropriate finding by the Authority of such violation --

(1) revoke the exclusive recognition status of the labor organization, which shall then immediately cease to be legally entitled and obligated to represent employees in the unit; or

(2) take any other appropriate disciplinary action.

Subchapter III
Grievances, Appeals, and Review
Grievance Procedures

(a)(1) Except as provided in paragraph (2) of this subsection, any collective bargaining agreement shall provide procedures for the settlement of grievances, including questions of arbitrability. Except as provided in subsections (d), (e) and (g) of this section, the procedures shall be the exclusive administrative procedures for resolving grievances which fall within its coverage.

(2) Any collective bargaining agreement may exclude any matter from the application of the grievance procedures which are provided for in the agreement.

(b)(1) Any negotiated grievance procedure referred to in subsection (a) of this section shall --

(A) be fair and simple,

(B) provide for expeditious processing, and

(C) include procedures that--

(i) assure an exclusive representative the right, in its own behalf or on behalf of any employee in the unit represented by the exclusive representative, to present and process grievances;

(ii) assure such an employee the right to present a grievance on the employee's own behalf, and assure the exclusive representative the right to be present during the grievance proceeding; and

(iii) provide that any grievance not satisfactorily settled under the negotiated grievance procedure shall be subject to binding arbitration which may be invoked by either the exclusive representative or the agency.

(2)(A) The provisions of a negotiated grievance procedure providing for binding arbitration in accordance with paragraph (1)(C)(iii) shall, if or to the extent that an alleged prohibited personnel practice is involved, allow the arbitrator to order --

(i) a stay of any personnel action in a manner similar to the manner described in section 1221(c) with respect to the Merit Systems Protection Board; and

(ii) the taking, by an agency, of any disciplinary action identified under section 1215(a)(3) that is otherwise within the authority of such agency to take.

(B) Any employee who is the subject of any disciplinary action ordered under subparagraph (A)(ii) may appeal such action to the same extent and in the same manner as if the agency had taken the disciplinary action absent arbitration.

(c) The preceding subsections of this section shall not apply with respect to any grievance concerning --

(1) any claimed violation of subchapter III of chapter 73 of this title (relating to prohibited political activities);

(2) retirement, like insurance, or health insurance;

(3) a suspension or removal under section 7532 of this title;

(4) any examination, certification, or appointment; or

(5) the classification of any position which does not result in the reduction in grade or pay of an employee.

(d) An aggrieved employee affected by a prohibited personnel practice under section 2302(b)(1) of this title which also falls under the coverage of the negotiated grievance procedure may raise the matter under a statutory procedure or the negotiated procedure, but not both. An employee shall be deemed to have exercised his option under this subsection to raise the matter under either a statutory procedure or the negotiated procedure at such time as the employee timely initiates an action under the applicable statutory procedure or timely files a grievance in writing, in accordance with the provisions of the parties' negotiated procedure, whichever event occurs first. Selection of the negotiated procedure in no manner prejudices the right of an aggrieved employee to request the Merit Systems Protection Board to review the final decision pursuant to section 7702 of this title in the case of any personnel action that could have been appealed to the Board, or, where applicable, to request the Equal Employment Opportunity Commission to review a final decision in any other matter involving a complaint of discrimination of the type prohibited by any law administered by the Equal Employment Opportunity Commission.

(e)(1) Matters covered under sections 4303 and 7512 of this title which also fall within the coverage of the negotiated grievance procedure may, in the discretion of the aggrieved employee, be raised either under the appellate procedures of section 7701 of this title or under the negotiated grievance procedure, but not both. Similar matters which arise under other personnel systems applicable to employees covered by this chapter may, in the discretion of the aggrieved employee, be raised either under the appellate procedures, if any, applicable to those matters, or under the negotiated grievance procedure, but not both. An employee shall be deemed to have exercised his option under this subsection to raise a matter either under the applicable appellate procedures or under the negotiated grievance procedure at such time as the employee timely files a notice of appeal under the applicable appellate procedures or timely files a grievance in writing in accordance with the provisions of the parties' negotiated grievance procedure, whichever event occurs first.

(2) In matters covered under sections 4303 and 7512 if this title which have been raised under the negotiated grievance procedure in accordance with this section, an arbitrator shall be governed by section 7701(c)(1) of this title, as applicable.

(f) In matters covered under section 4303 and 7512 of this title which have been raised under the negotiated grievance procedure in accordance with this section, section 7703 of this title pertaining to judicial review shall apply to the award of an arbitrator in the same manner and under the same conditions as if the matter had been decided by the Board. In matters similar to those covered under sections 4303 and 7512 of this title which arise under other personnel systems and which an aggrieved employee has raised under the negotiated grievance procedure, judicial review of an arbitrator's award may be obtained in the same manner and on the same basis as could be obtained of a final decision in such matters raised under applicable appellate procedures.

(g)(1) This subsection applies with respect to a prohibited personnel practice other than a prohibited personnel practice to which subsection (d) applies.

(2) An aggrieved employee affected by a prohibited personnel practice described in paragraph (1) may elect not more than one of the remedies described in paragraph (3) with respect thereto. For purposes of the preceding sentence, a determination as to whether a particular remedy has been elected shall be made as set forth under paragraph (4).

(3) The remedies described in this paragraph are as follows:

(A) An appeal to the Merit Systems Protection Board under section 7701.

(B) A negotiated grievance procedure under this section.

(C) Procedures for seeking corrective action under subchapters II and III of chapter 12.

(4) For the purpose of this subsection, a person shall be considered to have elected

(A) the remedy described in paragraph (3)(A) if such person has timely filed a notice of appeal under the applicable appellate procedures;

(B) the remedy described in paragraph (3)(B) if such person has timely files a grievance in writing, in accordance with the provisions of the parties; negotiated procedure; or

(C) the remedy described in paragraph (3)(C) if such person has sought corrective action from the Office of Special Counsel by making an allegation under section 1214(a)(1).

(h) Settlements and awards under this chapter shall be subject to the limitations in section 5596(b)(4) of this title.

7122 Exceptions to Arbitral Awards

(a) Either party to arbitration under this chapter may file with the Authority an exception to any arbitrator's award pursuant to the arbitration (other than an award relating to a matter described in section 7121(f) of this title). If upon review the Authority finds that the award is deficient --

(1) because it is contrary to any law, rule, or regulation; or

(2) on other grounds similar to those applied by Federal courts in private sector labor-management relations; the Authority may take such action and make such recommendations concerning the award as it considers necessary, consistent with applicable laws, rules, or regulations.

(b) If no exception to an arbitrator's award is filed under subsection (a) of this section during the 30-day period beginning on the date the award is served on the party, the award shall be final and binding. An agency shall take the actions required by an arbitrator's final award. The award may include the payment of backpay (as provided in section 5596 of this title).

7123 Judicial Review; Enforcement

(a) Any person aggrieved by any final order of the Authority other than an order under (1) section 7122 of this title (involving an award by an arbitrator), unless the order involves an unfair labor practice under section 7118 of this title, or (2) section 7112 of this title (involving an appropriate unit determination), may, during the 60-day period beginning on the date on which the order was issued, institute and action for judicial review of the Authority's order in the United States court of appeals in the circuit in which the person resides or transacts business or in the United States Court of Appeals for the District of Columbia.

(b) The Authority may petition any appropriate United States court of appeals for the enforcement of any order of the Authority and for appropriate temporary relief or restraining order.

(c) Upon the filing of a petition under subsection (a) of this section for judicial review or under subsection (b) of this section for enforcement, the Authority shall file in the court the record in the proceedings, as provided in section 2112 of title 28. Upon the filing of the petition, the court shall cause notice thereof to be served to the parties involved, and thereupon shall have jurisdiction of the proceeding and of the question determined therein and may grant any temporary relief (including a temporary restraining order) it considers just and proper, and may make and enter a decree affirming and enforcing, modifying and enforcing as so modified, or setting aside in whole or in part the order of the Authority. The filing of a petition under subsection (a) or (b) of this section shall not operate as a stay of the Authority's order unless the court specifically orders the stay. Review of the Authority's order shall be on the record in accordance with section 706 of this title. No objection that has not been urged before the Authority, or its designee, shall be considered by the court, unless the failure or neglect to urge the objection is excused because of extraordinary circumstances. The findings of the Authority with respect to questions of fact, if supported by substantial evidence on the record considered as a whole, shall be conclusive. If any person applies to the court for leave to adduce additional evidence and shows to the satisfaction of the court that the additional evidence is material and that there were reasonable grounds for the failure to adduce the evidence in the hearing before the Authority, or its designee, and to be made a part of the record. The Authority may modify its findings as to the facts, or make new findings by reason of additional evidence so taken and filed. The Authority shall file its modified or new findings, which, with respect to questions of fact, if supported by substantial evidence on the record considered as a whole, shall be conclusive. The Authority shall file its recommendations, if any for the modification or setting aside of its original order. Upon the filing of the record with the court, the jurisdiction of the court shall be exclusive and its judgment and decree shall be final, except that the judgment and decree shall be subject to review by the Supreme Court of the United States upon writ of certiorari or certification as provided in section 1254 of title 28.

(d) The Authority may, upon issuance of a complaint as provided in section 7118 of this title charging that any person has engaged in or is engaging in an unfair labor practice, petition any United States district court within any district in which the unfair labor practice in question is alleged to have occurred or in which such person resides or transacts business for appropriate temporary relief (including a restraining order). Upon the filing of the petition, the court shall cause notice thereof to be served upon the person, and thereupon shall have jurisdiction to grant any temporary relief (including a temporary restraining order) it considers just and proper. A court shall not grant any temporary relief under this section if it would interfere with the ability of the agency to carry out its essential functions or if the Authority fails to establish probable cause that an unfair labor practice is being committed.

Subchapter IV
Administration and Other Provisions
7131 Official Time

(a) Any employee representing an exclusive representative in the negotiation of a collective bargaining agreement under this chapter shall be authorized official time for such purposes, including attendance at impasse proceeding, during the time the employee otherwise would be in a duty status. The number of employees for whom official time is authorized under this subsection shall not exceed the number of individuals designated as representing the agency for such purposes.

(b) Any activities performed by any employee relating to the internal business of a labor organization (including the solicitation of membership, elections of labor organization officials, and collection of dues) shall be performed during the time the employee is in a nonduty status.

(c) Except as provided in subsection (a) of this section, the Authority shall determine whether any employee participating for, or on behalf of, a labor organization in any phase of proceedings before the Authority shall be authorized official time for such purpose during the time the employee otherwise would be in a duty status.

(d) Except as provided in the preceding subsections of this section –

(1) any employee representing an exclusive representative, or

(2) in connection with any other matter covered by this chapter, any employee in an appropriate unit represented by an exclusive representative.

shall be granted official time in any amount the agency and the exclusive representative involved agree to be reasonable, necessary, and in the public interest.

7132 Subpenas

(a) Any member of the Authority, the General Counsel, or the Panel, any administrative law judge appointed by the Authority under section 3105 of this title, and any employee of the Authority designated by the Authority may –

(1) issue subpenas requiring the attendance and testimony of witnesses and the production of documentary or other evidence from any place in the United States; and

(2) administer oaths, take or order the taking of depositions, order responses to written interrogatories, examine witnesses, and receive evidence.

No subpoena shall be issued under this section which requires the disclosure of intramanagement guidance, advise, counsel, or training within an agency or between an agency and the Office of Personnel Management.

(b) In the case of contumacy or failure to obey a subpoena issued under subsection (a)(1) of this section, the United States district court for the judicial district in which the person to whom the subpoena is addressed resides or is served may issue an order requiring such person to appear at any designated place to testify or to produce documentary or other evidence. Any failure to obey the order of the court may be punished by the court as a contempt thereof.

(c) Witnesses (whether appearing voluntarily or under subpoena) shall be paid the same fee and mileage allowances which are paid subpoenaed witnesses in the courts of the United States.

7133 Compilation and Publication of Data

(a) The Authority shall maintain a file of its proceedings and copies of all available agreements and arbitration decisions, and shall publish the texts of its decisions and the actions taken by the Panel under section 7119 of this title.

(b) All files maintained under subsection (a) of this section shall be open to inspection and reproduction in accordance with the provisions of sections 552 and 552a of this title.

7134 Regulations

The Authority, the General Counsel, the Federal Mediation and Conciliation Service, the Assistant Secretary of Labor for Labor Management Relations, and the Panel shall each prescribe rules and regulations to carry out the provisions of this chapter applicable to each of them, respectively. Provisions of subchapter II of chapter 5 of this title shall be applicable to the issuance, revision, or repeal of any such rule or regulation.

7135 Continuation of Existing Laws, Recognitions, Agreements, and Procedures

(a) Nothing contained in this chapter shall preclude (1) the renewal or continuation of an exclusive recognition, certification of an exclusive representative, or a lawful agreement between an agency and an exclusive representative of its employees, which is entered into before the effective date of this chapter; or (2) the renewal, continuation, or initial according of recognition for units of management officials or supervisors represented by labor organizations which historically or traditionally represent management officials or supervisors in private industry and which hold exclusive recognition for units of such officials or supervisors in any agency on the effective date of this chapter.

(b) Policies, regulations, and procedures established under and decisions issued under Executive Orders 11491, 11616, 11636, 11787, and 11838, or under any other Executive order, as in effect on the effective date of this chapter, shall remain in full force and effect until revised or revoked by the President, or unless superseded by specific provisions of this chapter or by regulations or decisions issued pursuant to this chapter.

Appendix B
10 Cases Recommended for Reading

Appendix B: 10 Cases Recommended for Reading

This appendix contains 10 cases recommended for reading to gain an insight into how the FLRA makes decisions and provides some of the most important concepts in federal labor relations. By no means is this an exhaustive list of cases you should know. The FLRA has issued over 66 Volumes of FLRA Decisions. These 10 cases are probably less than 1 % of all the cases that the FLRA has issued since its inception in 1978. It is hoped reading these cases will spark your interest in federal labor relations. Reading cases gives you an understanding of what takes place in federal labor relations and how the issues are handled by both labor and management.

Case #1 Flagrant Misconduct Standard

Department of the Air Force, Grissom Air Force Base, Indiana and American Federation of Government Employees, AFL-CIO, 51 FLRA NO.2 (1995)

See also, Federal Aviation Administration, 64 FLRA No. 66 (2010), *and Social Security Administration,* 64 FLRA 599 (2010).

Case #2 Bad Faith Bargaining

U.S. Department of the Air Force, Headquarters, Air Force Logistics Command, Wright-Patterson Air Force Base, Ohio and American Federation of Government Employees, Council 214, 36 FLRA No. 62 (1990)

See also, Dept. of Justice, Executive Office for Immigration Review, 61 FLRA No. 89 (2006)

Case #3 Definition of Working Conditions

Antilles Consolidated Education Association Union and Antilles Consolidated School System, 22 FLRA No. 23, (1986)

See also, Dept. of the Air Force, Luke Air Force Base, 64 FLRA 642 (2010).

Case #4 Discrimination Against Union Representatives

Letterkenny Army Depot and International Brotherhood of Police Officers, Local 358, 35 FLRA No. 15 (1990)

Case #5 Appropriate Arrangements

National Treasury Employees Union and U.S. Department of Commerce Patent and Trademark Office, 53 FLRA No. 59, 1997

See also, Internal Revenue Service, 66 FLRA No. 35 (2011); *Environmental Protection Agency,* 65 FLRA 113 (2010); and *Dept. of the Treasury, Bureau of the Public Debt,* 65 FLRA No.109 (2011)

Case #6 Particularized Need Criteria for Information Requests by the Union

United States Department of Justice, Immigration and Naturalization Service. Western Regional Office, Labor Management Relations, Laguna Niguel, California and United States Department of Justice, Immigration and Naturalization Service U.S. Border Patrol, Tucson Sector, Tucson, Arizona and American Federation of Government Employees, National Border Patrol Council, Local 2544, AFL-CIO 58 FLRA No. 16, (2003)

Case #7 Past Practice

United States Department of Homeland Security, Border and Transportation Directorate, Bureau of Customs and Border Protection and National Treasury Employees Union, 59 FLRA No. 165 (2004)

See also, U.S. Air Force Academy 65 FLRA No. 158 (2011)

Case #8 Appropriate Unit Criteria for Determining Whether a Petitioned for Bargaining Unit is Appropriate

United States Department of the Air Force, Lackland Air Force Base, San Antonio, Texas and American Federation of Government Employees, AFL-CIO, 59 FLRA No. 133 (2004)

Case #9 Right to Assign Work

American Federation of Government Employees, Local 3392 and U.S. Government Printing Office, Public Documents Distribution Center, Pueblo, Colorado, 52 FLRA No. 15, (1996)

Case #10 Limitation on Bargaining – Federal Statute

National Federation of Federal Employees, Local 29 and U.S. Department of the Army, Engineer District Kansas City, Missouri, 45 FLRA No. 53 (1992)

Case #1 Flagrant Misconduct Standard

51 FLRA No. 2
Federal Labor Relations Authority
Washington, D.C.

Department of the Air Force
Grissom Air Force Base, Indiana
(Activity/Respondent)
and
American Federation of Government
Employees, AFL-CIO
(Union/Charging Party)
CH-CA-30596

Decision and Order
August 18, 1995

Before the Authority: Phyllis N. Segal, Chair; and Tony Armendariz, Member

I. Statement of the Case

This unfair labor practice case is before the Authority on exceptions to the attached decision of the Administrative Law Judge filed by the General Counsel. The Respondent filed a motion to strike the General Counsel's exceptions and the General Counsel filed a motion to strike the Respondent's motion. The Respondent also filed a reply to the General Counsel's motion to strike.

The complaint alleges that the Respondent violated section 7116(a)(1) and (2) of the Federal Service Labor-Management Relations Statute (the Statute) by suspending the Union Vice- President for activities protected by the Statute.

Upon consideration of the Judge's decision and the entire record, we adopt the Judge's findings, conclusions, and recommended Order only to the extent consistent with this decision. We conclude that the Respondent violated the Statute, as alleged in the complaint.

II. Judge's Decision

The facts are fully set forth in the Judge's decision and are only briefly summarized here.

The Respondent suspended Union Vice-President Melvin Smith for 14 days based on his alleged: (1) use of discourteous, abusive, offensive, and sexually harassing language; (2) unauthorized absence of 2 hours; and (3) deliberate misrepresentation of the facts by failing to inform his supervisor that realignment negotiations had been canceled. The first allegation was based on the following statements by Smith to the Respondent's Chief Negotiator:

"You can't be that fu--ing stupid, lady... I always knew you was stupid, I knew you was goddamn stupid[.]"

Judge's Decision at 5, 6 (quoting Tr. at 91, 92). The statements were made during a negotiation session wherein the Union received a letter from the Respondent which canceled previously agreed-upon bargaining over realignment.

Citing *American Federation of Government Employees, National Border Patrol Council and U.S. Department of Justice, Immigration and Naturalization Service, El Paso Border Patrol Sector*, 44 FLRA 1395 (1992) (INS) and *Department of the Navy, Naval Facilities Engineering Command, Western Division San Bruno, California*, 45 FLRA 138 (1992) (Member Armendariz concurring in part and dissenting in part) (*Naval Facilities Engineering Command*), the Judge stated that Smith could not be disciplined for his remarks unless his remarks constituted "flagrant misconduct." Judge's Decision at 9. The Judge found that "the use of the 'f' word, as with other profane words, standing alone, does not constitute flagrant misconduct[,]" but that "vicious, vulgar[,] personal attacks of a highly sexual nature during negotiations is [sic] not protected activity." *Id.* In this regard, the Judge found that Smith and the Union President "combined in a vicious, vulgar, personal attack" on the Respondent's chief negotiator.[1] *Id.* The Judge concluded that "[t]heir language constituted flagrant misconduct[.]" *Id.* The Judge further concluded that, because the Union negotiators' conduct was not protected, the Respondent did not violate the Statute by disciplining Smith. Accordingly, the Judge dismissed the complaint.

III. Positions of the Parties

A. General Counsel's Exceptions

The General Counsel contends that Smith was engaged in protected union activity when he made the statements and that, under Authority precedent, Smith's statements were not of such an outrageous or insubordinate nature as to remove them from the protection of the Statute. Among other things, the General Counsel claims that Smith's statements were provoked by the Respondent's cancellation of the realignment negotiations.[2] The General Counsel also alleges that the Judge incorrectly "merged the remarks of [the Union President] and Smith and treated them as one for purposes of his analysis." Exceptions at 9.

The General Counsel alleges that the unauthorized absence and misrepresentation allegations were "nothing more than spurious make-weight charges." Id. at 6 n.2.[3] The General Counsel requests that the Authority order the Respondent to rescind Smith's 14-day suspension, expunge any reference to it from his records, and award him backpay, with interest, and any benefits lost due to the 14-day suspension.

B. Respondent's Motion to Strike, General Counsel's Response and Respondent's Reply

The Respondent moves to strike the General Counsel's exceptions on the ground that the exceptions raise an issue that was not previously raised before the Judge and, as such, are precluded from consideration by section 2429.5 of the Authority's Regulations.[4] The Respondent asserts that the General Counsel argues for the first time in its exceptions that Smith's conduct at the bargaining session should be analyzed separately from that of the Union President.

In response, the General Counsel contends that the Respondent's motion to strike constitutes an opposition or a cross-exception to the General Counsel's exceptions and, as such, is untimely under section 2423.28(b) of the Authority's Regulations.[5]

In reply, the Respondent argues that its motion to strike is not a response to the General Counsel's exceptions, but, rather, a request for legal relief from the opposing party's failure to adhere to section 2429.5 of the Authority's Regulations.

IV. Analysis and Conclusions

A. Procedural Issue

We reject the Respondent's motion to strike the General Counsel's exceptions because the Respondent has failed to comply with section 2423.28(b) of the Authority's Regulations. Despite its caption, the Respondent's motion presents arguments about the merits of the General Counsel's exceptions and, as such, is an opposition to the exceptions. As the Respondent did not request permission to file an additional submission, the opposition is untimely filed and will not be considered.[6] See *U.S. Department of Justice, Immigration and Naturalization Service, Border Patrol, El Paso, Texas*, 37 FLRA 1310, 1311-13 (1990).

Moreover, even if we were to find the submission properly filed as a motion to strike and, therefore, timely, the Respondent's assertions do not provide a basis for barring the General Counsel's argument under section 2429.5 of our Regulations as presenting an "issue which was not presented in the proceedings before the... Judge." The Judge found that the Respondent did not violate the Statute by disciplining Smith because the language of both the Union President and Smith constituted flagrant misconduct. The complaint does not allege, and it is not apparent that it was argued to the Judge, that Smith was or could be disciplined for comments other than his own. Given this, the General Counsel's arguments are in response to the Judge's findings and, as such, could not have been made prior to the Judge's decision. Accordingly, they are not precluded by our Regulations.

B. Merits

Section 7102 of the Statute guarantees employees the right to form, join, or assist any labor organization, or to refrain from such activity, without fear of penalty or reprisal. *INS*, 44 FLRA 1402. A union representative has the right to use "intemperate, abusive, or insulting language without fear of restraint or penalty" if he or she believes such rhetoric to be an effective means to make the union's point. *Naval Facilities Engineering Command*, 45 FLRA at 155 (quoting *Old Dominion Branch No. 46, National Association of Letter Carriers, AFL-CIO v. Austin*, 418 U.S. 264, 283 (1984)). Consistent with section 7102, however, an agency has the right to discipline an employee who is engaged in otherwise protected activity for remarks or actions that "exceed the boundaries of protected activity such as flagrant misconduct." *U.S. Air Force Logistics Command, Tinker Air Force Base, Oklahoma City, Oklahoma and American Federation of Government Employees, Local 916, AFL-CIO*, 34 FLRA 385, 389 (1990) (citation omitted) (Tinker AFB). Remarks or conduct that are of such "an outrageous and insubordinate nature" as to remove them from the protection of the Statute constitute flagrant misconduct. *Naval Facilities Engineering Command*, 45 FLRA at 156; Tinker AFB, 34 FLRA at 390.

In determining whether an employee has engaged in flagrant misconduct, the Authority balances the employee's right to engage in protected activity, which "permits leeway for impulsive behavior,... against the employer's right to maintain order and respect for its supervisory staff on the jobsite." *Department of Defense, Defense Mapping Agency Aerospace Center, St. Louis, Missouri*, 17 FLRA 71, 80 (1985) (Defense Mapping Agency) (quoting *Department of the Navy, Puget Sound Naval Shipyard, Bremerton, Washington*, 2 FLRA 54, 55 (1979) (*Puget Sound*)). Relevant factors in striking this balance include: (1) the place and subject matter of the discussion; (2) whether the employee's outburst was impulsive or designed; (3) whether the outburst was in any way provoked by the employer's conduct; and (4) the nature of the intemperate language and conduct. *Defense Mapping Agency*, 17 FLRA at 80-81 (1985) (Authority adopted Judge's decision which noted the foregoing factors to be considered in determining whether an action constitutes flagrant misconduct). However, the foregoing factors need not be cited or applied in any particular way in determining whether an action constitutes flagrant misconduct. *Cf. U.S. Department of Defense, Defense Logistics Agency and American Federation of Government Employees, Local 2693*, 50 FLRA 212, 217-18 (1995) (Authority denied agency's exceptions contending that an arbitration award was contrary to law because the arbitrator did not apply all of the Defense Mapping Agency factors in determining that the grievant's language did not constitute flagrant misconduct).

In this case, there is no contention that the remarks were made in front of other employees on the job site or that they disrupted the work of the unit. Moreover, it is undisputed that Smith's language was impulsive rather than designed. Although the extent to which Smith's comments were "provoked" by the Respondent's conduct is not clear, the record shows that the comments were made in reaction to a letter from the Respondent canceling certain previously agreed-upon negotiations about which the union had received no prior notification. In addition, while the remarks made by Smith were offensive and should not be condoned, when examined as a whole and in context, they were not of such an outrageous and insubordinate nature as to remove them from the protection of the Statute.[7] In this regard, Smith's remarks are similar to remarks found not to constitute flagrant misconduct in other cases. For example, *INS*, 44 FLRA at 1402 (grievant calling a supervisor an "asshole" and a "space cadet" did not constitute flagrant misconduct). *Cf. Puget Sound*, 2 FLRA at 75 (Authority concluded that, under Executive Order 11491, as amended, a union official was improperly suspended for remarking to a supervisor, "I am going to get your ass[,]" when seeking permission to meet with another union official).

Based on the foregoing, and on the Statute, prior precedent compels us to find that Smith's remarks did not constitute flagrant misconduct. Therefore, the Respondent violated section 7116(a)(1) and (2) by disciplining Smith, based, in part, on those remarks. See, e.g., *id.*

V. Remedy

The Authority will order a make-whole remedy where there is discrimination in connection with conditions of employment based on unlawful consideration of protected union activity and the respondent has not shown that it would have taken the same action in the absence of such consideration. *E.g., Department of the Army, Headquarters, XVIII Airborne Corps and Fort Bragg, Fort Bragg, North Carolina*, 43 FLRA 1414, 1418 (1992).

In this case, there is no evidence or contention that the Respondent would have disciplined Smith in the absence of consideration of the remarks he made at the negotiation session. Therefore, we find that a make-whole remedy, requiring that the Respondent expunge the suspension from Smith's records and make him whole for loss of pay and benefits he incurred, is appropriate and necessary to effectuate the purposes and policies of the Statute.[8] Accordingly, we will order the Respondent to: (1) rescind Smith's 14-day suspension; (2) expunge all references to the suspension from Smith's personnel records and any other agency files; (3) make Smith whole for any backpay, including interest, and benefits lost due to the suspension.

VI. Order

Pursuant to section 2423.29 of the Authority's Regulations and section 7118 of the Federal Service Labor-Management Relations Statute, the Department of the Air Force, Grissom Air Force Base, Indiana, shall:

1. Cease and desist from:

(a) Interfering with, restraining, or coercing its employees by disciplining Melvin Smith or any representative of the American Federation of Government Employees, AFL-CIO, the exclusive representative of a unit of its employees, for protected conduct engaged in while performing union representational duties.

(b) In any like or related manner, interfering with, restraining, or coercing its employees in the exercise of rights assured them by the Statute.

2. Take the following affirmative actions in order to effectuate the purposes and policies of the Statute:

(a) Expunge from its files all records of, and references, to the 14-day suspension given to Melvin Smith and make Smith whole by reimbursing him for the losses he incurred as a result of the 14-day suspension, including back pay with interest, and any other benefits lost due to the suspension.

(b) Post at its facilities throughout the Department of the Air Force, Grissom Air Force Base, Indiana, where bargaining unit employees represented by the American Federation of Government Employees, AFL-CIO, are located, copies of the attached Notice on forms to be furnished by the Federal Labor Relations Authority. Upon receipt of such forms, they shall be signed by the Commanding Officer, and they shall be posted and maintained for 60 consecutive days thereafter in conspicuous places, including all bulletin boards and other places where notices to employees are customarily posted. Reasonable steps shall be taken to ensure that such Notices are not altered, defaced, or covered by any other material.

(c) Pursuant to section 2423.30 of the Authority's Rules and Regulations, in writing, within 30 days from the date of this Order, as to what steps have been taken to comply.

NOTICE TO ALL EMPLOYEES AS ORDERED BY THE FEDERAL LABOR RELATIONS AUTHORITY AND TO EFFECTUATE THE POLICIES OF THE FEDERAL SERVICE LABOR-MANAGEMENT RELATIONS STATUTE

WE NOTIFY OUR EMPLOYEES THAT:

We will not interfere with, restrain, or coerce our employees by disciplining Melvin Smith or any representative of the American Federation of Government Employees, AFL-CIO, the exclusive representative of a unit of our employees, for protected conduct engaged in while performing union representational duties.

We will not in any like or related manner, interfere with, restrain, or coerce our employees in the exercise of rights assured them by the Federal Service Labor-Management Relations Statute.

We will expunge from our files all records of, and references to, the 14-day suspension given to Melvin Smith and make Smith whole by reimbursing him for the losses he incurred as a result of the 14-day suspension, including back pay with interest, and any other benefits lost due to the suspension.

_____
(Activity)

Dated:_____
By:_____
(Signature) (Title)

This Notice must remain posted for 60 consecutive days from the date of posting and must not be altered, defaced, or covered by any other material.

If employees have any questions concerning this Notice or compliance with its provisions, they may communicate directly with the Regional Director of the Chicago Regional Office, Federal Labor Relations Authority, whose address is: 55 West Monroe Street, Suite 1150, Chicago, Illinois 60603, and whose telephone number is: (312) 353-6306.

UNITED STATES OF AMERICA
FEDERAL LABOR RELATIONS AUTHORITY
OFFICE OF ADMINISTRATIVE LAW JUDGES
WASHINGTON, D.C. 20424-0001

Case No. CH-CA-30596

DEPARTMENT OF THE AIR FORCE GRISSOM AIR FORCE BASE, INDIANA
Respondent
and
AMERICAN FEDERATION OF GOVERNMENT EMPLOYEES, AFL-CIO
Charging Party

Major David L. Frishberg
For the Respondent
Philip T. Roberts, Esquire
For the General Counsel
Mr. Fred Hartig
For the Charging Party
Before: WILLIAM B. DEVANEY
Administrative Law Judge

DECISION

Statement of the Case

This proceeding, under the Federal Service Labor-Management Relations Statute, Chapter 71 of Title 5 of the United States Code, 5 U.S.C. § 7101, et seq.1, and the Rules and Regulations issued thereunder, 5 C.F.R. § 2423.1, et seq., concerns whether certain statements, made by Union officials at a bargaining session to a female representative of Respondent, which were vile, obscene and of an explicitly sexual nature, constituted protected activity. For reasons fully set forth hereinafter, I find the statements did not constitute protected activity and that the discipline imposed for misconduct did not violate §§ 16(a)(1) or (2) of the Statute.

This case was initiated by a charge filed on April 15, 1993 (G.C. Exh. 1(a)), which alleged violations of §§ 16(a)(1), (3), (4) and (8) of the Statute; and by an amended charge filed on July 22, 1993 (G.C. Exh. 4(b)), which alleged violations of §§ 16(a)(1), (2) and (4) of the Statute. The Complaint and Notice of Hearing issued on November 23, 1993 (G.C. Exh. 4(d)); alleged violations of §§ 16(a)(1) and (2) only; and ordered that the hearing be held at a date, time and place to be determined. By Notice dated December 8, 1993 (G.C. Exh. 4(h)), this case, and a number of other cases, were set for hearing on January 26, 1994, in Indianapolis, Indiana, pursuant to which a hearing was duly held in Indianapolis, Indiana, on January 26, 1994, before the undersigned. All parties were represented at the hearing, were afforded full opportunity to be heard, to introduce evidence bearing on the issues involved, and were afforded the opportunity to present oral argument, which Respondent exercised. At the conclusion of the hearing, February 28, 1994, was fixed as the date for mailing post-hearing briefs, which time was subsequently extended, on separate motions of Respondent and of General Counsel, to which the parties did not object, for good cause shown, to March 28, 1994. General Counsel and Respondent each timely mailed a brief, received on, or before, April 5, 1994, which have been carefully considered. Upon the basis of the entire record, including my observation of the witnesses and their demeanor, I make the following findings and conclusions:

Findings of Fact

1. The American Federation of Government Employees, Local 3254 (hereinafter, "Union") is the exclusive representative of a unit of all appropriated fund professional and non-professional employees at Grissom Air Force Base, Indiana (hereinafter, "Respondent")(G.C. Exhs. 4(d) and (f)).

2. The host unit at Respondent had been the 305th Air Refueling Wing, an active duty unit. The 434th Wing, a reserve unit that includes a fighter component and a tanker component, had been a tenant at Respondent (Tr. 41-42). In 1991, the Base Closure Commission recommended, and the President approved, that Grissom, while not to be closed, should be realigned; that the 305th Air Refueling Wing be deactivated and its planes sent to other bases; and that on, or about, September 30, 1994, Grissom be turned over to the reserves, i.e., the 434th Wing would then become the host (Tr. 42). The Union was notified of the realignment in 1991, requested bargaining and, on February 12, 1992, the parties signed off on ground rules for realignment and contract negotiations (G.C. Exh. 16; Tr. 46). The ground rules provided, inter alia, that each team would consist of four negotiators, including the Chief Negotiator; that realignment negotiations would be held on Thursday from 0800 to 1130 and that contract negotiations would be held on Fridays from 0800 to 1130; and that, '9.' The union teams (Contract and Realignment) will be given a total of 144 hours a week of official time... to be used for both negotiations and preparation time. This time is agreed to be used on Wednesdays, Thursdays and Fridays. 10. It is agreed that the 144 hours... will be used for both Realignment and on going Contract negotiations. 11. The union team will be given an aggregate total of 256 hours for preparation time (used for purpose of Realignment negotiations). This preparation time is to be used prior to 6 Mar 92...." (G.C. Exh. 16).

3. By letter dated March 25, 1992 (G.C. Exh. 18), the Union submitted a list of 18 issues over which it wished to negotiate (G.C. Exh. 18; Tr. 52). The parties negotiated over the items, one at a time, from March 1992, but by December 11, 1992, had resolved only about three or four of the issues listed in the Union's letter of March 25 (Tr. 55). Also, at some point (the date was not shown) after negotiating on two Articles of the Union's choice, one of which was resolved by agreement and the other the Union requested mediation, other contract negotiations had been postponed (G.C. Exh. 31).

4. Present at the December 3, 1992, negotiating session for the Union were: Fred Hartig,[2] Chief negotiator; Melvin David Smith3; James L. Dicken; and Troy Prior (Tr. 56, 88, 114, 140-141, 182, 198, 212). Present on December 3, 1992, for Respondent were: Ms. Sula C. Smith, Chief Negotiator; Lieutenant Colonel Michael A. Moran; Ms. Patricia Craddock; and John A. Pepper (Tr. 56, 140, 181-182, 198, 212). The first

order of business was to sign an agreement on training and development (Tr. 56). All four people on each team signed the agreement and Ms. Sula Smith made and distributed copies (Tr. 56). Then, Ms. Sula Smith handed Mr. Hartig the following letter:

FROM: 305 MSSQ/MSCE

3 December 1992

SUBJ: Negotiations, AFGE Local 3254 and Grissom Air Force Base

TO: Fred Hartig, President, AFGE Local 3254

1. You requested, on behalf of Local 3254, to enter into full contract negotiations. After much discussion, you and management agreed that negotiations could be postponed until August 1993. We requested that the verbal agreement be put in writing to assure complete understanding. You did submit to the Civilian Personnel Office an agreement to be signed by management and Local 3254 expressing that you would agree to postponing the contract negotiations if certain stipulations would be agreed to by management.

2. After consideration of the entire proposal to postpone the contract negotiations, management cannot agree to all the stipulations requested so therefore, we will enter into full contract negotiations as you previously requested.

3. This means that ground rules for full contract negotiations must be negotiated. The Parking Proposal submitted to the realignment negotiating team applies to current contract article XXXXV; as such, we will defer negotiations on that subject until full contract negotiations begin. Our original agreement regarding contract negotiations resulted in negotiating the two articles of your choice. Management did not agree to add, supplement, or change any other contract article. An agreement was reached on one of the articles, Performance Evaluations, and you have unilaterally requested mediation on the compressed work schedule portion of the Work Schedule article. Since we will be entering into full contract negotiations, we will be prepared to finalize that article at that time. With that said, the ground rules for realignment and contract negotiations are no longer valid.

4. All realignment negotiations, the ground rules associated with realignment negotiations, and all official time for realignment negotiations will cease as of the end of the negotiations meeting on 3 December 1992.

Any future meetings to discuss the Training Committee plans and recommendations will be by mutual consent of the current assigned chief negotiators.

5. Please contact me to discuss the date, time, and place for the initial meeting to discuss the ground rules for full contract negotiations. Management will appoint two members to negotiate the ground rules...." (G.C. Exh. 31).

Mr. Hartig became angry, his voice became louder and louder, his face became red and he made some vile comments to Ms. Smith (Tr. 142), including, "We're going to shove this up your a--" (Tr. 67, 142, 183, 200) and that "...the FLRA will shove this up your a--" (Tr. 67). Ms. Smith told Mr. Hartig that she didn't think that language was appropriate[4] (Tr. 92, 142, 183, 201) and Mr. Hartig replied, "I don't give a f--- what you think" (Tr. 68, 184). Mr. Hartig repeatedly screamed, are you, "...refusing to negotiate...." (Tr. 143) but Ms. Smith's reply that no, she was not refusing to negotiate but wanted to negotiate (Tr. 143, 202) was either ignored or fell on deaf ears. Only Mr. Hartig had the letter, but, at about this point, Mr. Melvin Smith reached over and pulled the letter over in front of himself so he could read it (Tr. 90). As he read the letter, he got mad and said loudly, "You can't be that f-----g stupid, lady" (Tr. 91), as Mr. Smith and Col. Moran (Tr. 183) stated; "You're f-----g stupid, lady" (Tr. 59-60, 78) as Mr. Hartig, Ms. Smith (Tr. 144) and Ms. Craddock (Tr. 202-203) said; "You're f-----g stupid" (Tr. 116), as Mr. Prior said. Mr. Melvin Smith stated that he then[5], "...started yelling. I says, 'I always knew you was stupid, I knew you was god damn stupid,' and all that." (Tr. 92), as Mr. Smith stated; "I always thought you were stupid and now I know it." (Tr. 144), as Ms. Smith and Ms. Craddock stated (Tr. 202) (Mr. Hartig seems by inference to have agreed with Ms. Smith's and Ms. Craddock's statement (Tr. 78)). Shortly, thereafter, Mr. Hartig called a caucus (Tr. 60) and the Union members left the negotiating room and went downstairs and outside to the covered porch area. (Tr. 60, 146). Respondent's negotiators remained in the negotiating room for a time, but after a while, someone asked, "Why are we staying" since it appeared that there was no prospect for productive negotiations (Tr. 146). All were taken aback by what had occurred and agreed that it would be best if they broke off and left. So, they got their coats, gathered up their papers and left (Tr. 147). As they approached the Union negotiators on the porch area, Mr. Hartig asked Ms. Smith, "Are you ending the negotiating session?" and Ms. Smith replied, "Yes, we are. And it's time for you folks to go back to work" or "You all should return to work." (Tr. 93, 147, 188, 206). Mr. Hartig told Ms. Smith, "You can suck my6 d---." (Tr. 147-148, 188, 206, 217). Mr. Hartig told his team members to contact their supervisors (Tr. 94).

6. Mr. Melvin Smith went to the Union office (Tr. 94) and he testified that he called his shop[7] but his supervisor, Mr. Daro Johnson, was not in and he had told Ms. Gross, another employee in the shop, who answered the telephone, that he would call back later (Tr. 95). Mr. Smith further testified that about 45 minutes later, he called his shop again, but again, Mr. Johnson was not in and that he told Mr. Bobby Stevens, another fellow employee, who answered the telephone, that he would call back later (Tr. 95). Mr. Smith called again "right before lunchtime" and talked to Mr. Johnson (Tr. 95). There is no dispute that Mr. Smith did not tell Mr. Johnson that realignment negotiations had ended (Tr. 107, 108, 226, 227). Mr. Smith testified that he, "...told him [Johnson] that I was going to be on official time in the afternoon for representational." (Tr. 95). Mr. Johnson testified that Mr. Smith, "...told me he needed some prep time because he was getting ready to go do some training in Cleveland. And I told him it was okay because, 'You were already on prep time for negotiation and the time that you needed to do the paperwork to go to this training... go ahead." (Tr. 226). I do not credit Mr. Smith's testimony. First, his statement that he told Mr. Johnson "I'm not going to be working contract negotiations this afternoon" (Tr. 96) is inconsistent with his later concession that he had not told Mr. Johnson that negotiations had been cancelled (Tr. 108). Second, Mr. Smith's statement that Mr. Johnson told him, "'Well, you didn't need to call me," and I said, 'Well, that's right. I just wanted to keep you informed,' and hung up." (Tr. 96), closely follows, and strongly supports, Mr. Johnson's testimony. Accordingly, I credit Mr. Johnson's testimony that Mr. Smith said he needed some prep time.

7. The conduct of Messrs. Hartig and Smith was immediately reported by Ms. Sula Smith to the legal office (Tr. 149). She was so upset and distraught that she had to go home (Tr. 149), but after about an hour and a half returned to work and prepared her statement of what had occurred that morning at the negotiating session (G.C. Exh. 47, Attachment 1). The other members of Respondent's negotiating team also prepared statements, either that day or the following day, December 4, 1992 (G.C. Exh. 47, Attach- ment 2, 3 and 4). Ms. Smith continued to have serious emotional problems and was required to seek mental counseling, at her personal expense (Tr. 154).

8 By memorandum dated December 16, 1992 (G.C. Exh. 47) Mr. Johnson gave Mr. Melvin Smith notice of a proposed 14 day suspension (G.C. Exh. 47; Tr. 97, 98). Three grounds were asserted: "a. *Use of discourteous, abusive, offensive, and sexually harassing language.*"; "b. *Unauthorized absence of 2 hours.*"; and "c. *Deliberate misrepresentation.*" (G.C. Exh. 47; Tr. 98). Mr. Smith made an oral reply to Mr. John Burks on February 8, 1993 (Tr. 98, 254) and by memorandum dated March 5, 1993, Mr. Burks, Aircraft Engine Mechanic Foreman, affirmed the proposed suspension (G.C. Exh. 48; Tr. 98, 225). Mr. Hartig also was disciplined for his conduct during the negotiating session of December 3, 1992 (Tr. 71); took his case to arbitration and lost (Tr. 71), although he stated, "It's under appeal." (Tr. 71).

Conclusions

The central and controlling issue in this case is whether the language used by the Union negotiators at the negotiating session of December 3, 1992, constituted protected activity. I am well aware that the Supreme Court, in a case under the Executive Order, held, *inter alia,* that, "...the same federal policies favoring uninhibited, robust, and wide-open debate in labor disputes are applicable...."[8] (*Old Dominion Branch No. 496, National Association of Letter Carriers, AFL-CIO v. Austin,* 418 U.S. 264, 273 (1974) (hereinafter referred to as, "Letter Carriers").

and that,

"...we see nothing in the Executive Order which indicates that it intended to restrict in any way the robust debate which has been protected under the NLRA. Such evidence as is available, rather, demonstrates that the same tolerance for union speech which has long characterized our labor relations in the private sector has been carried over under the Executive Order...." (id., at 275).

I am also well aware that the Authority has adopted the reasoning of *Letter Carriers, supra, Department of the Navy, Naval Facilities Engineering Command, Western Division, San Bruno, California,* 45 FLRA 138, 155-156 (1992) (hereinafter referred to as, "San Bruno"). Indeed, the Authority has made it clear that, "...to exceed the protection of the Statute... remarks must have constituted 'flagrant misconduct.'" *American Federation of Government Employees, National Border Patrol Council,* 44

FLRA 1395, 1402 (1992); San Bruno, supra, 45 FLRA at 156. Profanity and/or insults uttered during negotiations must be accepted as "intemperate, abusive, or insulting language", supra, n.7, which may be used without fear of restraint or penalty, see, for example: Department of Treasury, Internal Revenue Service, Memphis Service Center, 16 FLRA 687, 696 (1984). The use of the "f" word, as with other profane words, standing alone, does not constitute flagrant misconduct. Negotiations are not Sunday School exercises; nevertheless, vicious, vulgar, personal attacks of a highly sexual nature during negotiations is not protected activity. Messrs. Hartig and Smith combined in a vicious, uncouth, rude, vulgar and profane personal attack on Ms. Sula Smith. Mr. Hartig's voice was loud, his face red and his manner threatening when he shouted, inter alia, "We're going to shove this up your a--" and,"...the FLRA will shove this up your a--;" when Ms. Smith said that language was not appropriate, Mr. Hartig shouted in reply, "I don't give a f--- what you think." Mr. Smith joined in and said loudly, "you can't be that f------ stupid, lady;" and then yelled, "I always knew you was stupid, I knew you was god damn stupid" or "I always thought you were stupid and now I know it." Then, outside as they were leaving, Mr. Hartig told Ms. Smith, "You can suck my d---." Their language constituted flagrant misconduct; was not protected conduct; and both Mr. Hartig and Mr. Smith were disciplined for their flagrant misconduct. *Department of Defense, Defense Mapping Agency, Aerospace Center, St. Louis, Missouri*, 17 FLRA 71 (1985).

Perhaps Ms. Sula Smith earned no kudos for diplomacy by her letter of December 3, 1992, to Mr. Hartig; but even the most cursory examination would have shown that negotiations were not being terminated, but only that realignment negotiations were ended and the parties would now move to full contract negotiations. She did nothing to provoke the loud, obscene diatribe inflicted upon her by Messrs. Hartig and Smith. She did not raise her voice, she did not use abusive or foul language, and she did not make derogatory comments (Tr. 124). Union negotiator Dicken was embarrassed by the conduct of Hartig and Melvin Smith (Tr. 215). Col. Moran was "taken back"; disappointed that people he had worked with for 10 1/2 months would say those kind of things; disgusted (Tr. 184); asked, "Do we really have to take that kind of language?" (Tr. 186). Ms. Craddock was shocked, appalled and embarrassed (Tr. 201); and Ms. Sula Smith had never heard such language used (Tr. 146), was surprised, hurt and quite embarrassed (Tr. 142). Indeed, as noted above, as a result of the vile and abusive personal attack of Messrs. Hartig and Smith, Ms. Sula Smith had to seek counseling, at her personal expense.

There is no probative evidence that the disciplinary action taken was because of the engagement in protected activity as officers of the Union.9 To the contrary, there is no question that the conduct in question occurred; that the incident was reported immediately after it occurred; that an investigation was promptly activated by the report of the incident; and that discipline was imposed because of the flagrant misconduct. Whether the asserted charges of unauthorized absence of two hours and/or deliberate misrepresentation would have been sustained if grieved, they were factually correct, as I have found, and can not be deemed to demonstrate pretext10; but even if these two charges were without basis, the first and primary charge of "Use of discourteous, abusive, offensive, and sexually harassing language" was not pretextual in any manner.

Because the conduct was not protected, Respondent did not violate §§ 16(a)(1) or (2) of the Statute for its discipline of Mr. Melvin D. Smith for his flagrant misconduct on December 3, 1992. Accordingly, it is recommended that the Authority adopt the following:

Order

The Complaint in Case No. CH-CA-30596 be, and the same is hereby, dismissed.

WILLIAM B. DEVANEY

Administrative Law Judge

Dated: July 29, 1994

Washington, DC

Footnotes

(If blank, the decision does not have footnotes.)

Authority's Footnotes Follow

1. The Union President's comments are set forth in the Judge's decision and will not be repeated here.

2. The General Counsel requests the Authority to take official notice of the decision of the Administrative Law Judge in *Department of the Air Force, Grissom Air Force Base, Indiana*, Case No. OALJ 94-56 (July 19, 1994), to which no exceptions were filed with the Authority, that the Respondent's cancellation of the

realignment negotiations constituted an unfair labor practice. As there is no assertion or other basis on which to conclude that it would be improper to do so, pursuant to section 2429.5 of the Authority's Regulations, the request is granted.

3. The Judge concluded that, although he would give "no credence to [the unauthorized absence and misrepresentation] charges" if he were an arbitrator deciding their merits, "they were factually correct... and cannot be deemed to demonstrate pretext[.]" Judge's Decision at 10 n.10 (citing Tr. at 268).

4. 5 C.F.R. § 2429.5 provides, in pertinent part: The Authority will not consider evidence offered by a party, or any issue, which was not presented in the proceedings before the Regional Director, Hearing Officers, Administrative Law Judge, or arbitrator....

5. 5 C.F.R. § 2423.28(b) provides that any party may file an opposition to exceptions, and/or cross-exceptions, with the Authority within 10 days after service of any exceptions to an Administrative Law Judge's decision.

6. The exceptions were served on the Respondent, by mail, on September 26, 1994. Accordingly, under 5 C.F.R. §§ 2423.28 and 2429.22, the Respondent had until close of business on October 11, 1994, to file an opposition. The Respondent's motion was filed on October 26, 1994.

7. In addition to the circumstances in which Smith made his remarks, we note that, in a previous negotiation session between the Union and the Respondent, a management representative used similar language in referring to a Union negotiator. Specifically, there is uncontradicted testimony in the record that, during a previous bargaining session, the Agency's chief negotiator asked his Union counterpart: "Are you fu--ing stupid?" Tr. at 119. 8. We express no view regarding the merits of other charges against Smith or whether the Respondent may now institute discipline against Smith based on those charges.

ALJ's Footnotes Follow

1. For convenience of reference, sections of the Statute hereinafter are, also, referred to without inclusion of the initial "71" of the statutory reference, e.g., Section 7116(a)(2) will be referred to, simply, as, "§ 16(a)(2)".

2. Mr. Hartig was also President of the Union.

3. 11/ Mr. Smith was also Executive Vice President of the Union.

4. 12/ I do not credit Mr. Hartig's testimony that Ms. Smith's response to his language had been,

"...She said those type of words don't bother her, keep it up. That's exactly what she said." (Tr. 68).

First, it is directly contradicted by the testimony of Mr. Melvin Smith, Ms. Sula Smith, Col. Moran and Ms. Craddock. Second, I found the testimony of Ms. Smith, Col. Moran and Ms. Craddock convincing and wholly credible in all respects, while the testimony of Mr. Hartig concerning his conduct on December 3, 1992, was not convincing. Indeed, although Mr. Hartig admitted his statements about what would be done with her letter (Tr. 67) and that he used the "f" word (Tr. 68), he denied having made any vulgar remarks because he could perceive no vulgarity in his comments (Tr. 66, 67, 68). Accordingly, I fully credit the testimony of Ms. Smith, Col. Moran and Ms. Craddock.

5. I do not credit Mr. Smith's testimony that, after he told Ms. Smith, words to the effect, "You're f-----g stupid, lady", Ms. Sula Smith said to him, "You got anymore insults for me? Those don't bother me." (Tr. 91), before he said, I always knew you was stupid...." First, his statement is directly contradicted by the testimony of Ms. Sula Smith, Col. Moran and Ms. Craddock and is not supported by the testimony of Mr. Hartig (Tr. 59-60) or of Mr. Prior (Tr. 116). Second, I found the testimony of Ms. Smith, Col. Moran and Ms. Craddock convincing and wholly credible in all respects and, therefore, I credit their testimony.

6. Mr. Hartig admitted he made the statement but insisted he used the letter "a" (Tr. 74) rather than the personal pronoun "my"; but his testimony is contradicted by the testimony of Ms. Smith (Tr. 147-148), Col. Moran (Tr. 188), Ms. Craddock (Tr. 206) and Mr. James L. Dicken (Tr. 217), and Mr. Hartig's testimony is not credited. Accordingly, I find that Mr. Hartig said "my" in his statement to Ms. Smith.

7. The negotiating session ended at about 8:30 a.m. (Tr. 74, 107) so, presumably, his call would have been shortly thereafter.

8. I.e., as the Court stated,

"...Linn [Linn v. Plant Guard Workers, 383 U.S. 53 (1966)] recognized that federal law gives a union license to use intemperate, abusive, or insulting language without fear of restraint or penalty...." (*Letter Carriers, supra,* 418 U.S. at 283).

9. Proffered testimony which occurred after the date of the disciplinary action, by a person not involved in the disciplinary action was rejected (Tr. 128-129).

10. Mr. Smith conceded that he did not tell Mr. Johnson that negotiations had ended; conceded that he left no message that he had called before he reached Mr. Johnson at about 11:30 a.m.; and the record is clear that Mr. Johnson was not informed that Mr. Smith had called before about 11:30. Further, I have found that Mr. Smith either requested "prep." time or when Mr. Johnson mentioned "prep." time he acquiesced. While Mr. Johnson had a basis for these charges, I stated at the hearing that, on the basis of testimony and evidence, if I were an arbitrator deciding the merits, I would give no credence to these two charges (Tr. 268).

Case #2 Bad Faith Bargaining

36 FLRA No. 62
Federal Labor Relations Authority
Washington, D.C.

U.S. Department of the Air Force Headquarters
Air Force Logostics Command,
Wright-Patterson Air Force Base, Ohio
(Respondent)
and
American Federation of Government
Council 214
(Charging Party)
5-CA-80086

Decision and Order
August 3, 1990

Before Chairman McKee and Members Talkin and Armendariz

I. Statement of the Case

This unfair labor practice case is before the Authority on exceptions filed by the Respondent to the attached decision of the Administrative Law Judge. The General Counsel filed an opposition to the exceptions and a motion to strike portions of the Respondent's exceptions.

The complaint alleges that the Respondent violated section 7116(a)(1) and (5) of the Federal Service Labor-Management Relations Statute (the Statute) by "failing and refusing to bargain concerning 'Last Chance Agreements' and the issuance of temporary credentials for union representatives who are not Air Force employees." Judge's Decision at 2. The Judge found that the Respondent failed and refused to bargain in good faith and, thus, violated section 7116(a)(1) and (5) of the Statute.

For the following reasons, we conclude that the Respondent violated section 7116(a)(1) and (5) of the Statute by its failure and refusal to bargain in good faith with the Union.

II. Background and Administrative Law Judge's Decision

The Respondent and the Charging Party (the Union) are parties to a Master Labor Agreement (MLA) covering 73,000 employees located at several facilities throughout the United States.

By letters dated October 15 and November 3, 1987, respectively, the Union requested bargaining and submitted proposals concerning "Last Chance Agreements" and the issuance of temporary credentials for Union representatives who are not Air Force employees. *Id.* at 2. On November 6, 1987, the Respondent notified the Union that "it was not refusing to bargain over the Union's proposals... and that it would respond to those proposals once an agreement on procedures for conducting Union-initiated mid-term bargaining had been reached." *Id.* at 2-3. The Respondent included a list of 16 proposed procedures for conducting mid-term bargaining.[1] The Respondent also returned the Union's November 3, 1987, letter and its proposal concerning the issuance of temporary credentials.

On November 10, 1987, the Union's President, Paul Palacio, spoke with Dale Biddle, the Respondent's Labor Relations Specialist, who had been assigned to the Union-initiated mid-term bargaining, about setting up a meeting to discuss the Respondent's proposals. Biddle told Palacio that he "was real busy and that he may be available towards the latter part of the year." Transcript at 26. Later that day, Palacio complained to Biddle's supervisor, Sheila Hostler, that he could not get Biddle to schedule a meeting to discuss Respondent's proposals. Although Hostler replied that Biddle would meet with Palacio the following week, she did not mention a date, time or place for the meeting.

On November 13, 1987, Palacio sent three letters to Biddle which included, among other things, the Union's counterproposals to the Respondent's proposals and a reiteration of the Union's request to bargain over the two proposals which it had submitted on November 3. On November 17, 1987, Biddle returned Palacio's letters without action, and set up a 30-minute meeting for November 19, 1987.

The November 19 meeting between Biddle and Palacio had lasted for an hour when Biddle "abruptly got up and said he had to go home." Transcript at 29. The parties discussed some of the Respondent's proposals during the course of the meeting. They did not discuss all 16 proposals before Biddle left, however, and did not set a date for the next meeting.

The Union filed the unfair labor practice charge in this case on November 23, 1987. Shortly thereafter, Palacio met with Biddle and Hostler and explained that he had filed the unfair labor practice charge because he believed that the Respondent was refusing to bargain. Palacio also complained again to Hostler that Biddle would not meet with him. Biddle did schedule another meeting but informed Palacio that he was cancelling the meeting until the unfair labor practice charge filed by Palacio was resolved. Hostler required Biddle to reschedule the meeting and the parties met several times after that to discuss the Respondent's proposals. No agreement was reached on the procedures to be followed for the Union-initiated mid-term bargaining. At the time of the unfair labor practice hearing in this case, the parties had reached impasse on the procedures to be followed for Union-initiated mid-term bargaining and requested assistance from the Federal Service Impasses Panel.[2]

The Judge concluded that the Respondent violated section 7116(a)(1) and (5) of the Statute by refusing to bargain over "Last Chance Agreements" and the issuance of temporary credentials for Union representatives who are not Air Force employees. The Judge stated that, in his view, "the issue here is whether the parties were... engaged in ground rule negotiations or whether they [were] involved in substantive negotiations concerning the Respondent's proposals of November 6, 1987 entitled 'Procedures for Union Initiated Mid-Term Bargaining.'" Judge's Decision at 4. According to the Judge, if the parties were involved in ground rule negotiations only, no violation of the Statute would exist. The Judge stated, however, that if the parties were not involved in ground rule bargaining, then the Respondent's action to require bargaining on the Respondent's "substantive proposals before conducting mid term bargaining with the Union might well be violative of the Statute." Id. Consequently, the Judge found that the "first question to be resolved is what constitutes ground rules." Id. at 5.

The Judge found that, consistent with the Authority's decision in *Department of Health and Human Services, Region VII, Kansas City, Missouri,* 14 FLRA 258 (1984) (*Department of Health and Human Services, Region VII*), ground rules are comprised only of matters relating to the "framework" of negotiations. Id. at 5. In examining the proposals set forth by the Respondent in this case, the Judge found that the proposals included matters which clearly could not be classified as ground rules. The Judge noted, for example, that the Respondent's proposals included such issues as "negotiations on a 'zipper clause' by AFGE, about which the Union probably has no authority to bargain; waiver of the Union's right to obtain information or data; limitations on the number of proposals the Union can make; [and] waiver of date and times for negotiations." Id. The Judge concluded that "what was proposed as ground rules by Respondent constituted, at best, a mixed bag." Id.

The Judge determined further that the ground rules proposed by the Respondent were not offered in good faith. The Judge found that the "mere fact that Respondent offered as ground rules matters which were for the most part substantive and then sought to bargain to impasse on those matters in the name of 'ground rule' bargaining belies any good faith[] argument it might make." Id. Further, the Judge found that "what Respondent required to be completed before negotiations began on the 'Last Chance [Agreements]' and temporary credentials [were] not merely ground rule negotiations, but contained substantive matters on which it was conditioning bargaining on the two proposals requested by the Union." Id.

The Judge concluded that "[i]mposing such onerous conditions, in the name of 'ground rules' which had to be resolved prior to bargaining on any Union mid-term proposals,... subverts the collective bargaining process." Id. Consequently, the Judge rejected Respondent's assertion that it was engaged in good faith bargaining over ground rules and found that the Respondent violated section 7116(a)(1) and (5) of the Statute.

III. Exceptions

The Respondent excepts to the Judge's findings and conclusions on three grounds. First, the Respondent objects to the definition of ground rules relied on by the Judge. The Respondent contends that the definition of ground rules used by the Judge "unduly limits [the] parties." Respondent's Brief in Support of Exceptions at 2. The Respondent claims that ground rules have been defined "rather succinctly as merely '...the arrangements between [...] parties as to how [...] negotiations will [sic] be conducted.'" *Id.* (quoting *Environmental Protection Agency,* 16 FLRA 602, 613 (1984) (EPA)). According to the Respondent, the Authority has found that negotiating a ground rules agreement "is an *inherent* aspect of an agency's obligation to bargain in good faith[.]" Respondent's Brief in Support of Exceptions at 3 (emphasis in original) (quoting *Veterans Administration, Washington, D.C. and Veterans Administration Medical and Regional Office Center, Fargo, North Dakota,* 22 FLRA 612, 633 (1986) (VA Fargo)). The Respondent argues that if an agency is obligated to bargain on ground rules, then a union should also be required to bargain on ground rules in the circumstances of union-initiated mid-term bargaining.

Second, the Respondent disputes the Judge's conclusion that the Respondent's proposals were not offered in good faith. According to the Respondent, none of the proposals which were cited by the Judge as being substantive created the onerous conditions found by the Judge. The Respondent contends first that the "zipper" clause proposal "may be characterized as premature[,] but certainly not one which the [U]nion has no authority to bargain." Respondent's Brief in Support of Exceptions at 3. The Respondent argues that, as to its proposal concerning the waiver of the Union's right to obtain information, "[t]here is no right to any and all information. The Statute at [section] 7114 requires only data not excluded by law and further which is reasonably relevant and necessary." *Id.* at 4. Further, with respect to the proposal which would relieve the Respondent of the obligation to conduct a "meeting" when the Union initiates mid-term bargaining, the Respondent does not specify the type of meeting to which the proposal refers. The Respondent asserts, however, that provisions in the parties' master agreement require it to hold "a meeting upon the request of the union when a management midterm proposal is initiated." *Id.* The Respondent claims that "[i]t did not seem logical to require a similar meeting when the union initiates a midterm proposal." *Id.*

The Respondent also objects to the Judge's conclusion that the Respondent must bargain over the Union's mid-term bargaining proposals prior to establishing the procedures for mid-term bargaining. The Respondent argues that because there has been no finding that the parties did not meet at reasonable times and places, further restrictions "on the contents of [its] initial proposals would constitute form over substance." *Id.* at 4.

Finally, Respondent argues that the need for a bargaining order in this case has been rendered moot by subsequent action of the parties. According to the Respondent, the parties agreed to and signed procedures for mid-term bargaining on October 25, 1988, a copy of which was attached to Respondent's exceptions. The Respondent claims further that pursuant to the mid-term bargaining procedures adopted by the parties, the parties met and exchanged data on the two Union proposals involved in this case. Consequently, the Respondent contends that an "order to bargain would be duplicative and unnecessary." *Id.*

IV. Opposition and Motion to Strike Portions of Respondent's Exceptions

The General Counsel filed an opposition to, and motion to strike portions of, the Respondent's exceptions.

In the motion to strike, the General Counsel objects to the attempt by the Respondent to introduce into the record a copy of the "Procedures For Union Initiated Mid-Term Bargaining," which the Respondent attached to its exceptions. The General Counsel argues that this document is dated subsequent to the hearing and close of the record in this case. The General Counsel contends that to allow this document to become part of the record would deprive the General Counsel and the Union of their rights to question the admissibility of the document.

In its opposition to the Respondent's exceptions, the General Counsel contends that a party violates the Statute when the "party causes unnecessary delay" or "conditions bargaining upon the resolution of extraneous matters[.]" Brief to Administrative Law Judge attached to Opposition at 5. In the General Counsel's view, a duty to bargain arose when the Union submitted its proposals to the Respondent, and the Respondent's conduct in "[r]eturning the proposals, as compared to retaining them and delaying action on them," constitutes an "outright refusal to bargain." *Id.* at 6.

The General Counsel asserts that "ground rules are not separate from the collective bargaining process but are part of the mutual obligation to bargain in good faith[.]" *Id.* at 9. The General Counsel contends further that a party does not have a right "to refuse to consider any subject matter proposals until such time as general procedures for... bargaining" are agreed on. *Id.* The General Counsel contends that the Respondent "brought a halt to any negotiation of the Union's proposals[] by returning them and refusing to even consider them." *Id.* at 11 (emphasis in original). The General Counsel also contends that previous Authority decisions "point up the principle that bargaining obligations regarding ground rules are important because ground rules are part and parcel of the collective bargaining process, and should be in furtherance of that process, not because parties have an absolute right to ground rules, in a vacuum." *Id.* at 15 (emphasis in original).

The General Counsel claims further that, contrary to the allegations of the Respondent, *VA Fargo* does not stand for the proposition that a party has the right to insist on completing the negotiation of ground rules prior to bargaining on substantive proposals. Rather, according to the General Counsel, *VA Fargo* holds that "ground rules are part and parcel of the mutual obligation to bargain in good faith." *Id.* at 17 (emphasis in original). Finally, the General Counsel contends that "[n]o Authority case holds or even suggests that a party has a right to final agreement on general procedures for all bargaining before proceeding with the business of bargaining." *Id.* at 18 (emphasis in original).

V. Analysis and Conclusion

A. The General Counsel's Motion to Strike Portions of Respondent's Exceptions is Granted

We agree with the General Counsel's contention that the parties' agreed-upon procedures for Union-initiated mid-term bargaining, attached by the Respondent to its exceptions, should not be considered by the Authority. Section 2429.5 of the Authority's Rules and Regulations provides that the Authority will not consider evidence which was not presented in proceedings before the Administrative Law Judge. The procedures were not presented in the proceeding before the Administrative Law Judge and, accordingly, we will not consider them here. *See United States Department of Agriculture, Animal and Plant Health Inspection Service, Plant Protection and Quarantine,* 26 FLRA 630 (1987).

B. The Respondent Violated Section 7116(a)(1) and (5) of the Statute

We find that the Respondent violated section 7116(a)(1) and (5) of the Statute by its failure and refusal to bargain with the Union in good faith. We do so, however, for reasons other than those of the Judge.

Section 7103(a)(12) of the Statute defines collective bargaining as the "performance of the mutual obligation of the representative of an agency and the exclusive representative of employees in an appropriate unit in the agency to meet at reasonable times and to consult and bargain in a good-faith effort to reach agreement with respect to the conditions of employment affecting such employees[.]" Further, section 7114(b)(1) and (3) states that "[t]he duty of an agency and an exclusive representative to negotiate in good faith... shall include the obligation... to approach the negotiations with a sincere resolve to reach a collective bargaining agreement... [and]... to meet at reasonable times and convenient places as frequently as may be necessary, and to avoid unnecessary delays[.]" In determining whether a party has fulfilled its bargaining responsibility, the totality of the circumstances in a case must be considered. *See, for example, Department of Defense, Department of the Air Force, Armament Division, AFSC, Eglin Air Force Base,* 13 FLRA 492, 505 (1983).

We find that the totality of the circumstances in this case supports the conclusion that the Respondent did not bargain in good faith. First, we find that the record establishes that the Respondent did not approach negotiations with a sincere resolve to reach agreement on the proposals submitted by the Union. Rather, in our view, the record establishes that the Respondent was attempting to avoid bargaining on the Union's proposals. For example, we note that the Respondent did not respond at all to the Union's October 15 request to bargain. In addition, although the Respondent responded to the Union's second request to bargain, that response consisted of the Respondent's returning the Union's proposals with the statement that mid-term bargaining procedures would have to be agreed upon before the Union's proposals would be considered. The response, which included the Respondent's 16 proposals, did not set, or propose, a date for bargaining, however.

Thereafter, when the Union's representative, Palacio, sought to set a date for the parties to bargain, the Respondent's representative, Biddle, stated that he was too busy to meet until the end of the year. Although

Palacio complained to Biddle's supervisor about his inability to schedule a meeting with Biddle and the supervisor replied that a meeting would be scheduled, no date, time or place for bargaining was suggested. When Palacio made his third request to bargain on the Union's proposals and sought again to set a date for bargaining, Biddle responded by offering to meet with Palacio for 30 minutes on November 19. The parties met that date. However, Biddle walked out of the meeting before they had finished discussing all of the Respondent's proposals and when Palacio attempted to set a date for another meeting, Biddle refused. Palacio again complained to Biddle's supervisor about his difficulty in arranging a meeting with Biddle. Although Biddle set up a meeting for "a couple of days later," he cancelled the meeting. Transcript at 30. The supervisor again intervened and the meeting was rescheduled. Although the parties met on several occasions in December, no agreement was reached on the ground rules at that time and the Union's proposals were not discussed.

As a result of the Respondent's conduct between October 15, 1987, when the Union first requested bargaining, and November 23, 1987, when the Union filed its unfair labor practice charge, the parties met for only 1 hour and none of the Union's proposals were discussed. During this time period, the Union made three separate requests to bargain and three attempts to schedule dates for bargaining. The Union's representative was required, on two occasions, to seek assistance from the Respondent's representative's supervisor to schedule negotiations. Although, on one of these occasions, the supervisor stated that a bargaining session would be scheduled, a session was not scheduled until the Union made another request. In our view, Respondent's conduct establishes that it was not bargaining, or attempting to bargain, in good faith. *See Army and Air Force Exchange Service, McClellan Base Exchange, McClellan Air Force Base, California,* 35 FLRA 764, 769 (1990) ("Stated simply, the parties' disagreement could not be resolved without discussion between their representatives.")

We note that, at the hearing, Biddle testified that he was unable to set dates for bargaining because he had a vacation planned for the end of the year and he was scheduled for training. We also note, however, that section 7114(b)(2) of the Statute requires that the Respondent provide "duly authorized representatives... to discuss and negotiate on any condition of employment[.]" If Biddle was unable to meet with the Union, therefore, a duly authorized substitute representative should have been made available.

In addition, the nature of the 16 proposals offered by the Respondent further indicates that Respondent was seeking to delay, or avoid, the bargaining process. We find it unnecessary in this case to define, with precision, what would constitute purely ground rules proposals, as opposed to substantive proposals. Under the Statute, however, the obligation to bargain over any matter, including ground rules, stems from the parties' obligation to "bargain in a good faith effort to reach agreement with respect to.... conditions of employment[.]" 5 U.S.C. § 7103(a)(12). As the obligation to bargain over ground rules is inseparable from the parties' mutual obligation to bargain in good faith, it is clear that a party may not insist on bargaining over ground rules which do not enable the parties to fulfill their mutual obligation. Stated simply, we conclude that ground rules proposals must, at a minimum, be designed to further, not impede, the bargaining for which the ground rules are proposed.

In this case, we are unable to conclude that the Respondent's proposals were designed to enable the parties to fulfill their mutual obligation to bargain in good faith. The Respondent's first proposal provided that "[t]he employer [would] not be obligated to negotiate over union initiated mid-term bargaining proposals and failure to do so [would] not constitute an unfair labor practice." Appendix, Proposal 1. The Respondent's second and third proposals would have required the Union to negotiate a "zipper" clause when the MLA was renegotiated and would have limited the Union to one mid-term bargaining initiative per year until the "zipper" clause was negotiated into the MLA. The Respondent's thirteenth proposal would have waived the Union's statutory right to seek assistance from the Federal Mediation and Conciliation Service (FMCS) and the Federal Service Impasses Panel (the Panel).[3]

It strains credulity, in our view, to assert that the nature of these proposals, which would relieve the Respondent of its obligation to bargain over either or both of the Union's substantive proposals and preclude the Union from requesting third-party assistance in resolving impasses over those proposals, was such that the Respondent was privileged, consistent with its statutory obligation to bargain in good faith, to insist on bargaining over them before addressing the Union's proposals. Rather, when viewed in the context of the Respondent's actions noted above, we find that the record as a whole, including the proposals themselves, supports the conclusion that the Respondent was not bargaining, or attempting to bargain, in good faith.

We emphasize, in this regard, that we are not ruling on the negotiability, or the merits, of the Respondent's proposals. We find, however, that when viewed in the context of the totality of the circumstances in this case, the nature of the Respondent's proposals belies the Respondent's assertion that it merely was attempting to set forth the "'arrangements... as to how negotiations will [sic] be conducted.'" Respondent's Brief in Support of Exceptions at 2 (quoting *EPA*). Instead, we conclude that the Respondent's ground rules were designed to set forth arrangements so that negotiations over the two Union proposals would not be conducted.

Consequently, we find that the Respondent violated section 7116(a)(1) and (5) of the Statute by refusing to bargain with the Union over "Last Chance Agreements" and the issuance of temporary credentials for certain Union representatives.

VI. Remedy

We conclude that, in addition to a cease and desist order, a bargaining order also is appropriate to remedy the Respondent's violation of section 7116(a)(1) and (5) in this case. In so concluding, we reject the Respondent's argument that a bargaining order has been rendered moot by subsequent action of the parties and, thus, an "order to bargain would be duplicative and unnecessary." Respondent's Brief in Support of Exceptions at 4.

As found above, the Respondent's actions, taken as a whole, clearly indicate that the Respondent did not bargain in good faith over the Union's proposals. Although the parties may have bargained over, and agreed to, procedures for mid-term bargaining, there is no indication in the record before us that the parties have concluded negotiations over "Last Chance Agreements" or the issuance of temporary credentials. Consequently, there is no basis on which to conclude that a bargaining order has been rendered moot, duplicative, or unnecessary. We shall, therefore, order that the Respondent, upon request, and to the extent consistent with applicable law, rule and regulation, bargain with the Union over "Last Chance Agreements" and the issuance of temporary credentials for Union representatives who are not Air Force employees.4

VII. Order

Pursuant to section 2423.29 of the Federal Labor Relations Authority's Rules and Regulations and section 7118 of the Statute, the Department of the Air Force, Headquarters, Air Force Logistics Command, Wright-Patterson Air Force Base, Ohio, shall:

1. Cease and desist from:

    (a) Refusing to bargain in good faith with the American Federation of Government Employees, Council 214, AFLCIO, the exclusive representative of certain of its employees, concerning "Last Chance Agreements" and the issuance of temporary credentials for Union representatives who are not Air Force employees.

    (b) In any like or related manner interfering with, restraining, or coercing employees in the exercise of their rights assured by the Federal Service Labor-Management Relations Statute.

2. Take the following affirmative action in order to effectuate the purposes and policies of the Federal Service Labor-Management Relations Statute:

    (a) Upon request, and to the extent consistent with applicable law, rule and regulation, bargain with the American Federation of Government Employees, Council 214, AFLCIO, the exclusive representative of certain of its employees, concerning "Last Chance Agreements" and the issuance of temporary credentials for Union representatives who are not Air Force employees.

    (b) Post at all of its facilities where bargaining unit employees represented by the American Federation of Government Employees, Council 214, AFL-CIO, are located, copies of the attached Notice on forms to be furnished by the Federal Labor Relations Authority. Upon receipt of such forms, they shall be signed by the Commander and shall be posted and maintained for 60 consecutive days thereafter, in conspicuous places, including bulletin boards and other places where notices to employees are customarily posted. Reasonable steps shall be taken to ensure that such Notices are not altered, defaced, or covered by any other material.

    (c) Pursuant to section 2423.30 of the Authority's Rules and Regulations, notify the Regional Director, Region V, Federal Labor Relations Authority,

175 W. Jackson Blvd., Suite 1359-A, Chicago, IL 60604, in writing, within 30 days from the date of this Order, as to what steps have been taken to comply.

NOTICE TO ALL EMPLOYEES AS ORDERED BY THE FEDERAL LABOR RELATIONS AUTHORITY AND TO EFFECTUATE THE POLICIES OF THE FEDERAL SERVICE LABOR-MANAGEMENT RELATIONS STATUTE
WE NOTIFY OUR EMPLOYEES THAT:

We will not refuse to bargain in good faith with the American Federation of Government Employees, Council 214, AFL-CIO, the exclusive representative of certain of our employees, concerning "Last Chance Agreements" and the issuance of temporary credentials for union representatives who are not Air Force employees.

We will not in any like or related manner, interfere with, restrain, or coerce our employees in the exercise of their rights assured by the Federal Service Labor-Management Relations Statute. We will upon request, and to the extent consistent with applicable law, rule and regulation, bargain with the American Federation of Government Employees, Council 214, AFL-CIO, concerning "Last Chance Agreements" and the issuance of temporary credentials for union representatives who are not Air Force employees.

_____

(Activity)

Dated:_____

By:_____

(Signature) (Title)

This Notice must remain posted for 60 consecutive days from the date of posting and must not be altered, defaced, or covered by any other material.

If employees have any questions concerning this Notice or compliance with any of its provisions, they may communicate directly with the Regional Director of the Federal Labor Relations Authority, Region V, whose address is: 175 W. Jackson Blvd., Suite 1359-A, Chicago, IL 60604, and whose telephone number is: (312) 353-6306.

APPENDIX

PROCEDURES FOR UNION INITIATED MID-TERM BARGAINING

1. The employer will not be obligated to negotiate over union initiated mid-term bargaining proposals and failure to do so will not constitute an unfair labor practice.

In the event it is determined that the above management proposal is unacceptable then the following proposals are submitted:

2. AFGE promises to negotiate a "zipper clause" when the MLA is renegotiated.

3. Until (1) above is negotiated in the MLA, the AFGE will be limited to one (1) mid-term bargaining initiative per calendar year.

4. The subject the AFGE initiates for mid-term bargaining must not have been previously mentioned, discussed, or proposed at any bargaining table.

5. Union initiated mid-term bargaining must be accompanied by written proposals.

6. The employer will have 180 workdays to respond to the AFGE's initiated mid-term proposals.

7. Negotiations will begin on a date and time determined by the employer.

8. All disputes over union mid-term bargaining will be subject to resolution under Articles 6 and 7 of the MLA.

9. The employer will not be obligated to furnish the AFGE with any information, data, etc., when the union initiates mid-term bargaining.

10. The employer will not be obligated to conduct a meeting when the union initiates mid-term bargaining.

11. When the AFGE initiates bargaining they will provide the employer with any and all information requested by the employer on the subject. This will be accomplished so the employer can engage intelligently in negotiations with the union on their initiated subject.

12. When AFGE initiates bargaining they will provide the employer, upon request, a meeting to discuss the matter.

13. The parties may seek assistance of the FMCS or the FSIP only by mutual agreement.

14. The employer may delegate the subject matter proposed by the AFGE for mid-term bargaining to a field activity of their choice to negotiate.

15. The employer reserves its right to submit additional proposals on this subject.

16. Nothing herein is considered or intended to waive any management right.

Footnotes

(If blank, the decision does not have footnotes.)

1. The Respondent's proposals are contained in the Appendix to this decision.

2. For reasons discussed in connection with our disposition of the General Counsel's Motion to Strike portions of the Respondent's exceptions, we do not consider evidence offered by the Respondent concerning events subsequent to the hearing.

3. Section 7119 of the Statute provides that either party may request assistance from FMCS and the Panel.

4. We note that on January 23, 1989, over 1 year after the events occurring in this case, two Union proposals concerning the issuance of temporary credentials at the Respondent's Air Logistics Centers at Tinker and Robins Air Force Bases which had been submitted in collective bargaining were declared nonnegotiable by the Agency. In *American Federation of Government Employees, Council 214 and Department of the Air Force, Air Force Logistics Command, Wright-Patterson Air Force Base, Ohio*, 34 FLRA 977 (1990), the Union's proposals were found to be nonnegotiable. We also note that on January 25, 1989, also over 1 year after the events occurring in the instant case, Union proposals concerning Last Chance Agreements which had been submitted in collective bargaining were declared nonnegotiable by the Agency. A negotiability appeal involving those proposals on Last Chance Agreements is currently pending before the Authority in *American Federation of Government Employees, Council 214, AFL-CIO and U.S. Department of the Air Force, Air Force Logistics Command, Wright-Patterson Air Force Base, Ohio*, Case No. 0-NG-1658.C

Case #3 Definition of Working Conditions

22 FLRA No. 23
Federal Labor Relations Authority
Washington, D.C.

Antilles Consolidated Education Association
(Union)
and
Antilles Consolidated School System
(Agency)

Case No. 0-NG-784

DECISION AND ORDER ON NEGOTIABILITY ISSUE

I. Statement of the Case

This case is before the Authority because of a negotiability appeal filed under section 7105(a)(2)(D) and (E) of the Federal Service Labor-Management Relations Statute (the Statute), concerning the negotiability of one five-part Union proposal.

II. Union Proposal

Article 36. Base/Post Privileges

1. All unit employees will be granted the use of the following base/post facilities:

A. Base/Post Exchanges at the site to which the employee is assigned.

B. All retail food outlets operated by the Navy Exchange, AAFES, or coast Guard Exchange at the site to which the employee is assigned, or

C. Access to the nearest exchange system and its retail food outlets in any case in which an employee is assigned to a site at which the facilities described in subsection A and B are not operated.

D. Base/post/station/fort special services recreation and morale support facilities at the site to which the employee is assigned.

E. Hospital facilities on a paid basis.

A. Position of the Parties

The Agency asserts that the proposal is nonnegotiable for four reasons: (1) it does not concern matters affecting working conditions of bargaining unit employees, within the meaning of section 7103(a)(14) of the Statute; (2) the Agency is without authority to bargain over the proposed benefits; (3) bargaining on the proposal is barred by regulations for which a compelling need exists; (4) negotiation on parts D and E of the proposal is foreclosed by applicable law.

The Union did not provide any arguments in its petition for review supporting the negotiability of the proposal, nor did it file a replybrief.

We will examine the Agency's contentions, in turn.

B. Analysis

1. Conditions of Employment of Bargaining Unit Employees

Under the statutory scheme established by sections 7103(a)(12), 7106, 7114 and 7117 a matter proposed to be bargained which is consistent with Federal law, including the Statute, Government-wide regulations or agency regulations is, nonetheless, outside the duty to bargain unless such matter directly affects the conditions of employment of bargaining unit employees. The term "conditions of employment" is defined in Section 7103(a)(14) as "personnel policies, practices, and matters whether established by rule, regulation, or otherwise, affecting working conditions...."

In deciding whether a proposal involves a condition of employment of bargaining unit employees the Authority considers two basic factors:

(1) Whether the matter proposed to be bargained pertains to bargaining unit employees; and

(2) The nature and extent of the effect of the matter proposed to be bargained on working conditions of those employees.

For example, as to the first factor, the question of whether the proposal pertains to bargaining unit employees, a proposal which is principally focused on non bargaining unit positions or employees does not directly affect the work situation or employment relationship of bargaining unit employees. *See National Federation of Federal Employees, Local 1451 and Naval Training Center, Orlando, Florida,* 3 FLRA 88 (1980) aff'd sub nom. *National Federation of Federal Employees v. FLRA,* 652 F.2d 191 (D.C. Cir. 1981) (Proposal requiring management to designate a particular number of representatives to negotiations was held to be outside the duty to bargain). But, a proposal which is principally focused on bargaining unit position or employees and which is otherwise consistent with applicable laws and regulations is not rendered nonnegotiable merely because it also would have some impact on employees outside the bargaining unit. *See Association of Civilian Technicians, Pennsylvania State Council and Pennsylvania Army and Air National Guard,* 14 FLRA 38 (1982) (Union proposal 1 defining the competitive area for reduction-in-force as coextensive with the bargaining unit was held to be within the duty to bargain even though it had an impact on non bargaining unit employees).

Part 1 of the Appendix to this decision references other Authority decisions concerning the nature and extent of the affect of a proposal on bargaining unit employees.

As to the second factor, relating to the effect of a proposal on working conditions, the question is whether the record establishes that there is a direct connection between the proposal and the work situation or employment relationship of bargaining unit employees. For example, a proposal concerning off-duty hour activities of employees was found to be outside the duty to bargain where no such connection was established. *See International Association of Fire Fighters, AFL-CIO, CLC, Local F-116 and Department of the Air Force, Vandenberg Air Force Base, California,* 7 FLRA 123 (1981) (Proposal to permit employees to utilize on-base recreational facilities during off-duty hours found not to concern personnel policies, practices, or matters affecting working conditions of bargaining unit employees).

On the other hand, a proposal concerning off-duty hour activities of employees was held to affect working conditions of bargaining unit employees where the requisite connection was established. *National Federation of Federal Employees, Local 1363 and Headquarters, U.S. Army Garrison, Yongsan, Korea,* 4 FLRA 139 (1980) (Proposal to revise the agency's "ration control" policy was found to concern standards of health and decency which were conditions of employment under agency regulations).

Part 2 of the Appendix to this decision references other Authority decisions concerning the nature and effect of a proposal on bargaining unit employees' working conditions.

Applying the first factor to the disputed proposal we find that the proposal expressly pertains only to bargaining unit employees. No claim is made that the proposal has any impact on nonbargaining unit employees. However, we must also assess the nature and effect of the proposal on bargaining unit employees' working conditions under the second factor. Here the Agency argues without contravention that access to the retail, recreational and medical facilities denoted in the proposal would occur primarily during the employees' non-duty hours. Further, the Union has provided no evidence, whatever, and the record does not otherwise establish that access to the facilities in question is in any manner related to the work situation or employment relationship or is otherwise linked to the employees' assignments within the school system in Puerto Rico. As a result we find the disputed proposal is to the same effect as the proposal permitting employees to use on base recreational facilities during off-duty hours found outside the agency's obligation to bargain in Vandenberg Air Force Base, 7 FLRA 123 (1981). Thus, the disputed proposal also does not directly affect working conditions of bargaining unit employees and is outside the Agency's obligation to bargain.

2. Matters within the Agency's Authority to Bargain

It is well established that the duty of an agency under the Statute is to negotiate with an exclusive representative of an appropriate unit of its employees concerning conditions of employment affecting them to the extent of its discretion, the is, except as provided otherwise by Federal law including the Statute, or by Government-wide rule or regulation or by an agency regulation for which a compelling need exists. For example, *see National Treasury Employees Union and Department of the Treasury, Bureau of the Public Debt*, FLRA 76 (1980), aff'd sub nom. *National Treasury Employees Union v. FLRA*, 691 F.2d 553 (D.C. Cir. 1982).

It is also well established that an agency may not foreclose bargaining on an otherwise negotiable matter by delegating authority as to that matter only to an organizational level within the agency different from the organizational level of recognition. Rather, under section 7114(b)(2) of the Statute, an agency is obligated to provide representatives who are empowered to negotiate and enter into agreement on all matters within the statutorily prescribed scope of negotiations. *American Federation of Government Employees, AFL-CIO, Local 3525 and United States Department of Justice, Board of Immigration Appeals*, 10 FLRA 61 (1982) (Union Proposal 1). Thus, the Agency's claim that the Superintendent of the Department of Navy Antilles School System is without authority to bargain on access to Navy retail, recreational or medical facilities because such facilities are in separate chains of command within the Department of Navy from the school system cannot be sustained. *See American Federation of Government Employees, AFL-CIO, Local 1409 and U.S. Adjutant General Publications Center, Baltimore, Maryland*, 18 FLRA NO. 68 (1985). Similarly, the Agency's argument that the Superintendent is without authority to bargain on access to Army facilities which are under the jurisdiction of a separate subdivision of DOD also cannot be sustained. *See Defense Contract Administration Services Region, Boston, Massachusetts*, 15 FLRA 750 (1984).

As to Coast Guard facilities, there is nothing in the record in this case which indicates that the Agency lacks the discretion to at least request the Department of Transportation to extend access to such Coast Guard facilities to Antilles School System employees. Thus, the Agency is obligated to bargain on access to Coast Guard facilities to this extent. *See American Federation of State, County and Municipal Employees, AFL-CIO and Library of Congress, Washington, D.C.*, 7 FLRA 578 (1982) (Union Proposals XI-XVI), enf'd sub nom. *Library of Congress v. FLRA*, 699 F.2d 1280 (D.C. Cir. 1983).

3. Compelling Need

The Agency has argued that a compelling need exists for certain ofits regulations to bar civilian employee access to the retail and recreational facilities in Puerto Rico. We note, however, an apparent inconsistency between this argument and DOD Directive 1400.6 which could be interpreted to permit access to such facilities by the employees in Puerto Rico. Neither party in this case addressed this specific question or otherwise discussed the effect of DOD Directive 1400.6 on civilian employees in Puerto Rico. Therefore, we consider it inappropriate, based on the record in this case, to pass on the compelling need issue raised by the Agency.

4. Consistency with law of Parts D and E of the Proposal

a. Part D of the Proposal

According to the record this part of the proposal would permit the Antilles School System employees to patronize on-post retail liquor stores. While the Agency's claims that Puerto Rico law precludes the sale of Commonwealth tax-free alcoholic beverages to these civilian employees we find such claim unsupported in the record. That is, the DOD regulations, which were included in the record by the Agency, specifically permit patronage of on-post retail liquor stores by other categories of persons, such as dependents of military personnel, who, like the civilian employees in this case, are not expressly listed as exempt under the Puerto Rico Statute. *See Puerto Rico Laws Annotated tit. 13 Section 6019* (1976). Thus, we do not find that the Agency has established that Part D of the proposal is inconsistent with law.

b. Part E of the Proposal

Part E of the proposal would permit employees to use the local Navy hospital on a paid basis. However, under 24 U.S.C. Section 34 Federal Employees located outside the continental limits of the United States and in Alaska may receive medical care at a naval hospital only "where facilities are not otherwise available in reasonably accessible and appropriate non-Federal hospitals." Also, under 24 U.S.C. Section 35, such employees may be hospitalized in a naval hospital "only for acute medical and surgical conditions...." "Since Part E of the proposal contains no limitations on access to the local naval hospital, it is inconsistent with the express statutory provisions governing such access.

c. Conclusion

The Authority finds, for the reasons set forth in the preceding analysis, that the entire proposal in this case concerns matters which are not conditions of employment of bargaining unite employees. Consequently, it is not within the duty to bargain although the Agency could negotiate on the proposal if it chose to do so, except for Part E.

Further, the Authority concludes that as Part E of the proposal is inconsistent with Federal law, it is outside the scope of the duty to bargain pursuant to section 7117(a)(1) of the Statute.

III. Order

Accordingly, pursuant to section 2424.10 of the Authority's Rules and Regulations, it is ordered that the petition for review be, and it hereby is, dismissed.

Issued, Washington, D.C., June 24, 1986.
/s/ Jerry L. Calhoun, Chairman
/s/ Henry B. Frazier III, Member
FEDERAL LABOR RELATIONS AUTHORITY

APPENDIX

Part 1

The following cases involve examples of proposals found outside the duty to bargain because of the impact on individuals or positions outside the bargaining unit.

National Council of Field Labor Locals, American Federation of Government Employees, AFL-CIO and U.S. Department of Labor, Washington, D.C., 3 FLRA 290 (1980) (Proposal I establishing the method management will use in filling supervisory and management positions found not to affect working conditions of bargaining unit employees).

American Federation of Government Employees, National Council of EEOC Locals NO. 216, AFL-CIO and Equal Employment Opportunity Commission, Washington, D.C., 3 FLRA 504 (1980) (Proposal relating to the assessment and training of supervisors found not to affect working conditions of bargaining unit employees).

National Treasury Employees Union and Internal Revenue Service, 6 FLRA 522 (1981) (Proposal VI requiring management to notify individuals who telephone the agency for tax information that such calls are subject to monitoring found not to affect working conditions of bargaining unit employees).

National Association of Government Employees, Local R7-23 and Headquarters, 375th Air Base Group, Scott Air Force Base, Illinois, 7 FLRA 710 (1982) (Proposal concerning discipline of management officials and supervisors found not to affect working conditions of bargaining unit employees).

American Federation of Government Employees, AFL-CIO, Local 2272 and Department of Justice, U.S. Marshals Service, District of Columbia, 9 FLRA 1004 (1982) (The portion of Proposal 5 which required management to prosecute private citizens who file false reports found not to affect working conditions of bargaining unit employees).

Association of Civilian Technicians, State of New York, Division of Military and Naval Affairs, Albany, New York, 11 FLRA 475 (1983) (Proposal 2 concerning procedures for filling military positions found not to affect the working conditions of bargaining unit employees).

American Federation of Government Employees, AFL-CIO, Local 2302 and U.S. Army Armor Center and Fort Knox, Fort Knox, Kentucky, 19 FLRA NO. 95 (1985) (Proposal 4 prescribing the content of certain management records relating to employees, the manner in which such records are maintained and restrictions on management access to such records found not to affect working conditions of bargaining unit employees).

Part 2

A. The following cases involve examples of proposals found outside the duty to bargain because of the absence of a direct affect on bargaining unit employees' working conditions. National Association of Air Traffic Specialists and Department of Transportation, Federal Aviation Administration, 6 FLRA 588

(1981) (Proposal IV permitting employee allotments from pay for "Political Action Fund" to be used in "political efforts to improve working conditions" found to affect working conditions in only a remote and speculative manner).

National Federation of Federal Employees, Council of Consolidated Social Security Administration Locals and Social Security Administration, 13 FLRA 422 (1983) (Proposals 3 and 4 requiring management to utilize recycled paper products and to provide the Union with such recycled paper products upon request found not to directly affect bargaining unit employees' working conditions as there was no demonstration in the record of any such effect).

Maritime Metal Trades Council and Panama Canal Commission, 17 FLRA 890 (1985) (Proposals 1 and 2 permitting employees to cash personal checks at the agency's treasury found not to directly affect working conditions of bargaining unit employees).

B. The following cases involve examples of proposals found to directly affect working conditions of bargaining unit employees.

American Federation of Government Employees, AFL-CIO and Air Force Logistics Command, Wright-Patterson Air Force Base, Ohio, 2 FLRA 604 (1980) (Union Proposal 1), enf'd as to other matters sub nom. Department of Defense v. FLRA, 659 F.2d 1140 (D.C. Cir. 1981), cert. denied sub. nom. AFGE v. FLRA, 455 U.S. 945 (1982) (A proposal to establish a union operated day care facility on agency property was found to directly affect bargaining unit employees by enhancing an individual's ability to accept employment or to continue employment with the agency and to promote workforce stability and prevent tardiness and absenteeism).

National Treasury Employees Union and Internal Revenue Service, 3 FLRA 693 (1980) (Union Proposal I establishing criteria for approval of outside employment was found to directly affect working conditions of unit employees because agency regulations which set forth policies governing outside employment were determinative of employee eligibility for certain positions and even prescribed whether employees could continue to be employed).

Planners, Estimators and Progressmen Association, Local NO. 8 and Department of the Navy, Charleston Naval Shipyard, Charleston, South Carolina, 13 FLRA 455 (1983) (A proposal to permit bargaining unit employees to record their time and attendance manually instead of mechanically through use of a time clock found to directly concern working conditions of such employees).

United States Department of Justice, United States Immigration and Naturalization Service and American Federation of Government Employees, AFL-CIO, Local 2509, 14 FLRA 578 (1984) (Assignment of Government-owned housing to employees was found to directly affect working conditions of bargaining unit employees in circumstances where there was a lack of adequate housing in the geographic area and the Government-owned housing in question was constructed for the benefit and use of employees stationed at the hardship location).

American Federation of Government Employees, AFL-CIO, Local 1770 and Department of the Army, Headquarters, XVIII Airborne Corps and Fort Bragg, Fort Bragg, North Carolina, 17 FLRA 752 (1985) (Proposal 4 requiring the agency to provide lockers or other secure areas for employees' personal items during working hours found to directly affect working conditions of unit employees).

Case #4 Discrimination Against Union Representatives

35 FLRA No. 15
Federal Labor Relations Authority
Washngton, D.C.

Letterkenny Army Depot
(Respondent)
and
Internation Brotherhood of Police Officers, Local 358
(Charging Party)

Case No. 2-CA-70172

DECISION AND ORDER

March 14, 1990

Before Chairman McKee and Members Talkin and Armendariz.

I. Statement of the Case

This unfair labor practice case is before the Authority on exceptions to the attached decision of the Administrative Law Judge issued in the above-entitled proceeding. Both the General Counsel and the Charging Party (the

Union) filed exceptions to the Judge's Decision. The Respondent filed an opposition to the exceptions of the General Counsel and the Union.

The complaint alleged that the Respondent violated section 7116(a)(1) and (2) of the Federal Service Labor-Management Relations Statute (the Statute) by failing and/or refusing to promote an employee because he had engaged in protected activity on behalf of the Union. The Judge found that no violation of the Statute had occurred and recommended that the complaint be dismissed.

Pursuant to section 2423.29 of the Authority's Rules and Regulations and section 7118 of the Statute, we have reviewed the rulings of the Judge made at the hearing and find that no prejudicial error was committed. Those rulings are affirmed.

We find, however, contrary to the Judge, that the Respondent's conduct violated the Statute. Accordingly, we will order the Respondent to retroactively promote the employee with backpay and to restore such benefits as will make the employee whole.

II. Background

The facts, which are set out fully in the Judge's decision, are briefly summarized here.

George C. Webber, a guard at the Letterkenny Army Depot, was a "fairly active" Union president from January 1984 to early October 1986. Judge's Decision at 3. Mr. Webber was "involved in several... incidents which may not have pleased management." Id. at 4. In August 1986, Mr. Webber applied for a position as lead guard. On October 8, 1986, the second line supervisor "signed a selection register nominating Webber for the position[.]" Id. at 2.

Subsequently, Mr. Webber learned from another employee that his selection had been cancelled by the Respondent's Director of Administration on October 10, 1986. During a meeting to discuss the issue, Mr. Webber was informed by the Police Captain that "the wrong procedure had been used in making the selection and that the first line supervisor (a lieutenant) rather than the second line supervisor (the Chief), should have made the selection." Id.

The selection was rerun, with the same candidates being considered. Mr. Webber was not selected by the first line supervisor. Rather, "[o]f the same five candidates the position was given to the only non-union candidate[.]" Id.

III. Administrative Law Judge's Decision

Although the Judge stated that he regarded the "course of events here as highly suspicious[,]" he found "no evidence that any of [Mr. Webber's representational] activity invoked any threats or statements indicating that his supervisors/managers were disposed to seek revenge for such conduct." Id. at 7.

The Judge noted that subsequent to the cancellation of Mr. Webber's selection, the Police Captain stated to Mr. Webber's successor as Union president that "he was happy not to have to do business with Webber any longer and did not particularly care for unions." Id. The Judge characterized this statement as "rather mild evidence of animus[,]" and contrasted it with what he found to be "fairly firm evidence" that Mr. Webber's selection had been cancelled because the Director of Administration "strongly believed [that] first line supervisors should be required to choose their own right-hand men." Id.

The Judge found that the Director of Administration's belief that Mr. Webber's previous selection had been a "poor choice" was based, at least in part, on Mr. Webber's Union activities. Id. The Judge concluded, however, that:

> There is a difference between deciding an employee has no future simply because he is a union activist, and deciding that his discharge of representational responsibilities demonstrates a lack of judgement [sic], ability or other factors required for a given promotion. The line may be thin, and difficult to draw, but it must be recognized if the application of the law is to be realistic.

Id. at 8.

The Judge concluded that the General Counsel failed to prove by a preponderance of the evidence that Mr. Webber's nonselection was motivated by his Union activities. Accordingly, the Judge recommended that the unfair labor practice complaint be dismissed.

IV. Positions of the Parties

A. The General Counsel's Exceptions

The General Counsel claims that the Judge's findings of fact do not comport with his conclusion that no violation of the Statute occurred. In particular, the General Counsel disagrees with the Judge's conclusion that the Respondent's consideration of Mr. Webber's protected activity was permissible. The General Counsel states:

> Counsel for the General Counsel is unaware of any precedent for concluding that management may

discriminate against an employee based on his protected union activities if it is determined that these protected activities demonstrate a lack of judgement [sic] or effectiveness. It is unfair and unrealistic to demand that a union representative be willing to risk his opportunity for promotion on an evaluation of the effectiveness of his union activities.

General Counsel Exceptions at 3.

The General Counsel maintains that the Administrative Law Judge's findings of fact "compel the conclusion that Respondent's nonselection of Webber was motivated by his Union activities." Id. As a remedy, the General Counsel requests that the Authority direct the Respondent retroactively to promote Mr. Webber to the position of lead guard and make him whole for the wages he lost as a result of the unfair labor practice.

B. The Union's Exceptions

The Union excepts to the Judge's decision on two grounds. First, the Union asserts that consistent with the Authority's decision in *Internal Revenue Service, Washington, D.C.*, 6 FLRA 96 (1981) (IRS), the Judge failed to correctly allocate the burden of proof in this case. The Union claims that once the General Counsel made a prima facie showing that Mr. Webber was engaged in protected activity and that this activity was a motivating factor in the Respondent's decision not to select Mr. Webber, "the burden should have shifted to the [Respondent] to demonstrate by a preponderance of the evidence that it would have reached the same promotion decision absent Mr. Webber's protected activity."

Union Exceptions at 2.

Second, the Union excepts to the Judge's conclusion that the Respondent was entitled to consider Mr. Webber's conduct while engaged in protected activity in evaluating his suitability for promotion. The Union claims that the Judge's conclusion establishes "an inappropriately high standard for statutory violations." *Id.* at 3. According to the Union, "[t]he Authority does not require anti-union threats or promises of revenge for union activities to establish a violation of the [S]tatute." *Id.* at 4.

C. The Respondent's Opposition

The Respondent argues first that the General Counsel's and the Union's exceptions were untimely filed. The Respondent claims that because the exceptions are untimely, they should not be considered by the Authority.

Alternatively, the Respondent argues that the record establishes that Mr. Webber's nonselection was based on factors other than his Union activities. The Respondent concedes that "Mr. Webber's representational activities may have contributed to a judgment as to his potential" for promotion. Respondent's Opposition at 3. The Respondent maintains, however, that "[v]alid reasons for Mr. Webber's nonselection, outside of his union activities, existed, were testified to..., and were found to be credible" by the Administrative Law Judge. Id.

V. Timeliness of the Exceptions

For the following reasons, we find that the General Counsel's and the Union's exceptions were timely filed.

The time limit for filing exceptions to an Administrative Law Judge's decision is 25 days after service of the decision. 5 C.F.R. § 2423.26(c). The date of service is the day the decision is deposited in the U.S. mail or is delivered in person. 5 C.F.R. § 2429.27(d). If the decision is served by mail, 5 days are added to the time period for filing exceptions. 5 C.F.R. § 2429.22. If the last day of the time limit falls on a Saturday, Sunday, or Federal legal holiday, the time limit is extended until the end of the next business day. 5 C.F.R. § 2429.21(a).

The Judge's decision is dated September 22, 1988, and was served on the parties by mail on that same date. By operation of 5 C.F.R. §§ 2429.21 and 2429.22, the parties had until October 22 to file their exceptions. However, since October 22 fell on a Saturday, the due date for filing exceptions was extended to the end of the next business day – Monday, October 24. The General Counsel's and the Union's exceptions were postmarked on October 24, 1988. Accordingly, the exceptions were timely filed.

VI. Analysis

A. Analytical Framework

Before discussing the specific facts of this case, we wish to address the analytical framework to be applied in cases alleging violations of section 7116(a)(2) of the Statute. In particular, we note the Union's assertion that once the General Counsel made a prima facie showing of discrimination, the burden "should have shifted" to the Respondent to demonstrate that it would have reached the same decision in the absence of Mr. Webber's protected activity. Union Exceptions at 2. In response to this assertion, we emphasize two points.

First, the burden of proof always rests with the General Counsel. Section 2423.18 of the Authority's Rules and Regulations provides that "[t]he General Counsel...

shall have the burden of proving the allegations of the complaint by a preponderance of the evidence." This is true in all cases of alleged discrimination, including "pretext" and "mixed motive" cases. In fact, the analytical framework applied to discrimination cases under section 7116(a)(2) is the same whether the case is labelled a "pretext" or a "mixed motive" case.

In all cases of alleged discrimination, whether "pretext" or "mixed motive," the General Counsel must establish that: (1) the employee against whom the alleged discriminatory action was taken was engaged in protected activity; and (2) such activity was a motivating factor in the agency's treatment of the employee in connection with hiring, tenure, promotion, or other conditions of employment. *22nd Combat Support Group (SAC), March Air Force Base, California*, 27 FLRA 279 (1987) (*March Air Force Base*). If the General Counsel fails to make the required prima facie showing, the case ends without further inquiry. *See, for example, Veterans Administration, Washington, D.C. and Veterans Administration Medical Center, Cincinnati, Ohio*, 26 FLRA 114 (1987), *petition for review denied sub nom. American Federation of Government Employees, Local 2031 v. FLRA*, 878 F.2d 460 (D.C. Cir. 1989); *and Department of the Air Force, Ogden Air Logistics Center, Hill Air Force Base, Utah*, 25 FLRA 342 (1987), where the particular conduct engaged in by employees was found not to be protected under the Statute. *See also Veterans Administration Medical Center, Leavenworth, Kansas*, 31 FLRA 1161 (1988) and *Department of Health and Human Services, Social Security Administration, Baltimore, Maryland*, 18 FLRA 55 (1985), where there was no evidence of discrimination.

Even if the General Counsel makes the required "prima facie" showing, an agency will not be found to have violated section 7116(a)(2) if the agency can demonstrate, by a preponderance of the evidence, that: (1) there was a legitimate justification for its action; and (2) the same action would have been taken even in the absence of protected activity. For example, IRS, 6 FLRA at 99 where the Authority referenced the approach taken by the Supreme Court in *Mt. Healthy City School District Board of Education v. Doyle*, 429 U.S. 274 (1977) (*Mt. Healthy*). In *Mt. Healthy*, which involved conduct protected by the U.S. Constitution, the Supreme Court established a "test of causation" for the purpose of "protect[ing] against the invasion of [protected] rights without commanding undesirable consequences not necessary to the assurance of those rights." *Id.* at 286-87. The Court held that the burden was on the moving party to show that his/her conduct was protected and that this conduct was a motivating factor in the employment decision. At that point, the employer could demonstrate, by a preponderance of the evidence, that it would have reached the same decision even in the absence of the protected conduct. It is erroneous to conclude, however, that because a respondent agency has an opportunity to establish that it had legitimate justification for taking the disputed action, the ultimate burden of proof shifts to the respondent to do so. The burden of proving the allegations of the unfair labor practice complaint rests solely with the General Counsel.

Second, even if the General Counsel makes the required *prima facie* showing, it is necessary to determine whether the General Counsel has proved the allegation in the complaint by a preponderance of the evidence. In this regard, a prima facie case consists only of "sufficient evidence... to get plaintiff past... a motion to dismiss[.]" Black's Law Dictionary 1071 (5th ed. 1979) (citation omitted). Only if the respondent offers no evidence in its support does a *prima facie* showing alone equate to proof by a preponderance of the evidence. See *id.* (noting that courts use the concept of a prima facie case to mean "not only that plaintiff's evidence would reasonably allow conclusion plaintiff seeks but also that plaintiff's evidence compels such a conclusion if the defendant produces no evidence to rebut it.") (citation omitted).

If, in response to a prima facie case established by the General Counsel, the respondent offers evidence, it is necessary to determine whether the respondent's evidence rebuts the General Counsel's *prima facie* showing. This determination is made on the basis of the entire record, including any evidence the General Counsel offers in rebuttal to the respondent's showing. If the respondent rebuts the General Counsel's *prima facie* showing by a preponderance of the evidence, thereby establishing that it would have taken the allegedly unlawful action even in the absence of protected activity, the General Counsel has not established a violation of the Statute.

In this regard, "pretext" and "mixed motive" cases differ in one respect only: in a "mixed motive" case, both lawful and unlawful reasons (motives) for the respondent's actions have been established. Because both lawful and unlawful motives have been established, it is necessary to determine whether the respondent would have taken the allegedly discriminatory action even without the unlawful motive. *See, for example, United States Department of the Treasury, Internal Revenue Service and United States Department of the Treasury, Internal Revenue Service, New Orleans District, New Orleans, Louisiana*, 30 FLRA 1013 (1988) (involving the evaluation of an employee's performance while he served as a union steward) *and Equal Employment Opportunity Commission*, 24 FLRA 851 (1986), *aff'd sub nom. Martinez v. FLRA*, 833 F.2d 1051 (D.C. Cir. 1987) (concerning the discharge of an employee following the filing of grievances). In each of these cases, the respondent established a lawful motive for the action that was taken and demonstrated that it would have acted in the same manner even in the absence of the protected conduct.

In a "pretext" case, on the other hand, a motive asserted by a respondent to be lawful is found to be unlawful (pretextual). Accordingly, unless the respondent establishes that there was an additional lawful (nonpretextual) motive for its allegedly discriminatory action, it is not necessary to determine whether the respondent would have taken the disputed action even without the unlawful motive. *See, for example, United States Forces Korea/ Eighth United States Army*, 11 FLRA 434 (1983) (the Authority found that the respondent's refusal to approve an extension of the local union president's overseas tour of duty was motivated by his union activity and that the reason for denying the extension was pretextual).

We note that the General Counsel may seek to establish, as part of its *prima facie* case, that the reasons asserted by a respondent for its allegedly discriminatory action are pretextual. The General Counsel may also, however, seek to establish as its *prima facie* case, only that the respondent took action based on consideration of protected activity and, after presentation of a respondent's evidence of nondiscriminatory reasons, seek to establish that those reasons are pretextual. In addition, an administrative law judge, or the Authority, may conclude that a respondent's asserted reasons for taking an action are pretextual, even if those reasons were not asserted to be such during the unfair labor practice hearing.

We note also the Authority's holding in *March Air Force Base*, where the General Counsel asserted that the respondent had lowered an employee's performance appraisal because the employee had sought union assistance and filed a grievance. The respondent asserted that the appraisal was lowered for performance-related reasons. The administrative law judge found that the General Counsel had not established a prima facie case of discrimination.

The Authority disagreed with the judge's finding and concluded that "the alleged reasons for the lowered appraisal were pretextual." 27 FLRA at 282. The Authority stated:

The Judge... declined to draw an inference that the protected activity was a motivating factor in the treatment complained of by [the employee]. We find not only that such an inference is proper, but on careful consideration we conclude that the protectedactivity alone was the motivating factor, because the asserted performance-related reasons have not been established.

Id. The Authority emphasized its holding as follows:

Since we find that the asserted reason for the [r]espondent's action was pretextual, this is not a case where both legitimate and improper motives are found which would require us to consider whether the [r]espondent would have acted as it did even absent the improper motive. In other words, this is not a "mixed motive" case, subject to the analysis outlined in *Mt. Healthy*[.]

Id. at 285 n.2.

The Authority's statement in *March Air Force Base* that it was unnecessary to determine whether the respondent would have taken the allegedly discriminatory action without the unlawful motive because no other motive was established is consistent with the analytical framework discussed above. The Authority's statement concerning the applicability of *Mt. Healthy*, however, may be misleading. As previously noted, a respondent always may seek to rebut the General Counsel's prima facie case, whether or not that case includes evidence that the respondent's asserted reasons for taking the allegedly discriminatory action were pretextual. It is erroneous to conclude, therefore, that the *Mt. Healthy* analysis does not apply in a "pretext" case. Rather, a conclusion that a respondent's asserted reasons for taking allegedly discriminatory action are pretextual is based on consideration of all the evidence presented in a case, including evidence presented by a respondent to rebut the General Counsel's *prima facie* case.

Finally, we note that the analytical framework discussed herein is consistent with the framework applied in the private sector. The National Labor Relations Board (the Board) adopted the same test in discrimination cases arising under the National Labor Relations Act (the Act). *See Wright Line*, 251 NLRB 1083 (1980), *enforced*, 662 F.2d 889 (1st Cir. 1981), *cert. denied*, 455 U.S. 989

(1982). Under a regulatory scheme that is comparable to that of the Statute, the Board held that its General Counsel bears the burden of proving the existence of unlawful discrimination by a preponderance of the evidence. An employer may attempt to rebut the General Counsel's allegations but this rebuttal is viewed by the Board as an affirmative defense. Although the Board characterized the *Mt. Healthy* test as a "shifting of burdens," the Board cautioned that:

[T]his shifting of burdens does not undermine the established concept that the General Counsel must establish an unfair labor practice by a preponderance of the evidence. The shifting burden merely requires the employer to make out what is actually an affirmative defense... to overcome the prima facie case of wrongful motive. Such a requirement does not shift the ultimate burden.

251 NLRB at 1088 n.11.

The Board's application of *Mt. Healthy* was sustained by the Supreme Court in *NLRB v. Transportation Management Corp.*, 462 U.S. 393 (1983). There, the Court emphasized that the General Counsel bears the burden of proving the elements of an unfair labor practice and that the employer's advancement of an affirmative defense does not alter the elements of an unfair labor practice that the General Counsel must prove under the Act. *Id.* at 401.

In summary, we reaffirm that the General Counsel bears the burden of proving, by a preponderance of the evidence, that an unfair labor practice has been committed. In a case involving alleged discrimination under section 7116(a)(2) of the Statute, the General Counsel must establish that the respondent's allegedly discriminatory action was motivated by consideration of protected activity. The General Counsel may also seek to establish, as part of its *prima facie* case, that respondent's asserted reasons for taking the allegedly discriminatory action are pretextual, or after presentation of respondent's evidence of lawful reasons, may seek to establish that those reasons are pretextual. *See Wright Line*, 251 NLRB at 1088 n.12 ("The absence of any legitimate basis for an action, of course, may form part of the proof of the General Counsel's case.") (citation omitted).

If the General Counsel makes the required *prima facie* showing, a respondent may seek to rebut that showing by establishing, by a preponderance of the evidence, the affirmative defense that: (1) there was a legitimate justification for its action; and (2) the same action would have been taken in the absence of protected activity. The analytical framework is the same in all cases involving alleged discrimination. *Compare Wright Line,* 251 NLRB at 1083 n.4 ("under the *Mt. Healthy* test, there is no real need to distinguish between pretext and dual motive cases.").

B. Application of Analytical Framework

The Judge concluded that the General Counsel failed to establish that Mr. Webber's nonselection was motivated by his Union activities. For the following reasons, we disagree with the Judge's conclusion. We find that Mr. Webber's Union activity was the sole reason for the cancellation of the selection register and that the Respondent did not demonstrate that it would have taken the same action in the absence of the protected activity. We further find that had the Respondent not unlawfully cancelled the selection register, Mr. Webber would have been selected for the lead guard position.

Our analysis requires an in-depth review of the testimony adduced at the hearing. We begin with a look at Mr. Webber's Union activities followed by an examination of the practice of lead guard selections.

The record indicates, and the Judge found, that Mr. Webber was an active Union president who was involved in several incidents "which may not have pleased management." Judge's Decision at 4. At least two of the incidents involved direct confrontations with the Director of Administration. Other incidents were elevated to higher levels of management. The record also indicates that for many years, possibly as long as 20 years, the selecting official for lead guard positions was the Chief of Police, who was the second level supervisor. With regard to this practice, the Respondent's personnel staffing specialist testified that prior to October 1986, at which time the selection register at issue was voided, "it would have been [the] Chief" who made lead guard selections. Transcript of Proceedings at 126. Additionally, the first line supervisor, who was designated the selecting official when the register was reissued, also testified that the Chief had always made selections in the past and that the first line supervisor was surprised when he was given the task of making the selection. *Id.* at 111.

The record also indicates that on learning of Mr. Webber's selection, the Director of Administration questioned the Chief as to why the Chief had been the selecting official. The Chief replied that he had always made the selections.

Id. at 98. The Director of Administration responded by saying "you're not going to do that any more. That's not the way I want to do it." *Id.* The Director of Administration also asked the Police Captain why the Chief was the selecting official rather than the first line supervisor. The Police Captain replied "that's the way it had been done before, in the past[.]" *Id.* at 147. The Director of Administration also testified that because of the size of the organization he was managing, he was unaware of who was making lead guard selections until the register at issue came to his attention. *Id.* at 75. The Director of Administration testified that at that time, "I changed it." *Id.*

The Respondent maintained throughout this proceeding that the register was voided because the correct procedure of having the first line supervisor be the selecting official for lead guard positions was not followed. In support of its position, the Respondent argued that: (1) the Director of Administration believed that because the first line supervisor had to supervise the lead guard, the first line supervisor should be able to decide with whom he wants to work; and (2) the position description of the first line supervisor and an agency regulation require the first line supervisor to make lead guard selections.

The first reason asserted by the Respondent must be contrasted with the fact, noted by the Judge, that the employee selected for the lead guard position would not necessarily work under the first line supervisor. Judge's Decision at 5 n.5. The record reveals that although applicants may know that a vacancy exists on a particular shift, a successful applicant for the position is not necessarily placed on that shift. Transcript at 45-46. This is so because other lead guards have an opportunity to bump into the shift. The selected employee would then be placed on the shift on which a vacancy was created by virtue of the exercise of bumping rights.

The second reason advanced by the Respondent is that the first line supervisor is required by his/her position description and an agency regulation to be the selecting official. Neither the position description nor the regulation was introduced into evidence. In fact, the Respondent's personnel staffing specialist testified that neither of those documents specifically identified the first line supervisor as the selecting official. *Id.* at 113 and 129. The specialist also stated that it was a violation of merit promotion procedures to allow the second level supervisor to make lead guard selections. *Id.* at 118 and 126. When asked by the Judge how a long-standing policy of allowing the Chief to be the selecting official could exist where such a practice was claimed to be a violation of merit promotion procedures, the specialist replied "I can't give you an answer on that[.]" *Id.* at 130.

The record also indicates that the Director of Administration and the Police Captain expressed concern about the choice of Mr. Webber to occupy a lead guard position. The Director of Administration testified that "Mr. Webber was not a good choice" based on his conduct on the Respondent's premises. Id. at 93. All of this conduct appears to have occurred during Mr. Webber's non-duty time with some of the conduct, though not all, involving representational activities. The Police Captain expressed his concern about the selection to the Director of Administration before the register was voided. As indicated by the Judge, the Police Captain also made statements to Mr. Webber's successor as Union president concerning Mr. Webber, and unions generally, which the Judge found to constitute "mild evidence of *animus*." Judge's Decision at 7. We note, additionally, the Respondent's concession that "Mr. Webber's representational activities may have contributed to a judgment as to his potential to be a [lead guard]." Respondent's Opposition at 3.

Finally, the Respondent claimed, in its post-hearing brief to the Judge, that from the time the register was voided, "all selections within the guard force have been made by the first line supervisors." Respondent's Post-Hearing Brief at 7. (Emphasis in original.) However, the record contains no evidence that there were any lead guard selections following the selection action in this case. The evidence that was introduced indicated only that first line supervisors had made selections for Police Officer positions. Respondent's Exhibits 6 and 7.

As indicated above, the Judge concluded that although he regarded the "course of events here as highly suspicious[,]" the General Counsel failed to establish that Mr. Webber's nonselection was motivated by his Union activities. Judge's Decision at 7. In our view, the record clearly establishes otherwise.

There is no dispute that Mr. Webber was an active Union president and that he was engaged in protected activity when he was selected for the lead guard position. The selection of Mr. Webber was made in accordance with the long-standing practice of having the second level supervisor serve as the selecting official. It was only when the Director of Administration learned of Mr. Webber's selection that the Respondent insisted upon following what it claimed to be the correct procedure of having the first line supervisor make the selection. However, no evidence was presented by the Respondent to demonstrate that this was the correct procedure or that there was a policy in effect of having the first line supervisor make lead guard selections. To the contrary, the Director of Administration testified that he was changing the policy and that the second level supervisor would not be making lead guard selections in the future. Moreover, the record establishes, and the Respondent concedes, that Mr. Webber's protected activity played a part in the decision that Mr. Webber was a poor choice for the position.

Based on the foregoing, we conclude that the General Counsel has established by a preponderance of the evidence that the voiding of the selection register, which resulted in Mr. Webber not being selected for the lead guard position, was motivated solely by his protected activity. Therefore, we find that the Respondent's alleged reasons for its actions were pretextual. Accordingly, we find that the Respondent violated section 7116(a)(1) and (2) of the Statute.

VII. Remedy

The General Counsel has requested that Mr. Webber be retroactively promoted and made whole for any loss in wages as a result of the Respondent's unlawful conduct. We agree.

Sections 7105(g) and 7118 of the Statute vest the Authority with broad remedial powers to correct violations of the Statute. Such remedial powers have been exercised, in appropriate circumstances, by ordering reinstatement of a wrongfully discharged employee and directing the retroactive promotion of an employee who had been unlawfully discriminated against on the basis of protected union activity. See, respectively, *United States Marine Corps, Marine Corps Logistics Base, Barstow, California*, 5 FLRA 725 (1981) and *United States Department of Defense, Department of the Air Force, Headquarters 47th Flying Training Wing (ATC), Laughlin Air Force Base, Texas*, 18 FLRA 142 (1985).

The Authority has consistently held that in order to direct a retroactive promotion with backpay which meets the requirements of the Back Pay Act, 5 U.S.C. § 5596, there must be a determination that the aggrieved employee was affected by an unjustified or unwarranted personnel action and also that such action directly resulted in the denial of a promotion to the aggrieved employee. See *American Federation of Government Employees*, Local 17, AFL-CIO and Veterans Administration Central Office, 24 FLRA 424 (1986).

In this case, the unlawful discrimination which formed the basis of the unfair labor practice constituted the unjustified or unwarranted personnel action. We find, moreover, that such action directly resulted in the failure to promote Mr. Webber.

As previously indicated, Mr. Webber was the selectee on the register that was cancelled on October 10, 1986. The Director of Administration testified that he "would have left the selection stand" had it been made by the first line supervisor. Transcript at 94. We have concluded, however, that Mr. Webber's Union activity was the sole reason for cancellation of the selection register. Although the personnel staffing specialist testified at the hearing that a selection register must be processed through various steps before it is finalized, there was no testimony or evidence that these additional steps would have changed the outcome of the selection. In other words, the record is entirely devoid of evidence that Mr. Webber would not have been selected had the register been properly processed. As we have found the Respondent's reason for cancelling the register to have been unlawfully motivated by Mr. Webber's protected activity, and not for any lawfully motivated reason, the record establishes that Mr. Webber would have been selected. A retroactive promotion with backpay and a restoration of benefits to make Mr. Webber whole is thus compelled by the circumstances of this case and can provide the only meaningful remedy for the unfair labor practice.(*/)

VIII. Order

Pursuant to section 2423.29 of the Authority's Rules and Regulations and section 7118 of the Federal Service Labor-Management Relations Statute, the Letterkenny Army Depot, shall:

1. Cease and desist from:

(a) Refusing to promote George C. Webber to the position of Lead Guard because of Mr. Webber's protected union activities.

(b) In any like or related manner interfering with, restraining or coercing its employees in the exercise of the rights assured them by the Statute.

2. Take the following affirmative action in order to effectuate the purposes and policies of the Statute:

(a) Retroactively promote George C. Webber to the position of Lead Guard, GS-085-05, reimburse him for the loss of pay suffered by reason of the cancellation of the selection register on October

10, 1986, which resulted in the failure to promote him, due to his protected union activities, and restore to him any rights or privileges he may have lost by such action.

(b) Post at its facility at the Letterkenny Army Depot, copies of the attached Notice on forms to be furnished by the Federal Labor Relations Authority. Upon receipt of such forms, they shall be signed by the Commanding Officer, Letterkenny Army Depot, and shall be posted and maintained for 60 consecutive days thereafter, in conspicuous places, including all bulletin board and other places where notices to employees are customarily posted. Reasonable steps shall be taken to ensure that such notices are not altered, defaced, or covered by any other material.

(c) Pursuant to section 2423.30 of the Authority's Rules and Regulations, notify the Regional Director, Region II, in writing, within 30 days from the date of this Order, as to what steps have been taken to comply.

NOTICE TO ALL EMPLOYEES AS ORDERED BY THE FEDERAL LABOR RELATIONS AUTHORITY AND TO EFFECTUATE THE POLICIES OF THE FEDERAL SERVICE LABOR-MANAGEMENT RELATIONS STATUTE

WE NOTIFY OUR EMPLOYEES THAT:

We will not refuse to promote George C. Webber because he engaged in protected union activities.

We will not in any like or related manner, interfere with, restrain, or coerce our employees in the exercise of the rights assured them by the Federal Service Labor-Management Relations Statute.

We will retroactively promote George C. Webber to the position of Lead Guard, GS-085-05, reimburse him for the loss of pay suffered by reason of the cancellation of the selection register on October 10, 1986, which resulted in the failure to promote him, due to his protected union activities, and restore to him any rights or privileges he may have lost by such action.

_____

(Agency)

Dated:_____

By:_____

(Signature) (Title)

This Notice must remain posted for 60 consecutive days from the date of posting and must not be altered, defaced, or covered by any other material.

If employees have any questions concerning this Notice or compliance with its provisions, they may communicate directly with the Regional Director, Region II, Federal Labor Relations Authority, whose address is: 26 Federal Plaza, Room 3700, New York, NY 10278, and whose telephone number is: (212) 264-4934.

Footnotes

(If blank, the decision does not have footnotes.)

* In directing the Respondent to retroactively promote Mr. Webber, we do not address what action, if any, might be necessary with respect to the employee who was selected when the register was reissued.

Case #5 Appropriate Arrangements

53 FLRA No. 59
Federal Labor Relations Authority
Washngton, D.C.

_____

National Treasury Employees Union
(Union)
and
U.S. Department of Commerce Patent & Trademark Office
(Agency)

_____

Case No. 0-NG-2159-001

DECISION AND ORDER ON NEGOTIABILITY ISSUES

September 30, 1997

Before the Authority: Phyllis N. Segal, Chair; and Donald S.

Wasserman, Member.

I. Statement of the Case

This case is before the Authority on a negotiability appeal filed by the Union under section 7105(a)(2)(E) of the Federal Service Labor-Management Relations Statute (the Statute).[1] We address here 4 proposals that were declared outside the duty to bargain during contract negotiations and 14 provisions that were disapproved by the Agency head under section 7114(c) of the Statute. Other proposals and provisions that were contained in the Union's appeal were addressed by the Authority in *National Treasury Employees Union and U.S. Department of Commerce, Patent and Trademark Office*, 52 FLRA 1265 (1997) (*Department of Commerce*).

For the reasons fully explained in sections III through XVII of this decision, we reach the following conclusions with respect to the proposals and provisions examined herein.[2] We find that Proposals 1, 3, 5 and 6 are within the duty to bargain. We further find that the following provisions are not contrary to law: Article 7, Section 11; Article 35, Section 9; Article 36, Section 9; Article 12, Section 4(G); Article 12, Section 5; Article 13, Section 3(M); Article 18, Section 1(G); Article 18, Section 1(H); and Article 18, Section 3(A). We dismiss the petition for review as to the following provisions: Article 14, Section 2(E); Article 14, Section 12; Article 15, Section 4; Article 19, Section 2(A); and Article 28, Section 5.

More particularly, we find the following:

Proposal 1, which would require the Agency to remove certain letters of reprimand and oral admonishments confirmed in writing from employee records, is within the duty to bargain. See Part III, *infra*.

Proposal 3, which establishes conditions for the reopening and renegotiation of contract provisions, is within the duty to bargain. See Part IV, *infra*.

Proposals 5 and 6, which require the use of progressive disciplinary actions and adverse actions under prescribed circumstances, are within the duty to bargain. See Part V, *infra*.

Article 7, Section 11, which states that inquiries and investigations into off-duty misconduct must be based on activity that would have some nexus to the employee's position, is not contrary to law. See Part VI, *infra*.

Article 35, Section 9 and Article 36, Section 9, which provide for written statements of the nexus between off-duty misconduct and the efficiency of the service and an opportunity to respond to changes in the statements of that nexus, are not contrary to law. See Part VI, *infra*.

Article 12, Section 4(G), which prescribes the composition of rating and ranking panels and the duties of the selecting official and the Office of Personnel, is not contrary to law. See Part VII, *infra*.

Article 12, Section 5, which provides that no employee will be placed in a disadvantageous position by virtue of service on a detail or work project, is not contrary to law. See Part VIII, *infra*.

Article 13, Section 3(M), which gives an employee an opportunity to resign before a written decision to effect a reduction in grade or removal is issued, is not contrary to law. See Part IX, *infra*.

Article 14, Section 2(E), which would require the use of an electronic access system to secure law office suites, is contrary to law. See Part X, *infra*.

Article 14, Section 12, which would grant administrative leave under certain circumstances, is contrary to law. See Part XI, *infra*.

Article 15, Section 4, which conditions the assignment of overtime on the assignment of training in connection with overtime assignments, is contrary to law. See Part XII, *infra*.

Article 18, Section 1(G), which permits the Agency to issue a written warning prior to placing an employee on sick leave restriction, is not contrary to law. See Part XIII, *infra*.

Article 18, Section 1(H), which would allow employees to use sick leave that they have not yet earned, is not contrary to law. See Part XIV, *infra*.

Article 18, Section 3(A), which would allow the use of advanced sick leave for maternity purposes, is not contrary to law. See Part XV, *infra*.

Article 19, Section 2(A), which would require the Agency to assign career development details in a fair and equitable manner, is contrary to law. See Part XVI, *infra*.

Article 28, Section 5, which would require the Agency to provide training on automated systems, is contrary to law. See Part XVII, *infra*.

II. Preliminary Matters

A. The Union's General and Unsupported Claims Under Sections 7106(b)(2) and 7106(b)(3) of the Statute Are Not Properly Raised

In its petition for review, the Union makes a general claim that the provisions "all set forth procedures concerning a variety of working conditions. In the alternative, they are all appropriate arrangements under section 7106(b)(3) for employees adversely affected by the Agency's decision to exercise various management rights." Petition for Review at 5. Where a union offers no arguments or authority to support its bare assertion that a particular provision is within the duty to bargain on either or both of these grounds, we do not consider the assertion. *See American Federation of Government Employees, Council of Locals No. 163 and U.S. Department of Defense, Defense Contract Audit Agency*, 51 FLRA 1504, 1513-14 (1996) (*Defense Contract Audit Agency*) (Authority rejected a union's bare assertion that a proposal was a negotiable procedure under section 7106(b)(2)); *American Federation of Government Employees, National Border Patrol Council and U.S. Department of Justice, Immigration and Naturalization Service*, 51 FLRA 1308, 1317 (1996) (*Immigration and Naturalization Service*) (Authority determined that because the union did not explain, and the proposal did not speak to, the manner in which a disputed portion would address adversely affected employees, that portion did not constitute an arrangement under section 7106(b)(3)). Accordingly, we address and resolve in this decision only those claims under sections 7106(b)(2) and 7106(b)(3) as to which the Union has provided support for its specific assertions.

B. Determining the Meaning to be Ascribed to the Proposals and Provisions [3]

In interpreting a disputed provision, the Authority looks to its plain wording and any union statement of intent. If the union's explanation is consistent with the plain wording, the Authority adopts that explanation for the purpose of construing what the provision means and, based on its meaning, deciding whether it is, or is not, contrary to law. *E.g., American Federation of Government Employees, Local 1900 and U.S. Department of the Army, Headquarters, Forces Command, Fort McPherson, Georgia*, 51 FLRA 133, 138-39 (1995) (*Fort McPherson*). Where a provision is silent as to a particular matter, a union's statement clarifying the matter will be adopted if it is otherwise consistent with the wording of the provision. *E.g., Laurel Bay*, 51 FLRA at 737. When a union's explanation is not supported by a reasonable construction, however, the explanation is deemed inconsistent with the plain wording, and the Authority does not adopt it for the purpose of determining whether the provision is contrary to law. *E.g., International Federation of Professional and Technical Engineers, Local 3 and U.S. Department of the Navy, Philadelphia Naval Shipyard, Philadelphia, Pennsylvania*, 51 FLRA 451, 459 (1995) (*Philadelphia Naval Shipyard*).

C. We Consider Only the Disputed Portions of the Provisions

As we stated in *Department of Commerce*, the Union has not requested the Authority to sever and separately consider portions of the provisions that are not in dispute and, further, that there is no other basis on which to do so. 52 FLRA at 1288 n.18. See also *American Federation of Government Employees, Local 1336 and Social Security Administration, Mid-America Program Service Center*, 52 FLRA 794, 797 (1996); *Patent Office Professional Association and Department of Commerce, Patent and Trademark Office*, 39 FLRA 783, 807 n.7 (1991). Here, as in *Department of Commerce*, where the Agency objects only to portions of provisions and we find that the disputed portions are not contrary to law, we order the Agency head to rescind its disapproval of the provisions in their entirety. Where, on the other hand, disputed portions are found to be contrary to law, we dismiss the petition for review as to the entire provisions. *E.g., Immigration and Naturalization Service*, 51 FLRA 1308 (Provisions 2 and 4).

III. Proposal 1

Article 7, (Employee Rights) Section 4(c)

A letter of reprimand will be removed from the employee's record no later than 12 months from the date of issuance. Oral admonishments confirmed in writing will be removed after 3 months.

A. Positions of the Parties

1. Agency

The Agency contends that the proposal interferes with management's right to discipline under section 7106(a)(2)(A) of the Statute and that it is not a negotiable appropriate arrangement within the meaning of section 7106(b)(3) of the Statute. The Agency states that the proposal would preclude management from relying on a letter of reprimand more than 12 months after it was issued and from relying on an oral admonishment, confirmed in writing, more than 3 months after it was issued. The Agency explains that because letters of reprimand and oral admonishments would be expunged from employees' files, they would no longer be "of record" and could not be relied on in future penalties. Agency's Supplemental Brief at 2. As a result, the Agency claims that the proposal would restrict the Agency's ability to determine the degree of discipline it could impose by preventing it from using prior disciplinary records.

2. Union

The Union agrees with the Agency that, under the proposal, the Agency could not rely on letters of reprimand and oral admonishments confirmed in writing that had been removed from employee files. The Union contends that the proposal is an appropriate arrangement under section 7106(b)(3) of the Statute. The Union maintains that employees would benefit because the reprimands would no longer form the basis for more severe disciplinary action. The Union asserts that the removal of letters of reprimand after 12 months is a reasonable exercise of the Agency's discretion and would not impose a significant burden. In this regard, the Union states that if additional discipline has not been brought against an employee within 12 months, the reprimand would have served its purpose "of reforming an employee's conduct[.]" Response at 4. In addition, with respect to oral admonishments confirmed in writing, the Union notes that such records are not included in the contractual definition of disciplinary action and argues that "[t]he Agency loses little when it relinquishes its right to base real disciplinary action" on oral admonishments because "[t]hese actions are not significant enough to be treated as disciplinary actions." *Id.* at 5.

The Union also asserts that the proposal "records a procedure by which letters of reprimand and oral admonishments confirmed in writing will be removed from the records of employees." Petition for Review at 2. Finally, the Union argues that the proposal is consistent with regulations that were contained in the Federal Personnel Manual (FPM) and afforded management the discretion to remove letters of reprimand or similar documents at any time.

B. Analysis and Conclusions

1. Meaning of the Proposal

This proposal would establish a time schedule for the removal of certain documents from employee records. The Agency would be required to remove letters of reprimand no later than 12 months from the date of issuance, and to remove oral admonishments, confirmed in writing, 3 months after issuance. The Union acknowledges that the intent of the proposal is to preclude the Agency from relying on the documents, once they have been removed from employee records, as the basis for more severe progressive disciplinary action. As the Union's statement of intent is consistent with the proposal's wording, we adopt it. *Laurel Bay,* 51 FLRA at 737.

2. The Proposal Is Within the Duty to Bargain

a. The Proposal Affects the Right to Discipline

The Authority has long held that proposals that would restrict the evidence an agency may rely on to support a disciplinary action directly interfere with the agency's right to discipline employees. See *International Association of Machinists and Aerospace Workers, Lodge 39 and U.S. Department of the Navy, Naval Aviation Depot, Norfolk, Virginia,* 41 FLRA 1452, 1454 (1991) (*Naval Aviation Depot*), and cases cited therein. Proposal 1 would establish a time limit on the use of prior written reprimands and oral admonishments to determine the penalty in subsequent discipline. Accordingly, the proposal affects management's right to discipline employees under section 7106(a)(2)(A) of the Statute. See *International Association of Machinists and Aerospace Workers, District Lodge 110, Local Lodges 1859, 2296, 2297, 2316 and U.S. Department of the Navy, United States Marine Corps Air Station and Naval Aviation Depot, Cherry Point, North Carolina,* 42 FLRA 192 (1991).

b. The Proposal Is an Appropriate Arrangement

The approach for determining whether a proposal is within the duty to bargain under section 7106(b)(3) is set out in *National Association of Government Employees, Local R14-87 and Kansas Army National Guard,* 21 FLRA 24 (1986) (*KANG*). Under that approach, the Authority initially determines whether the proposal is intended to be an "arrangement" for employees adversely affected by the exercise of a management right. An arrangement must seek to mitigate adverse effects "flowing from the exercise of a protected management right." *United States Department of the Treasury, Office of the Chief Counsel, Internal Revenue Service v. FLRA,* 960 F.2d 1068, 1073 (D.C. Cir. 1992) (*IRS, Chief Counsel*). See also *Fort McPherson,* 51 FLRA at 141; *American Federation of Government Employees, Council of Prison Locals, Local 3974 and U.S. Department of Justice, Federal Bureau of Prisons, Federal Correctional Institution, McKean, Pennsylvania,* 48 FLRA 225, 230-31 (1993) (*Federal Correctional Institution*). The adverse effect need not flow from the management right that a given proposal affects. *E.g., National Treasury Employees Union, Chapter 243 and U.S. Department of Commerce, Patent and Trademark Office,* 49 FLRA 176, 184 (1994) (Member Armendariz concurring in part and dissenting in part) (*PTO*).

The claimed arrangement must also be sufficiently "tailored" to compensate or benefit employees suffering adverse effects attributable to the exercise of management's right(s). *E.g., id.* As the Authority reaffirmed, relying on *United States Department of the Interior, Minerals Management Service, New Orleans, Louisiana v. FLRA*, 969 F.2d 1158, 1162 (D.C. Cir. 1992) (*Minerals Management Service*), section 7106(b)(3) brings within the duty to bargain proposals that provide "balm" to be administered "only to hurts arising from" the exercise of management rights. *Immigration and Naturalization Service*, 51 FLRA at 1319. That section of the Statute does not bring within the duty to bargain proposals that are so broad in their sweep that the "balm" would be applied to employees indiscriminately without regard to whether the group as a whole is likely to suffer, or has suffered, adverse effects as a consequence of management action under section 7106. Id. *See also PTO*, 49 FLRA at 184.

If the proposal is an arrangement that is sufficiently tailored, the Authority then determines whether it is appropriate, or whether it is inappropriate because it excessively interferes with the relevant management right(s).[4] *KANG*, 21 FLRA at 31-33. In doing so, the Authority weighs the benefits afforded to employees under the arrangement against the intrusion on the exercise of management's rights. *Id.*

Proposal 1 would insulate employees from more severe progressive discipline under specified circumstances. As such, the proposal is designed to address the adverse effects flowing from the exercise of management's right to discipline. E.g., *United Power Trades Organization and U.S. Department of the Army, Corps of Engineers, Walla Walla, Washington*, 44 FLRA 1145, 1149-50 (1992) (Proposal 1) (*Corps of Engineers*). The proposal also is tailored to compensate employees who suffer those adverse effects because it applies only to employees who receive letters of reprimand or oral admonishments confirmed in writing. E.g., *National Federation of Federal Employees, Local 1214 and U.S. Department of the Army Headquarters, U.S. Army Training Center and Fort Jackson, Fort Jackson, South Carolina*, 51 FLRA 1362, 1365-66 (1996) (Member Armendariz concurring) (*Fort Jackson*). Accordingly, we find that the proposal is an arrangement.

We also find that the proposal is appropriate. Employees would benefit by being protected against the imposition of more severe progressive discipline in the future based on letters of reprimand and oral admonishments confirmed in writing that have been effective in deterring conduct for which discipline is warranted. In particular, the Agency's inability to use such information to support more severe subsequent discipline would reward employees who have taken steps to avoid conduct for which progressive discipline could be imposed.

The constraints that would be imposed on the exercise of management's right to discipline are slight. First, there would still be a not insubstantial period of time during which the Agency could rely on letters of reprimand and oral admonishments confirmed in writing. For example, the Agency could exercise its right to impose more severe discipline on an employee if, during the 12-month period following receipt of a letter of reprimand, the employee engaged in conduct warranting further discipline. Second, the Agency maintains the right to rely on more severe disciplinary actions, such as suspensions and removals that are imposed based on more serious or egregious misconduct, in cases where subsequent discipline is warranted.

This proposal is unlike the proposal in *Naval Aviation Depot*, 41 FLRA at 1454-56, which precluded consideration of suspensions or reductions in grade or pay that occurred more than 3 years prior to the date of a proposed adverse action and was found to excessively interfere with management's right to discipline. Proposal 1 would preclude the Agency from considering only less severe penalties. Management retains the right to consider the full range of other penalties that may have been imposed in determining an appropriate disciplinary action. Although the proposal here permits management to rely on prior penalties for a shorter period of time than the proposal in *Naval Aviation Depot*, we find it more significant, as set forth above, that management can consider the full range of other penalties in imposing subsequent discipline.

Finally, the Agency's statement that the proposal "goes beyond an appropriate arrangement," is an unsupported assertion and, as such, does not warrant a conclusion that the proposal excessively interferes with management's right to discipline. Agency's Supplemental Statement on Petition for Review at 2. Accordingly, we find, on balance, that the benefits afforded to employees under the proposal outweigh the intrusion on management's right to discipline. Therefore, we conclude that Proposal 1 constitutes an appropriate arrangement under section 7106(b)(3) and that it is within the duty to bargain.

In reaching our conclusion, we recognize that the Authority has reached a contrary result with respect to similar proposals and provisions...., *American Federation of Government Employees, Local 900 and U.S. Department of the Army, U.S. Army Reserve Personnel Center, St. Louis, Missouri,* 46 FLRA 1494 (1993) (Provision 5); *Corps of Engineers,* 44 FLRA at 1149-52. In those cases, the Authority did not consider the severity of disciplinary action that agencies were precluded from using when imposing future disciplinary action. In our view, the Authority did not appropriately take into account in those decisions the minor nature of the infractions and penalties at issue and, as a result, did not properly weigh the effect of the proposals on the exercise of the right to discipline against the benefits that would be afforded to employees. We will no longer follow that precedent to the extent that it is inconsistent with our decision here.

IV. Proposal 3

Article 21 (Duration and Amendment), Sections 2 and 3

Section 2: This Agreement may be reopened at any time for the following purposes:

A. Amending articles or negotiating new articles which are required by changes in law or regulations. No changes shall be considered except those bearing directly on and falling within the scope of such laws or regulations.

B. Negotiating new articles on subject [sic] not previously negotiated.

C. Negotiating matters for which new or extended bargaining rights are provided by appropriate authority.

Section 3: Any time during the term of this Agreement, the parties may by mutual accord, terminate, extend, change or revise this Agreement. The party requesting the reopening will submit proposals to the other in writing. Within thirty (30) calendar days after proposals have been received by the receiving party such party will indicate either a willingness or refusal to negotiate. If consent is obtained, the receiving party will submit counterproposals and/or proposals and negotiations will commence with the procedures set forth in Article 33. A failure to consent to reopen under this Section by either party will not be the basis for filing any grievance under this Agreement.

A. Positions of the Parties

1. Agency

The Agency contends that the proposal is outside the duty to bargain based on *Social Security Administration v. FLRA,* 956 F.2d 1280 (4th Cir. 1992) (*SSA v. FLRA*), in which the court held that, under the Statute, Federal unions may not compel union-initiated midterm bargaining over issues not addressed in parties' agreements. Although the Agency acknowledges that the Authority has not accepted the court's decision or agreed to follow it in other circuits, the Agency claims that the Authority conceded, in a different case before the U.S. Court of Appeals for the Fourth Circuit, that it is bound to follow *SSAv. FLRA* within that jurisdiction. The Agency adds that it "resides" in the Fourth Circuit's jurisdiction. Supplemental Statement of Position at 5.

The Agency also contends that, despite the Union's intent, Section 3 of the proposal does not make bargaining discretionary. The Agency asserts that although Section 3 states that the refusal to bargain is not grievable, it does not preclude the Union from compelling the Agency to bargain through other proceedings, such as an unfair labor practice proceeding.

2. Union

The Union contends that the Authority has declined to follow the court's decision in *SSAv. FLRA,* and that it has found, instead, that unions have the right to initiate midterm bargaining.

The Union also distinguishes between Sections 2 and 3, noting that the former mandates bargaining while the latter makes bargaining discretionary. The Union also explains that Section 2 applies when "changes in the agreement are required by changes in law or regulation, if either party proposes new articles not previously negotiated, or if new or extended bargaining rights are provided by appropriate authority." Petition for Review at 3. Section 3 applies to "bargain[ing] changes to the existing provisions in the agreement." Id.

More specifically as to Section 2, the Union explains that Section 2(A) is "limited in its scope to bargaining over changes that are required by changes in law and regulation." Response at 11 (emphasis omitted). The Union adds that a provision of the agreement that is not in dispute (Article 3, Section 1) obligates the parties to follow existing and future laws. On this basis, the Union asserts that the agreement would have to be modified to comport with changes in law in any event. The Union also claims that "only Section 2B represents the type of mid-term bargaining proscribed by the Fourth Circuit." *Id.* at 8. The Union adds that, even if *SSA v. FLRA* were applied to Sections 2(A), 2(C) and 3, there is nothing in the court's decision that would render the proposal outside the duty to bargain. The Union maintains that if new or extended bargaining rights are provided by appropriate authority, a situation not addressed in *SSA v. FLRA*, there would be an obligation to bargain and the Agency could not lawfully refuse to do so.

As to Section 3, the Union claims that this part of the proposal would not permit the Union to compel midterm bargaining. Specifically, the Union notes that the phrase "may by mutual accord" signifies that if one party to the agreement does not consent to mid-term bargaining, there can be no negotiations. Response at 9 (emphasis omitted). The Union maintains that its interpretation of Section 3 is reinforced by the use of the terms "willingness" and "consent" in the remaining sentences of the section and by the final sentence, which precludes a grievance over a party's decision to withhold consent. Id. The Union also claims that, because bargaining under Section 3 is predicated on mutual consent, "the Union does not believe that it has any right to compel mid-term negotiations... by means of an unfair labor practice." *Id.* at 10. The Union adds that if an unfair labor practice charge were filed, it would be dismissed based on the language of Section 3.

B. Analysis and Conclusions

1. Meaning of the Proposal

By its terms, Section 2 of the proposal would permit either party to reopen the agreement for negotiations under prescribed circumstances. The Union explains that, once reopened, Section 2 would require bargaining. Section 3 provides for renegotiations under different circumstances. The Union explains that Section 3 bargaining is contingent on mutual assent. The Union's explanations regarding Sections 2 and 3 are consistent with their wording and we adopt them. *Laurel Bay,* 51 FLRA at 737. In addition, although the wording of Section 3 is silent with respect to the filing of an unfair labor practice charge, the Union's explanation as to how this section will operate shows its intention that it could not compel bargaining. As this explanation is consistent with the language of Section 3, we adopt it. *Id.*

2. The Proposal is Within the Duty to Bargain

The Agency objects to the proposal on two grounds. The first ground applies to Sections 2 and 3. The second ground applies to Section 3 only. We address each objection separately. For the reasons explained below, we find that Proposal 3 is within the duty to bargain.

a. Sections 2 and 3 Are Consistent With Bargaining Obligations Under the Statute

Sections 2 and 3 seek to establish the circumstances under which the parties are authorized to bargain during the term of the agreement. Under Authority precedent, the duty to bargain in good faith imposed by the Statute requires an agency to bargain during the term of a collective bargaining agreement over union-initiated proposals that are not contained in or covered by the agreement unless the union has waived its right to bargain on the subject matter involved. *Internal Revenue Service,* 29 FLRA 162, 166 (1987). In *Internal Revenue Service,* the Authority adopted the holding and statutory construction of the *U.S. Court of Appeals for the D.C. Circuit in National Treasury Employees Union v. FLRA,* 810 F.2d 295 (D.C. Cir. 1987) (*NTEU v. FLRA*). There, the court determined that the Statute's obligation to bargain encompasses union-initiated midterm bargaining based on the language of the Statute, congressional intent, and private sector precedent under the National Labor Relations Act.

As the Agency points out, the U.S. Court of Appeals for the Fourth Circuit interprets the Statute differently. In *SSA v. FLRA,* that court expressly rejected the reasoning of the D.C. Circuit, and held that bargaining over union-initiated proposals during the term of an agreement is not required by the Statute. 956 F.2d at 1281. In the face of this irreconcilable split in the circuits, the Authority has continued to adhere to the view of the D.C. Circuit, adopted in *Internal Revenue Service,* for the reasons that are set forth in that decision.

The proposal in this case, however, presents an issue different from that over which the Fourth and D.C. Circuits disagree in *SSA v. FLRA* and *NTEU v. FLRA,* respectively. This case concerns whether a bargaining proposal, offered as part of term negotiations and authorizing the parties to negotiate midterm, is within the Agency's duty to bargain. As such, the case before us is akin to *U.S. Department of Energy, Washington, D.C.,* 51 FLRA 124 (1995) (Department of Energy), reversed sub nom. *U.S. Department of Energy v. FLRA,* 106 F.3d 1158 (4th Cir. 1997) (*DOE v. FLRA*). In *Department of Energy,* the Authority found that a collective bargaining provision obligating the agency to bargain over union-initiated midterm proposals was not inconsistent with the Statute or any other law, Government-wide regulation, or agency rule for which a compelling need had been established.[5] 51 FLRA at 129. The Fourth Circuit reversed the Authority's decision, finding that the rationale of SSA v. FLRA applied to that case as well. DOE v. FLRA, 106 F.3d at 1163.[6]

The Agency contends that because it "resides" in the Fourth Circuit, the Authority is required to apply the law of the Fourth Circuit in this case.[7] Even assuming that the Fourth Circuit would apply DOE v. FLRA to this case and find the proposal outside the Agency's obligation to bargain, the Agency's assertion is flawed in two respects: First, the Agency fails to take into account the judicial review provisions of section 7123(a) of the Statute; and second, the Agency ignores the importance of a uniformly administered Federal laborrelations program.

Under section 7123(a), a person aggrieved by a final order of the Authority may "institute an action for judicial review of the Authority's order in the United States court of appeals in the circuit in which the person resides or transacts business or in the United States Court of Appeals for the District of Columbia. Accordingly, even when, as here, an agency's offices are located within the geographical jurisdiction of the Fourth Circuit, it is not certain that an Authority decision concerning the Agency's actions will be reviewed by that court. Were the Authority to accept the Agency's argument and find the proposal outside the Agency's duty to bargain, the Union could seek judicial review in the District of Columbia Circuit claiming, accurately, that the proposal was within the duty to bargain because it merely restates what that circuit has found to be a statutory obligation. If that court were to review such a determination, the Authority's decision would be reversed. Accordingly, irrespective of the course chosen, the Authority could find itself in the position of defending a determination which is inconsistent with precedent of the United States court of appeals in which review is obtained.[8]

Second, the Authority is charged with providing leadership in establishing policies and guidance relating to the Statute, 5 U.S.C. § 7105(a), as well as interpreting the Statute in a manner consistent with the requirements of an effective and efficient government, 5 U.S.C. § 7101(b). Such leadership can be accomplished in an efficient manner only through a consistent and uniform administration of the Statute. Cf. *NLRB v. Natural Gas Utility District*, 402 U.S. 600, 603-604 (1971) (National Labor Relations Act is Federal legislation, administered by a national agency, intended to solve a national problem on a national scale). This interest in a national, uniformly administered Federal labor-management relations program would be undercut if the Authority were to resolve cases based on the geographic locale of the origin of the dispute. Moreover, in light of the multiple forum options provided by section 7123(a) of the Statute, resolution of cases on this basis would be futile in any event.

Accordingly, when faced with an irreconcilable split in the circuit courts, the Authority must apply its expertise and reach a determination as to which view best effectuates congressional intent.[9] For the reasons first expressed in *Internal Revenue Service*, the Authority continues to hold that the duty to bargain in good faith encompasses union-initiated midterm bargaining. Consequently, we respectfully decline to apply the contrary precedent of the Fourth Circuit to this case. Instead, we adhere to the rationale set forth in *Department of Energy*.

b. Section 3 Is Not Contrary to Law

We reject the Agency's contention that this section is contrary to law because it could compel the Agency, through an unfair labor practice proceeding, to engage in midterm bargaining with respect to terminating, extending, changing or revising provisions of the agreement. Based on the Union's explanation that we have adopted, Section 3 would not operate in this manner. That is, nothing in Section 3 would obligate the Agency to consent to enter into midterm bargaining and, if it chose not to do so, there would be no basis on which to file an unfair labor practice charge.[10]

V. Proposals 5 and 6 (11)

Proposal 5

Article 35 (Disciplinary Actions), Section 2

The parties recognize the Agency's discretion to determine an appropriate penalty in accordance with Section 3 below. Unless inconsistent with established office policy, disciplinary actions shall generally be progressive in nature and fairly relate to the offense.

Proposal 6

Article 36 (Adverse Actions), Section 2

The parties recognize the Agency's discretion to determine an appropriate penalty in accordance with Section 3 below. Unless inconsistent with established office policy, adverse actions shall generally be progressive in nature and fairly relate to the offense.

A. Positions of the Parties

1. Agency

The Agency contends that Proposals 5 and 6 impose substantive requirements on, and therefore directly interfere with, management's right to discipline under section 7106(a)(2)(A) of the Statute by: (1) requiring the Agency to use progressive discipline; and (2) insuring that penalties fairly relate to the offenses for which they are imposed. The Agency cites a number of Authority decisions in support. The Agency further contends that in *American Federation of Government Employees, AFL-CIO, Local 3732 and U.S. Department of Transportation, United States Merchant Marine Academy, Kings Point, New York*, 39 FLRA 187 (1991) (*Merchant Marine Academy*) (Provision 2), the Authority found that a provision requiring an agency to apply progressive discipline was not negotiable as an appropriate arrangement under section 7106(b)(3) of the Statute.

2. Union

The Union acknowledges that the Authority has found proposals similar to Proposals 5 and 6 nonnegotiable. However, the Union contends that the proposals here are distinguishable because they "preserve[] the Agency's right to deviate from its current policy of progressive discipline during the life of the [parties'] agreement." Response at 16. In this regard, the Union asserts that the proposals "tip] the balance of the *KANG* test in favor of the benefit to employees." *Id.* The Union further argues that, unlike *American Federation of Government Employees, Local 1426 and U.S. Department of the Army, Fort Sheridan, Illinois*, 45 FLRA 867 (1992) (*Fort Sheridan*), Proposals 5 and 6 do not restrict the Agency's right to determine an appropriate penalty and, therefore, that they constitute appropriate arrangements under section 7106(b)(3) of the Statute.

B. Analysis and Conclusions

1. Meaning of the Proposals

By their express terms, these proposals require that, as a general matter and unless inconsistent with established office policy, disciplinary and adverse actions will be progressive and fairly relate to the offense. The proposals do not define the meaning of the phrase "established office policy." However, the Union makes two points that serve to explain the phrase. First, the Union explains that the Agency retains the right to deviate from its "current policy" of progressive discipline. Second, the Union contrasts these proposals with a proposal at issue in *Fort Sheridan*.

As to the first point, there is no further explanation as to whether "current policy" refers to policy that was in existence at the time the parties negotiated the agreement or to policy in effect during the term of the agreement, which may include changes to the preexisting policy. The fact that the Union contrasts these proposals to the proposal in *Fort Sheridan* persuades us that it is the latter. In *Fort Sheridan*, the union explained that the intent of its proposal mandating the use of progressive discipline, which the union claimed was required under an agency regulation, was to obligate such usage "without regard to whether the regulation is rescinded or a decision made to eliminate the use of progressive discipline as to certain forms of employee conduct." 45 FLRA at 875. By stating that Proposals 5 and 6 do not restrict the Agency's right to determine an appropriate penalty, we construe these proposals to mean that, unlike the situation in *Fort Sheridan*, the Agency would have the flexibility to promulgate new policy during the life of the agreement. Accordingly, in view of the Union's statements, which are consistent with the wording of the proposals and which we adopt, we find that the phrase "established office policy" means that policy in effect at the time that progressive disciplinary and adverse actions are taken. See *Fort McPherson*, 51 FLRA at 138-39.

2. The Proposals Are Within the Duty to Bargain

a. The Proposals Affect the Right to Discipline

Both parties acknowledge that the Authority previously has found nonnegotiable proposals requiring the use of progressive discipline. *E.g., Merchant Marine Academy*, 39 FLRA at 198-99; *U.S. Department of the Navy, Naval Aviation Depot, Marine Corps Air Station, Cherry Point, North Carolina and International Association of Machinists and Aerospace Workers, Local 2297*, 36 FLRA 28, 32-36 (1990) (*Marine Corps Air Station*). In those cases, the Authority held that restrictions on an agency's ability to choose the specific penalty to impose in disciplinary actions directly interfere with the right to discipline employees under section 7106(a)(2)(A) of the Statute. The same conclusion applies here. Although Proposals 5 and 6 are not written in mandatory terms and would permit management to deviate from the use of progressive discipline, as we have explained above, they would nonetheless require the use of progressive discipline in some circumstances. Accordingly, they affect the exercise of management's right to discipline under section 7106(a)(2)(A) of the Statute.

c. The Proposals Are Appropriate Arrangements

The Authority previously has recognized that, as a general matter, a provision that requires an agency to administer discipline in a fair or consistent manner is intended to ameliorate the adverse effects on employees who are subject to the exercise of management's right to take disciplinary action. *Fort Jackson*, 51 FLRA at 1365. Proposals 5 and 6, under which disciplinary actions are "generally" to be progressive and fairly relate to the offense, similarly are intended to address the adverse effects on employees flowing from the exercise of management's right to discipline. In as much as the proposals would apply to those employees against whom disciplinary and adverse actions have been taken, they are also sufficiently tailored to administer "balm" "only to hurts arising from" the exercise of management rights. *Minerals Management Service*, 969 F.2d at 1162. Accordingly, we find that the proposals constitute arrangements.

We also find that the proposals are appropriate because they would not excessively interfere with the right to discipline. The proposals would ameliorate the adverse effects on employees by insulating them from more severe discipline than that which is progressive and proportional to the infraction. At the same time, management's ability to determine an appropriate penalty would not be seriously circumscribed for the following reasons.

First, the proposals explicitly provide for the use of progressive discipline unless doing so would be inconsistent with "established office policy." As explained above, the Agency retains the right to change its policy of progressive discipline and to apply the policy in effect at the time disciplinary and adverse actions are taken. Thus, the Agency would not, in fact, be required to use progressive discipline in all instances unless its own policies so dictate.

Second, the proposals incorporate Section 3 of Articles 35 and 36, which were not disapproved and which each set forth a non-exhaustive list of "mitigating and/or aggravating circumstances" that the Agency will apply in deciding what discipline or adverse actions are appropriate. Thus, the Agency has already agreed to apply factors that may affect the exercise of its right to discipline. We do not view the requirement that the Agency "generally" use progressive discipline as a more severe restriction on the exercise of management's right than management has already agreed to impose on itself. In our view, the intrusion on the exercise of management's right to discipline that is engendered by the proposals has less weight in view of other restrictions the Agency has agreed to apply. *Cf. Department of Interior, Bureau of Land Management v. FLRA*, 873 F.2d 1505, 1510-11 (D.C. Cir. 1989) (court rejected agency argument that provision authorizing 10-day delay in employee suspensions substantively diminished agency's right to suspend immediately disruptive employees; court found that agency had already agreed to negotiate over procedures that would have had the effect of retaining disruptive employees for more than 10 days).

As the proposals do not mandate that progressive discipline be used in all instances, they are distinguishable from proposals and provisions in other cases, including those cited by the Agency, that were deemed to excessively interfere with the right to discipline. In such cases, the agencies would have been required to either use progressive discipline or impose a minimum penalty in disciplinary actions. *E.g., Merchant Marine Academy*, 39 FLRA at 198-99; *Marine Corps Air Station*, 36 FLRA at 32-36; *American Federation of Government Employees, AFL-CIO, Local 1931 and Department of the Navy, Naval Weapons Station, Concord, California*, 32 FLRA 1023, 1044-47 (1988), *rev'd as other matters sub nom. Department of the Navy, Naval Weapons Station, Concord, California v. FLRA*, Nos. 88-7408/7470 (9th Cir. Feb. 7, 1989) (Order); *International Plate Printers, Die Stampers and Engravers Union of North America, AFL-CIO, Local 2 and Department of the Treasury, Bureau of Engraving and Printing, Washington, D.C.*, 25 FLRA 113, 133-34 (1987). Here, there are no such absolute requirements.

Finally, the proposals are similar, in effect, to the provision at issue in *Fort Jackson*. The provision there stated that "discipline and adverse actions will be based on just cause and be consistently applied equitably and promote the efficiency of the Federal Service." 51 FLRA at 1363. The Authority found that the provision did not excessively interfere with the right to discipline because, as relevant here, the provision did not require the agency to apply the same penalties under all circumstances and it preserved the agency's ability to take into account all the circumstances surrounding the disciplinary or adverse action. Although Proposals 5 and 6 are different in that they focus on the use of progressive discipline, they are similar in that they preserve management's ability to determine appropriate discipline in a manner comparable to *Fort Jackson*.

In sum, and on balance, we find that the benefits afforded to employees under Proposals 5 and 6 outweigh the intrusion on the exercise of management's right to discipline. Accordingly, the proposals are within the duty to bargain.

VI. Article 7, Section 11; Article 35, Section 9; Article 36, Section 9

Article 7 (Employee Rights), Section 11

Any inquiry and investigation into allegations of off-duty misconduct must be based on activity which, if verified, would have some nexus (i.e., some relationship) to the employee's position. The parties agree that the conduct of employees while off duty shall result in action only when there is a nexus between that conduct and the employee's official position. Employees will not be subject to harassment or frivolous inquiries.

Article 35 (Disciplinary Actions), Section 9

In cases where discipline is proposed for reasons of off-duty misconduct, the Office's written notification shall contain a statement of the nexus between the off-duty misconduct and the efficiency of the service. If the deciding official decides to substantively change the nexus statement in the proposal with adverse effect on the employee, notice of such change will be provided with the summary of the oral reply. Three work days will normally be provided for the employee and/or representative to supplement the record on this subject.

Article 36 (Adverse Actions), Section 9

In cases where discipline is proposed for reasons of off-duty misconduct, the Office's written notification shall contain a statement of the nexus between the off-duty misconduct and the efficiency of the service. If the deciding official decides to substantively change the nexus statement in the proposal with adverse affect [sic] on the employee, notice of such change will be provided with the summary of the oral reply. Three work days will normally be provided for the employee and/or representative to supplement the record or [sic] this subject.

A. Positions of the Parties

1. Agency

The Agency contends that all three provisions directly interfere with management's right to discipline under section 7106(a)(2)(A) of the Statute. The Agency claims that these provisions would place the Agency under a contractual obligation to establish a nexus between off-duty misconduct and the employee's position despite the fact that such a nexus requirement "may not always exist" under applicable laws. Statement of Position at 2. In support, the Agency relies on *National Federation of Federal Employees, Council of Veterans Administration Locals and Veterans Administration*, 31 FLRA 360, 410-13 (1988) (Council of VA Locals) (discussing Executive Order 12564), remanded *sub nom. Veterans Administration v. FLRA*, No. 88-1314 (D.C. Cir. Sep. 27, 1988), decision on remand, 33 FLRA 349.

The Agency also contends that all three provisions are inconsistent with 5 C.F.R. Part 735, which prohibits an employee from engaging in criminal, infamous, dishonest, immoral, or notoriously disgraceful misconduct. The Agency further argues that Article 7, Section 11 is inconsistent with 5 C.F.R. Part 2635, which sets forth specific standards of conduct for Federal employees and authorizes agencies to supplement those standards. The Agency explains that 5 C.F.R. § 2635.106 "states that [a] violation of this part or of an Agency supplement may be cause for appropriate corrective or disciplinary action[,]" and that the Office of Personnel Management did not intend to limit discipline for these violations to instances where the Agency could demonstrate a direct relationship between the misconduct and job performance. Statement of Position at 3. In support of this latter contention, the Agency cites *Defense Logistics Agency, Council of AFGE Locals, AFL-CIO and Department of Defense, Defense Logistics Agency*, 24 FLRA 367, 367-70 (1986) (*Defense Logistics Agency*). Finally, the Agency contends that Article 35, Section 9 and Article 36, Section 9 are inconsistent with Executive Order 12564 because there is no nexus requirement for discipline based on a violation of the Drug Free Workplace Program.

2. Union

The Union contends that Article 7, Section 11 is identical to a provision found negotiable by the Authority in *United States Department of Justice, Immigration and Naturalization Service and American Federation of Government Employees, National Border Patrol Council*, 31 FLRA 1123 (1988) (*AFGE, National Border Patrol Council*). The Union further states that Article 7, Section 11 is intended "only to restrict investigations or inquiries into off-duty misconduct that could not form the basis for any action by the Agency against an employee." Union's Response at 20. According to the Union, the provision "does not preclude investigations or inquiries which could lead to some disciplinary action." Id. More particularly as to Article 35, Section 9 and Article 36, Section 9, the Union states that they require "only that the Agency act in accordance with the nexus requirement that exists in the law." Id. at 55-56.

The Union also contends that in *AFGE, National Border Patrol Council,* the Authority rejected the argument that provisions that contain nexus requirements interfere with Executive Order 12564 and found, instead, that such provisions would not prevent any investigation required by executive orders, their implementing regulations, or management's internal security practices. The Union asserts that the Authority's reasoning should extend as well to the Agency's assertions regarding 5 C.F.R. § 735.203 and Part 2635. The Union also cites *American Federation of Government Employees, AFL-CIO, Council of Marine Corps Locals, Council 240 and Department of the Navy, United States Marine Corps,* 35 FLRA 108 (1990) (U.S. Marine Corps), in support.

B. Analysis and Conclusions

1. Article 7, Section 11

a. Meaning of the Provision

Article 7, Section 11 would permit inquiries and investigations into allegations of off-duty misconduct only where the activity, if verified, would have some relationship to an employee's position. The Union explains that the provision is intended to restrict inquiries and investigations where off-duty misconduct could not form the basis for any action by the Agency against an employee. This explanation as to how the provision would operate is, in effect, synonymous with the provision's express requirement that inquiries and investigations have some relationship to an employee's position. As the Union's explanation is consistent with the plain language of the provision, we adopt it. *Fort McPherson,* 51 at 138-39. Thus, a relationship between the alleged off-duty misconduct and the employee's position would be established whenever the Agency is entitled to take disciplinary action against an employee for such off-duty misconduct.

b. The Provision Is Not Contrary to Law

Based on the above interpretation, Article 7, Section 11 would not preclude any investigations or inquiries into off-duty misconduct that could lead to some disciplinary action against an employee. Consequently, the provision would not affect management's right to discipline employees under section 7106(a)(2)(A) of the Statute. See also *U.S. Marine Corps,* 35 FLRA at 110-12 (proposal requiring nexus standard for adverse actions did not interfere with management's right to discipline).

We reject the Agency's arguments that the provision would conflict with the Agency's obligations under Executive Order 12564 and 5 C.F.R. Parts 735 and 2635. First, Executive Order 12564 seeks to eliminate the use of illegal drugs by Federal employees, either on or off-duty, and requires that employees found to be using such drugs be disciplined. Accordingly, Executive Order 12564 relates to conduct, including off-duty conduct, that could form the basis for agency action against an employee. Similarly, as 5 C.F.R. Parts 735 and 2635 prescribe standards of conduct for Federal employees, an employee who fails to comply with those standards would be subject to disciplinary action, thereby establishing a relationship between off-duty misconduct and the employee's position. Thus, as the Agency could take action against an employee for illegal drug use and for violations of standards of conduct governing Federal employees, a nexus would exist between the activity and the employee's position. See *AFGE, National Border Patrol Council,* 31 FLRA at 1131-32 (provision that would restrict investigations and inquiries that have no relationship to an employee's employment would not prevent investigations that are required or authorized by, among other things, executive orders, including Executive Order 12564, and regulations). As such, the provision would not prevent the Agency from taking actions that are required by laws and regulations.

The Agency's reliance on *Council of VA Locals* is misplaced. The proposal in that case would have prevented the agency from disciplining an employee based on the use of drugs unless the usage would have adversely affected the employee's job performance or behavior at work. The Authority found that the proposal was outside the duty to bargain, as relevant here, because it would have prevented the agency from disciplining an employee unless the employee's conduct adversely affected the employee's job performance. Unlike that proposal, which was limited to conduct affecting job performance, this provision encompasses matters relating more broadly to an employee's position. It would not restrict the Agency's ability to investigate off-duty misconduct in accordance with Executive Order 12564 and 5 C.F.R. Parts 735 and 2635. We also reject the Agency's reliance on *Defense Logistics Agency.* The provision in that case addressed employees' privacy. Based on the union's intent, the Authority concluded that the provision limited the agency's ability to discipline employees to instances where it could establish a direct relationship between conduct and job performance. In contrast, the provision here would not limit inquiries and investigations into an employee's off-duty misconduct where such misconduct could form the basis for Agency action against the employee under laws and regulations.

2. Article 35, Section 9; Article 36, Section 9

a. Meaning of the Provisions

These provisions require that where discipline is proposed for reasons of off-duty misconduct, the written notification provided to employees will contain a statement of the nexus between the off-duty misconduct and the "efficiency of the service." Thus, under these provisions, the Agency must tell the employee the relationship, if any, between the employee's asserted misconduct and the efficiency of the service. The provisions also require that the Agency provide an opportunity for the employee and/or a representative to "supplement the record" where changes are made to that nexus statement.

b. The Provisions Are Not Contrary to Law

We reject the Agency's contentions that the provisions are inconsistent with 5 C.F.R. Part 735 and Executive Order 12564, and with management's right to discipline under section 7106(a)(2)(A) of the Statute because they contain a nexus standard. The provisions simply set forth notification requirements. They do not require the establishment of any nexus. The Agency makes no argument that the furnishing of such written notification is in any way contrary to law, rule or regulation. Accordingly, we find that these provisions are not contrary to law. See, *e.g., National Treasury Employees Union and U.S. Nuclear Regulatory Commission, Washington, D.C.,* 43 FLRA 1279, 1314-18 (1992) (furnishing written notification of reasonable suspicion for employee drug test and providing reasons therefor held to be within the duty to bargain).

VII. Article 12, Section 4(G)

G. In order to provide a fair ranking of more than eight (8) candidates subject to panel evaluation, an evaluation panel will be utilized. The panel will be constituted in the following manner:

A panel for a particular position will consist of at least three members, selected by the Office of Personnel, one of whom shall be from an office or unit other than the one in which the vacancy is located. At least one of these members must be familiar with the work where the vacancy is located. When advice and guidance on the interpretation of qualifications is considered essential, the selecting official may advise the panel but has no vote. Such advice should normally be provided before the panel receives the names and applications of the candidates.

A. Positions of the Parties

1. Agency

The Agency contends that the provision directly interferes with its right to assign work under section 7106(a)(2)(B) of the Statute for the following reasons: (1) the provision makes a specific assignment of work to the Office of Personnel, by requiring that office to select employees to serve on an evaluation panel; (2) the selection of employees to serve on the evaluation panel involves an assignment of work to those employees; and (3) the provision mandates that the selecting official act as an advisor to the panel and prohibits that same official from being assigned the task of voting with the panel. In support of each of these reasons, the Agency cites: (1) *American Federation of State, County, and Municipal Employees, AFL-CIO, Local 2910 and Library of Congress,* 11 FLRA 632 (1983) (Proposals 1 and 2); (2) *Patent Office Professional Association and U.S. Department of Commerce, Patent and Trademark Office,* 41 FLRA 795 (1991) (Provision 4) and *National Treasury Employees Union and Department of the Treasury, Bureau of the Public Debt,* 3 FLRA 769, 775 (1980), enf'd sub nom. *NTEU v. FLRA,* 691 F.2d 553 (D.C. Cir. 1982); and (3) *National Treasury Employees Union and Department of the Treasury,* 21 FLRA 1051 (1986) (Provision 7).

2. Union

The Union contends that the provision is a negotiable procedure within the meaning of section 7106(b)(2) of the Statute because it merely specifies the circumstances in which applicants for vacancies will be rated by a panel. In support, the Union cites *National Federation of Federal Employees, Local 2099 and Department of the Navy, Naval Plant Representative Office, St. Louis, Missouri,* 35 FLRA 362 (1990) (Naval Plant). The Union claims that the provision does not interfere with management's right to assign work because it: (1) preserves management's discretion to select the particular individuals to serve on the evaluation panel; and (2) permits the Agency to designate the individual within the Office of Personnel who will select the members of the evaluation panel. In this latter connection, the Union cites *Service and Hospital Employees International Union, Local 150 and Veterans Administration Medical Center, Milwaukee, Wisconsin*, 35 FLRA 521 (1990) (Member Armendariz, concurring in part and dissenting in part) (*VAMC, Milwaukee*) (Provision 3).

Alternatively, the Union contends that the provision is negotiable as an appropriate arrangement under section 7106(b)(3) of the Statute. The Union explains that the provision is intended to ensure that at least one member of the panel has some familiarity with the work where the vacancy is located. According to the Union, the benefit to the employees is substantial because if employees are rated by a panel with some knowledge of the job for which the employees are competing, the panel will be more likely to rate employees based on their qualifications for the job. The Union maintains that the burden on management's right is slight because only one member of the panel selected by the Agency must have knowledge of the work. The Union also states that the Agency would benefit from the provision by receiving a more accurate rating of employee qualifications. More particularly as to the third sentence of the provision, regarding the duties of the selecting official, the Union claims that allowing that official to vote with the panel would undermine the objectivity of the process. The Union claims that the provision would protect employees from the adverse effects resulting from the selecting official's exercise of influence in the rating process. The Union also asserts that employees will benefit by having their qualifications for the vacancy evaluated objectively and that the burden on the Agency is minimal because the selecting official retains the authority to select from among objectively rated candidates.

B. Analysis and Conclusions

1. Meaning of the Provision

This provision would require the use of an evaluation panel for selection actions when there are more than eight candidates who are being considered for a position. The provision also provides for: a minimum of three panel members; selection of panel members so that one member is from an office or unit other than the one at which the vacancy is located and at least one member is familiar with the work where the vacancy is located; the designation of the Office of Personnel to select panel members; the authorization of the selecting official to provide advice and guidance, but not vote, on interpretations of qualifications; and the time frame for providing such advice to panel members.

The Agency objects only to three portions of the provision: (1) the specific assignment of work to the Office of Personnel; (2) the composition of the panel; and (3) "mandating that the selecting official act as an advisor" while prohibiting the assignment of the task of voting to that official. To the extent the Agency's third argument interprets the provision to require the selecting official to provide advice and guidance, we reject that interpretation. The express wording of the provision states that the selecting official "may" advise the panel. Accordingly, the provision would permit, but would not require, the selecting official to advise the panel. We also note that the Agency does not object to the use of panels *per se* nor to their use when there are more than eight candidates.

2. The Provision Is Not Contrary to Law

a. The Provision Affects the Right to Assign Work

The right of an agency to assign work under section 7106(a)(2)(B) of the Statute includes the authority to determine the particular duties to be assigned, when work assignments will occur, and to whom or what positions the duties will be assigned. *American Federation of Government Employees, Local 3392 and U.S. Government Printing Office, Public Documents Distribution Center, Pueblo, Colorado*, 52 FLRA 141, 143 (1996). Employees appointed to ranking panels are performing work for the Agency and the selection of employees involves a work assignment by the Agency. See *American Federation of Government Employees, Local 2298 and U.S. Department of the Navy, Navy Resale Activity/Navy Exchange, Naval Weapons Station, Charleston, South Carolina*, 35 FLRA 1128, 1136 (1990) (*Navy Resale*). In contrast, proposals that simply require the use of rating and ranking panels do not affect the exercise of management rights, including the right to assign work, and have been found to be within the duty to bargain. *E.g., National Treasury Employees Union and U.S. Department of the Treasury, Customs Service, Washington, D.C.*, 46 FLRA 696, 778-79 (1992) (*Customs Service*). As explained below, we find that portions of Article 12, Section 4(G) affect the right to assign work.

The first portion of the provision to which the Agency objects would require the Office of Personnel to select panel members. Although the Union claims that this portion does not affect the right to assign work because it permits the Agency to designate the individual within the Office of Personnel who will select the members of the evaluation panel, the portion nonetheless assigns a specific task to the Office of Personnel. In this manner, the provision is comparable to a proposal that was found outside the duty to bargain in *National Federation of Federal Employees, Local 1437 and United States Army Armament Research, Development and Engineering Center, Picatinny Arsenal, New Jersey*, 35 FLRA 1052, 1057-63 (1990) (*Picatinny Arsenal*). Proposal 2 in that case would have required: (1) the Civilian Personnel Office to appoint employees to rating and ranking panels; and (2) the Equal Employment Opportunity Office to compile a list of nominees for the panel. The Authority held that those portions of the proposal directly interfered with the right to assign work because they dictated the specific duties that would be performed by the designated offices.

The Union does not distinguish Picatinny Arsenal but, instead, cites for support a provision in *VAMC, Milwaukee*, 35 FLRA at 526-29, that required a supervisor to post a notice, at least two weeks in advance, indicating which employees would be expected to work on holidays. However, *VAMC, Milwaukee* is distinguishable because, in that case, the agency did not assert that management would be required to designate a particular individual to perform a specified task. In this case, the Agency expressly argues that the assignment of work to the Office of Personnel is inconsistent with its right to assign work. Nothing in *VAMC, Milwaukee* supports a conclusion that the first disputed portion of Article 12, Section 4(G) does not affect the right to assign work.

The second portion of the provision to which the Agency objects concerns employee service on evaluation panels, which the Agency claims involves the assignment of work. This portion of the provision specifies that at least one panel member must come from an office or unit other than the one in which the vacancy is located, and that at least one member who is familiar with the work where the vacancy is located must be appointed to serve on a panel. The Authority previously has found that proposals that dictate the types or grades of employees assigned to rating panels directly interfere with the exercise of management's right to assign work. *E.g., Patent Office Professional Association and U.S. Department of Commerce, Patent and Trademark Office*, 41 FLRA 795, 816-18 (1991) (POPA) (Provision 4); *American Federation of Government Employees, Local 85 and Veterans Administration Medical Center, Leavenworth, Kansas*, 30 FLRA 400, 409-11 (1987) (Proposal 8). Although the Union claims that management's ability to select the particular individuals to perform the duties of the evaluation panel is preserved, this portion does more than simply require the assignment of panel duties to employees whom management has selected. This portion would limit management's assignment of evaluation panel duties to employees from particular offices and who have familiarity with the work where the vacancy is located. Thus, this portion of the provision is distinguishable from a provision in *Naval Plant*, 35 FLRA at 367-68, which the Authority found established a ranking panel but did not violate the right to assign work because it did not require the agency to assign duties to ranking panel members it had not chosen.

The third portion of the provision to which the Agency objects provides that the selecting official may advise the panel but has no vote. The Authority previously has found that proposals that limited the role of selecting officials directly interfered with the right to assign work. *E.g., Customs Service*, 46 FLRA at 777-79 (Section 8A); *Navy Resale*, 35 FLRA at 1134-36 (Proposal 4). Similarly, here, this portion of the provision affects management's assignment of duties to the selecting official.

b. The Provision Is Not a Procedure

The Authority previously has held that provisions that are inconsistent with the exercise of a management right do not constitute procedures under section 7106(b)(2) of the Statute.[12] *E.g., Customs Service*, 46 FLRA at 726. Applying that precedent to our finding that Article 12, Section 4(G) affects the right to assign work, we conclude that it is not a procedure under section 7106(b)(2) of the Statute.

c. The Provision Is an Appropriate Arrangement

The adverse effects the Union identifies in this case flow from the exercise of management's right to select. In this connection, it is well established that rating and ranking panels are part of the process an agency uses to select candidates to fill vacant positions. *E.g., Picatinny Arsenal*, 35 FLRA at 1061. The Union claims that, without the protections afforded by this provision, employees who are rated by evaluation panels will not be accurately rated on their qualifications. The Union also asserts that, in exercising its right to select, the selecting official could influence the rating process, resulting in unfair ratings and a lack of objectivity in the rating process. We find that the Union has established that the provision is designed to address adverse effects flowing from management's right to select.

With regard to the part of the *KANG* test that requires tailoring, we recognize that the provision is not directed only to those employees who would be unfairly and inaccurately rated. Instead, it would include all employees who are rated by evaluation panels when there are more than eight candidates. As we stated earlier, see Part III.B.2.b., provisions that are so broad in their sweep as to be applied without regard to whether employees have suffered, or are likely to suffer, adverse effects are not sufficiently tailored. At the same time, however, the Authority has held that "[p]roposals that are prophylactic in nature, in that they are intended to eliminate the possibility of an adverse effect, may constitute appropriate arrangements negotiable under section 7106(b)(3) of the Statute." *PTO,* 49 FLRA at 191.

Article 12, Section 4(G) is designed to be prophylactic in that it seeks to eliminate the possibility of unfair or inaccurate ratings by individuals who are unfamiliar with an employee's work or by selecting officials who have predetermined choices. Significantly, the provision applies only to employees who apply for positions and who, given a sufficient number of candidates, are subject to the panel evaluation process. As such, the scope of this provision is limited to that group of employees who apply for a particular position. Within that group, employees who may be harmed as a result of unfair or inaccurate ratings cannot be determined in advance. Realistically, it is only after an evaluation panel has completed its role and a selection made that an unsuccessful candidate is likely to challenge the fairness and accuracy of the evaluation process. Only then can employees who were harmed by that process be identified. Also at that time, only corrective actions can be taken to ameliorate any harm engendered by the selection process. However, section 7106(b)(3) contemplates that parties may negotiate ways of preventing harm from occurring in the first instance. See *Minerals Management Service,* 969 F.2d at 1163 (the court rejected the theory that the "use of the past tense in the phrase 'adversely affected' creates a temporal wall forbidding any negotiability except as to harm that has already occurred.")

Article 12, Section 4(G) is designed to prevent the occurrence of unfair or inaccurate ratings in the selection process. Accordingly, we find that the provision is sufficiently tailored so that it constitutes an arrangement. See *also PTO,* 49 FLRA at 194-95 (provision prohibiting immediate supervisors from soliciting or collecting charitable pledges found sufficiently tailored because, even though it would encompass some employees in addition to those who would be coerced, it targeted a group of employees that was likely to be harmed and sought to address or prevent actual or anticipated adverse effects on those employees).

Having found that Article 12, Section 4(G) is an arrangement, we will no longer follow decisions that suggest that proposals concerning rating and ranking panels can never constitute appropriate arrangements. See, *e.g., American Federation of Government Employees, Local 3434 and National Aeronautics and Space Administration, Marshall Space Flight Center, Alabama,* 49 FLRA 382 (1994) (Authority rejected union claim that proposal, which sought to include union participation on rating and ranking panels that were used when filling positions under a competitive placement plan, constituted an arrangement). For the reasons stated above, proposals that seek to mitigate forseeable adverse effects on employees who are subject to a rating and ranking panel evaluation process can constitute arrangements.[13]

We next address whether the arrangement is appropriate or whether it excessively interferes with management's rights. In this connection, the provision protects employees by ensuring that they are evaluated fairly and objectively by members of an evaluation panel who have some knowledge of the qualifications necessary to perform the work of the vacant position and without the selecting official's influence. We find that the advantages afforded by such review are significant.

We further find that the effect on management's right to assign work is minimal. In this regard, the provision requires that only one member of the panel have some familiarity with the work entailed by the position that is vacant and that one member of the panel be located in an office or unit other than the one in which the vacancy is located. The Agency retains the discretion to appoint employees with these specified characteristics to the panel as well as all other panel members. Furthermore, there is no indication in the record that service on a panel by any employee would be on other than an occasional basis and no evidence that management would be unable to assign other, non-panel related work to employees during the pendency of their panel service. As such, management's ability to assign work would not be seriously impaired.

Additionally, requiring the Office of Personnel to make panel assignments is not alleged to be, and there is no basis in the record on which to conclude that it would be, a burdensome task. Also, nothing in the provision would prevent that Office from soliciting input from managers or supervisors regarding the availability of employees to serve on panels. Finally, although the Agency may not appoint the selecting official as a voting member of the panel under the provision, the provision permits the selecting official to participate by offering advice and guidance to the other members of the panel. Furthermore, the selecting official retains the ultimate authority to select from among fairly rated candidates.

On balance, we find that the burden placed on management's right to assign work is outweighed by the benefits afforded to employees and that, therefore, the provision does not excessively interfere with that right.[14] Accordingly, we conclude that Article 12, Section 4(G) is negotiable as an appropriate arrangement under section 7106(b)(3) of the Statute.

VIII. Article 12 (Promotion and Reassignment), Section 5

No member of the unit shall be placed in a disadvantageous position with regard to promotions by virtue of officially initiated service on a detail or work project.

A. Positions of the Parties

1. Agency

The Agency contends that the provision directly interferes with management's right to assign employees under section 7106(a)(2)(A) of the Statute because it would prohibit the Agency from detailing or assigning employees under certain circumstances. In support, the Agency relies on *National Association of Government Employees, Local R14-52 and U.S. Department of the Army, Red River Army Depot, Texarkana, Texas,* 44 FLRA 738 (1992) (Provision 5) (*Red River Army Depot*). The Agency states that its right to assign employees would be "drastically impair[ed]" and notes, by way of example, that if an employee performed poorly while on detail, the provision would prohibit management from considering that performance when the employee applied for a promotion. Agency's Supplemental Brief at 3. The Agency also explains that the term "officially initiated service" reflects a detail that has been initiated by the Agency and not at the request of an employee.

2. Union

Without addressing how the provision affects management's rights, the Union contends that the provision is an appropriate arrangement under section 7106(b)(3) of the Statute in that it is designed to limit the adverse effects on employees of being detailed to another position even if, as the Union explains, employees volunteer for such assignments. According to the Union, "virtually the same language as Article 12, Section 5 concerning the potential adverse impact of assignments to detail work" was found negotiable in *Internal Revenue Service, Washington, D.C. and Internal Revenue Service, Denver District, Denver, Colorado,* 27 FLRA 664, 672 (1987) (*IRS, Denver*). Union's Response at 23. The Union claims that the provision in that case was "broader and more inclusive" than the provision here and relies on the Authority's reasoning in *IRS, Denver* to support its position that Article 12, Section 5 is within the duty to bargain.

The Union also asserts that, unlike the provision in *Red River Army Depot*, this provision would not require the Agency to consider alternate personnel practices, such as recruiting, promotion, or transfer, before assigning an employee to a detail. The Union states that the term "officially initiated service" refers to a work project or detail that is officially sanctioned or initiated by the Agency.

B. Analysis and Conclusions

1. Meaning of the Provision

This provision operates when employees are assigned to a detail or work project that is "officially initiated." The Union's explanation that employees can volunteer for a detail or work project is consistent with the wording of the provision and we adopt it. *Laurel Bay*, 51 FLRA at 737. The Union's further explanation that the provision would not require the Agency to consider the use of other personnel actions, such as promotions or transfers, before assigning an employee to a detail is also consistent with the wording of the provision and we adopt it. *Id.*

Additionally, as neither the wording of the provision nor the Union's explanation makes clear how the term "disadvantageous" is to be defined, we interpret the Union's reliance on *IRS, Denver* and the Authority's rationale expressed therein, to reflect the Union's view that the provision is intended to operate in the same manner as the provision in *IRS, Denver*. In that case, the Authority found negotiable a provision that provided that detailed employees would not be adversely affected with regard to promotions or evaluations because they had performed lower-graded work on details. Based on the Union's reliance on IRS, Denver, we construe this provision as designed to ensure that work performed on details will not disadvantage employees who later seek promotions. In *IRS, Denver*, the Authority found no indication that the provision was intended to shield poor performance of lower-graded work from appropriate remedial action. We also construe the Union's position to mean that the Agency would not be prevented by Article 12, Section 5 from evaluating an employee's performance while on a detail. The Union's position that Article 12, Section 5 is intended to operate in the same manner as the provision in IRS, Denver is consistent with the wording of the provision before us. We adopt that position for the purpose of ascertaining the meaning of Article 12, Section 5. *Laurel Bay,* 51 FLRA at 737.

In sum, this provision operates when employees are assigned to or volunteer for a detail or work project that is initiated by the Agency. Although employees are assured that they will not be placed at a disadvantage with regard to promotions because they have received such work assignments, the Agency retains the right to evaluate their performance while on the detail or work project.

2. The Provision Is Not Contrary to Law

Based on the meaning of the provision described above, we reject the Agency's assertion that it would be prevented from considering an employee's performance while on a detail or work project when the employee applied for a promotion. In addition, this provision does not prohibit the Agency from detailing or assigning employees. Instead, the Agency retains the right to assign employees to details or work projects. As such, the provision does not affect management's right to assign employees under section 7106(a)(2)(A). The provision is distinguishable from the provision in *Red River Army Depot* that, in relevant part, was found nonnegotiable. The provision in that case specifically precluded management from assigning employees to details in lieu of other appropriate personnel actions. In contrast, Article 12, Section 5 does not limit the Agency's ability to assign employees to details or work projects. Rather, it operates after management has made one of these work assignments to ensure that employees are not placed at a disadvantage in terms of promotional opportunities. Accordingly, we find that Article 12, Section 5 is not contrary to law.

IX. Article 13 (Performance Appraisal), Section 3(M)

Whenever management has decided to effect a reduction in grade or removal, the employee will be offered an opportunity to resign before the written decision is issued.

A. Positions of the Parties

1. Agency

The Agency contends that the provision directly interferes with management's rights under section 7106(a)(2)(A) of the Statute. The Agency states that by requiring management to give an employee the opportunity to resign before implementing a reduction in grade or a removal, the provision would preclude the Agency from exercising its right to take disciplinary action under certain situations. In support, the Agency relies on *National Federation of Federal Employees, Local 405 and U.S. Department of the Army, Army Information Systems Command, St. Louis, Missouri,* 42 FLRA 1112 (1991) (Army Information Systems Command).

The Agency also claims that the provision is contrary to Government-wide regulations. The Agency explains that, if an employee resigns, the provision would prevent the Agency from including in the Notification of Personnel Action, SF-50, a statement that the employee resigned after receiving a Notice of Proposed Removal. The Agency cites a provision of FPM Supplement 296-33, Paragraph S31-4c(2)(c), which, prior to the FPM's abolishment, provided that "[w]hen an employee submits a request for resignation after receiving written notice of proposed disciplinary or adverse action, the pending action must be listed as the agency finding on the SF 50...." Agency's Supplemental Brief at 4 (emphasis omitted). According to the Agency, this regulation was incorporated into a Guide for Processing Personnel Actions (Guide) issued by the Office of Personnel Management (OPM) after the FPM's abolishment. The Agency maintains that, in order to comply with OPM regulations and maintain accurate personnel records, it is required to annotate an employee's official personnel file with a comment that an employee resigned after receiving written notice of a proposed decision to separate or demote the employee.

Additionally, the Agency states that, while an employee can resign at any time, the intent of the provision is to permit an employee to resign with a "clean record," thereby prohibiting the required annotation on the employee's official personnel record. Agency's Supplemental Brief at 4.

2. Union

The Union states that the provision "forces affected employees to choose between reduction in grade or removal... and resignation from the job...." Response at 27. The Union asserts that the loss of a job under these circumstances is tantamount to disciplinary action and, consequently, that the provision does not restrict management's right to discipline. The Union also claims that the provision does not affect the basis on which disciplinary action is proposed and, as such, that the provision is distinguishable from that at issue in *Army Information Systems Command*.

Alternatively, the Union argues that the provision is negotiable as an appropriate arrangement under section 7106(b)(3) of the Statute. The Union claims that a reduction in grade or removal may prevent or reduce future employment opportunities and may cause the employee "psychological, financial, or family problems." Id. at 29. The Union argues that the provision would mitigate these adverse effects without a significant burden on management's rights. The Union maintains that the Agency's goal of removing an unsatisfactory employee from the workforce would still be accomplished under the provision.

The Union also states that it is unaware of any conflict between the provision and applicable law or regulation and urges the Authority to disregard the Agency's argument regarding one of those regulations, which the Union claims was incorrectly cited. Finally, in response to a question posed by the Authority with regard to whether an employee can resign at any time, the Union states the following:

This provision memorializes an employee's opportunity to resign before the employee's file is blemished by recordation of a reduction in grade or removal. To the extent not prohibited by law, discretion can be exercised to notate reasons for resignation that may have less severe an impact on the employee's future employment opportunities than a notation that the employee resigned under threat of reduction in grade or removal.

Union's Supplemental Brief at 5

B. Analysis and Conclusions

1. Meaning of the Provision

The provision requires that when management "has decided to effect" a reduction in grade or removal an employee will be given an opportunity to resign before a "written decision" is issued. Neither of the quoted phrases is defined or clearly explained. The thrust of the Union's argument is to permit an employee to resign before any written recordation of a reduction in grade or removal is made. Consistent with the Union's intent, we construe this provision to mean that when management has made the initial determination to reduce an employee's grade or remove an employee, the Agency must offer the affected employee an opportunity to resign before that employee is given a written notice of proposed reduction in grade or removal. In construing the provision in this manner, we note that the provision is silent with regard to what steps the Agency must take in providing the opportunity to resign and the period of time that offer is available. The provision simply requires the Agency to extend that opportunity.

2. The Agency's Argument Is Properly Before the Authority

We deny the Union's request that we not consider the Agency's argument concerning a Government-wide regulation that was not correctly cited. The Agency has maintained throughout this proceeding that the provision is inconsistent with the requirement of properly annotating personnel records. Further, the parties were asked to supplement the record with regard to the applicable statutory or regulatory provisions governing the documentation of personnel actions and to specify those provisions. The Agency provided correct citations at that time and both parties had an opportunity to present their positions in full. Thus, the argument was properly raised before the Authority.

3. The Provision Is Not Contrary to Law

We reject the Agency's argument that the provision is inconsistent with regulatory requirements concerning the proper annotation of an employee's resignation. The Agency relies on a regulation in OPM's Guide to Processing Personnel Actions that concerns "Separations by Other than Retirement." It governs, among other things, performance-based removals under 5 C.F.R. Part 432.15 The regulation addresses appropriate documentation on the SF-50 when an employee submits a resignation after receiving written notice of proposed disciplinary or adverse action. As we have explained above, this provision operates before an employee has received a written notice that management proposes to remove the employee. Indeed, in such circumstances, the regulation on which the Agency relies prohibits an agency from annotating on the SF-50 any information regarding a proposed or pending disciplinary or adverse action when an employee has resigned before receiving notification, in writing, of such proposed action.[16]

We also reject the Agency's argument that the provision is inconsistent with section 7106(a)(2)(A) of the Statute, which includes the right to remove and reduce in grade. The Authority previously has found that proposals or provisions that preclude management from taking actions against an employee for a particular offense directly interfere with that management right. *E.g., International Federation of Professional and Technical Engineers, Local 1 and U.S. Department of the Navy, Norfolk Naval Shipyard, Portsmouth, Virginia*, 49 FLRA 225, 230 (1994). The "offense" may include unacceptable performance. See *Patent Office Professional Association and Patent and Trademark Office, Department of Commerce*, 29 FLRA 1389, 1405 (1987), petition for review denied, 873 F.2d 1485 (D.C. Cir. 1989). The provision here does not preclude management from removing an employee or reducing an employee's grade. Because an employee can resign at any time, as the Agency recognizes, the provision does not implicate the exercise of management's right to remove employees or reduce their grade or pay. Stated otherwise, even in the absence of such a provision, the Agency could not refuse to accept an employee's resignation in order to remove the employee or effect a reduction in grade.

The Agency's reliance on *Army Information Systems Command* is misplaced.[17] As relevant here, the proposal in that case would have prevented management from using approved leave as the basis for disciplinary action. Because the proposal restricted the agency's ability to discipline, there was an impermissible effect on the exercise of that management right. There is no such restriction on the right to discipline here.

X. Article 14 (Physical Facilities), Section 2(E) (18)

Management will provide a secured work space. Law Office suites will be secured via an electronic access system.

A. Positions of the Parties
1. Agency

The Agency contends that this provision interferes with its right to determine internal security practices under section 7106(a)(1) of the Statute. The Agency claims that section 7106(a)(1) includes the right to determine what is necessary to safeguard the Agency's physical property against internal or external risks, improper or unauthorized disclosure of information, and the disruption of the Agency's operations. The Agency asserts that, by mandating the use of an electronic access system to secure law office suites, the provision precludes management from selecting any other security system. The Agency explains that its offices presently are secured by electronic, key-controlled access systems.

2. Union

The Union contends that employee safety and security at the workplace are general conditions of employment and that the Authority has found that proposals concerning building security are negotiable. The Union cites various Authority decisions in support. Without addressing how the provision affects management's rights, the Union further claims that the provision is an appropriate arrangement under section 7106(b)(3) of the Statute in that it is intended to provide security and safety to employees. The Union adds that the provision does not prevent the Agency from implementing additional security measures and that the "impact" of this provision is identical to the impact of the proposal in *American Federation of Government Employees, Local 3302 and U.S. Department of Health and Human Services, Social Security Administration, Dunbar Branch Office, Baltimore, Maryland*, 37 FLRA 350, 354-55 (1990) (*SSA, Dunbar*). Union's Response at 31. The Union also states, as relevant here, that "[t]he use of an electronic system would not preclude, subject to negotiations, the implementation of an additional system to increase security."

Union's Supplemental Brief at 6
B. Analysis and Conclusions
1. Meaning of the Provision

The portion of the provision that is in dispute would require the Agency to secure law office suites through the use of an electronic access system. Although the Authority sought clarification from the parties regarding the manner in which this provision was intended to operate, it is unclear from their statements what type of electronic access system is envisioned and, more particularly, whether the system the Union proposes to use is the same as the electronic, key-controlled access system that the Agency states it is presently using. It is unnecessary to resolve these matters, however, in view of our disposition of this provision.

2. The Provision is Contrary to Law

a. The Provision Affects the Right to Determine Internal Security Practices

It is well established that the right to determine internal security practices under section 7106(a)(1) includes the authority to determine the policies and practices that are part of an agency's plan to secure or safeguard its personnel, physical property or operations against internal and external risks. *E.g., American Federation of Government Employees, Federal Prison Council 33 and U.S. Department of Justice, Federal Bureau of Prisons*, 51 FLRA 1112, 1115 (1996). Provisions that require management to take specific actions to safeguard an agency's personnel and operations directly interfere with the right to determine internal security practices...., *SSA, Dunbar*. Because the instant provision would require the Agency to use an electronic access system to protect the security of its property and personnel, we find that the provision affects management's right to determine its internal security practices under section 7106(a)(1) of the Statute.

b. The Provision Is Not an Appropriate Arrangement

Applying the first prong of the *KANG* standard, we find that the Union has not established that the provision is an arrangement. The Union has not identified any adverse effects on employees, either actual or reasonably foreseeable, that flow from the exercise of management's right to determine its internal security practices. The only argument advanced by the Union to support its claim that the provision is intended as an arrangement is the contention that the provision is designed to provide security and safety to employees. However, the Union has not explained how management's choice of its internal security measures has failed to provide adequate security.

Previously, in determining whether provisions were intended to ameliorate the adverse effects flowing from the exercise of an agency's right to determine its internal security practices, the Authority examined the existence or absence of security measures at the agency's facilities. *E.g., American Federation of Government Employees, AFL-CIO, Local 2782 and U.S. Department of Commerce,* *Bureau of the Census, Washington, D.C.*, 49 FLRA 470, 475 (1994) (Census); *SSA, Dunbar*, 37 FLRA at 360. The Authority also took into account actual or foreseeable effects on employees and agency property. *E.g., POPA*, 41 FLRA at 839; *National Federation of Federal Employees, Local 2050 and Environmental Protection Agency*, 36 FLRA 618, 620-22 (1990) (EPA). For example, in *EPA*, the record showed that there had been numerous incidents involving employees' security in and around the agency's facilities, including one fatality caused by an individual who had improperly gained access to the building in which that employee worked. 36 FLRA at 621. There was also evidence of threats to the security of the agency's facilities, including thefts, vandalism, and bullet holes found in windows of employee offices. *Id.* Considering these factors, the Authority found that a proposal requiring that employees in two agency facilities receive the same level of protection provided to employees in a third facility was an arrangement to address the adverse effects of the internal security practices that the agency had employed.

In this case, there is no evidence or assertion that the security measure currently provided by the Agency, which consists of an electronic key-controlled access system, fails to provide adequate security for employees and the Agency's property and operations. We reject the Union's claim that, as the impact of the proposal in *SSA, Dunbar* is identical to the impact of the provision here, the Authority should find this provision to be an appropriate arrangement. In *SSA, Dunbar*, the union proposed adoption of a practice in order to deal with irate or potentially dangerous claimants where no practice to deal with that situation existed. The Authority found that the proposal was intended to address the adverse effects of employee work assignments based on union arguments that specifically addressed the danger to employees. In contrast, the Union here has failed to demonstrate that management's choice of its internal security practices has resulted in actual or foreseeable adverse effects on employees that the provision is intended to ameliorate.

Finally, the Union's contention that employee safety and security at the workplace are general conditions of employment that the Authority has found negotiable does not persuade us to reach a different result. The negotiability of each provision must be assessed based on the record presented to the Authority. Not all provisions relating to safety and security have been found negotiable. *E.g., Census*, 49 FLRA at 473-76; *EPA*, 36 FLRA at 629-32.

In sum, we find that the Union has failed to establish that the provision satisfies the first prong of the KANG standard. Accordingly, we conclude that the provision does not constitute an appropriate arrangement and that the Agency head properly disapproved it.

XI. Article 14 (Physical Facilities), Section 12

The Office shall grant excused administrative leave when physical conditions at an employee's work station endanger the safety or health of an employee if the Office is unable to provide an alternative work station.

A. Positions of the Parties

1. Agency

The Agency contends that the provision is outside the duty to bargain because it interferes with management's right to assign work under section 7106(a)(2)(B) of the Statute. According to the Agency, the provision would eliminate management's discretion to determine whether to grant leave or whether an employee's presence is required to accomplish necessary work.

2. Union

The Union relies on the Authority's decision in *National Federation of Federal Employees, Local 1994 and Military Entrance Processing Station, Boston, Massachusetts*, 27 FLRA 968 (1987) (*Military Entrance Processing Station*). According to the Union, the Authority found negotiable in that case a provision that is "more generous to affected employees" than this provision. Response at 32. The Union also claims that the cases relied on by the Agency to support its position do not apply because they concern provisions related to the granting of administrative leave for specific purposes and not to the health and safety issues referenced by this provision.

B. Analysis and Conclusions

1. Meaning of the Provision

This provision would require the Agency to grant administrative leave to employees when conditions are unsafe or unhealthful and alternative work stations cannot be provided. The express language of this provision does not establish who – management or the employee--would determine when physical conditions at an employee's work station endanger the safety or health of that employee. The Agency contends, and the Union does not disagree, that the provision would divest management of the discretion to determine whether to grant leave. Although the Union quotes *Military Entrance Processing Station*, in which the Authority found that the agency retained the discretion to grant employees excused absences, the Union does not indicate that this provision is intended to give the Agency the same discretion as in *Military Entrance Processing Station*.[19] Under these circumstances, we construe the provision as allowing employees to determine when physical conditions at their work stations would endanger their safety or health.

2. The Provision Is Contrary to Law

The Authority has held that provisions concerning the use of administrative leave directly interfere with the right to assign work under section 7106(a)(2)(B) of the Statute if they eliminate management's discretion to determine whether an employee is to remain on duty to perform necessary work. *National Treasury Employees Union and U.S. Department of the Treasury, Office of Chief Counsel, Internal Revenue Service*, 39 FLRA 27, 43 (1991), *aff'd in part, vacated in part and remanded as to other matters, IRS, Chief Counsel*, 960 F.2d at 1068. In this case, based on our construction of the provision, as explained above, employees could determine whether the conditions that exist at their work stations are unsafe or unhealthful. As such, employees could determine the circumstances under which the Agency would have to grant administrative leave. As the provision fails to preserve management's discretion to decide whether an employee's absence will conflict with the accomplishment of necessary work, it impermissibly affects management's right to assign work under section 7106(a)(2)(B) of the Statute. Contrary to the Union's claim, the fact that this provision is concerned with employee safety and health does not eliminate the effect on management's right to assign work. *E.g., National Federation of Federal Employees, Local 1655 and U.S. Department of Defense, National Guard Bureau, Alexandria, Virginia*, 49 FLRA 874 (1994) (Provision 6).

The Union's reliance on *Military Entrance Processing Station* does not compel a different result. Provision 3 in that case required the agency to assign work to employees in a safe and healthy area, if "conditions" could not be corrected immediately, or to excuse employees without charge to leave until the condition was corrected. The Authority adopted the Union's explanation that the provision applied to emergency situations where the continued presence of employees at their normal work places would place them in imminent danger. The Authority found that the provision was comparable in effect to a proposal found to be within the duty to bargain in *American Federation of Government Employees, AFL-CIO, Local 3511 and Veterans Administration Hospital, San Antonio, Texas,* 12 FLRA 76, 91 (1983) (Proposal 37) (VA, San Antonio), which required employees to return to their worksite during a smoke notification or fire alarm unless that was the location of the emergency. Although it is not clear in *Military Processing Entrance Station* and *VA, San Antonio* whether the emergency situations that existed were declared by management, nothing in those decisions compels a finding that the provision here would permit management to determine that the work environment is unsafe or unhealthful. Instead, this provision could operate whenever an employee, in his or her own view, believes that there is an unsafe or unhealthful work environment. As such, it would allow employees to determine whether or not to perform work.

In sum, we conclude that this provision impermissibly affects management's right to assign work under section 7106(a)(2)(B) of the Statute. As there is no cognizable assertion that the provision is a negotiable procedure or appropriate arrangement, we conclude that the Agency head properly disapproved it.

XII. Article 15 (Overtime), Section 4 [20]

Within the above criteria, overtime shall be assigned uniformly within any Law Office or other organizational unit for which overtime is authorized. "Uniformly" means that whenever practicable all qualified employees will be trained prior to the beginning of overtime, if training is necessary for the specific overtime project as distinguished from regular training on the job and given the opportunity to begin overtime work on the same date. Complaints or disagreements concerning overtime shall be processed in accordance with the negotiated grievance procedure.

A. Positions of the Parties

1. Agency

The Agency contends that the provision interferes with its right to assign work under section 7106(a)(2)(B) of the Statute by requiring it to provide training to employees. The Agency argues that when training is necessary for an overtime project, this provision would require that all qualified employees be provided training prior to the commencement of overtime. According to the Agency, even if some employees had already received the necessary training to perform the overtime work, the provision would preclude management from assigning overtime to those employees. The Agency maintains that the provision is not rendered negotiable by limiting the training requirement to qualified employees.

2. Union

The Union contends that the provision would not require the Agency to provide training in all circumstances because the provision states that qualified employees will be trained "whenever practicable." According to the Union, the provision merely encourages the Agency to provide training to employees who otherwise would not be eligible for overtime.

B. Analysis and Conclusions

1. Meaning of the Provision

This provision is part of a contract article involving overtime. The provision states that, "whenever practicable," qualified employees will be trained prior to the commencement of overtime. Although the Union explains that the provision would not require management to provide training in all circumstances, neither that explanation nor the wording of the provision defines what the quoted term means. It is unnecessary for us to define it, however, because it is clear that, under any definition, the provision would obligate management to provide training in some circumstances. Thus, for at least some employees, Article 15, Section 4 conditions the assignment of overtime on the assignment of training.

2. The Provision Is Contrary to Law

It is well established that the right to assign work includes the right to train, or not to train, employees. *E.g., American Federation of Government Employees, Local 3407 and U.S. Department of Defense, Defense Mapping Agency, Hydrographic/Topographic, Washington, D.C.,* 39 FLRA 557, 560 (1991). The right to assign work also includes the right to assign overtime and to determine when the overtime will be performed. *E.g., American Federation of Government Employees, Local 3157 and U.S. Department of Agriculture, Federal Grain Inspection Service,* 44 FLRA 1570, 1596 (1992) (Proposal 5). This provision affects management's right to assign work because, based on our construction above, it would require the Agency to provide training to some employees before the employees could be assigned overtime duties.

As this provision impermissibly affects management's right to assign work, and there is no cognizable assertion that the provision is a negotiable procedure or appropriate arrangement, the Agency head properly disapproved it.

XIII. Article 18 (Leave), Section 1(G) [21]

Where the Office has reasonable ground to believe that an employee has abused sick leave, a written warning may be issued informing the employee that if the described abuse continues, sick leave restriction may be imposed. If subsequently imposed, another written notice will be provided explaining that, for a stated period, but not to exceed 6 months, request for approval of sick leave must be accompanied by a medical certificate. At the end of the stated period, the Office shall review the employee's situation and shall give the employee notice of recession [sic] or renewal of the restriction due to continued abuse.

A. Positions of the Parties

1. Agency

The Agency contends that the provision interferes with the right to discipline under section 7106(a)(2)(A) of the Statute because it would require management to provide an employee with a written warning prior to placing the employee on sick leave restriction. In support, the Agency cites *National Association of Government Employees, Local R5-82 and U.S. Department of the Navy, Navy Exchange, Naval Air Station, Jacksonville, Florida*, 43 FLRA 25, 26-29 (1991) (Naval Air Station).

2. Union

The Union claims that the provision does not require management to provide an employee with a written warning before placing the employee on sick leave restriction. Rather, the Union contends that the provision gives the Agency discretion to take such action. The Union asserts that the term "may" is permissive. As such, the Union claims that the provision is distinguishable from provisions found nonnegotiable because they mandated the issuance of a written warning prior to the imposition of sick leave restriction.

B. Analysis and Conclusions

1. Meaning of the Provision

This provision permits, but does not require, the furnishing of a written warning to an employee who is suspected of abusing sick leave. The Union's explanation that the provision would not require the Agency to issue a written warning prior to placing an employee on sick leave restriction is consistent with the wording of the provision. Therefore, we adopt it. *Fort McPherson*, 51 FLRA at 138-39.

2. The Provision Is Not Contrary to Law

The Authority previously has found that provisions precluding an agency from imposing sick leave restrictions affect management's right to discipline under section 7106(a)(2)(A). *E.g., Naval Air Station*, 43 FLRA at 28. Consistent with the interpretation of Article 18, Section 1(G) stated above, by allowing the Agency, in its discretion, to issue a warning before placing an employee on sick leave restriction, the provision does not affect the Agency's ability to discipline employees in any way. Thus, the provision does not prohibit the Agency from placing an employee who is suspected of abusing sick leave on sick leave restriction immediately without a written warning. Accordingly, we find that the disputed portion of the provision does not affect management's right to discipline under section 7106(a)(2)(A) of the Statute.

The Agency's reliance on *Naval Air Station* is misplaced. The provision in that case required management to provide oral and written warnings before placing an employee suspected of abusing sick leave on leave restriction. The provision was found to directly interfere with management's right to discipline. As noted, the provision here does not restrict management's right to discipline. Accordingly, it is not contrary to law.

XIV. Article 18 (Leave), Section 1(H)

H. Requests for advanced sick leave will normally be granted in accordance with governing regulations when all of the following conditions are met:

1. the employee is eligible to earn sick leave;

2. the employee's request does not exceed 240 hours, or for temporary employees only the amount to be earned during the period of temporary employment if appropriate;

3. there is no reason to believe the employee will not return to work after having used the leave, and the employee has sufficient funds in his or her retirement account or any other source of monies owed to the employee by the Government to reimburse the Employer for the advance, should the employee not return to work;

4. the employee has provided acceptable medical documentation of the need for advanced sick leave; and

5. the employee is not subject to leave restriction.

A. Positions of the Parties

1. Agency

The Agency contends that this provision interferes with management's right to assign work under section 7106(a)(2)(B) of the Statute because it would require the Agency "to identify some type of 'abnormal situation'" in the event that the Agency refuses to grant a request for advanced sick leave when an employee meets the criteria described in the provision. Statement of Position at 16. The Agency argues that the provision would create an entitlement to advanced sick leave for some employees without providing for the consideration of staffing needs or workload requirements.

2. Union

The Union states that the provision does not interfere with management's right to assign work and that it is intended to be applied in accordance with governing regulations. The Union claims that the provision would not obligate or direct management to perform any particular action and that it is consistent with Authority precedent in *Customs Service*, 46 FLRA 696 (Provision 6) and *National Association of Government Employees, Local R12-29 and U.S. Department of the Navy, Naval Facilities Contracts Training Center, Construction Battalion Center, Port Hueneme, California*, 43 FLRA 810 (1991) (Proposal 2) (*Port Hueneme*). The Union further contends that the provision constitutes an appropriate arrangement within the meaning of section 7106(b)(3) of the Statute and that it has a "minimal impact on management's right to assign work." Union's Response at 42. The Union explains that advanced sick leave is sought by an employee "when an employee has exhausted his or her current sick leave balance and anticipates the need for additional sick leave." Union's Supplemental Brief at 7. According to the Union, in order for employees to plan necessary medical procedures in advance and "maintain their health," they must be able to request and receive advanced sick leave. Union's Brief at 41. The Union claims that, without this opportunity, employees could suffer severe medical hardship. The Union adds that the provision contains safeguards to protect against the arbitrary use or abuse of advanced sick leave by employees.

B. Analysis and Conclusions

1. Meaning of the Provision

This provision requires the granting of advanced sick leave under prescribed circumstances. The Union explains that advanced sick leave refers to leave that employees may request and use if they have exhausted their accrued sick leave. This explanation is consistent with the wording of the provision and we adopt it. *Laurel Bay*, 51 FLRA at 737. As such, this provision would allow employees to use sick leave that they have not yet earned. We construe the provision to apply when an employee requests an advance of sick leave for a specific purpose but has no accrued sick leave available for use.

2. The Provision Is Not Contrary to Law

a. The Provision Affects the Right to Assign Work

Proposals that require agencies to grant sick leave or advanced sick leave to employees, including proposals that condition the grant of leave on compliance with Government-wide regulations, have been held to directly interfere with management's right to assign work under section 7106(a)(2)(B) of the Statute. *E.g., Army Information Systems Command*, 42 FLRA at 1127; *National Association of Government Employees, SEIU, AFL-CIO and Veterans Administration, Veterans Administration Medical Center, Department of Memorial Affairs*, 40 FLRA 657, 680 (1991) (*Department of Memorial Affairs*). As the provision here would require the Agency normally to grant requests for advanced sick leave if employees meet certain conditions, the provision affects the exercise of management's right to assign work. Therefore, contrary to the Union's claim, this provision is unlike Provision 6 in *Customs Service* and Proposal 2 in *Port Hueneme*, which merely required each agency "to consider" certain actions but did not impose a substantive limitation on management's right to assign work. Use of the term "normally" does not warrant a different result because that term imposes a substantive limitation on the Agency's right to assign work. *E.g., Army Information Systems Command*, 42 FLRA at 1127 (proposal that management ordinarily will approve employees' requests to use and be advanced sick leave found to directly interfere with management's right to assign work). *See also* Part XVI, *infra*, discussing a similar limitation on the right to assign work.

b. The Provision Is an Appropriate Arrangement

Applying the first prong of the KANG analysis, the Union has established that the provision is intended as an arrangement for employees who are adversely affected by the exercise of management's right to assign work. It is undisputed that management has the ability to grant requests for advanced sick leave. Decisions as to whether to grant such a request involve an exercise of the right to assign work because they determine whether or not an employee may be absent from duty. When management decides that an employee may not be absent from duty and assigns work to that employee, management has effectively denied the advanced sick leave request. The Union identifies essentially two adverse effects on employees who have no accrued sick leave balances that would result from management's decision to assign work to employees who otherwise would be absent from duty: (1) the inability of employees to maintain their health, with possibly serious repercussions if they are unable to take sick leave or have access to the health care system; and (2) the inability to plan necessary medical procedures in advance. Insofar as these adverse effects flow from the exercise of a management right, Article 18, Section 1(H) is distinguishable from the provisions in *IRS, Chief Counsel*, 960 F.2d 1068, and its progeny, in which there was no evidence that the claimed adverse effects flowed from the exercise of a management right. *E.g., Federal Correctional Institution*, 48 FLRA at 230-31.

We also find that the provision is tailored, consistent with the *KANG* standard. The provision addresses those employees who have no accrued sick leave available and who would be required to remain on duty and perform work, as assigned by management, rather than attending to their medical needs.

As to the appropriateness prong of the KANG analysis, we find, on balance, that the provision is appropriate because it does not excessively interfere with management's right to assign work.[22] First, the benefits that would be afforded to employees under the provision are significant. The provision would give employees who have exhausted their sick leave balances, and who have a legitimate need to be on sick leave, the assurance that up to 30 days of sick leave would be available for their use at the time they need such leave. As such, employees would be able to plan and schedule medical appointments and otherwise maintain their health. In addition, employees would not be placed in the position of having to obtain approval for some other type of leave, such as leave without pay or annual leave, and could thereby avoid incurring the financial detriment and other consequences that would flow from the use of such other leave.

Although the Agency contends that the provision would require management to grant advanced sick leave without regard to staffing needs and workload requirements, we find that the impact on the right to assign work is minimal. Employees must satisfy a number of conditions that are specified in the provision before management can be required to grant advanced sick leave. The provision preserves management's ability to refuse a request for such leave if, for example, a requesting employee has not supplied sufficient medical documentation of the need for advanced sick leave or if management has reason to believe that an employee will abuse a grant of advanced sick leave or not return to work after having used the leave. The intrusion on management's right is further limited by the fact that, where an employee requests advanced sick leave before the employee wishes to use that leave, management could prepare for the employee's absence and lessen the impact on workload considerations.

Accordingly, we conclude that this provision is an appropriate arrangement within the meaning of section 7106(b)(3) of the Statute.

XV. Article 18 (Leave), Section 3(A)[23]

In accordance with Federal Personnel Manual Chapter 630, a female employee may be absent on leave for maternity purposes. The length of such absence shall be determined by the employee, her physician and her supervisor. She may use sick leave, annual leave or leave without pay to the extent that she has available annual and sick leave time, provided however, that requests for advanced sick leave, shall be treated by the Office the same as any other available annual leave time. Any absence in excess of available annual or sick leave time will be recorded and treated as leave without pay.

A. Positions of the Parties

1. Agency

The Agency objects only to that portion of the provision that provides for the use of advanced sick leave. It makes two arguments that are predicated on law and regulation. There is no claimed effect on the exercise of a management right. First, the Agency contends that the provision is contrary to 5 C.F.R. § 630.403, which requires that "[a]n agency may grant sick leave only when supported by evidence administratively acceptable." Second, the Agency argues that the provision is contrary to 5 U.S.C. § 6307(c), which states, in part, that a "maximum of 30 days sick leave with pay may be advanced for serious disability or ailment[.]"[24]

2. Union

The Union explains, consistent with Article 18, Section 1(H) discussed above, that requests for advanced sick leave would be limited to 240 hours (*i.e.*, 30 days) and would have to be accompanied by acceptable medical documentation of the need for such leave. The Union also contends that the parties are required to follow applicable statutes and regulations by a different provision of the agreement that is not in dispute. The Union also states that the Authority has found a comparable provision to be within the duty to bargain, citing *National Federation of Federal Employees and Department of the Interior, Bureau of Land Management*, 29 FLRA 1491 (1987) (Provision 13).

B. Analysis and Conclusions

1. Meaning of the Provision

As relevant here, the disputed portion of this provision relates to the availability of advanced sick leave for maternity purposes. The Union explains that this provision would authorize 30 days of advanced sick leave for such purposes and would require acceptable medical documentation in connection with requests for advanced sick leave. As this explanation is consistent with the wording of the provision, we adopt it. *Laurel Bay*, 51 FLRA at 737. In so doing, we note that the Union has not explained how, under the wording of the provision, requests for advanced sick leave are to be treated "as any other available annual leave time." However, we find that it is unnecessary to resolve this uncertainty. First, the Agency makes no arguments concerning this portion of the provision. Indeed, the Agency's arguments focus on statutory and regulatory requirements governing sick, not annual, leave. Second, nothing in the provision addresses management's ability to impose requirements attendant to the granting of annual leave.

2. The Provision Is Not Contrary to Law

The Agency claims that this provision is contrary to law on two narrow grounds: (1) the provision does not limit to 30 days the amount of advanced sick leave available; and (2) the provision does not require the submission of evidence to support such a sick leave request. We reject these contentions.

First, 5 U.S.C. § 6307(d) provides, in relevant part, that "[w]hen required by the exigencies of the situation, a maximum of 30 days sick leave with pay may be advanced for serious disability or ailment[.]"[25] Given the Union's explanation that requests for advanced sick leave would be limited to 30 days, the provision is consistent with 5 U.S.C. § 6307(d).

Second, 5 C.F.R. § 630.403 provides that an agency may grant sick leave only when supported by administratively acceptable evidence. Given the Union's explanation that requests for advanced sick leave would have to be accompanied by administratively acceptable evidence, which we have adopted, the provision is consistent with 5 C.F.R. § 630.403.

In sum, we find that the provision is not contrary to the law and regulation relied on by the Agency.

XVI. Article 19 (Career Development Details), Section 2(A)[26]

Assignments to career development details shall be made and administered in a fair and equitable manner among every qualified employee who has expressed an interest in a detail. The Office and the Union encourage highly qualified individuals to participate in career development details. Three weeks advance notification of a career development detail shall be made by means of an announcement to all unit employees.

A. Positions of the Parties

1. Agency

The Agency contends that the provision interferes with management's right to assign work under section 7106(a)(2)(B) of the Statute. The Agency claims that the provision places a substantive limitation on the exercise of management's right to assign work because it would enable arbitrators to substitute their subjective judgment for that of the Agency. In support, the Agency relies on *Customs Service*, 46 FLRA at 707-09.

2. Union

The Union contends that the provision does not interfere with management's right to assign work. The Union also contends that in *Customs Service* the Authority found that the possibility that an arbitrator's judgment may be substituted for that of an agency was not a basis for precluding negotiations over a provision. In addition, the Union claims that the Authority has found that provisions containing the phrase "fair and equitable" are negotiable. The Union explains that the use of such a phrase is intended to ensure that assignments to career development details are not made on the basis of favoritism, nepotism, illegal discrimination, or other similar grounds. The Union maintains that the provision addresses the manner in which the Agency's program is applied and not the establishment of the elements of the program.

The Union further asserts that the provision is an appropriate arrangement under section 7106(b)(3) of the Statute. According to the Union, the provision specifies that only qualified employees are eligible to participate in career development details. The Union adds that employees "who are unfairly or inequitably not chosen will very likely suffer in their opportunities for career advancement and, therefore, in pay and choice of jobs." Union's Response at 46. The Union also notes that selection for career development details is beyond the control of the employees.

B. Analysis and Conclusions

1. Meaning of the Provision

The disputed portion of the provision would require the Agency to assign and administer career development details in a fair and equitable manner among every qualified employee who has expressed an interest in a detail.(27)

2. The Provision Is Contrary to Law

a. The Provision Affects the Right to Assign Work

The right to assign work includes, among other things, the right to decide whether employees will be detailed to perform various work assignments. *E.g., Federal Professional Nurses Association, Local 2707 and U.S. Department of Health and Human Services, Division of Federal Employee Occupational Health, Region III,* 43 FLRA 385, 392-93 (1991). Provisions that restrict the range of management action under section 7106 of the Statute constitute limitations on the exercise of that right and for that reason have been held to directly interfere with the exercise of the right. Customs Service, 46 FLRA at 718-19. The Authority has held that terms such as "fair and equitable," "equitable," and "equitably," when used in proposals that govern the exercise of a management right, constitute substantive limitations on the exercise of that right. *E.g., American Federation of Government Employees, Local 3258 and U.S. Department of Housing and Urban Development, Boston Regional Office,* 48 FLRA 232, 234 (1993). In this case, because the provision would require the Agency to assign career development details in a fair and equitable manner, it imposes a substantive restriction on the Agency's right to assign work. Accordingly, we conclude that this provision affects management's right to assign work under section 7106(a)(2)(B) of the Statute. See also Part XIV, supra, discussing a similar limitation on the exercise of the right to assign work.

The fact that assignments would be made among qualified employees does not alter this result in view of the additional requirement in the provision that assignments be made from among employees who had expressed an interest in a detail. Even assuming that management could unilaterally determine whether employees were qualified, management would be unable to assign an employee to a career development detail unless that employee had expressed an interest in such an assignment. This limitation on management's ability to assign an employee to perform the duties associated with a detail affects management's right to assign work.

b. The Provision Is Not an Appropriate Arrangement

As stated earlier, see Part III.B.2.b., a provision will not constitute an arrangement within the meaning of section 7106(b)(3) of the Statute if the adverse effects it seeks to mitigate do not flow from the exercise of a management right. This is the view espoused by the D.C. Circuit in IRS, Chief Counsel, 960 F.2d 1068. See also the decision and order on remand in *National Treasury Employees Union and U.S. Department of the Treasury, Office of Chief Counsel, Internal Revenue Service,* 45 FLRA 1256, 1259 (1992). Neither of the parties disputes the application of that precedent here. We find, consistent with the decisions that have applied this doctrine, that Article 19, Section 2(A) is not an arrangement.

In *IRS, Chief Counsel,* the court rejected the Authority's finding that a provision was an arrangement for employees adversely affected by management's right to assign employees. The provision would have required supervisors to refrain from rotating or scheduling assignments to avoid compensating employees who, consistent with a different provision of the agreement, were entitled to the pay of a higher-level position if they were detailed for at least one pay period. The court noted the absence of any contention "that a temporary assignment to a higher-level position itself has an adverse effect on employees." 960 F.2d at 1073. The court determined that the adverse effect the Authority identified was "evidently nothing more than the denial of a benefit... that the existing contract does not provide and that the union wishes to obtain." Id. The court remanded the case to the Authority essentially for the purpose of assessing how the provision constituted an arrangement. In its remand decision, the Authority found that the provision was "expressly and solely" directed at preventing the curtailment of details to avoid the negotiated requirement for higher pay and, as such, that it did not constitute an arrangement. 45 FLRA at 1258.

In this case, the Union states that if employees are not chosen for career development details based on unfair or inequitable reasons, they are likely to suffer in their "opportunities for career advancement and, therefore, in pay and choice of jobs." Union's Response at 46. The only reference in the record before us to the existence of career development details is that which appears in Article 19, Section 1, which was not disapproved.[28] There is no evidence or argument that management has previously utilized career development details.[29] We find that the Union has failed to establish that the adverse effects it has identified flow from the exercise of a management right. The only adverse effects that are identified, namely, the potential for lost or diminished job opportunities and pay, would flow from management's failure to adhere to the terms of the provision.

In material respects, this provision is comparable to the provision discussed above in *IRS, Chief Counsel*. In both cases, the disputed provisions essentially sought to ensure full compliance with other, non-disputed portions of the same provisions. Here, as there, it is management's refusal to abide by a provision's terms, as distinct from the exercise of a management right, that gives rise to the adverse effects. See also *Federal Correctional Institution*, 48 FLRA at 230-31.

In sum, we find that Article 19, Section 2(A) does not constitute an arrangement under section 7106(b)(3). In view of this result, we need not address whether the provision is "appropriate" consistent with that prong of the *KANG* standard.

XVII. Article 28 (Automation), Section 5[30]

Training may be provided by the Office when the Office determines that such training is required. The Office will provide adequate instruction and guidance on any automated system before the use of any system is made mandatory. Requests for additional training made by the Union or individual employees will be given due consideration.

A. Positions of the Parties

1. Agency

The Agency argues that the disputed portion of this provision would infringe on management's right to assign work because it would require the Agency to provide training to employees prior to assigning them duties on automated systems and would preclude the assignment of such duties until training is approved. The Agency maintains that the Authority has held that provisions that require management to provide training in order for employees to perform new tasks are nonnegotiable. The Agency also explains that the term "adequate" is fact-sensitive and that the Authority has found such qualifying terms to impose substantive conditions on the exercise of management's rights. The Agency further states that the phrase "made mandatory" refers to a system that employees would be required to use.

2. Union

The Union asserts that Article 28, Section 5 is an appropriate arrangement under section 7106(b)(3) of the Statute. According to the Union, the provision "is directly linked to and [sic] actual exercise of management rights associated with the introduction of new equipment and operational procedures. It would apply only in the event that these rights were exercised." Union's Response at 52. The Union explains that the provision is designed for employees who are adversely affected by the Agency's decision to introduce new equipment and procedures and that training would be provided "to all employees who use the automated system prior to making the use of the system mandatory." Union's Supplemental Brief at 7. According to the Union, the provision is similar to a proposal that was found negotiable in *American Federation of Government Employees, AFL-CIO, Local 2317 and U.S. Marine Corps, Marine Corps Logistics Base, Nonappropriated Fund Instrumentality, Albany, Georgia*, 29 FLRA 1587, 1603-05 (1987) (*Marine Corps Logistics Base*). The Union explains that reasonably foreseeable adverse effects could occur to both the Agency and employees who are not trained in the new automated system. The Union states that untrained employees would be unproductive and that their performance and evaluations would be severely affected. The Union further contends that the provision does not excessively interfere with management's right to assign work because the nature of the training required by the provision is linked to the change in the work requirements and, further, that the provision does not dictate either the type of training that will be given or when it will be given. The Union states that the "adequacy of training would depend on the nature and complexity of the automated system." Union's Supplemental Brief at 7.

B. Analysis and Conclusions

1. Meaning of the Provision

By its express terms, the portion of the provision that is in dispute would require that adequate instruction and guidance be provided on automated systems before their use is made mandatory. The parties have expressed a common understanding that the provision would require the Agency to provide training before employees are required to use the systems. Our decision is based on this common understanding as to how the provision is intended to operate. In addition, the Union's explanation that the provision would apply to all employees who use automated systems is consistent with the wording of the provision and we adopt it. *Laurel Bay*, 51 FLRA at 737.

2. The Provision Is Contrary to Law

a. The Provision Affects the Right to Assign Work

This provision affects management's right to assign work under section 7106(a)(2)(B) because it would prevent management from assigning duties involving the use of an automated system until training is provided to all employees. The provision is comparable to a proposal in *National Federation of Federal Employees, Local 29 and U.S. Department of the Army, Engineer District, Kansas City, Missouri*, 45 FLRA 603, 615-17 (1992), that was found to be outside the duty to bargain because it conditioned management's ability to assign work on the completion of appropriate training.

b. The Provision Is Not an Appropriate Arrangement

Under the portion of the KANG standard that addresses whether a provision is an arrangement, the Union must establish that the provision addresses the adverse effects flowing from the exercise of a management right and that it is sufficiently tailored. In this connection, the Union claims, and we find, that this provision is intended to address the adverse effects on employees flowing from the exercise of management's assignment of work. Specifically, the Union states that employee productivity and performance evaluation could be negatively affected as a consequence of the lack of training.

However, we find that the Union has failed to establish that the provision is sufficiently tailored. While it is possible that some employees would experience the adverse effect the Union identifies, the Union has not demonstrated that all employees are likely to suffer such consequences. As the provision would apply to all employees who use automated systems, the Agency would be required to provide training even for those employees who do not need it. In finding that the provision is not tailored, we note that we have not been presented with a situation where it is impossible to determine reliably, in advance, which employees are likely to suffer adverse consequences. In view of this, the Union could have limited the reach of the provision to those employees who needed training or whose productivity and performance foreseeably could be harmed by a lack of training.

The Union's reliance on *Marine Corps Logistics Base* is unavailing. The Authority found that the provision in that case required that training be given "only where there is a need for it, not in all circumstances without regard to its relevance or necessity." 29 FLRA at 1605. Because the provision here is not so "tailored," it is distinguishable.

As the provision does not constitute an arrangement under section 7106(b)(3) of the Statute, we need not address whether the provision is "appropriate," consistent with that prong of the KANG standard. In sum, we find that this provision is contrary to law and that the Agency head properly disapproved it.

XVIII. Order 31

The petition for review is dismissed as to Article 14, Section 2(E); Article 14, Section 12; Article 15, Section 4; Article 19, Section 2(A); and Article 28, Section 5. The Agency shall, upon request, or as otherwise agreed to by the parties, negotiate over Proposals 1, 3, 5 and 6. Further, the Agency shall rescind its disapproval as to Article 7, Section 11; Article 35, Section 9; Article 36, Section 9; Article 12, Section 4(G); Article 12, Section 5; Article 13, Section 3(M); Article 18, Section 1(G); Article 18, Section 1(H); and Article 18, Section 3(A).[32]

APPENDIX

Article 35 – Disciplinary Actions

Section 3

In deciding what discipline is appropriate, the Office will give due consideration to the relevance of mitigating and/or aggravating circumstances. The following factors, not intended to be exhaustive or applied mechanically, outline the tolerable limits of reasonableness which will be applied to the circumstances of each case.

1. The nature or seriousness of the offense and its relation to the employee's duties;
2. The employee's job level and type of employment, including supervisory or fiduciary role, contacts with the public, and prominence of the position;
3. The employee's past disciplinary record;
4. The employee's past work record, including length of service, performance, ability to relate to other employees, and dependability;
5. The effect of the offense on the employee's ability to perform at a satisfactory level and its effect on the supervisor's confidence in the employee;
6. Consistency of the penalty with those imposed upon other employees for the same or similar offenses;
7. Consistency of the penalty with the applicable table of penalties;
8. The notoriety of the offense and its impact upon the reputation of the Office;
9. The clarity with which the employee was on notice of any rules that were violated in committing the offense, or had been warned about the conduct in question;
10. Potential for the employee's rehabilitation;
11. Mitigating circumstances surrounding the offense such as unusual job tensions, personality problems, mental impairment, harassment, bad faith, malice or provocation on the part of others.
12. The adequacy and effectiveness of alternative sanctions to deter such conduct in the future by the employee or others.

Article 36 – Adverse Actions
Section 3

In deciding what discipline is appropriate, the Office will give due consideration to the relevance of mitigating and/or aggravating circumstances. The following factors, not intended to be exhaustive or applied mechanically, outline the tolerable limits of reasonableness which will be applied to the circumstances of each case.

1. The nature or seriousness of the offense and its relation to the employee's duties;
2. The employee's job level and type of employment, including supervisory or fiduciary role, contacts with the public, and prominence of the position;
3. The employee's past disciplinary record;
4. The employee's past work record, including length of service, performance, ability to relate to other employees, and dependability;
5. The effect of the offense on the employee's ability to perform at a satisfactory level and its effect on the supervisor's confidence in the employee;
6. Consistency of the penalty with those imposed upon other employees for the same or similar offenses;
7. Consistency of the penalty with the applicable table of penalties;
8. The notoriety of the offense and its impact upon the reputation of the Office;
9. The clarity with which the employee was on notice of any rules that were violated in committing the offense, or had been warned about the conduct in question;
10. Potential for the employee's rehabilitation;
11. Mitigating circumstances surrounding the offense such as unusual job tensions, personality problems, mental impairment, harassment, bad faith, malice or provocation on the part of others;
12. The adequacy and effectiveness of alternative sanctions to deter such conduct in the future by the employee or others.

Footnotes
(If blank, the decision does not have footnotes.)

1. The parties also filed supplemental submissions in response to Authority requests for additional information.
2. The proposals are numbered according to the Union's numbering scheme. The provisions are denoted by their article and section numbers.
3. The Authority uses the same approach for determining the meaning of proposals and provisions for purposes of ascertaining whether the former

are within the duty to bargain and the latter are not contrary to law. In addition, the meanings that we adopt here for a particular provision would apply in resolving other disputes, such as arbitration proceedings, where the construction of that provision is at issue. See *National Education Association, Overseas Education Association, Laurel Bay Teachers Association and U.S. Department of Defense, Department of Defense Domestic Schools, Laurel Bay Dependents Schools, Elementary and Secondary Schools, Laurel Bay, South Carolina*, 51 FLRA 733, 741-42, n.8 (1996) (Laurel Bay). For convenience, we use the terms "proposal" and "provision" interchangeably here and elsewhere in this decision where it is appropriate to do so.

4. As explained more fully in Part VII at note 14, a different standard may apply for determining whether a provision is appropriate.

5. The Authority noted that although the negotiability of the provision did not depend on finding a statutory obligation to bargain midterm, the proposal did restate the statutory obligation and was negotiable on that ground as well. 51 FLRA at 128 n.5 (citing *Merit Systems Protection Board Professional Assoc. and Merit Systems Protection Board, Washington, D.C.*, 30 FLRA 852 (1988) (Proposal 4)).

6. *Department of Energy* involved unfair labor practice allegations that raised the legality of a provision imposed by the Federal Service Impasses Panel (Panel). In contrast, the case before us concerns the duty to bargain over a proposal in a negotiability proceeding. The Fourth Circuit has not applied the reasoning of *DOE v. FLRA* to a case not involving provisions imposed by the Panel. Such a case is currently pending before that court in *U.S. Department of the Interior v. FLRA*, Nos. 96-2855, 97-1135 (4th Cir., oral argument scheduled Oct. 1, 1997).

7. We acknowledge that, if review is obtained in the Fourth Circuit, that court is bound to apply the law of the circuit as established by previous panels unless that law is overturned by the court en banc or by the Supreme Court. See *Busby v. Crown Supply, Inc.*, 896 F.2d 833, 840-41 (4th Cir. 1990). This acknowledgment differs from the Agency's contention that the Authority has conceded that it must follow Fourth Circuit precedent in any case where review might lie in the Fourth Circuit.

8. Further, as both the Agency and the Union are potentially "aggrieved" by other negotiability determinations in this multi-proposal and multi-provision case, it is by no means a certainty that the Authority's decision concerning the negotiability of this proposal will be determinative of the circuit in which judicial review is sought.

9. The Fourth Circuit itself has recognized that "the Authority is in a difficult position when the circuit courts of appeals that may review its decisions have reached differing conclusions[.]" *DOE v. FLRA*, 106 F.3d at 1162 n.8.

10. We do not decide what conduct, if any, might form the basis of an unfair practice allegation once the parties have agreed to bargain on the matters set forth in Section 3.

11. Proposals 5 and 6 reference, respectively, Section 3 of Articles 35 and 36, which are not in dispute. The relevant text of those sections is set forth in the Appendix to this decision.

12. The Union argues that, in light of the Authority's decision in *National Association of Government Employees, Local R5-184 and U.S. Department of Veterans Affairs Medical Center, Lexington, Kentucky*, 51 FLRA 386 (1995), (VA Lexington), the Authority must revise its analytical framework for determining whether a proposal or provision is a procedure within the meaning of section 7106(b)(2). In that decision, the Authority addressed the relationship between sections 7106(a) and 7106(b) of the Statute in dealing with proposals that were asserted to be within the duty to bargain under section 7106(b)(1). The Authority stated that "§ 7106(b) is indisputably an exception to § 7106(a)." 51 FLRA at 392. According to the Union, "the same principle" applied to proposals encompassed by section 7106(b)(1) "must also be applied to proposals or provisions claimed to be negotiable procedures under section 7106(b)(2)." Union's Supplemental Submission at 2. While we agree with the Union that our precedent addressing section 7106(b)(2) warrants reexamination, we decline to do so in this case. In addressing the applicability of VA Lexington, the parties made no specific arguments with regard to this provision, and we do not believe there is a sufficient record in this case to undertake such a reexamination here.

We will do so when the matter is clearly presented to us and there is an adequate record on which to base our adjudication. We do not wish to delay the resolution of this case by soliciting further input on this matter at this time.

13. We view the Authority's decision in *American Federation of Government Employees, AFL-CIO, Local 2317 and U.S. Marine Corps, Marine Corps Logistics Base, Nonappropriated Fund Instrumentality, Albany, Georgia,* 29 FLRA 1587, 1600-02 (1987) (Provision 6) as distinguishable from Article 12, Section 4(G). In the former case, the union failed to establish that a provision requiring the selection of certain candidates referred by a rating panel established by the provision was an arrangement. The Authority found that the provision would apply without regard to whether any employee had been adversely affected by a selection action and would totally preclude the agency from making selections from other appropriate sources. In contrast, Article 12, Section 4(G) would not apply to all selection actions and would not preclude the selecting official from making a selection from any appropriate source, consistent with section 7106(a)(2)(C) of the Statute.

14. We believe, for the reasons expressed by Chair Segal in *Department of Commerce,* 52 FLRA at 1309-11, that the inquiry for determining whether negotiated provisions, in contrast to bargaining proposals, are appropriate may more properly involve whether the management right(s) at issue have been "abrogated," rather than the excessive interference test applied above. The abrogation inquiry would require a different assessment of the burdens that a provision would impose and, in general, could permit a different degree of interference with the exercise of management's rights. In particular, that inquiry would defer to the parties' assessment of the burdens imposed, as evidenced by their agreement to abide by the provision. We find it unnecessary to address that inquiry here, however, because we have determined that, under the excessive interference test, this provision is appropriate. As such, the judgment of the negotiating parties about the amount of interference they considered appropriate is upheld, and an application of the abrogation standard would not alter this determination.

15. As the OPM regulation does not, on its face, govern reductions-in-force, we address the applicability of that regulation only with regard to the part of the provision dealing with removals.

16. For employees who have rights to appeal separations, the Guide states in relevant part:

"Unless the employee was notified in writing *before* the resignation was submitted, you may not place on the SF 52/50, or on the employee's OPF or EPF, any information: – regarding a proposed or pending disciplinary or adverse action[.]"

Guide, Chapter 31, 4.c.(2)(c). (Emphasis in original).

For employees who are serving in a probationary or trial period and who have no appeal rights, the Guide states: no agency comments or findings regarding the employee's resignation may be placed on the SF 52, SF 50, in the employee's OPF (Official Personnel Folder), or in the EPF (Employee Performance Folder).

Id. at 4.c.(1)(a). (Emphasis in original).

17. The Agency did not identify which of the 21 proposals at issue in *Army Information Systems Command* it was referencing. We assume that the Agency was citing to Proposal 20, as that is the only one in which there was a claimed effect on the right to discipline.

18. Only the second sentence of the provision is in dispute.

19. We treat the Union's reliance on Authority precedent differently here than we did with respect to Article 12, Section 5 because the Union relied on precedent there to explain the manner in which its provision was intended to operate. The Union did not similarly explain the application of precedent to the operation of Article 14, Section 12.

20. Only the first two sentences of this provision are in dispute.

21. Only the first sentence of this provision is in dispute.

22. We apply the excessive interference standard here for the reasons expressed in note 14, *supra*.

23. In response to an Authority inquiry regarding the provision's reference to the FPM, both parties

23. ...agree that the FPM's abolishment has no effect on the provision.

24. Amendments to 5 U.S.C. § 6307(c) that were enacted in 1994, Pub. L. No. 103-329, redesignated subsection (c) as subsection (d) with modifications not here relevant. Our analysis refers to the current provision.

25. The Agency makes no claim that absence "for maternity purposes" is not covered by this statutory provision.

26. Only the first sentence of this provision is in dispute.

27. Other portions of Article 19 that were not disapproved by the Agency head require management to designate recurring details as career development details, identify selection factors and provide selection preference to various candidates, and specify the duration and commencement of details, among other things. Thus, management has already agreed to make assignments to details based on enumerated selection factors and to give preference to employees who have never served on details. However, there is no assertion in this case that, in evaluating the effect of Section 2(A) on the exercise of management's right to assign work, the Authority should consider either Article 19 in its entirety or any specific portions of the article that were not disapproved.

28. Article 19, Section 1 provides that:

The Office shall designate certain recurring details as "career development details." Career development details are temporary assignments of at least 90 days to a different position, with the primary purpose of providing training directly related to development of an employee's career as an Attorney Advisor. It will also provide employees an opportunity to develop their skills and interests, and to improve efficiency in administrative and technical fields so that a reservoir of developed employees will be in existence for possible selection to higher level vacancies. Union's Response, Attachment 4 at 49.

29. As such, we do not address the extent to which the Union could have bargained over a provision similar to Article 19, Section 2(A) had there been an existing practice or agreement provision concerning career development details.

30. Only the second sentence of this provision is in dispute.

31. The issuance of our decision today brings to 28 the total number of proposals and provisions that we have resolved in this case and in *Department of Commerce*, 52 FLRA 1265. Originally, the Authority was presented with an entire collective bargaining agreement that had been disapproved along with 7 proposals that had not been resolved through the bargaining process. In view of the Agency's subsequent withdrawal of its disapproval with regard to a number of provisions, it appears that the Agency recognized that disapproval of the entire agreement was not consonant with section 7114(c)(2) of the Statute, which limits disapprovals to agreements that are not in accordance with laws, rules or regulations. Of the provisions that remained in dispute, only portions of many of them were actually disapproved. Had the parties resolved, or at least narrowed, the number of issues in dispute, this case would have not have required such a significant expenditure of Authority resources.

The Authority's resolution of this case also could have been greatly advanced had the parties made a more diligent effort to present an adequate record on which the Authority could rule. Deficiencies in the record required us to solicit input from the parties on several occasions, principally with regard to the meaning of various proposals and provisions, their intended operation, and an identification of which proposals and provisions were actually in dispute. We remind all parties that it is their obligation to provide a sufficient basis on which the Authority can make negotiability rulings.

32. In finding these proposals to be within the duty to bargain and the provisions not contrary to law, we make no judgments as to their merits.

Case #6 Particularized Need Criteria for Information Requests by the Union

58 FLRA No. 165
United States Department of Justice
Immigration & Naturalization Service,
U.S. Border Patrol
Tucson Sector
Tucson, Arizona
(Respondents)n2
and

United States Department of Justice
Immigration & Naturalization Service,
Western Regional Office
Labor Management Relations
Laguna Niguel, California
and
American Federation of Government Employees
National Border Patrol Council
Local 2544, AFL-CIO
(Charging Party)

Case No. DE-CA-01-0497
DE-CA-01-0498

July 14, 2003

Before the Authority: Dale Cabaniss, Chairman, and Carol Waller Pope and Tony Armendariz, Members[n2]

I. Statement of the Case

This unfair labor practice (ULP) case is before the Authority on exceptions to the attached decision of the Administrative Law Judge (Judge) filed by the Respondents. The General Counsel (GC) filed an opposition and a cross-exception, to which the Respondents did not file an opposition.

The amended, consolidated complaint alleges that the Respondents violated § 7116(a)(1), (5) and (8) of the Federal Service Labor-Management Relations Statute (the Statute) by refusing to furnish the Union with certain data. The Judge found that the Respondents violated the Statute with regard to certain items, but not others.

Upon consideration of the Judge's decision and the entire record, we adopt the Judge's findings, conclusions, and recommended Order only to the extent consistent with this decision. We set aside the portion of the Judge's Order directing that the Respondents respond in writing within ten days of data requests and conduct meetings or phone conferences with the Union when the requests are denied. Further, we direct that, to the extent that the arbitration proceeding regarding the employee's removal is not yet final, Respondent Tucson Sector (Respondent Sector) will permit the Union, within ten days after receiving the data, to reply in writing to the data and to request that the Arbitrator suspend the arbitration proceeding and consider the Union's written reply.

II. Background and Judge's Decision

The facts are set forth fully in the Judge's decision and are only briefly summarized here.

In response to the proposed removal of an employee, the Union requested several categories of data from Respondent Sector, including items 1, 6, 7, and 9. Respondent Sector denied the Union's request with regard to items 1 and 7, and forwarded the request regarding items 6 and 9 to Respondent Western Region (Respondent Region). Respondent Region told the Union that it would respond after it considered whether it had any antidisclosure interests, but did not respond further.

The Union filed two charges alleging that Respondent Sector violated the Statute by (1) failing to furnish items 1 and 7 and (2) failing to "respond appropriately to items 6 and 9." GC Ex. 1(a). Later, the Union amended the second charge to name Respondent Region as the charged party with regard to items 6 and 9. On the same day, the GC issued a consolidated complaint naming both Respondent Region and Respondent Sector as Respondents with regard to all of the items, and identifying an individual (Aguilar) as the responsible Respondent Sector agent.

At the hearing, the Judge granted the GC's pre-hearing motion to amend the complaint to clarify that Respondent Sector refused to furnish items 1 and 7, Respondent Region refused to furnish items 6 and 9, and [v58 p657] a different individual (Pyeatt) was the responsible Respondent Region agent. In addition, the Judge ruled that he would not consider defenses that the data was not reasonably available or normally maintained in the regular course of business, because the Respondents failed to raise those arguments to the Union at or near the time of the Union's request.

The Judge found that the Union had established particularized need for items 1 and 7, and that Respondent Sector violated the Statute by failing to furnish those items. Further, the Judge found that the Union had established particularized need for item 6 and that Respondent Region violated the Statute by both failing to provide that item, and by failing to respond to the Union's request. Moreover, the Judge found that, although the Union had not established particularized need for item 9 and that Respondent Region thus did not violate the Statute by failing to provide that item, Respondent Region violated the Statute by failing to respond to the Union's request for that item.

The Judge directed that, if Respondent Sector's deciding official had not yet made a determination regarding the employee's proposed discipline, then that official must consider any reply filed by the Union within ten work days of receiving the requested data, without raising a timeliness argument. In addition, the Judge considered the Respondents' actions in the instant case and previous cases, and he found that the Respondents follow a practice of "stonewalling" the Union. Judge's Decision at 32. Modifying a remedy from one of those previous cases, he directed the Respondents, within ten work days after receiving future data requests, to respond by specifically addressing certain issues in writing and to meet or conduct a phone conference with the Union, at the Union's request, in cases where the Respondents refuse to provide the data.

III. Positions of the Parties

A. Respondents' Exceptions

The Respondents contend that the issuance of the complaint failed to comply with: 5 C.F.R. § 2423.9 and Article 2.H of the Unfair Labor Practice Case Handling Manual (ULP Manual) because the GC could not have received the amended charge prior to issuing the complaint; 5 C.F.R. § 2423.6(d) because Respondent Region was not served with a charge "prior to the issuance of the Complaint[;]" and 5 C.F.R. § 2423.8(a), and Articles 2H-4 and 2H-6 of the ULP Manual, because Respondent Region was not given an opportunity to respond to the amended charge prior to issuance of the complaint.[n3] Exceptions at 2.

Further, the Respondents object to the Judge's decision to permit amendment of the complaint at the hearing. In this connection, the Respondents argue that the initial complaint discussed only Aguilar, a Respondent Sector agent, and only when the complaint was amended to name Pyeatt did the complaint list any actions taken by a Respondent Region agent. According to the Respondents, the amendment "created a new theory of violation... close to [the] hearing" and "prejudiced the ability of Respondent to present evidence/defenses and fully participate in the hearing." *Id.* at 6.

In addition, the Respondents assert that the Judge erred by precluding Respondent Region from arguing that item 6 was not reasonably available or normally maintained in the regular course of business.[n4] The Respondents contend that, although Respondent Region did not raise this argument at or near the time of the information request, doing so would have been futile. With respect to the merits, the Respondents argue that the Judge erred in finding particularized need for items 1 and 7. According to the Respondents, the Union did not need that data in order to argue, in another forum such as arbitration, that the Respondents' actions were improper. The Respondents cite *United States DOJ, Fed. Bureau of Prisons, Fed. Corr. Inst., Forrest City, Ark.*, 57 FLRA 808, 813-14 (2002) (*Forrest City*) (Member Pope dissenting in pertinent part), *petition for review withdrawn*, No. 02-1239 (D.C. Cir. Feb. 24, 2003), and claim that *United States Department of the Navy, Puget Sound Naval Shipyard, Bremerton, Wash.*, 38 FLRA 3, 6-7 (1990) (Puget Sound) – relied on by the Judge – is distinguishable from this case because the data requested there was specifically referenced in the management document that prompted the data request.

[v58 p658] Additionally, the Respondents claim that the Judge's particularized need findings effectively require them to perform legal research for the Union. The Respondents also claim that the Judge's decision puts them in a "catch 22" situation because it requires them to reveal whether they have authority for their actions, and that it requires them to "answer[] a query" rather than "respond[] to an information request." Resp't Exceptions at 8, 9. Moreover, according to the Respondents, the Judge stated that the Respondents spent more effort in denying the Union's request than in complying with it, and this statement indicates that the Judge is "less-th[a]n neutral" and suggests that the Respondents should "give in" to unreasonable information requests. *Id.* at 9.

Finally, the Respondents claim that the Judge's direction that they respond within ten days of data requests, and meet or conduct phone conferences with the Union when they deny such requests, is unwarranted because the Respondents have prevailed in other cases and on some of the issues in the instant case.

B. GC's Opposition and Cross-Exception

The GC argues that the Judge correctly found that it issued the amended charge and the complaint in compliance with 5 C.F.R. § 2423.9. The GC also argues that the Judge correctly precluded the Respondents from raising defenses, and that this was based not only on their failure to raise those defenses previously, but also on their failure to comply with the Judge's subpoenas. In addition, the GC argues that the Judge properly permitted amendment of the complaint because the Respondents had a full and fair opportunity to defend themselves at the hearing. The GC claims that the Judge properly evaluated items 1 and 7 and properly granted the challenged, nontraditional remedy.

In the cross-exception, the GC states that Respondent Sector has decided to remove the employee, and that an arbitration hearing concerning the proposed removal was scheduled for November 2002. The GC requests that Respondent Sector "be directed to furnish the requested information for the Union's use at arbitration and, upon the Union's request (following its review of the information), allow the Union to seek postponement of the arbitration hearing to permit the use of such information at arbitration." GC Opp'n & Cross-Exception at 16.

V. Analysis and Conclusions

A. The alleged deficiencies in the issuance of the complaint against Respondent Region do not provide a basis for dismissing the complaint

The Respondents allege that the complaint was issued in a manner that violated three Regulations, specifically, 5 C.F.R. §§ § 2423.9, 2423.6(d) and 2423.8(a). [n5] In order for procedural irregularities to provide a basis for dismissing a complaint, a respondent must show that it was prejudiced by those irregularities. See *Department of the Army, Harry Diamond Labs., Adelphi, Md.,* 9 FLRA 575, 575 n.1 (1982). See also *United States Penitentiary, Florence, Colo.,* 53 FLRA 1393, 1394, 1403 (1998) (adopting judge's decision); *United States DOJ, Bureau of Prisons, Allenwood Fed. Prison Camp, Montgomery, Pa.,* 40 FLRA 449, 455 (1991), *rev'd on other grounds sub nom. United States DOJ v. FLRA,* 988 F.2d 1267 (D.C. Cir. 1993).

The Respondents argue that the complaint was not issued in accordance with 5 C.F.R. § 2423.9, which provides that a charging party may amend the charge "[p]rior to the issuance of a complaint." The Judge determined that the charge was amended prior to the issuance of the complaint, as evidenced by the fact that the complaint "expressly refer[s] to the charge having already been amended." Judge's Decision at 12. As the Respondents provide no basis for finding that determination erroneous, we reject the Respondents' argument.[n6]

The Respondents also argue that the complaint was not issued in accordance with 5 C.F.R. § 2423.6(d) because Respondent Region was not served with a charge "prior to the issuance of the Complaint." Exceptions [v58 p659] at 2. Section 2423.6(d) provides, in pertinent part, that the charging party "shall serve a copy of the charge" on the charged party, and that the Authority's Regional Office investigating the charge also "routinely serves a copy of the charge on the Charged Party[.]" Nothing in § 2423.6(d) requires that the charge be served prior to the complaint. Accordingly, we reject the Respondents' argument.

With regard to 5 C.F.R. § 2423.8(a), that Regulation provides that "[d]uring the course of the investigation [of the charge], all parties involved are afforded an opportunity to present their evidence and views to the Regional Director." It is undisputed that Respondent Region did not have the opportunity to respond to the amended charge prior to issuance of the complaint. Thus, the Respondents have established that the GC did not follow the requirements of 5 C.F.R. § 2423.8(a).

The Respondents do not explain how Respondent Region was prejudiced by the GC's failure to give Respondent Region an opportunity to respond prior to issuance of the complaint naming Respondent Region. Although Respondent Region was deprived of the opportunity to present evidence to the FLRA prior to being named in the amended charge, this in no way establishes that it was prejudiced by the fact that it fully presented its position after the issuance of the complaint, rather than before. In this connection, the Respondents do not assert that there is evidence or any other matter that Respondent Region would have introduced during the pre-complaint investigation that would have affected the course of the case. Thus, while we do not condone the GC's failure to follow the requirements of 5 C.F.R. § 2423.8(a), we find that Respondent Region was not prejudiced by that procedural irregularity.

B. The Judge did not abuse his discretion by permitting amendment of the complaint

The Authority will reverse a judge's ruling on a motion to amend a complaint only where the judge abused his or her discretion. See *Department of Transportation, FAA, Fort Worth, Tex.,* 55 FLRA 951, 954 (1999). In resolving this issue, the Authority assesses whether the respondent had sufficient notice regarding the issue sought to be included in the complaint by the amendment, or whether the respondent was prejudiced by the amendment to the complaint. See *id.*

The original complaint alleged that Respondent Region failed to furnish items 6 and 9, among other items. Consequently, the complaint put Respondent Region on notice that it would need to defend against its failure to furnish items 6 and 9. The amendment to the complaint, which was requested thirteen days before the hearing, narrowed the allegations to state that Respondent

Region failed to furnish only items 6 and 9 and to add a responsible official, Pyeatt, from Respondent Region. As the Respondents were able to call Pyeatt as a witness and fully question him, see Tr. at 162-90, and do not in any way explain how they were prejudiced by the amendment narrowing the allegation against it, they have not demonstrated that the Judge abused his discretion by permitting that amendment.

C. The Judge did nor err by declining to consider Respondent Region's defenses that item 6 was not reasonably available or normally maintained.[n7]

The Authority has held that an agency is responsible for raising, at or near the time of the union's data requests, any countervailing anti-disclosure interests. See *Forrest City*, 57 FLRA at 812.

The Respondents argue that Respondent Region raised its antidisclosure interests at the first reasonable opportunity, in its answer to the complaint. However, Respondent Region's first opportunity to raise those interests was not in the answer to the complaint, because it could have raised those interests at any time after receiving the data request. Instead, after informing the Union that it would consider whether it had anti-disclosure interests and respond further, Respondent Region waited more than three months before raising those interests in, and only in, its answer to the complaint. In these circumstances, we find that the Judge did not err by finding that Respondent Region failed to raise antidisclosure interests at or near the time of the data request.

In addition, we reject as unsupported the Respondents' argument that it would have been futile for Respondent Region to respond to the data request after the charge was filed against Respondent Sector. Instead, we find it reasonable to conclude that, if Respondent Region had articulated anti-disclosure interests to the Union, then the Union may have withdrawn the charge or the GC may have determined not to issue a complaint naming Respondent Region, thereby resolving the dispute. Further, as found by the Judge, the Union's need for the information continued after the filing of the charge against Respondent Sector because the action against the employee was going forward. [v58 p660]

In these circumstances, we conclude that the Judge did not err in finding that Respondent Region failed to timely raise antidisclosure interests and thus could not rely on those interests in this case.[n8] Therefore, we adopt the Judge's finding that the Respondent violated the Statute by failing to disclose item 6.

D. The Union established particularized need for items 1 and 7[n9]

In order to demonstrate that requested information is "necessary" under § 7114(b)(4) of the Statute, a union "must establish a particularized need for the information by articulating, with specificity, why it needs the requested information, including the uses to which the union will put the information, and the connection between those uses and the union's representational responsibilities under the Statute." *IRS, Wash., D.C.*, 50 FLRA 661, 669 (1995) (IRS). The union's responsibility for articulating its interests in the requested information requires more than a conclusory assertion and must permit an agency to make a reasoned judgment as to whether the disclosure of the information is required under the Statute. *Id.* at 670.

In item 1, the Union requested the "statutory or regulatory basis" that permitted Respondent Sector to rescind two adverse actions and reissue a single, proposed removal. GC Ex. 5 at 1. The Union informed Respondent Sector that it needed the data to determine whether discipline of the employee was in accordance with the requested policies, and explained that it anticipated using the data in connection with its representational responsibilities under the Statute. In these circumstances, we conclude that, consistent with precedent, the Union established particularized need for item 1. See *Forrest City*, 57 FLRA at 812-13; *United States Department of Justice, Wash., D.C.*, 46 FLRA 1526, 1534-35 (1993).

In item 7, the Union requested "written policies and/or instructions in existence prior to October of 1998" that require employees to obtain supervisory permission before leaving their work areas. GC Ex. 5 at 3. The Union explained that it needed the information "in order to determine whether [the employee's] actions constitute a violation of policy or regulation[,]" and that it "anticipate[d] that this information will be used in the written and oral replies." *Id.* The Union also later elaborated that the employee was charged with failure to remain in his designated work area, the exact subject matter of the written policies and/or instructions it was seeking. In these circumstances, we conclude, consistent with precedent, that the Union established particularized need for item 7. See *Forrest City*, 57 FLRA at 812-13.

We reject the Respondents' contention that the Union did not need the requested data in order to argue, in another forum such as arbitration, that the Respondents' actions were improper. In this connection, data concerning the Respondents' legal authority was necessary for the Union to evaluate whether arbitration was appropriate, and if it was appropriate, to prepare for that arbitration. We also reject the Respondents' reliance on *Forrest City* because, unlike the request in this case, the request involved in the portion of Forrest City relied on by the Respondents involved an overlybroad data request. [n10] See *Id.* at 813-14 (Member Pope dissenting). With regard to the Respondents' discussion of Puget Sound, 38 FLRA 3, the Authority has not held that a union is entitled to requested information only if management previously has cited that information as the basis for a management action. *See, e.g., Forrest City,* 57 FLRA 808. Accordingly, the Respondents do not demonstrate that the Union was not entitled to the data here.

In addition, although the Respondents assert that the Judge effectively required them to perform legal research, the Judge explicitly stated that they are not required to do so and are only required to provide *documents* that they already possess. Further, although the Respondents contend that the Judge's decision puts them in a "catch 22" situation because it requires them to admit that they have no authority for the disciplinary action, the fact that the Respondents are required to state that they do not possess documents supporting the disciplinary action does not require them to state that they lack authority for that action. Resp't Exceptions at 8. [*v58 p661*] Additionally, while the Respondents assert that the Judge's decision requires them to "answer[ ] a query" rather than "respond[ ] to an information request[,]" they do not explain why that is the case, or why that alleged distinction would excuse their failure to respond to the requests. *Id.* at 9.

For the foregoing reasons, we adopt the Judge's finding that Respondent Sector violated the Statute with regard to items 1 and 7.[n11]

E. We set aside the portion of the remedy challenged by the Respondents and deny the Respondents' request to direct the Union to cease submitting requests for unnecessary information

In *F.E. Warren Air Force Base, Cheyenne, Wyo.,* 52 FLRA 149 (1996), the Authority set forth the standard for assessing whether nontraditional remedies are appropriate in an individual case:

[A]ssuming that there exist no legal or public policy objections to a proposed, nontraditional remedy, the questions are whether the remedy is reasonably necessary and would be effective to recreate the conditions and relationships with which the unfair labor practice interfered, as well as to effectuate the policies of the Statute, including the deterrence of future violative conduct.

Id. at 161 (citation and internal quotations omitted). Nontraditional remedies will be fashioned only where traditional remedies will not adequately redress the wrong incurred by the ULP. *Fed. Bureau of Prisons, Wash., D.C.,* 55 FLRA 1250, 1259 (2000) (then-Member Cabaniss dissenting as to other matters). The Authority has found nontraditional remedies appropriate where, for example, a respondent has engaged in a pattern of statutory violations. *See, e.g., United States Penitentiary, Leavenworth, Kan.,* 55 FLRA 704, 718 (1999).

The Judge based the challenged remedy on his finding that the Respondents have engaged in a pattern of "stonewalling" the Union. Judge's Decision at 32. However, the Judge cited only one previous case -- *United States INS, Border Patrol, Tucson, Ariz.,* Case Nos. DE-CA-60715 and DE-CA-60791 (July 16, 1997), an administrative law judge decision to which no exceptions were filed – where Respondent Sector was found to have violated the Statute, and no cases where Respondent Region was found to have violated the Statute. See Judge's Decision at 3 and 31. In the other cited case – *United States Border Patrol, Tucson Sector, Tucson, Ariz.,* 52 FLRA 1231 (1997) – the Authority found that the Respondents did not violate the Statute. Further, even in the instant case, the Judge found that the Respondents provided some of the requested information, did not violate the Statute in denying other requests, and noted that in a separate decision issued the same day, he had found that the Respondent did not violate the Statute, see Judge's Decision at 32 n.12. Thus, we find no basis for concluding that the Respondents have engaged in a pattern of statutory violations, such that the challenged remedy is reasonably necessary. Moreover, neither the Judge nor the GC explain why a traditional remedy will not adequately redress this aspect of the wrong incurred by the ULP. In these circumstances, we set aside the portion of the Judge's Order directing that the Respondents respond in writing within ten days of data requests and conduct meetings or phone conferences with the Union when the requests are denied.

We reject the Respondents' request that the Authority direct the Union to no longer submit requests for information that is unnecessary for representational duties, because the Respondents have not demonstrated that the Union's requests for items 1 and 7 were unnecessary.

F. We grant a modified version of the remedy requested in the GC's cross-exception

The Judge directed that, in the event the deciding official has not made a determination regarding the employee's proposed discipline, then that official must consider any written reply filed by the Union within ten work days of receiving the requested data, without an objection on timeliness grounds by the Respondents. The Respondents did not except to this portion of the remedy.

The GC asserts that Respondent Sector has decided to remove the employee and that an arbitration hearing concerning the proposed removal was scheduled for November 2002. See *Id.* at 16 n. 3. Accordingly, the GC requests that this portion of the remedy be modified to provide that the Respondents be directed "to furnish the requested information for the Union's use at arbitration and, upon the Union's request (following its review of the information), allow the Union to seek postponement [v58 p662] of the arbitration hearing to permit the use of such information at arbitration." GC's Opp'n and Cross-Exception at 16. The Respondents do not object to the GC's request.

The record provides no basis for determining whether the arbitration hearing occurred as scheduled and/or whether a final and binding arbitration award has issued. If these events have occurred, then the GC's requested remedy cannot be effectuated and is moot. On the other hand, if the hearing has not occurred and/or if a final and binding arbitration award has not yet issued, then a modified version of the requested remedy would provide the Union with essentially the same relief as the unchallenged portion of the Judge's remedy described above; it would merely take into account the fact that circumstances have changed since the Judge's decision.

We find that a modified version of the requested remedy would recreate the conditions and relationships with which the ULP interfered and would effectuate the policies of the Statute. See *F.E. Warren*, 52 FLRA at 161. Accordingly, we modify the Judge's proposed Order and direct that, to the extent that the arbitration proceeding is not yet final, Respondent Sector will permit the Union, within ten days after receiving the data, to reply in writing to the data and to request that the Arbitrator suspend the arbitration proceeding and consider the Union's written reply.

V. Order

Pursuant to § 2423.41 of our Regulations and § 7118 of the Federal Service Labor-Management Relations Statute, it is hereby ordered that:

A. The Immigration and Naturalization Service, United States Border Patrol, Tucson Sector, Tucson, Arizona shall:

1. Cease and desist from:

(a) Failing or refusing to furnish the American Federation of Government Employees, National Border Patrol Council (the Union), with Items 1 and 7 of the Union's data request of March 5, 2001, which information is necessary for the investigation and processing of the Union's response to the proposed discipline of employee Jason Wood and any grievance that may arise, or has arisen, therefrom;

(b) In any like or related manner interfering with, restraining, or coercing employees in the exercise of their rights assured by the Statute.

2. Take the following affirmative action in order to effectuate the purposes and policies of the Statute:

(a) Furnish the Union with Items 1 and 7 of the Union's data request of March 5, 2001;

(b) Reply in a timely and proper manner to requests for information made by the Union pursuant to the Statute.

(c) To the extent that the arbitration proceeding regarding the employee's removal is not yet final, permit the Union, within ten days after receiving the data, to reply in writing to the data and to request that the Arbitrator suspend the arbitration proceeding and consider the Union's written reply.

(d) Post at its facilities in the Tucson Sector used by bargaining unit employees represented by the Union, copies of the attached Notice (Appendix A), on forms to be furnished by the Federal Labor Relations Authority. Upon receipt of such forms, they shall be signed by the Chief Patrol Agent of the Tucson Sector and shall be posted and maintained for 60 consecutive days thereafter, in conspicuous places, including all bulletin boards and other places where notices to employees are customarily posted. Reasonable steps shall be taken to ensure that these Notices are not altered, defaced, or covered by other material.

(e) Pursuant to § 2423.41(e) of the Authority's Regulations, notify the Regional Director, Denver Regional Office, Federal Labor Relations Authority, in writing within 30 days from the date of this Order, as to what steps have been taken to comply.

B. The Immigration and Naturalization Service, Western Regional Office, Labor Management Relations, Laguna Niguel, California shall:

1. Cease and desist from:

(a) Failing or refusing to furnish the American Federation of Government Employees, National Border Patrol Council (the Union), with Item 6 of the Union's data request of March 5, 2001, which information is necessary for the investigation and processing of the Union's response to the proposed discipline of employee Jason Wood and any grievance that may arise, or has arisen, therefrom;

(b) In any like or related manner interfering with, restraining, or coercing employees in the exercise of their rights assured by the Statute.

2. Take the following affirmative action in order to effectuate the purposes and policies of the Statute:
[v58 p663]

(a) Furnish the Union with Item 6 of the Union's data request of March 5, 2001;

(b) Reply in a timely and proper manner to requests for information made by the Union pursuant to the Statute.

(c) Post at its facilities in the Western Region of the Immigration and Naturalization Service used by bargaining unit employees represented by the Union, copies of the attached Notice (Appendix B), on forms to be furnished by the Federal Labor Relations Authority. Upon receipt of such forms, they shall be signed by an appropriate official of the Respondent and shall be posted and maintained for 60 consecutive days thereafter, in conspicuous places, including all bulletin boards and other places where notices to employees are customarily posted. Reasonable steps shall be taken to ensure that these Notices are not altered, defaced, or covered by other material.

(d) Pursuant to § 2423.41(e) of the Authority's Regulations, notify the Regional Director, Denver Regional Office, in writing, within 30 days from the date of this Order, as to what steps have been taken to comply.

Appendix A

NOTICE TO ALL EMPLOYEES POSTED BY ORDER OF THE FEDERAL LABOR RELATIONS AUTHORITY

The Federal Labor Relations Authority has found that the Immigration and Naturalization Service, United States Border Patrol, Tucson Sector, Tucson, Arizona, violated the Federal Service Labor-Management Relations Statute (the Statute) and has ordered us to post and abide by this Notice.

We hereby notify employees that:

We will not fail or refuse to furnish the American Federation of Government Employees, National Border Patrol Council (the Union), with Items 1 and 7 of the Union's data request of March 5, 2001, which information is necessary for the Union to represent employee Jason Wood.

We will not, in any like or related manner, interfere with, restrain, or coerce our employees in the exercise of their rights assured by the Statute.

We will, upon request, furnish the Union with Items 1 and 7 of the Union's data request of March 5, 2001.

We will reply in a timely and proper manner to requests for information made by the Union pursuant to the Statute.

We will, to the extent that the arbitration proceeding regarding the employee's removal is not yet final, permit the Union, within ten days after receiving the data, to reply in writing to the data and to request that the Arbitrator suspend the arbitration proceedings and consider the Union's written reply.

Dated:_____
By:_____

Chief Border Agent

United States Border Patrol

Tucson Sector

This Notice must remain posted for 60 consecutive days from the date of posting, and must not be altered, defaced, or covered by any other material.

If employees have any questions concerning this Notice or compliance with its provisions, they may communicate directly with the Regional Director, Denver Regional Office, whose address is: 1244 Speer Boulevard, Suite

100, Denver, Colorado 80204, and whose telephone number is: (303) 844-5226. [v58 p664]

Appendix B

NOTICE TO ALL EMPLOYEES POSTED BY ORDER OF THE FEDERAL LABOR RELATIONS AUTHORITY

The Federal Labor Relations Authority has found that the Immigration and Naturalization Service, Western Regional Office, Labor Management Relations, Laguna Niguel, California, violated the Federal Service Labor-Management Relations Statute (the Statute) and has ordered us to post and abide by this Notice.

We hereby notify employees that:

We will not fail or refuse to furnish the American Federation of Government Employees, National Border Patrol Council (the Union), with Item 6 of the Union's data request of March 5, 2001, which information is necessary for the Union to represent employee Jason Wood.

We will not, in any like or related manner, interfere with, restrain, or coerce our employees in the exercise of their rights assured by the Statute.

We will, upon request, furnish the Union with Item 6 of the Union's data request of March 5, 2001.

We will reply in a timely and proper manner to requests for information made by the Union pursuant to the Statute.

Dated:_____
By:_____

(Signature) (Title)

Immigration and Naturalization Service

Western Regional Office

This Notice must remain posted for 60 consecutive days from the date of posting, and must not be altered, defaced, or covered by any other material.

If employees have any questions concerning this Notice or compliance with its provisions, they may communicate directly with the Regional Director, Denver Regional Office, whose address is: 1244 Speer Boulevard, Suite 100, Denver, Colorado 80204, and whose telephone number is: (303) 844-5226.

Concurring Opinion of Chairman Cabaniss

Although I agree with the conclusions in this case, I write separately to point out that the scope of our review with regard to Item 1 of the Union's information request was limited to the Agency's argument that the information was not necessary. As noted in Footnote 9 of the majority opinion, the only issue presented to the Authority by the Agency was whether the data was necessary, or put another way, whether the Union had articulated a particularized need with sufficient clarity. Having determined that it did, the questions of whether the "data" was normally maintained in the regular course of business or was reasonably available were not before us. See, *Fed. Bureau of Prisons, S. Cent. Region, Dallas, Tex.*, 55 FLRA 1250 (2000)(Member Cabaniss dissenting).

More importantly, we do not view the data request as broadly as that alleged by the Agency and our finding the language of Item 1 to be a valid data request to which the Agency should have responded does not mean that a response consistent with the Agency's characterization of the request was required. In my view, the Agency could have fully complied with the request in Item 1 by providing a copy of the regulation(s) or statute(s) covering removal actions for that agency. As indicated in *Internal Revenue Service, Washington, D.C. and Internal Revenue Service, Kansas City Service Center, Kansas City, Missouri*, 50 FLRA 661 (1995) (IRS, Kansas City), the parties should articulate and exchange their respective interests in disclosing information and an Agency should not frustrate that purpose by viewing a request in the broadest terms possible and then using that interpretation as their basis for refusing to provide any response. Such an all or nothing approach does not facilitate the exchange of interests called for in *IRS, Kansas City*.

Case #7 Past Practice

59 FLRA No. 165
United States Department of Homeland Security,
Border and Transportation
Directorate, Bureau of Customs & Border Protection
(Respondent)
and
National Treasury Employees Union
(Charging Party)

Case No. WA-CA-02-0485
Decision and Order
May 6, 2004

Before the Authority: Dale Cabaniss, Chairman, and Carol Waller Pope and Tony Armendariz, Members

I. Statement of the Case

This unfair labor practice case is before the Authority on exceptions and cross exceptions to the attached decision of the Administrative Law Judge filed by the Respondent and the General Counsel (GC), respectively. Each party filed an opposition. The Respondent also filed a motion to supplement the record, to which the GC filed an opposition.

The complaint alleges that the Respondent violated § 7116(a)(1) and (5) of the Federal Service Labor-Management Relations Statute (the Statute) by implementing interim guidelines on the use of personal cell phones and pagers without giving the Charging Party notice and an opportunity to bargain over the interim guidelines or, in the alternative, by not informing the Charging Party that an overriding exigency required immediate implementation of the interim guidelines. The Judge found that the Respondent did not violate the Statute by implementing the interim guidelines because doing so did not change a condition of employment and because an overriding exigency warranted immediate implementation of the interim guidelines. Nevertheless, the Judge found that the Respondent violated the Statute by not responding to the Charging Party's request to rescind the interim guidelines and to bargain post-implementation. As a remedy, the Judge recommended a cease and desist order and a notice posting. [v59 p911]

Upon consideration of the Judge's decision and the entire record, we adopt the Judge's findings, conclusions, and recommended Order and Notice, as modified below.

II. Background and Judge's Decision

The employees at issue work at various ports-of-entry throughout the United States, where they perform inspections of persons, vehicles, and containers entering the United States. Upon discovering that an Immigration Inspector had used a personal cell phone in an attempt to allow drug smugglers to enter the United States without an inspection, the Respondent implemented a policy entitled "Interim Guidelines on Cell Phones and Pagers in Primary and Secondary Inspection Areas."[n1] Judge's Decision at 2. The Respondent implemented the policy without giving the Charging Party notice and an opportunity to bargain. After the interim guidelines were implemented, the Charging Party requested that they be rescinded until the parties could bargain over them. The Respondent did not respond to the Charging Party's request.

The GC issued a complaint alleging that the Respondent violated § 7116(a)(1) and (5) of the Statute by implementing the interim guidelines without giving the Charging Party notice of and an opportunity to bargain over them or, in the alternative, by failing to inform the Charging Party that an overriding exigency required implementation of the interim guidelines prior to bargaining.

The Judge found that the GC and the Charging Party did not show "by a preponderance of the evidence... that, prior to [the interim guidelines being implemented], the Respondent generally permitted bargaining unit employees to carry and use personal communication equipment in primary and secondary inspection areas." Id. at 10. In reaching this conclusion, the Judge considered the testimony of two GC witnesses and five Respondent witnesses. He also considered an excerpt from the Respondent's Uniform Handbook, which states that "[o]nly authorized uniform items officially approved by the Commissioner of Customs... are authorized to be worn by Customs employees." Id. at 10. The Judge found that the "quoted language tends to corroborate the Respondent's contention that the practices at Champlain, as described by [the GC's witness] were not typical of conditions throughout the country." Id. The Judge acknowledged the Respondent's witness' testimony that the interim guidelines "changed the working conditions of bargaining unit employees[,]" but he found that the statement did not amount to an admission that implementation of the interim guidelines changed bargaining unit employees' conditions of employment. Id. at 15.

The Judge further found that, although there was no written policy concerning the use of cell phones and pagers, there was a "general prohibition against carrying and using" those devices. Id. at 6 n. 6. According to the Judge, there was "some divergence of practice," Id. at 10, because some ports "departed from this general prohibition" by allowing employees to carry and/or use personal cell phones and pagers in the primary and secondary inspection areas. Id. at 6 n. 6. However, he found that "such isolated incidents do not amount to a past practice." Id. at 14. Based on the foregoing, the Judge concluded that the implementation of the interim guidelines did not change bargaining unit employees' conditions of employment and that "the Respondent did not violate the Statute by failing to give advance notice to the Union or to bargain...." Id. at 16 (citing *United States Department of the Air Force, 6th Support Group, MacDill AFB, Fla.*, 55 FLRA 146, 152 (1999)).

The Judge further found that "the circumstances which caused the Respondent to issue the [g]uidelines also justified their immediate implementation." *Id.* at 13. In this connection, the Judge found that "the Respondent immediately implemented the [g]uidelines in order to close... a serious 'loophole' in border security." Id. Consequently, the Judge concluded that the Respondent "had no duty to give the Union advance notice of its reliance on an overriding exigency" and, therefore, did not violate the Statute in this regard. Id. at 16 n. 17.

Nevertheless, as relevant here, the Judge found that the Respondent violated the Statute by failing to respond to the Charging Party's request to rescind the interim guidelines and bargain post-implementation. In so finding, the Judge explained that "the duty to bargain requires, at the very least, a response to a demand to bargain and an explanation of the reason for an agency's refusal to negotiate[.]" *Id.* at 16 (citing *Army and Air Force Exchange Serv., McClellan Base Exchange, McClellan AFB, Ca.*, 35 FLRA 764, 769 (1990)). As a remedy, the Judge recommended a cease and desist order and a notice posting. [*v59 p912*]

III. Positions of the Parties[n2]

A. GC's Exceptions

The GC excepts to the Judge's finding that cell phones and pagers generally were prohibited in the primary and secondary inspection areas and to his conclusion that implementation of the interim guidelines did not change a condition of employment. In this connection, the GC asserts that the Judge should not have relied on the Uniform Handbook to corroborate the Respondent's position that the working conditions at the Champlain port were atypical of the conditions throughout the country.[n3] According to the GC, the Uniform Handbook is relevant only to the question of whether employees wore personal communication devices on their uniform belts. See GC's Exceptions at 19. The GC also argues that the Judge should not have found its witness' work experience at the Champlain port atypical of the work experience of other employees at that port simply because his work was performed in overtime capacity. See *Id.* at 20.

The GC asserts that the Judge correctly found that the use of personal communication equipment in the inspection areas is a condition of employment. However, according to the GC, the Judge should have found that the Respondent changed that condition of employment when it implemented the interim guidelines. In addition, the GC asserts that the Judge should have found that bargaining unit employees were adversely affected by the change and that the effect of the change was more than *de minimis*. See Id. at 24. The GC does not dispute the Judge's finding that the Respondent was entitled to implement the interim guidelines without notice due to an overriding exigency. See GC's Exceptions at 29. However, the GC argues that the Judge should have found that the Respondent was required to bargain post-implementation with the Charging Party.

According to the GC, the reason that the Judge did not find that the Respondent was required to bargain post-implementation was because he incorrectly relied on past practice case law in determining that there was no change in conditions of employment. See id. at 29-30. In this connection, the GC asserts that, under the Authority's precedent, adopting a new policy to replace numerous different policies is analyzed as a change in working conditions, and not as a change in past practice. Id. at 30 (citing *Federall Bureau of Prisons, Federall Corrections Institute, Bastrop, Tex.*, 55 FLRA 848 (1999)). In any event, the GC argues that the interim guidelines "constituted a change from the practice that had been in place prior to the [implementation of the] [g]uidelines." *Id.* at 21.

Finally, the GC excepts to two aspects of the Judge's remedy. First, the GC asserts that the Judge should have recommended that the parties be ordered to bargain over the interim guidelines because those guidelines are still in effect and will remain in effect until bargaining over the permanent directive is complete. Second, the GC argues that the Judge should have recommended a posting in all of the Respondent's facilities where Customs inspectors who are represented by the Charging Party work, and not just in the Central Region.

B. Respondent's Opposition

The Respondent asserts that the Judge's reliance on the Uniform Handbook and his evaluation of the GC witness' testimony regarding his work experiences were proper. According to the Respondent, this evidence, coupled with corroborating testimony from Respondent witnesses, support the Judge's conclusion that the Respondent did not change a condition of employment by implementing the interim guidelines. See Respondent's Opposition 4-7.

The Respondent also asserts that evidence of local exceptions to a national policy is insufficient to prove the existence of an established past practice. See *Id.* at

10. According to the Respondent, "in virtually all locations[,] employees were prohibited from using their personal cell phones and pagers in the primary and secondary areas." *Id.* at 11.

Finally, the Respondent argues that post-implementation bargaining is not warranted "now that the parties have already engaged in bargaining over the Customs Directive which is intended to supersede the Interim Guidelines and contains the same prohibition at issue in this case." *Id.* at 18.

C. Respondent's Cross Exceptions

According to the Respondent, the Judge's Order should be modified to delete "any language... regarding the Agency's implementation of changes in conditions [v59 p913] of employment without informing the Union" because the Judge "clearly made the finding that the Respondent's implementation of the [g]uidelines involved in this case did not cause a change in conditions of employment...." Cross Exceptions at 2 (emphasis omitted). In addition, the Respondent asserts that, because the Judge found only one violation and concluded that the Respondent acted properly by implementing the interim guidelines without notice, "it is appropriate to add the 'in any like or related manner' language to the Order and Notice provisions." *Id.* at 3. According to the Respondent, the Judge's recommended order is too "broad and sweeping" without this "qualifying language." *Id.* at 4. Based on the foregoing, the Respondent asks that sections 1(b) and 2(b) be excluded from the Order, that section 1(c) be modified in the Order, and that paragraphs 2 and 5 be excluded from the Notice.

D. GC's Opposition

The GC does not oppose the Respondent's request to add the "in any like or related manner" wording to the Order. Cross-Exceptions at 3. However, the GC argues that the Respondent's cross exceptions as to the other sections of the Order and Notice should be denied. In this regard, the GC asserts that the Judge's Order is consistent with his finding that, by failing to inform the Charging Party that it implemented the change due to an overriding exigency, the Respondent "deprived the Charging party of information necessary for the effective representation of the bargaining unit." GC's Opposition at 3 (quoting Judge's Decision at 16).

IV. Preliminary Matter

After the interim guidelines were implemented, the Respondent advised the Charging Party of its intent to implement a permanent directive to replace the interim guidelines. Bargaining over the permanent directive took place, and as a result, a negotiability petition was filed with the Authority. In addition, the parties requested assistance from the Federal Service Impasses Panel (FSIP). See Judge's Decision at 7. Pursuant to 5 C.F.R. § 2423.21, the Respondent moves to supplement the record with certain documents related to the parties' negotiability dispute that is now before the Authority and their request for assistance from FSIP. The Respondent explains that these documents were issued after the close of the hearing and asserts that they are relevant to the question of whether the Respondent has engaged in bargaining with the Charging Party over the permanent directive. The GC opposes the motion as irrelevant, arguing that the dispute at hand concerns only the interim policy, and not the permanent directive.

Under § 2429.5 of the Authority's Regulations, the Authority may take official notice of the record of other FLRA proceedings, including FSIP, as would be proper. *See, e.g., SSA, Office of Hearings and Appeals, Region II, Buffalo Office of Hearings and Appeals, Buffalo, N.Y.*, 58 FLRA 722, 724 n.6 (2003) (taking official notice of FSIP's decision and Order resolving the parties' impasse); *Nat'l Guard Bureau*, 57 FLRA 240, 244 (2001); *United States Dep't of VA*, 57 FLRA 515, 518 n.5. (2001). The Respondent's supplemental submissions relate to other FLRA proceedings involving the parties in this case. In addition, the Judge considered the parties' bargaining history over the Directive in his discussion of an appropriate remedy. See Judge's Decisions at 17. Therefore, we take official notice of the records of the parties' negotiability appeal and request to FSIP.

V. Analysis and Conclusions

A. The Judge Did Not Err In Concluding that there Was No Change In Conditions of Employment

The determination of whether a change in conditions of employment has occurred involves an inquiry into the facts and circumstances regarding the Respondent's conduct and the employees' conditions of employment. See *92 Bomb Wing, Fairchild Air Force Base, Spokane, Wash.*, 50 FLRA 701, 704 (1995) (citing *United States Department of Transportation, Federal Aviation Administration, Wash., D.C.*, 44 FLRA 482, 493 n.3 (1992)). In addition, when reviewing a Judge's factual findings, the Authority reviews the record to determine whether those factual findings are supported by substantial evidence in the record as a whole. *See, e.g., United States Department of Transportation*, 48 FLRA 1211, 1215 (1993). The GC disputes the Judge's conclusion that there was no change in conditions of employment when the interim guidelines were implemented. The Judge's conclusion in this regard is based on his finding that there was already a "general prohibition" against the use of personal cell phones and pagers in the primary and secondary inspection areas. Judge's Decision at 6 n.6. As more fully explained below, we find that the Judge's conclusion that there was no change in conditions of employment is supported by substantial evidence in the record as a whole.

An examination of the record reveals that two witnesses testified for the GC. One testified that, prior to the issuance of the interim guidelines, he and three other employees at the Champlain port used personal cell phones and pagers in the primary and secondary inspection areas. See Judge's Decision at 8. The other testified that, before the interim guidelines were implemented, [v59 p914] employees were allowed to carry and use personal cell phones in the inspection areas. Five witnesses testified for the Respondent. The Director of the Buffalo port testified that he supervises 500 employees and that, at the Buffalo port, the use of personal cell phones and pagers is prohibited in the primary and secondary inspection areas. See *Id.* at 9. A Labor Relations Specialist testified that the interim guidelines were implemented to "reaffirm" the Respondent's prohibition on the use of personal cell phones and pagers in the primary and secondary inspection areas. Transcript at 154. She also testified that the Respondent later discovered that the interim guidelines "did constitute a change" in the practices at some ports. *Id.* at 160, 162. Two other management officials testified that the Respondent's policy was to prohibit employees from making calls in the primary and secondary inspection areas. See *Id.* at 178, 191. The fifth witness testified that he once saw an employee using a cell phone at the Arizona port. See *Id.* at 210. In addition, the evidence shows that the Respondent operates approximately 300 ports around the country, see Transcript at 174, and that it has a policy against unauthorized items being worn on employee uniforms. See Judge's Decision at 10.

The Judge's conclusion, that the Union had demonstrated that some employees at the Champlain port used cell phones and pagers in the primary and secondary inspection areas but that this was atypical of the practices throughout the country, is supported by substantial evidence in the record. In this connection, the Respondent's witnesses presented consistent testimony that the Agency's policy was to prohibit such use, even though they acknowledged that some ports may have deviated from this policy. Moreover, the Union's evidence that at least 3 employees at the Champlain port used personal cell phones and pagers is diminished by the fact that there are approximately 300 ports across the country. In this connection, although there is no evidence of the Respondent's total number of employees, the record shows that the Buffalo port has approximately 500 employees, and the policy in Buffalo is that no cell phones and pagers are permitted in the primary and secondary inspection areas. In addition to the Union's evidence, the Respondent's evidence shows only two specific instances of an inspector using a cell phone in the primary and secondary inspection areas. That is, one of the Respondent's witnesses testified to seeing an inspector use a cell phone at the Arizona port, see transcript at 210, and other evidence establishes that an Immigration Inspector used a cell phone to communicate with drug smugglers, which is what prompted this written policy. See Judge's Decision at 6.

In this connection, the GC disputes the Judge's consideration of the Respondent's Uniform Handbook, in which the Respondent prohibits the inspectors from wearing certain items on their uniforms. According to the GC, the Uniform Handbook is relevant only to the question of whether employees wore personal communication devices on their uniform belts. See GC's Exceptions at 19. The Judge found, in this regard, that the Uniform Handbook "tends to corroborate the Respondent's contention that the practices at Champlain... were not typical of conditions throughout the country." *Id.* The Judge's conclusion that there was no change in conditions of employment is supported by substantial record evidence, notwithstanding his reliance on the Uniform Handbook. Accordingly, the GC's exception is not persuasive, and we deny the exception.

B. The Judge Correctly Found No Past Practice of Using Personal Cell Phones and Pagers In the Primary and Secondary Inspection Areas

The GC argues that "there was no general prohibition of carrying and using personal communication equipment in primary and secondary inspection areas." Exceptions at 23. It is well established that parties may establish terms and conditions of employment by practice, or other form of tacit or informal agreement, and that this, like other established terms and conditions of employment, may not be altered by either party in the absence of agreement or impasse following good faith bargaining. *See, e.g., Department of the Navy, Naval Underwater Systems Ctr., Newport Naval Base*, 3 FLRA 413, 414 (1980). In order to establish a condition of employment by past practice, there must be a showing that the practice has been consistently exercised over a significant period of time and followed by both parties, or followed by one party and not challenged by the other. *See, e.g., USDA-Forest Service, Pacific N.W. Region, Portland, Or.,* 48 FLRA 857 (1993); *see also United States Department of Health and Human Services, Social Security Administration and Social Security Administration Field Operations, Region II,* 38 FLRA 193, 207 (1990). Essential factors in finding that a past practice exists are that the practice must be known to management, responsible management must knowingly acquiesce in the practice, and the practice must continue for a significant period of time. *See, e.g., Department of Health, Education and Welfare, Region V, Chicago, Ill.,* 4 FLRA 736 (1980).

Applying these standards, we agree with the Judge's conclusion that there was no established past practice of permitting employees to use personal cell phones and pagers in the primary and secondary inspection areas. In this regard, the record supports the Judge's finding that the use of personal cell phones and [v59 p915] pagers in the Champlain port and other ports amounts to "isolated incidents [that] do not amount to a past practice." Judge's Decision at 14. In particular, the evidence shows that there are a large number of ports as compared to the small number of reported incidents of cell phone use. *Compare Tr. at 210 with* Tr. at 174 and Judge's Decision at 6. In addition, the Respondent's witnesses consistently testified that such use was generally prohibited prior to the implementation of the interim guidelines. Specifically, the Director of the Buffalo port testified that the use of personal cell phones and pagers is prohibited in the primary and secondary inspection areas at the Buffalo port. See Judge's Decision at 9. Also, another witness testified that the interim guidelines were implemented to "reaffirm" the Respondent's prohibition on the use of personal cell phones and pagers in the primary and secondary inspection areas. Tr. at 154. In our view, the few instances of cell phone use that have been shown are insufficient to establish a widespread practice of using personal cell phones and pagers in the primary and secondary inspection areas or demonstrate that management was aware of, and acquiesced to, the practice. Consequently, we conclude that the Judge's finding that the Respondent's practice was to prohibit the use of personal cell phones and pagers in the primary and secondary inspection areas is supported by substantial evidence in the record as a whole. Accordingly, we deny the GC's exception.

C. The Judge's Recommended Order and Notice Must Be Modified

According to the GC, the Judge should have ordered the Respondent to engage in post-implementation bargaining to remedy the violation of not responding to the Charging Party's request to rescind the interim guidelines and bargain postimplementation. However, we agree with the Judge that this remedy is unnecessary in the circumstances of this case. Because the implementation of the interim guidelines did not change a condition of employment and the parties are bargaining over a permanent directive that will replace the interim guidelines, we find that bargaining over the interim guidelines is not warranted and would serve no useful purpose to the parties. In this connection, we note that the GC does not contend that the subject matters of the interim guidelines and the directive are different, such that an agreement over the directive would not resolve the parties' dispute over the interim guidelines. We also note that the Authority recently determined that certain Union proposals over the permanent directive were not within the duty to bargain. See *NTEU,* 59 FLRA No. 154 (2004). Consequently, we deny the GC's request to modify the Order by requiring bargaining over the interim guidelines.

The GC requests that the scope of the posting be expanded to include all of the Respondent's facilities where Customs inspectors who are represented by the Charging Party work, and not just the Central Region. The GC's request is consistent with the Authority's precedent holding that a nationwide posting is appropriate when the ULP is committed at the national level. See *FDIC, Wash., D.C.,* 48 FLRA 313, 331 (1993), *petition for review denied,* No. 93-1694, (D.C. Cir. Dec. 22, 1994). As it is undisputed that the Respondent's interim guidelines establish a national policy that applies to all Customs inspectors who work in primary and secondary inspection areas, we will modify the Order and Notice to require posting consistent with the GC's request.

The Respondent requests that the Judge's recommended Order and Notice posting be modified to omit all wording regarding changing conditions of employment because the Judge found that the Respondent did not change a condition of employment. Because the only violation found in this case is the Respondent's failure to respond to the Charging Party's request to rescind the interim guidelines and bargain thereafter, we will modify the Order and Notice to exclude the paragraphs regarding changing conditions of employment.

Finally, the Respondent requests that section 1(C) of the Order be modified to include the words "in any like or related manner." Cross Exceptions at 3. Because the GC does not oppose the Respondent's request and the requested wording is consistent with the wording commonly used in the Authority's orders, we will modify the Order and Notice as requested.

VI. Decision

The GC's exceptions as to the merits of the Judge's decision are denied. The Judge's recommended Order and Notice is adopted, as modified consistent with this decision.

VII. Order

Pursuant to § 2423.41(c) of the Authority's Regulations and § 7118 of the Federal Service Labor-Management Relations Statute, it is hereby ordered that the United States Department of Homeland Security, Border and Transportation Directorate, Bureau of Customs and Border Protection, shall:

1. Cease and desist from:

(a) Failing to respond to requests to bargain by the National Treasury Employees Union. [v59 p916]

(b) In any like or related manner, interfering with, restraining or coercing employees in the exercise of their rights assured by the Federal Service Labor-Management Relations Statute.

2. Take the following affirmative action:

(a) Respond to requests to bargain by the National Treasury Employees Union.

(b) Post at all of its facilities copies of the attached Notice on forms to be furnished by the Authority. Upon receipt of such forms they shall be signed by the Commissioner of Customs, and shall be posted and maintained for 60 consecutive days thereafter in conspicuous places, including all bulletin boards and other places where notices to employees are customarily posted. Reasonable steps shall be taken to ensure that such Notices are not altered, defaced or covered by any other material.

(c) Pursuant to § 2423.41(e) of the Authority's Regulations, notify the Regional Director of the Washington Region, Federal Labor Relations Authority, in writing, within 30 days of the date of this Order, as to what steps have been taken to comply.

NOTICE TO ALL EMPLOYEES POSTED BY ORDER OF THE FEDERAL LABOR RELATIONS AUTHORITY

The Federal Labor Relations Authority has found that the United States Department of Homeland Security, Border and Transportation Directorate, Bureau of Customs and Border Protection violated the Federal Service Labor-Management Relations Statute and has ordered us to post and abide by this Notice.

We hereby notify employees that:

We will not fail to respond to requests to bargain by the National Treasury Employees Union.

We will not in any like or related manner, interfere with, restrain or coerce employees in the exercise of their rights assured by the Federal Service Labor-Management Relations Statute.

We will respond to requests to bargain by the National Treasury Employees Union.

_____
(Agency)

Dated:_____ By:_____
(Signature)

This Notice must remain posted for 60 consecutive days from the date of posting, and must not be altered, defaced, or covered by any other material.

If employees have any questions concerning this Notice or compliance with its provisions, they may communicate directly with the Regional Director, Washington Regional Office, whose address is: Federal Labor Relations Authority, Tech World Plaza, 800 K Street, NW, Suite 910, Washington, DC 20001, and whose telephone number is: 202-482-6700.

Case #8 Appropriate Unit Criteria for Determining Whether a Petitioned for Bargaining Unit is Appropriate

59 FLRA No. 133

———

United States Department of the Air Force
Lackland Air Force Base
San Antonio, Texas
(Activity)

and
American Federation of Government Employees,
AFL-CIO
(Petitioner)

Case No. DA-RP-03-0010
Order

Denying Application for Review
March 10, 2004

Before the Authority: Dale Cabaniss, Chairman, and Carol Waller Pope and Tony Armendariz, Members

I. Statement of the Case

This case is before the Authority on an application for review filed by the Activity under § 2422.31 of the Authority's Regulations. The Activity seeks review of the Regional Director's (RD) Decision and Order and Direction of Election, in which the RD found the Petitioner's proposed unit appropriate and ordered an election. No opposition to the application was filed.

For the reasons set forth below, we conclude that the Activity has failed to establish that review of the RD's decision is warranted. Accordingly, we deny the application for review.

II. Background and RD's Decision

The Petitioner filed a representation petition seeking an election to represent all non-appropriated fund (NAF), non-supervisory employees of the Activity's Services Division. At the hearing, the Activity contended that the Services Division employees should be split into three separate bargaining units for representational purposes, rather than the single bargaining unit sought by the Petitioner.

In considering the appropriateness of the Petitioner's proposed unit, the RD set out the standard contained in § 7112(a) of the Federal Service Labor-Management Relations Statute (the Statute).[n1] The RD explained that "[i]n order for a unit to be considered appropriate, all three criteria -- community of interest, effective dealings, and efficiency of agency operations --must be met." RD's Decision at 24. The RD further explained that "[t]he Statute does not, however, require that the proposed unit be the only appropriate unit or the most appropriate unit." *Id.*

Turning to the first criterion, the RD concluded that the employees included in the Petitioner's proposed unit share a community of interest. Specifically, the RD found that the affected employees are "subject to the same chain of command" and health and personnel policies and that they all "support the same... mission[.]" *Id.* at 26. The RD further found that the employees are geographically co located and share such things as parking, child care services, and eating and entertainment facilities. According to the RD, these factors outweigh the facts that there is "a small degree of interchange between NAF employees in the performance of their duties" and that "a number of working conditions do not match up across the board[.]" *Id.*

With respect to the second criterion, the RD found "no evidence on which to find that the petitioned-for unit would impede effective dealings with the Activity." *Id.* at 27. In this regard, the RD found that NAF employees' personnel files are co-located and that NAF employees are serviced by the same human resources and payroll offices. According to the RD, "the record established that no lines of authority had been established for carrying out labor relations with the petitioned-for unit[.]" *Id.* at 27. Therefore, she concluded that the proposed unit would promote effective dealings.

As to the third criterion, the RD found that the proposed unit would promote efficiency of the Activity's operations. In this connection, the RD found "no reason why the Activity would need to establish any new organizational structures to accomplish labor relations." *Id.* In addition, she found that the proposed unit would "eliminate the possibility of fragmenting into separate units a group of employees that share a strong community of interest." *Id.* Accordingly, she concluded that the proposed unit would promote efficiency of the Activity's operation.

Rejecting the Activity's argument to the contrary, the RD determined that flexible, probationary, and temporary [v59 p740] employees with reasonable expectations of continued employment of more than 90 days should be included in the unit.[n2] According to the RD, regular and flexible employees have different entitlements to benefits and only regular employees are guaranteed a minimum number of hours of work. Nevertheless, she found that "these facts do not negate the overwhelming community of interest shared by the regular and flexible employees alike, or management's ability to deal with both categories of employees as a single group." *Id.* at 29. The RD also found that flexible, probationary, and temporary employees have a reasonable expectation of continued employment. Consequently, the RD concluded that these employees share a community of interest with regular employees and that including them in the unit would promote effective dealings and efficiency of Activity's operations. *Id.*

Based on the foregoing, the RD concluded that the Petitioner's proposed unit was an appropriate unit and that it should include flexible, probationary, and temporary employees who have reasonable expectations of continued employment of more than 90 days. The RD ordered an election.

III. The Activity's Application for Review

The Activity disputes the RD's representation determination on three grounds.

First, the Activity argues that the Services Division would more appropriately be divided into three units that correspond to its three sections: the Family Member Program, the Business Operations Unit, and the Lodging Operations Unit. It claims that these units have distinct missions and perform "three entirely different functions." Application for Review at 52-53. In particular, the Activity asserts that there is "virtually no commingling among the employees of the three organizations." *Id.* at 74. According to the Activity, employees in the Family Member Program are required to have "more education, more training, and more background checks[,]" *Id.* at 54, as distinguished from the Business and Lodging Operations, which have a goal of making a profit. *See id.* at 61, 72. The Activity also asserts that the three units are governed by different rules and regulations. *See, e.g., Id.* at 56, 67, 72. To support its claim that three separate units are appropriate, the Activity cites several Authority decisions in which it claims the Authority has found units appropriate that were composed of "numerous occupational groups" such as "firefighters, security officers, air traffic controllers, nurses and professionals." *Id.* at 46.

Second, the Activity argues that "the unit proposed by the Petitioner would not constitute an appropriate unit" because "the Services Division is made up of three distinct functional groups of employees." *Id.* at 80. In this regard, the Activity argues that "[t]here is no integration as a general rule among the three organizations." *Id.* at 82. According to the Activity, with a single unit, "it would be impossible" to bargain over matters such as uniforms or dress codes, hours of work, duty assignments, overtime callback procedures, and training requirements. See *Id.* at 80. The Activity also argues that managers may become confused about which contract provisions apply to which employees. Based on these arguments, the Activity disputes the RD's conclusions that the employees included in the petition share a community of interest and that including them in a bargaining unit would promote effective dealings and efficiency of the Activity's operations.

Finally, the Activity argues that flexible employees should be excluded from the proposed unit because they do not work a regular schedule, see id. at 75, and because they have little or no career opportunity. See *Id.* at 14. The Activity also argues that probationary employees should be excluded because "they are subject to removal at any given time basically at the convenience of the organization." *Id.* at 78. According to the Activity, "it is illegal for probationary employees to be covered by a collective bargaining agreement that covers the separation of probationary employees." *Id.* at 83-84 (citing NTEU v. FLRA, 848 F.2d 1273 (D.C. Cir. 1988)).

IV. Analysis and Conclusions

The Activity does not specifically rely on any of the grounds for review that are set forth in § 2422.31(c) of the Authority's Regulations.[n3] However, the Activity challenges the RD's legal conclusion that the proposed unit is appropriate under § 7112(a) of the Statute. We, therefore, construe the Activity's application as raising a claim that the RD failed to apply established law. *[v59 p741]*

A. The RD Did Not Fail To Apply Established Law by Concluding that the Petitioner's Proposed Unit Is Appropriate Under § 7112(a) of the Statute

In determining whether a petitioned-for unit is appropriate under § 7112(a) of the Statute, the Authority considers whether the unit would: (1) ensure a clear and identifiable community of interest among employees in the unit; (2) promote effective dealings with the agency involved; and (3) promote efficiency of the operations of the agency involved. *See, e.g., Defense Mapping Agency, Aerospace Ctr., St. Louis, Mo.,* 46 FLRA 502, 509 (1992). A proposed unit must meet all three appropriate unit criteria in order to be found appropriate. See *Department of the Interior, National Park Serivce, Lake Mead National Recreation Area, Boulder City, Nev.,* 57 FLRA 582, 584 (2001). Determinations as to each of these three criteria are made on a case-by-case basis. See *United States Department of the Navy, Fleet and Industrial Supply Center, Norfolk, Va.,* 52 FLRA 950, 960 (1997) (FISC). The Authority has set out factors for assessing each criterion, but has not specified the weight of individual factors or a particular number of factors necessary to establish an appropriate unit. See *AFGE, Local 2004,* 47 FLRA 969, 972 (1993) (Local 2004).

The Activity's initial objection to the RD's decision is that three separate units would be more appropriate than the unit the Petitioner seeks and the RD found to be appropriate. However, as the RD explained, the relevant determination in this case is "the appropriateness of the unit sought by the Petitioner." RD's Decision at 2. In this regard, the Authority's precedent holds that a proposed unit need not be the "most appropriate" or the "only appropriate" unit in order to be an appropriate unit under the Statute. Local 2004, 47 FLRA at 973. Consequently, the Activity's insistence that "three units would be more effective" than one does not provide a basis for concluding that the Petitioner's proposed unit is not appropriate or for overturning the RD's decision. Application for Review at 79.

In addition to its claim that three units would be more appropriate, the Activity objects to the RD's decision that the proposed unit is appropriate. As fully explained below, we conclude that the RD did not fail to apply established law in concluding that the proposed unit is appropriate.

1. Community of Interest

In order to determine whether employees share a clear and identifiable community of interest, the Authority examines such factors as whether the employees in the proposed unit are a part of the same organizational component of the agency; support the same mission; are subject to the same chain of command; have similar or related duties, job titles and work assignments; are subject to the same general working conditions; and are governed by the same personnel and labor relations policies that are administered by the same personnel office. See *United States Department of the Air Force, Air Force Materiel Command, Wright-Patterson Air Force Base,* 47 FLRA 602 (1993). In addition, factors such as geographic proximity, unique conditions of employment, distinct local concerns, degree of interchange between other organizational components, and functional or operational separation may be relevant. See FISC, 52 FLRA at 960-61 and cases cited therein.

Here, the RD found only a small degree of interchange between the affected employees in the performance of their duties, and she found some variance in the employees' working conditions. However, the RD found that the affected employees are subject to the same chain of command and health and personnel policies, and that they share parking, child care services, and eating and entertainment facilities. The RD also found that the affected employees support the same mission and are geographically colocated. These findings support the RD's conclusion that the affected employees share a community of interest, consistent with the Authority's precedent. See, e.g., *United States Securities and Exchange Commission, Wash., D.C.,* 56 FLRA 312, 316 (2000) (finding consolidated nation-wide unit appropriate where RD found that all employees support same mission and are subject to same personnel policies).

The Activity disputes this finding, arguing that there is virtually no commingling among the affected employees and that the Services Division consists of three distinct groups of employees that perform different [v59 p742] duties. The Activity relies on Authority precedent finding appropriate units structured around a functional grouping of employees who possess characteristics and concerns limited to that group to support its argument. See, e.g., *Department of the Navy, Naval Station, Norfolk, Va.,* 14 FLRA 702, 704 (1984) *(Naval Station).* However, the Activity's reliance on this precedent is misplaced because the Authority has never held that appropriate units must include only employees who share functions or occupations. Indeed, in *Naval Station,* where the Authority held that a unit of firefighters was appropriate under § 7112(a) of the Statute, the Authority also held that these same firefighters "may appropriately be included in the comprehensive, Activity-wide unit...." *Id.*

As explained above, the RD considered the level of interaction among the employees and the varying duties performed by them. Nevertheless, she found that these considerations were outweighed by other factors, such as the employees' shared location, mission, and chain of command. The RD was not bound to weigh any one factor more heavily than another, see Local 2004, 47 FLRA at 972, and the Activity does not dispute the RD's findings regarding the other factors. Consequently, the Activity has not provided a basis to conclude that the RD erred in her conclusion that the affected employees share a community of interest.

2. Effective Dealings

The effective dealings criterion pertains to the relationship between management and the exclusive representative selected by the proposed unit. See FISC, 52 FLRA at 961. The factors bearing on this criterion include: the past collective bargaining experience of the parties; the locus and scope of authority of the personnel administering personnel policies covering employees in the proposed unit; the limitations, if any, on the negotiation of matters of critical concern to employees in the proposed unit; and the level at which labor relations policy is set in the agency. *Id.*

The RD found that the affected employees' personnel files are jointly located and that the employees are all serviced by the same human resources and payroll offices. She also found that there are no established lines of authority to conduct labor relations. The Activity does not dispute these findings. Indeed, the Activity agrees that there is "no pattern or history of a unit as proposed by the Petitioner for labor relations at Lackland AFB." Application for Review at 84. Nevertheless, the Activity insists that it would be "impossible" for the parties to bargain over certain matters, such as training and uniforms. The Activity has not provided any evidence or support for this contention. Moreover, the RD specifically found that "[n]o evidence was offered to show that employees would not be able to negotiate with the same officials who exercise authority over personnel decisions." RD's Decision at 27. Consequently, we conclude that the Activity's arguments do not demonstrate that the RD erred in finding that the proposed unit would promote effective dealings.

3. Efficiency of Operations

The efficiency of operations criterion pertains to whether the structure of the bargaining unit bears a rational relationship to the operational and organizational structure of the agency. See *Miss. Army National Guard, Jackson, Miss.,* 57 FLRA 337, 342 (2001). The RD found "no reason why the Activity would need to establish any new organizational structures to accomplish labor relations" and the Activity does not provide any such reasons. RD's Decision at 27. In addition, although the Activity insists that three units would be "more effective" than one, it does not make any claims that its operations would be impaired if there was only one bargaining unit. Application for Review at 79. Consequently, the Activity has not demonstrated that the RD erred in finding that the proposed unit would not impede the efficiency of operations.

B. The RD Did Not Fail To Apply Established Law by Including Flexible, Probationary, and Temporary Employees In the Appropriate Unit

The Authority has found that various classes of employees, other than regular or permanent employees, may be included in bargaining units with regular or permanent employees, so long as they share a community of interest with the regular or permanent employees. *See, e.g., United States Department of the Treasury, United States Mint,* 32 FLRA 508 (1988) (including certain temporary employees in the bargaining unit); see also *United States Department of Commerce, National Oceanic and Atmospheric Administration, National Marine Fisheries Service, N.E. Region,* 24 FLRA 922 (1986) (temporary intermittent observers with 1-year appointments extendable by 3 years included in bargaining unit with permanent part-time observers). When determining whether such employees share a community of interest with permanent employees, the Authority considers whether the employees have a reasonable expectation of continued employment. See *United States Army Enginnering Activity, Capital Area, Fort Myer, Va.,* 34 FLRA 38, 42 (1989). The Authority also will consider other factors. For example, the Authority has found that temporary employees who (1) held 6-month appointments which could be renewed; (2) shared the same general supervision, [v59 p743] work schedules, office conditions and common working environment with other bargaining unit employees; (3) had regular and frequent contacts with other unit employees; and (4) performed substantially the same duties as other permanent unit employees, had a clear and identifiable community of interest with the other employees in the unit and that their inclusion in the unit would promote effective dealing with, and efficiency of the operations of, the activity. See *United States Small Business Administration, Lower Rio Grande Valley District Office,* 16 FLRA 180, 181 (1984).

In concluding that flexible, probationary, and temporary employees are included in the appropriate unit, the RD found that these employees have the same conditions of employment, services, and requirements as regular employees. In addition, the RD explained that "[e]mployees who have a reasonable expectation of continued employment beyond a defined, brief period (such as 90 days), are routinely found to be appropriately included in bargaining units with other similarly situated employees." RD's Decision at 29 (citing *United States Department of the Air Force, 90th Missile Wing (SAC), F.E. Warren Air Force Base, Cheyenne, Wyo.,* 48 FLRA 650

(1993)). The RD, found that the flexible and probationary employees at issue have reasonable expectations of employment of more than 90 days, and that they, along with the temporary employees who have a reasonable expectation of employment of more than 90 days, share a community of interest with regular employees. Moreover, according to the RD, including flexible, probationary, and temporary employees in the bargaining unit would promote effective dealings and efficiency of agency operations. The RD's findings are consistent with longstanding Authority precedent finding it appropriate to include various nonregular employees in bargaining units with regular employees. See *Fort Buchanan Installation, Club Management. System, Fort Buchanan, P.R.*, 9 FLRA 143 (1982) (on-call and intermittent employees with reasonable expectancy of continued employment shared community of interest with regular full-time employees and including them promotes effective dealings and efficiency of agency operations).

The Activity has not offered any evidence to rebut the RD's factual findings, which support his conclusion that flexible, probationary, and temporary employees share a community of interest with regular employees and that including them in the bargaining unit would promote effective dealings and efficiency of agency operations. In this connection, although the Activity accurately asserts that flexible employees do not work regular hours and that probationary employees may not grieve termination actions, these facts, standing alone, do not indicate that such employees do not share a community of interest with regular employees. Moreover, although probationary employees may not challenge their separations under a negotiated grievance procedure, there is no basis for finding that they may not be included in a bargaining unit or covered by a collective bargaining agreement for other purposes. Accordingly, the Activity has not demonstrated that the RD failed to apply established law by including these employees in the bargaining unit.

V. Order

The Activity's application for review is denied.

Footnote # 1 for 59 FLRA No. 133 – Authority's Decision

As relevant here, 5 U.S.C. § 7112(a) provides that "[t]he Authority... shall determine any unit to be an appropriate unit only if the determination will ensure a clear and identifiable community of interest among the employees in the unit and will promote effective dealings with, and efficiency of the operations of the agency involved."

Footnote # 2 for 59 FLRA No. 133 – Authority's Decision

Flexible employees are "employees whose schedules vary based on operational needs and who... are not guaranteed any number of hours." RD's Decision at 5; cf. 5 C.F.R. § 340.403 (intermittent employment is performed when the nature of the work is sporadic and unpredictable so that a tour of duty cannot be regularly scheduled in advance). Probationary employees are employees whose employment is subject to a probationary period. See 5 C.F.R. § 315.801. Temporary employees are employees that are hired to fill positions for a short duration of time, usually no longer than one year. See id. at § 316.401.

Footnote # 3 for 59 FLRA No. 133 – Authority's Decision

Section 2422.31(c) provides, in pertinent part, that the Authority may grant an application for review when the application demonstrates that review is warranted on one or more of the following grounds:

(1) The decision raises an issue for which there is an absence of precedent;

(2) Established law or policy warrants reconsideration; or,

(3) There is a genuine issue over whether the Regional Director has:

(i) Failed to apply established law;

(ii) Committed a prejudicial procedural error;

(iii) Committed a clear and prejudicial error concerning a substantial factual matter.

5 C.F.R. § 2422.31(c).

Case #9 Right to Assign Work

52 FLRA No. 15
Federal Labor Relations Authority
Washington, D.C.

American Federation of Government Employees, Local 3392
(Union)
and
U.S. Government Printing Office
Public Documents Distribution Center
Pueblo, Colorado
(Agency)

Case No. 0-NG-2259

Decision and Order on a Negotionability Issues
September 11, 1996

Before the Authority: Phyllis N. Segal, Chair; Tony Armendariz and Donald S. Wasserman, Members.

I. Statement of the Case

This case is before the Authority on a negotiability appeal filed by the Union under section 7105(a)(2)(E) of the Federal Service Labor-Management Relations Statute (the Statute), and concerns the negotiability of one proposal providing that certain duties will be performed by a supervisor. For the reasons that follow, we find that the proposal affects management's right to assign work and is, therefore, outside the duty to bargain.

II. Proposal

The duties of Postage Report information for SSU, and Reimbursable reports for Unit II be returned to supervisory duties.

III. Positions of the Parties

A. Union

The Union asserts that as a result of an unfair labor practice charge filed by the Union, the parties agreed to bargain over proposed changes related to the assignment of duties to employees.[1] The Union maintains that, as management was willing to negotiate and did agree to other matters related to the assignment of duties to the employees, the remaining proposal is also negotiable. According to the Union, the duties of postage and reimbursable report preparation were formerly performed exclusively by supervisors. The Union maintains that these duties "place an unfair burden on bargaining unit employees, in that errors made in these two (reporting) duties may seriously affect the operation of [the] Agency, as well as damage the yearly evaluation of [the] employees." Petition for Review at 1-2.

B. Agency

The Agency argues that the proposal violates its rights, under sections 7106(a)(2)(A) and (B) of the Statute, "to assign and direct work." Statement of Position at 1. Contrary to the Union's claim that the duties of postage and reimbursable report preparation were exclusively performed by supervisors, the Agency asserts that these duties are included in the position descriptions of unit employees, although previous supervisors had undertaken these duties. The Agency contends that because it is clearly established that proposals concerning the assignment of work to supervisors are nonnegotiable, the proposal is nonnegotiable. Finally, the Agency maintains that the proposal is not an appropriate arrangement within the meaning of section 7106(b)(3).

IV. Analysis and Conclusion

Although the Agency claims that the proposal violates its right under section 7106(a)(2)(A) to direct work, section 7106(a)(2)(A) concerns the right to direct employees.[2] It is clear from the Agency's brief, as well as the cases on which the Agency relies, that the Agency is claiming that the proposal violates its right to assign particular duties to particular employees under section 7106(a)(2)(B) of the Statute. Consequently, we construe the Agency's claim that the proposal violates its right to direct work as a claim that the proposal affects the Agency's right to assign work under section 7106(a)(2)(B) of the Statute.[3]

The right of an agency to assign work under section 7106(a)(2)(B) of the Statute includes the right to determine the particular duties to be assigned, the right to decide when work assignments will occur, and the right to decide to whom or what positions the duties will be assigned. *American Federation of Government Employees, National Border Patrol Council and U.S. Department of Justice, Immigration and Naturalization Service*, 51 FLRA 1308, 1315 (1996). Additionally, proposals or provisions that concern the assignment of specific duties to particular management officials directly interfere with an agency's right to assign work. *Id.*

The proposal seeks to require the Agency to assign the duties of preparing the postage and reimbursable reports to a supervisor rather than to a member of the bargaining unit. As such, the proposal affects management's right to assign work under section 7106(a)(2)(B) of the Statute. Id. As the Union makes no claim that its proposal is intended to be an appropriate arrangement under section 7106(b)(3), there is no need to address the Agency's argument that the proposal is not an appropriate arrangement.[4] Accordingly, we conclude that the proposal is outside the duty to bargain.

V. Order

The petition for review is dismissed.

Footnote #1

The settlement agreement between the parties provided that the "Agency and the Union will commence bargaining over the proposed changes... and negotiate to agreement or impasse...." Attachment to Petition for Review.

Footnote #2

The right to direct employees has been defined as the right to supervise and guide the employees in the performance of their duties on the job. National Association of Government Employees, Local R1-109 and U.S. Department of Veterans Affairs, Medical Center, Newington, Connecticut, 47 FLRA 651, 656 (1993).

Footnote #3

TIn this regard, the Agency makes no claim, and thus we do not address, whether the proposal also would be found to be outside the duty to bargain because it determines the terms and conditions of employment of non-unit employees.

Footnote #4

TThe Union makes no claim that the Agency's refusal to bargain over the proposal violates the settlement agreement. Therefore, there is no need for us to address that matter. We note, in this regard, that the settlement agreement does not address the negotiability of the proposals.

Case #10 Limitation on Bargaining – Federal Statute

45 FLRA No. 53

Federal Labor Relations Authority
Washington, D.C.

National Federation of Federal Employees, Local 29
(Union)

and

U.S. Department of the Army Engineer District
Kansas City, Missouri
(Agency)

Case No. 0-NG-1919

Decision and Order on a Negotionability Issues
July 22, 1992

Before Chairman McKee and Members Talkin and Armendariz

I. Statement of the Case

This case is before the Authority on a negotiability appeal filed by the Union under section 7105(a)(2)(E) of the Federal Service Labor-Management Relations Statute (the Statute). It concerns the negotiability of four proposals relating to the Agency's implementation of the procurement integrity provision of the Office of Federal Procurement Policy Act, (Procurement Act), codified as amended at 41 U.S.C. § 423 (1988).1/

For the reasons stated below, we find that the record is insufficient to assess the negotiability of the first sentence of Proposal 2, which requires the Agency to invite the Union to participate in all training sessions on procurement integrity. Accordingly, we will dismiss the petition for review as to that portion of the proposal. The second sentence of Proposal 2, which requires that procurement officials receive periodic update training, is negotiable as an appropriate arrangement under section 7106(b)(3) of the Statute.

Proposal 7, which requires that the Agency provide bargaining unit employees with appropriate training, a synopsis of the procedures and requirements of the procurement integrity program, and an opportunity to discuss their concerns about the program before executing the "Procurement Integrity Certification," directly and excessively interferes with management's right to assign work. Therefore, the proposal is nonnegotiable.

Proposal 8, which defines the term "familiar" as used in the "Procurement Integrity Certification for Procurement Officials," is negotiable.

Proposal 9, which constitutes the Union's proposed "Procurement Integrity Certification for Procurement Official" form, is inconsistent with 41 U.S.C § 423(l)(2) and, therefore, is nonnegotiable under section 7117(a)(1) of the Statute.

II. Preliminary Matters

A. The Timeliness of the Union's Response

On February 25, 1991, the Union filed its petition for review with the Authority. On March 7, 1991, the Authority issued an Order suspending the processing of the negotiability case because the Union filed concurrent unfair labor practice charges and had selected to proceed first with the unfair labor practice proceedings. On August 9, 1991, the Authority issued an Order resuming processing of the negotiability case following the disposition of the charges. The Agency was given 30 days from the date of receipt of the Authority's Order to file a statement of position, as provided under section 2424.6 of the Authority's Rules and Regulations. The Union was given 15 days from the date of receipt of the Agency's statement of position to file a response with the Authority, as provided under section 2424.7 of the Authority's Rules and Regulations. The Agency filed its statement of position on September 11, 1991, and the Union claims to have received it on September 26, 1991.

The Union's response was hand-delivered to the Authority's docket room after 5:00 p.m. on Friday, October 11, 1991. The actual date of filing, therefore, was Tuesday, October 15, 1991.2/ On October 18, 1991, the Authority issued an Order requiring the Union to show cause why its response should be considered by the Authority, noting that the response was due by October 11, 1991. The Authority granted the Union until October 25, 1991, to file a submission and stated that a failure to comply with the Order would result in the Authority not considering the Union's response. The Union did not respond to the Authority's Order. Consequently, we will not consider the Union's untimely response. See *National Association of Government Employees, Local R1-109 and U.S. Department of Veterans Affairs, Veterans Administration Medical Center, Newington, Connecticut*, 35 FLRA 513, 514 (1990).

B. The Union's Appropriate Arrangements Contentions

The Agency contends that the Union "has failed to make any showing in support of its claim that the proposals are appropriate arrangements." Statement of Position at 8. The Agency argues that the Union did not fully address the issue of appropriate arrangements as required by National Association of Government Employees, Local R14-87 and Kansas Army National Guard, 21 FLRA 24 (1986) (*Kansas Army National Guard*). The Agency adds that the Union's failure to make any showing in support of its claim is similar to the situations presented in *American Federation of Government Employees, Local 2062 and U.S. Department of Veterans Affairs, New Orleans Regional Office, New Orleans, Louisiana*, 39 FLRA 857, 861 (1991), and *International Association of Fire Fighters, Local F-159 and U.S. Department of the Navy, Naval Station Treasure Island, San Francisco, California*, 37 FLRA 836, 839 (1990), in which the Authority noted the absence of sufficient records on which to determine whether the proposals were negotiable as appropriate arrangements. The Agency urges the Authority to reach the same result here.

We reject the Agency's contention that the Union has failed to support its claim that the proposals constitute negotiable appropriate arrangements. Instead, we find there is a sufficient basis on which to address the Union's assertion that the proposals are appropriate arrangements for employees adversely affected by the implementation of the Procurement Act.

C. Whether the Proposals Concern Conditions of Employment

The Agency states that "[i]t is long established that if the subject matter of a proposal is covered by law then the proposal is not negotiable." Statement of Position at 2. The Agency also states that the "proposals at issue impinge on requirements dictated by Congress to Federal agencies under the Office of Federal Procurement Policy Act (41 USC 423)." *Id.*

Under the Statute, parties are obligated to bargain over proposals concerning conditions of employment, provided that the proposals do not violate law, Government-wide regulation, or an agency regulation for which there is a compelling need. Conditions of employment are defined as personnel policies, practices, and matters whether established by rule, regulation, or otherwise, affecting working conditions. 5 U.S.C. § 7103(a)(14). However, matters that are specifically provided for by federal statute are excluded from the definition of conditions of employment. 5 U.S.C. § 7103(a)(14)(C).

It is well established that where an agency has discretion under applicable law and regulation over a matter affecting conditions of employment, the agency is obligated under the Statute to exercise that discretion through bargaining unless the governing law or regulation specifically requires that only the agency may exercise that discretion. *For example, National Federation of Federal Employees and U.S. Department of Agriculture, Forest Service*, 35 FLRA 1008, 1014 (1990); *National Treasury Employees Union and Department of the Treasury, U.S. Customs Service*, 21 FLRA 6 (1986), *aff'd sub nom. Department of the Treasury, U.S. Customs Service v. FLRA*, 836 F.2d 1381 (D.C. Cir. 1988); *National Treasury Employees Union, Chapter 6 and Internal Revenue Service, New Orleans District*, 3 FLRA 748, 759-60 (1980). Thus, it is only where law or applicable regulation vests an agency with exclusive authority or unfettered discretion over a matter that the exercise of the agency's discretion is not subject to negotiation. See, *for example, Illinois National Guard v. FLRA*, 854 F.2d 1396 (D.C. Cir. 1988); *Police Association of the District of Columbia and Department of the Interior, National Park Service, U.S. Park Police*, 18 FLRA 348 (1985).

Additionally, the Authority has rejected any interpretation of section 7103(a)(14)(C) that would hold that reference to a particular matter in a statute is sufficient to except that matter from the definition of conditions of employment. *For example National Association of Government Employees, Local R1-144, Federal Union of Scientists and Engineers and U.S. Department of the Navy, Naval Underwater Systems Center, Newport, Rhode Island,* 38 FLRA 456, 487-88 (1990), *decision on remand,* 43 FLRA 47 (1991). Rather, "where a statute specifically provides for or establishes a particular aspect of a matter, *that aspect* of the matter is not included within the conditions of employment about which an agency is obligated to bargain." *Id.* at 488 (emphasis in original). We have reviewed the record before us and find that the proposals do not concern matters that are specifically provided for by federal law. Consequently, the proposals are not excepted from the duty to bargain on that basis.

The Agency also states that "not all actions required of an employee by his or her Federal employer lead to a concomitant right to negotiate." Statement of Position at 2. In support, the Agency cites *National Treasury Employees Union and Internal Revenue Service,* 6 FLRA 522 (1981), in which, among other things, the Authority found nonnegotiable a proposal that did not directly relate to conditions of employment of unit employees. As we stated above, the proposals are not excepted from the definition of conditions of employment under section 7103(a)(14)(C) of the Statute. Moreover, as the proposals involve training for employees and other matters that directly relate to the work situation of bargaining unit employees, we find, as a general matter, that the proposals directly relate to conditions of employment of bargaining unit employees. See, *for example, American Federation of Government Employees, Department of Education Council of AFGE Locals and Department of Education,* 35 FLRA 56, 59-60 (1990) (Education) (proposals relating to training of unit employees concern personnel policies, practices and working conditions within the meaning of section 7103(a)(14) of the Statute).

III. Proposal 2

The union shall be invited to participate in all training sessions regarding procurement integrity. Each employee identified as a "procurement official" will receive periodical [sic] update training.

A. Positions of the Parties

1. The Agency

The Agency contends that the proposal interferes with management's right to assign work because it mandates that a specific type of training course be developed, that employees affected by the Procurement Act attend that training, and that participation be extended to the Union. The Agency also states that, to understand the intent of Proposal 2, the two sentences of the proposal must be read together. The Agency explains that the Union cannot be expected to participate in the training, and employees cannot receive periodic training, unless the Agency is required to develop a training course.

The Agency notes that the Authority consistently has held that an agency's right to assign work encompasses the right to train, or not to train, employees. In support, the Agency cites *American Federation of Government Employees, Local 3407, and U.S. Department of Defense, Defense Mapping Agency, Hydrographic-Topographic, Washington, D.C.,* 39 FLRA 557, 560 (1991) *(Defense Mapping, Washington).* The Agency states that the training at issue in Proposal 2 concerns aspects of procurement integrity for which all procurement and contracting personnel are responsible, is directly related to the duties of the employees, and directly affects employees' work performance. The Agency further explains that the procurement integrity provisions of the Procurement Act not only addresses employees' responsibilities regarding improper business practices and conflicts of interest but also involves the requirement that employees sign certain procurement integrity certification forms. The Agency notes that a "[f]ailure to fulfill these certification responsibilities will result in the employee's violation of the law and [G]overnment wide regulation governing procurement integrity." Statement of Position at 3.

The Agency also argues that Proposal 2 is similar to a proposal in *National Federation of Federal Employees, Local 1437 and United States Army Armament Research, Development and Engineering Center, Picatinny Arsenal, New Jersey,* 35 FLRA 1052, 1055-56 (1990) *(Army Research, Picatinny),* which required the agency to allow five employees designated by the union to attend a specific training course at least once each year during the life of the parties' agreement and which the Authority found was nonnegotiable. The Agency argues that Proposal 2 is similar in that it proposes that all procurement officials attend periodic procurement integrity training. The Agency states that the only difference between Proposal 2 and Army Research, Picatinny is that a specific count of employees was not made and the Union did not specify the length of time between each class.

The Agency also argues that Proposal 2 mandates that training be given and, on this basis, is distinguishable from Proposal 1 in Education, 35 FLRA at 61, in which a proposal requiring the agency to consider employee training requests was found negotiable. The Agency maintains that, by the use of the words "will receive," Proposal 2 mandates that training be given and does not suggest that the Agency can only "consider" a request for training. Statement of Position at 4. The Agency also states that the proposal "mandates participation of [U]nion representatives in the training, rather than allowing the [A]gency to consider for the training only those who need and are eligible for the training." Id.

2. The Union

As noted above, the Union's response was untimely filed and has not been considered. In its petition for review, the Union did not specifically address each proposal but rather made statements that are applicable to all the proposals in dispute. The Union stated that the proposals are intended to apply only to bargaining unit employees, are appropriate arrangements for employees adversely affected by the implementation of the Procurement Act, and are "clear on their face when read in the context of the entire proposal." Petition for Review at 1. The Union maintained that the proposals are not in conflict with the Procurement Act, the Statute, or Government-wide rules and regulations.

B. Analysis and Conclusions

We find that there is insufficient information in the record on which to make a negotiability determination with respect to the first sentence of the proposal. Therefore, we will dismiss the petition for review as to that sentence. We also find that, although the second sentence of the proposal directly interferes with management's right to assign work, it is negotiable as an appropriate arrangement.

1. The First Sentence

The first sentence of the proposal states that the Union shall be invited to participate in all procurement integrity training sessions. When read in conjunction with the second sentence of the proposal, it is apparent that the training sessions are those the Union seeks to establish for employees identified as procurement officials. The Agency contends that the proposal interferes with the right to assign work by preventing the Agency from considering for training "only those who need and are eligible for the training." Statement of Position at 4. The Union did not explain the intent of Proposal 2 other than to state that it is clear on its face.

Based on the record before us, we are unable to determine the negotiability of the first sentence. Critical to an assessment of its negotiability is the meaning to be ascribed to the term "participate." However, neither party has addressed the meaning of that term. For example, if the intent of the proposal is to give the Union an opportunity to assist in conducting the training sessions, the proposal would be found nonnegotiable on the basis that it interferes with the right to assign work. See *National Treasury Employees Union and U.S. Department of the Treasury, Bureau of Alcohol, Tobacco and Firearms*, 45 FLRA No. 30, slip op. at 19-22 (1992) (proposal providing a union representative an opportunity to address formal training classes for up to 15 minutes during duty hours, at which job-related training would be given, excessively interfered with management's right to assign work). We would reach a similar result if the proposal is intended to provide instruction to the Union representatives in connection with the performance of their job-related duties. See *Defense Mapping, Washington*, 39 FLRA at 560. Alternatively, if the proposal is designed to permit the Union to attend and observe the training sessions, then we would examine whether the Union had a representational interest in addressing employee concerns related to the training. Without a clear indication of the meaning of the term participate, however, we are unable to assess the negotiability of the first sentence of the proposal.

The parties bear the burden of creating a record on which a negotiability determination can be made. See *National Federation of Federal Employees, Local 1167 v. FLRA*, 681 F.2d 886, 891 (D.C. Cir. 1982). A party failing to meet this burden acts at its peril. Accordingly, as we are unable to determine whether the first sentence of Proposal 2 is negotiable, we will dismiss the petition for review as to that sentence. See also *National Federation of Federal Employees, Local 1655 and U.S. Department of Defense, National Guard Bureau, Department of Military Affairs, Illinois Air National Guard*, 35 FLRA 740, 747 (1990).

2. The Second Sentence

The second sentence of the proposal provides that employees identified as procurement officials will receive periodic update training. The Union states that the proposal applies only to bargaining unit employees. As explained by the Agency, the training concerns aspects of the procurement integrity process for which all procurement and contracting personnel are responsible, is directly related to the duties of employees, and directly affects their work performance. Thus, we find that the training encompassed by the second sentence is directly related to the duties of those bargaining unit employees who are identified as procurement officials. The Authority previously has held that proposals requiring agencies to provide training to employees consisting of instruction on their duties and responsibilities directly interfere with the right to assign work. See *Defense Mapping, Washington,* 39 FLRA at 560. As the second sentence requires the Agency to provide training for employees relating to the performance of their duties, we conclude that the second sentence directly interferes with management's rights under section 7106(a)(2)(B) of the Statute.

However, we further find that the second sentence is negotiable as an appropriate arrangement. To determine whether a proposal constitutes an appropriate arrangement, we must decide whether it is intended as an arrangement for employees adversely affected by the exercise of a management right, and whether it is appropriate because it does not excessively interfere with the exercise of a management right. *Kansas Army National Guard,* 21 FLRA at 31-33.

Initially, we find that the second sentence is intended as an arrangement for employees who may be adversely affected by the exercise of management's right to assign work. As noted by the Agency, the procurement integrity provisions of the Procurement Act address various employee responsibilities and require that employees sign certain procurement integrity certification forms. The Agency acknowledges that an employee who fails to fulfill the certification responsibilities will be found to have violated law and Government-wide regulations. In this connection, we note that 41 U.S.C. § 423(h) provides that employees who engage in conduct prohibited by the Procurement Act "shall be subject to removal or other appropriate adverse personnel action pursuant to the procedures specified in chapter 75 of title 5 or other applicable law or regulation." 41 U.S.C. § 423(h)(2). By requiring the Agency to provide periodic update training to procurement officials, the second sentence of the proposal is designed to apprise employees of new or changed requirements relating to the performance of their duties. Thus, with the training, employees would be provided with the information needed to avoid the legal consequences of failing to fulfill the requirements of the Procurement Act.

We further find, after balancing the competing interests of the Agency in being able to assign work and the interests of employees in ensuring that they have appropriate training to perform the requirements of the Procurement Act, that the second sentence would not excessively interfere with the right to assign work. Periodic update training would afford obvious benefits to employees. For example, it would be easier for employees to keep abreast of changes in law or regulation that affect the performance of their duties if the Agency were to provide a systematic means of dispensing that information. Additionally, as a general matter, employees would benefit from such training by improving their knowledge, proficiency, ability, and skill in carrying out their official duties. It is also noteworthy that a logical consequence of improved individual performance would be the beneficial effect on the Agency's administration of its procurement program.

On the other hand, the second sentence would require the Agency to take whatever measures are necessary to provide training for employees on a recurring basis. However, both the Procurement Act and its implementing regulations already require the head of each federal agency to establish training on procurement ethics.3/ At a minimum, the Procurement Act and the implementing regulations require that the training program include the distribution of a written explanation of certain provisions of the Procurement Act. Thus, the second sentence simply requires the Agency to supplement the training that is required by law and regulation. In addition, the Agency would retain the discretion to determine the content, duration, and timing of the training. In this regard, the second sentence does not specify the type of training that the Agency will provide, such as formal classes or on-the-job training, nor does it dictate the schedule of training, its duration, or who will provide the actual training. See *Patent Office Professional Association and Department of Commerce, Patent and Trademark Office,* 39 FLRA 783, 837-38 (1991) (Commerce, Patent Office) (portion of proposal requiring that agency provide adequate training for examiners found not to excessively interfere with right to assign work insofar as agency retained discretion to determine the type of training, its schedule, duration, and who would conduct the training).

In our view, the burden imposed on the Agency to provide periodic update training is minimal when compared with the benefits afforded to employees by providing such training. Consequently, we conclude that the second sentence of Proposal 2 constitutes a negotiable appropriate arrangement under section 7106(b)(3) of the Statute. Finally, we find that *Army Research, Picatinny*, relied on by the Agency, is distinguishable. Although the Authority found that a proposal requiring the agency to provide training directly interfered with the right to assign work, a result we also reach here, the Authority did not address whether the proposal constituted a negotiable appropriate arrangement because that issue was not before the Authority. In contrast, the Union claimed that the second sentence constitutes a negotiable appropriate arrangement and, based on the foregoing analysis, we have concluded that it does. IV. Proposal 7 4/

No bargaining unit employee will be required to execute the "Procurement Integrity Certification" until they have been provided appropriate training, the synopsis identified in item 4 above, and the opportunity to discuss areas of concern with the agency official charge [sic] with oversight of the procurement integrity program.

A. Positions of the Parties

The Agency contends that the proposal is outside the duty to bargain pursuant to section 7117(a)(1) of the Statute because it prevents the Agency from complying with law and regulation. More specifically, the Agency contends that if Proposal 7 were found negotiable, it would require federal officials to provide training before employees could be required to execute procurement integrity certifications. The Agency argues that 41 U.S.C. § 423(e)(3),5/ provides that a procurement official may be required to execute a procurement integrity certification at any time "during the conduct of any federal agency procurement of products or services." Statement of Position at 2. The Agency also states that the proposal is inconsistent with 48 C.F.R. § 3.104-9(c)(2), which "mandates that employees will execute the procurement integrity certification form when a contract award or modification is made." *Id.* at 5. Additionally, the Agency claims that the proposal is inconsistent with 48 C.F.R. § 3.104-12(a)(2), which provides that "as a condition of serving as a procurement official, each employee must certify that he or she is familiar with certain provisions of [the] Act." *Id.*

The Agency further contends that Proposal 7 interferes with management's right to assign work under section 7106(a)(2)(B) of the Statute. The Agency explains that employees engaged in executing contracts for the Agency are required to execute certifications when work is completed. The Agency argues, however, that the proposal would prevent the assignment of work involving the execution of contracts until employees had completed the training provided by Proposal 2. The Agency states that Proposal 7 is similar to *Service and Hospital Employees International Union, Local 150 and Veterans Administration Medical Center, Milwaukee, Wisconsin*, 35 FLRA 521, 537 (1990) (VAMC, Milwaukee), in which the Authority found nonnegotiable a proposal limiting the assignment of work to those employees who were qualified to perform the work or were undergoing training to perform such work. The Agency also asserts that Proposal 7 has the identical effect of imposing conditions on management's right to assign work as Proposal 14 in *National Union of Hospital and Health Care Employees, AFL-CIO, District 1199 and Veterans Administration Medical Center, Dayton, Ohio*, 28 FLRA 435, 461 (1987), *decision on remand*, 33 FLRA 281 (1988), which required management to provide some form of training to newly hired employees as a condition precedent to making specific work assignments and which was held nonnegotiable.

The Union's position is as stated in connection with Proposal 2.

B. Analysis and Conclusions

We conclude that Proposal 7 is nonnegotiable because it directly and excessively interferes with management's right to assign work. Initially, we note that the Agency has made a number of arguments with respect to certification requirements that are imposed on a variety of persons and at various stages of the procurement process. We find, however, that the type of certification encompassed by the proposal is limited to that which procurement officials are required to complete as a condition of serving as a procurement official. We reach this conclusion because the proposal itself refers to the "Procurement Integrity Certification." That is the title of a specific form, referred to in 48 C.F.R. §§ 3.104-12(a)(2) and (3), and an example of which is set forth at 48 C.F.R. § 53.302-333.6/ The requirement that procurement officials complete a certification as a condition of serving in that capacity emanates from 41 U.S.C. § 423(l)(2). This certification is different from that which procurement officials may be required to complete under 41 U.S.C. § 423(e)(3) that is relied on by the Agency. Additionally, although the proposal refers to bargaining unit employees, we find that the proposal is intended to apply to procurement officials only and not to contracting officers, to whom 48 C.F.R. § 3.104-9(c)(2) applies. We reach this conclusion because the Procurement Integrity Certification form itself applies only to procurement officials. Moreover, the synopsis identified in Proposal 4, which the proposal requires the Agency to provide to employees, applies only to procurement officials.

In sum, we conclude that the certification referred to in Proposal 7 is that which procurement officials are required to complete as a condition of serving in that capacity. Therefore, the Agency's arguments as to the applicability of 41 U.S.C. § 423(e)(3) and 48 C.F.R. § 3.104-9(c)(2) are inapposite and we need not address them further.

The Agency's remaining arguments are that the proposal is inconsistent with 48 C.F.R. § 3.104-12(a)(2) and with the right to assign work under section 7106(a)(2)(B) of the Statute. For the following reasons, we find that Proposal 7 directly and excessively interferes with the right to assign work. In view of this conclusion, we will not address the claimed inconsistency with the cited regulation.

Proposal 7 provides that before employees can be required to execute the Procurement Integrity Certification, they will be given adequate training, information concerning the regulations and procedures of the procurement integrity program, and an opportunity to discuss concerns with a specified Agency representative. According to the Agency, the proposal would prevent management from assigning duties involving the execution of procurement contracts until all the requirements set forth in the proposal have been met. This assertion is uncontradicted. Therefore, we find that by requiring the Agency to provide training and information to employees before requiring them to complete the requisite certification, the proposal would limit the assignment of duties attendant to the procurement process for an unspecified period of time until the requirements of the proposal have been satisfied. It is well established that management's right to assign work under section 7106(a)(2)(B) of the Statute includes the right to determine the particular duties to be assigned, when work assignments will occur, and to whom or what positions the duties will be assigned. See, for example, *National Weather Service Employees Organization and U.S. Department of Commerce, National Oceanic and Atmospheric Administration, National Weather Service,* 37 FLRA 392, 399 (1990); *VAMC, Milwaukee,* 35 FLRA at 537-39. Proposal 7 would place conditions on management's ability to assign work involving the procurement process until the requirements set forth in the proposal have been met. We find that such restrictions on the Agency's ability to assign duties to employees constitute a direct interference with the right to assign work. Accordingly, we find that the Proposal 7 directly interferes with the Agency's right to assign work under section 7106(a)(2)(B) of the Statute.

Next, we address whether the proposal constitutes a negotiable appropriate arrangement. As noted in our discussion concerning the second sentence of Proposal 2, there are possible penalties for employees who fail to comply with provisions of the procurement integrity program. By requiring the Agency to provide employees with appropriate training and information relevant to the procurement integrity program before they execute the applicable certification that enables them to operate as procurement officials, Proposal 7 constitutes an arrangement for employees who may be adversely affected by management's exercise of its right to assign work relating to the procurement integrity process. Therefore, we find that Proposal 7 is intended as an arrangement.

We further find, however, that the proposal would excessively interfere with the right to assign work. On the one hand, requiring management to provide employees with appropriate training and other information relevant to the procurement integrity program would assist employees in avoiding the adverse consequences of failing to adhere to the requirements of the Procurement Act and would serve to improve their performance in carrying out the provisions of the Procurement Act. On the other hand, the proposal would preclude the Agency from assigning duties involving the procurement process until the Agency fulfilled the requirements of the proposal. Thus, the proposal would place a severe limitation on the Agency's right to assign work. As a result, until the required training, information, and discussion period was provided, procurement officials would not be able to complete the assigned duties necessary for the Agency to obtain the property or services to support the Agency's mission, such as drafting, reviewing, and approving specifications for particular procurement actions; preparing or issuing procurement solicitations; evaluating bids or proposals; selecting sources for procurements; conducting negotiations for procurements; and reviewing and approving awards or modifications of procurement contracts. See 41 U.S.C. § 423(p)(3)(A). See, also, *Overseas Education Association and U.S. Department of Defense Dependents Schools, FPO, Seattle,* 42 FLRA 197, 206-07 (1991), *petition for review denied sub nom. Overseas Education Association v. FLRA,* 961 F.2d 36 (2d Cir. 1992) (proposal that students be dismissed to allow teachers to prepare for open house program excessively interfered with right to assign work insofar as proposal would have unduly hampered agency's ability to efficiently and effectively conduct its operations). On balance, therefore, we conclude that Proposal 7 excessively interferes with management's right to assign work under section 7106(a)(B)(2) of the Statute.

V. Proposal 8

The term "familiar" as used in the "Procurement Integrity Certification For Procurement Officials" shall have the following meaning:

Familiar - a general knowledge of, rather than practical application.

A. Positions of the Parties

The Agency contends that the proposal's definition of the word "familiar" is contrary to that ascribed by Congress in 41 U.S.C. § 423(e)(1)(B)(i).[7] The Agency states that under that section, "contracting officers, and others participating in the preparation or submission of a contract bid, must certify he or she is familiar with particular sections of the procurement integrity provision and its applicable implementing regulations." Statement of Position at 6. The Agency argues, citing various dictionary definitions of the word, that the Union is attempting to bargain a broader meaning of "familiar" than that normally accepted. The Agency states that, "absent discussion in the legislative history, Congress did not intend to attach a meaning to the word familiar other than the one generally accepted[,]" and that "[i]t is not appropriate for the [U]nion to substitute its judgment for that of Congress[.]" *Id.*

The Union's position is the same as that stated in connection with Proposal 2.

B. Analysis and Conclusions

Proposal 8 concerns the meaning of the term "familiar" as used in the Procurement Integrity Certification for procurement officials. Consistent with the plain language of the proposal and our discussion of Proposal 7, we find that the procurement integrity certification encompassed by the proposal is that which procurement officials must execute as a condition to serving in that capacity. In contrast, 41 U.S.C. § 423(e)(1)(B)(i), which the Agency claims is inconsistent with the proposal, involves certifications by officers or employees of contractors with respect to participation in bids or offers by competing contractors. Thus, the certification required under section 423(e)(1)(B)(i) is different from that set forth in the proposal and does not provide a basis on which to find the proposal nonnegotiable.

We note, however, that the term "familiar" does appear in the procurement integrity certification form set forth at 48 C.F.R. § 53.302-333 that agencies may use. The Agency makes no argument that defining "familiar" for purposes of that form in the manner set forth in the proposal is inconsistent with any law, rule, or regulation, and none is apparent to us. Consequently, we find that Proposal 8 is negotiable.

VI. Proposal 9

"Procurement Integrity Certification for Procurement Official"

As a condition of serving as a procurement official, I (type or print name) hereby certify that I am familiar with of [sic] the provisions of subsections 27(b), (c), and (e) of the Office of Federal Procurement Policy Act (41 USC 423) as amended by section 814 of Public Law 101-189. I further certify that I will not engage in any conduct prohibited by such subsections and will report to the contracting officer any information concerning a violation or possible violation of subsections 27(a), (b), (d), or (f) of the Act. A written explanation of subsections 27(a) through (f) has been made available to me. I understand that should I leave the Government during the conduct of a procurement for which I have served as a procurement official, I have a continuing obligation under section 27 not to disclose proprietary or source selection information relating to that procurement and a requirement to so certify.

This certification shall not be construed in any way to be a waiver of my Constitutional rights.

A. Positions of the Parties

According to the Agency, the proposal constitutes the Union's proposed procurement integrity certification form. The Agency argues that, as such, the proposal is inconsistent with 48 C.F.R. §§ 3.104-9(c)(2) and 3.104-12(a)(2). The Agency explains that, under those regulations, procurement officials are required to report not only violations of the Procurement Act, but violations of the implementing regulations as well. The Agency states that the proposal deletes any reference to the implementing regulations that are contained in the Federal Acquisition Regulation.8/ The Agency also states that it would withdraw its allegation of nonnegotiability if the Union's intent is to include a reference to the applicable implementing regulations.

The Union's position is as stated in connection with Proposal 2.

B. Analysis and Conclusions

As we noted previously, 41 U.S.C. § 423(l)(2) and 48 C.F.R. § 3.104-12(a)(2) require procurement officials to execute certifications as a condition of serving in that capacity. An optional certification form that agencies may use is referenced in 48 C.F.R. § 3.104-12(a)(3) and, as noted earlier, is set forth at 48 C.F.R. § 53.302-333. The Union's proposal constitutes an attempt to negotiate the certification form that procurement officials will execute. For the following reasons, we find that the proposal is inconsistent with federal law. Therefore, the proposal is outside the duty to bargain under section 7117(a)(1) of the Statute.

As relevant to our disposition of the proposal, 41 U.S.C. § 423(l)(2) of the Procurement Act states that the procurement ethics program shall (2) require each such procurement official, as a condition of serving as a procurement official, to certify that he or she... will report immediately to the contracting officer any information concerning a violation or possible violation of subsection (a), (b), (d), or (f) of this section, or applicable implementing regulations.

Clearly, the Procurement Act requires procurement officials to certify that they will report violations and possible violations of both the Procurement Act and the applicable implementing regulations. The proposal, however, does not include the statutory requirement to certify that employees will report actual and possible violations of the applicable implementing regulations. Although the Agency did not expressly note any differences in unlawful conduct specified in the regulations, as compared with that set forth in the referenced sections of the Procurement Act, it is an elementary rule of statutory construction that effect must be given to every word, clause, and sentence of a statute so that no part is rendered inoperative or insignificant. See, for example, United States v. Menasche, 348 U.S. 528, 538-39 (1955). Thus, 41 U.S.C. § 423(l)(2) requires that violations of both law and regulation must be reported. By deleting the reference to applicable implementing regulations, the proposal effectively eliminates that requirement. As such, the proposal is inconsistent with federal law. Pursuant to section 7117(a)(1) of the Statute, the proposal is nonnegotiable.

Because of this finding, we need not address the Agency's contentions that the proposal is inconsistent with various regulatory provisions. Likewise, we need not address the Union's contention that the proposal constitutes an appropriate arrangement under 7106(b)(3) of the Statute. That section applies only when management exercises one of the reserved rights set out elsewhere in section 7106 and not when a proposal is found to be inconsistent with law. See, for example, *National Association of Government Employees, Local R1-109 and U.S. Department of Veterans Affairs, Veterans Administration Medical Center, Newington, Connecticut*, 37 FLRA 500, 511 (1990).

VII. Order

The Agency must upon request, or as otherwise agreed to by the parties, bargain concerning the second sentence of Proposal 2 and Proposal 8.9/ We dismiss the petition for review as to the first sentence of Proposal 2, Proposal 7, and Proposal 9.

Appendix
41 U.S.C. § 423(e)(1)(B)(i) Provides in Part
(e) Certification and Enforcement Matters

(1) A Federal agency may not award a contract for the procurement of property or services to any competing contractor... unless the officer or employee of such contractor responsible for the offer or bid for such contract[.]

(B) certifies in writing to such contracting officer that each officer, employee,... of such competing contractor who has participated personally and substantially in the preparation or submission of such bid or offer,... has certified to such competing contractor that he or she –

(i) is *familiar* with, and will comply with, the requirements of subsection (a) [entitled "[p]rohibited conduct by competing contractors"] of this section and applicable implementing regulations; (emphasis added)

41 U.S.C. § 423(e)(3) Provides

(e) Certification and Enforcement Matters

(3) The head of a Federal agency may require any procurement official or any competing contractor, at any time during the conduct of any Federal agency procurement of property or services –

(A) to certify in writing to the head of such agency that such procurement official or the officer or employee of the competing contractor responsible for the offer or bid for such contract or the modification or extension of such contract, as the case may be, has no information concerning a violation or possible violation of subsection (a), (b), (d), or (f) or this section, or applicable implementing regulations, pertaining to such procurement; or

(B) to disclose to the head of such agency any and all such information and to certify in writing that any and all such information has been disclosed.

41 U.S.C. § 423(l) Provides

The head of each Federal agency shall establish a procurement ethics program for its procurement officials. The program shall, at a minimum –

(1) provide for the distribution of written explanations of the provisions of subsections (b), (c), and (e) of this section to such procurement officials; and

(2) require each such procurement official, as a condition of serving as a procurement official, to certify that he or she is familiar with the provisions of subsections (b), (c), and (e) of this section, and will not engage in any conduct prohibited by such subsection, and will report immediately to the contracting officer any information concerning a violation or possible violation of subsection (a), (b), (d), or (f) of this section, or applicable implementing regulations.

48 C.F.R. § 3.104-9(c)(2) Provides

Immediately prior to contract award or execution of a contract modification, the contracting officer shall execute the ["Contracting Officer Certificate of Procurement Integrity"] the following certificate and maintain the completed certificate in the contract file.

48 C.F.R. § 3.104-12 Provides

(a) Subsection 27(l) of the [Office of Federal Procurement Policy] Act provides that the head of each Federal agency shall establish a procurement ethics training program for its procurement officials. The program shall, as a minimum –

(1) Provide for the distribution of a written explanation of subsections 27 (a) through (f) of the Act to such procurement officials; and

(2) Require each such procurement official, as a condition of serving as a procurement official, to certify in writing that he or she is familiar with the provisions of subsections 27 (b), (c), and (e) of the Act and will not engage in any conduct prohibited by such subsections, and will report immediately to the contracting officer any information concerning a violation or possible violation of subsection 27 (a), (b), (d), or (f) of the Act as implemented in the [Federal Acquisition Regulation] FAR.

(3) Certification made under section 27 as originally enacted and implemented in the FAR do not satisfy the certification requirements of subparagraph (a)(2) of this subsection. Agencies may use Optional Form 333 at 53.302-333 to obtain the certifications required by subparagraph (a)(2) of this subsection.

48 C.F.R. § 53.302-333, Provides

As a condition of serving as a procurement official, I hereby certify that I am familiar with the provisions of subsections 27(b), (c), and (e) of the Office of Federal Procurement Policy Act (41 USC 423) as amended by section 814 of Public Law 101-189. I further certify that I will not engage in any conduct prohibited by such subsections and will report immediately to the contracting officer any information concerning a violation or possible violation of subsections 27(a), (b), (d), or (f) of the Act and applicable implementing regulations. A written explanation of subsections 27(a) through (f) has been made available to me. I understand that, should I leave the Government during the conduct of a procurement for which I have served as a procurement official, I have a continuing obligation under section 27 not to disclose proprietary or source selection information relating to that procurement and a requirement to so certify.

Footnote #1

The petition for review contained an additional proposal. However, in its statement of position, the Agency claims that after the petition for review was filed the parties reached agreement on that proposal. As there is no basis in the record on which to hold otherwise, we find that the proposal is not in dispute and we will not consider it further.

Footnote #2

Under section 2429.24(a) of the Authority's Rules and Regulations, "[d]ocuments hand-delivered for filing must be presented in the Docket Room not later than 5 p.m. to be accepted for filing on that day." The response was considered filed on Tuesday, October 15, 1991, because, due to a Federal holiday on October 14, 1991, that was the next business day following delivery.

Footnote #3

The pertinent provisions of 41 U.S.C. § 423(l) and 48 C.F.R. § 3.104-12(a) are set forth in the Appendix to this decision.

Footnote #4

The reference to "item 4" is to Proposal 4 in the petition for review. Proposal 4, which is not in dispute, states:

> All "procurement officials" in the bargaining unit shall be given a clear and complete synopsis of the requirements and procedures of the procurement integrity program.

Petition for Review, Enclosure No. 1

Footnote #5

For the text of 41 U.S.C. § 423(e)(3), as well as the cited regulations, see the Appendix to this decision.

Footnote #6

The text of 48 C.F.R. § 53.302-333 is set forth in the Appendix.

Footnote #7

The text of 41 U.S.C. § 423(e)(1)(B)(i) is set forth in the Appendix.

Footnote #8

The implementing regulations are set forth in various provisions of title 48 of the Code of Federal Regulations.

Footnote #9

In finding these matters to be negotiable, we make no judgment as to their merits.

OTHER BOOKS BY

JOSEPH SWERDZEWSKI

Labor Law and Labor Relations 4th Edition
A Practical Guide to Federal Labor Relations

The ALL NEW 4th EDITION of Labor Law and Labor Relations has been updated with a new chapter covering Pre-Decisional Involvement (PDI), to help you understand the law even better. It is an easy to read practical guide that every manager, supervisor, and union steward who spends 25% of their time on Labor Relations needs to have, in order to understand their role in Federal Sector Labor Relation! This is a practical guide to federal labor relations and does not attempt to explain the intricacies of the complex federal system but instead gives federal supervisors, working managers, and union representatives a general understanding of what they need to know to be effective in labor relations.

For more information visit the JSA website at www.jsafed.com.

Communication and Trust
A Guide to a Successful Work Place

Learn to develop more effective communication skills and build work place trust!

"Developing effective communication skills, attitudes and processes and improving employee trust in management and the organization will lead to a more productive and effective workplace as well as increasing employee satisfaction and retention."

Learn how communication and trust work hand-in-hand in the workplace.

"A lack of trust is one of the greatest inhibitors to developing effective communication. A lack of effective communication is one of the greatest inhibitors to creating trust."

Read real life workplace scenarios where employer/employee communication went wrong and learn what to do in similar situations.

For more information visit the JSA website at www.jsafed.com.

How to Conduct a Workplace Investigation

How to Conduct a Workplace Investigation will give your Managers, Supervisors, Union Representatives, and Lawyers all the information they need to know when conducting workplace investigations.

GET THE ANSWERS – INVESTIGATE!

Topics covered in this easy to read guide include, but are not limited to: The Investigator's Authority, Conduct and Role of an Investigator, Common Problems of Investigators, Preparation for an Investigation, Developing an Investigative Plan, Interviewing and/or Questioning Witnesses, Investigator Communication Skills, Witness Right and Representation, Understanding Evidence, and Investigative Reports.

For more information visit the JSA website at www.jsafed.com.

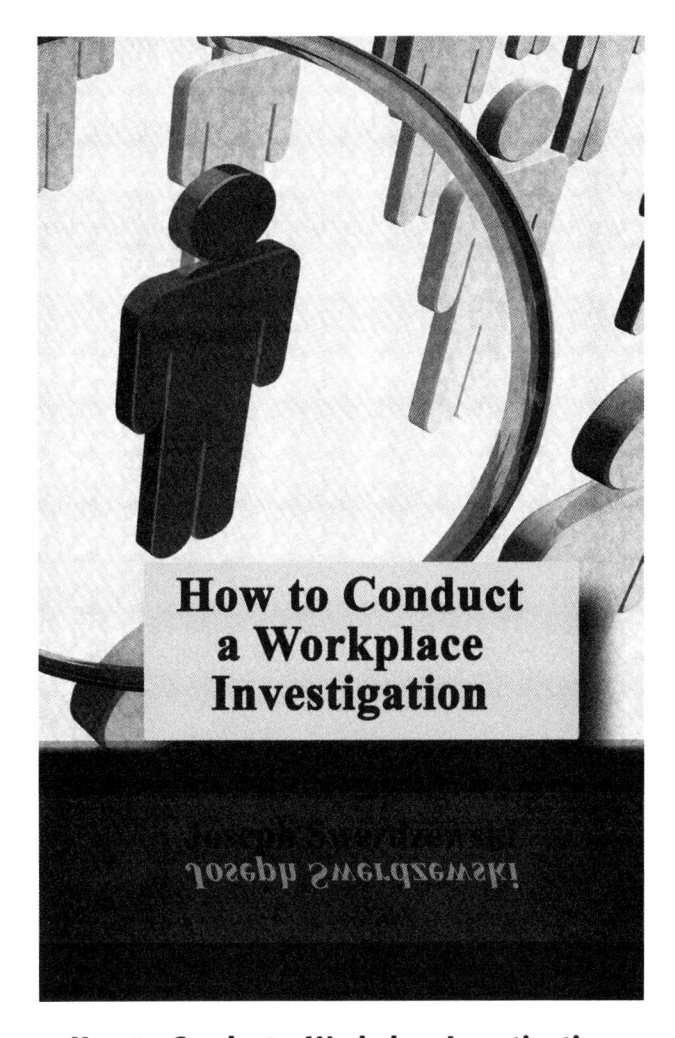

Your Partner For Success

HELPING YOU MEET YOUR HUMAN RESOURCES AND LABOR RELATIONS GOALS.

JSA Services:
- Collective Bargaining
- Mediation & Dispute Resolution
- Advice & Counsel
- Training
- Human Resources
- Personnel Actions
- Labor / Employee Relations
- Recruitment & Internal Placement
- Misconduct Investigations
- Position Classification

JSA has an established record within the federal government of providing the highest level of quality advice and assistance to their clients. Mr. Swerdzewski, founder of JSA, is a nationally known federal attorney who served two terms as the General Counsel to the Federal Labor Relations Authority. He and his staff are dedicated to providing their clients with the best services in a cost effective and professional manner.

" Gaining an in-depth understanding of our customers' needs and goals is a fundamental step in the way we work! "

One of our acknowledged specialties is federal sector labor relations. We have assisted agencies in the negotiation of their collective bargaining agreement through labor relations advice on a whole gamut of issues, mediation and facilitation services as well as training on numerous areas of labor relations. Beyond labor relations we have assisted agencies in training and consulting on a myriad of human resources issues.

Please call for more information ▶▶▶

JSA

6586 Highway 431 South
Suite E457
Hampton Cove, AL 35763 USA
(256)970-5514 | Fax: (256)288-0628

NOTES

NOTES